MODERN LEGAL STUDIES

GRIEVANCES, REMEDIES AND THE STATE

Second Edition

Australia
The Law Book Company
Brisbane, Sydney, Melbourne, Perth

Canada
Carswell
Ottawa, Toronto, Calgary, Montreal, Vancouver

AGENTS

India
N.M. Tripathi (Private) Ltd
Bombay

Eastern Law House (Private) Ltd
Calcutta

M.P.P. House
Bangalore

Universal Book Traders
Delhi

Aditya Books
Delhi

Israel
Steimatzky's Agency Ltd
Tel Aviv

Pakistan
Pakistan Law House
Karachi, Lahore

MODERN LEGAL STUDIES

GRIEVANCES, REMEDIES AND THE STATE

Second Edition

by

PATRICK BIRKINSHAW, LL.B., Barrister at Law

Professor at the Faculty of Law,
University of Hull

LONDON
SWEET & MAXWELL
1994

First Edition 1985

Published by Sweet & Maxwell Limited of
South Quay Plaza, 183 Marsh Wall, London E14 9FT
Typeset by The Midlands Book Typesetting Company,
Loughborough, Leics.
Printed by Information Press, Eynsham, Oxford

No natural forests were destroyed to make this product;
only farmed timber was used and replanted.

A CIP catalogue record for this book is available from
the British Library

ISBN 0 421 48510 8

To Jane, Daniel, Rachel, Sarah and Emily

PREFACE TO THE FIRST EDITION

This book has had a long gestation period. The idea developed while I was working with Norman Lewis on local government in the late 1970s. It seemed to me then, and now, that neither lawyers nor researchers in other disciplines had explored adequately the internal processes of governmental institutions and the way they respond to complaints, complainants or allow informal opportunities for consultation or even participation in decision-making; or, most cherished of all, simply leave organisations or interests to regulate their own affairs within the framework of the general law. The plan was to examine a section of the institutions of the contemporary British State, to establish what they did in relation to grievances from the public affected by their administration, and to study what connections there were between these informal practices and the more formal procedures for complaint resolution or dispute settlement culminating with Ombudsmen and Courts of Law. In other words, I was inverting the traditional approach which begins with the courts and, sometimes, works "down" as it were. As such, the idea was ambitious, possibly over-ambitious. There was a necessity for much original empirical field-work; in government departments, (comprising interviews and visits between 1982 and 1984), local authorities, with nationalised industry consumer councils, health authorities and public corporations etc. I did not want simply to go and examine and report. I wanted also to explain how these processes tied in with a representative-democratic model of government, and how our public institutions operated when set beside the ideals which our system of government and law are supposed to foster; and to ask what was there about the ideals which needed developing, advancing or strengthening and was this possible given political, economic and cultural constraints? A phrase of Roberto Unger's – the dialectic interplay between the organisation of power and its legitimation – seemed to sum up what I had in mind.

This is a study of public institutions. This is not to deny the importance of individuals. Far from it. Rather it is an acknowledgement of the fact that the institutions of the State, comprising

vii

individual politicians and officials, and their operations, set the political climate in which our lives, rights and liberties flourish; or otherwise.

On the acknowledgements side, my debt is embarrassing. First and foremost to my wife, Jane, who typed, and re-typed, and re-typed most of the manuscript, the tables and index. Literally countless civil servants, local government officials, public officials and appointees have shown enormous forbearance and assistance. My thanks to all of them. Tony Prosser, Ian Harden, Chris Himsworth, Tony Bradley, Richard Thomas and Ray Smith all read chapters and made helpful criticisms and suggestions. Patrick McAuslan provided encouragement and much constructive advice. Norman Lewis has, as tutor, colleague and friend, more responsibility than anyone else for stimulating my interest in the present subject and making me realise the limits of my knowledge of the field. The shortcomings, oversights and errors in the work are mine alone. I have been able to refer to developments up to December 31, 1984. Finally, I would like to thank my colleagues in the Faculty of Law at Hull for covering for me while on study leave, and Pat Wilson, Melanie Bucknell and Joan Wilson who typed various sections of the book.

Notice of *R. v. H.M. Treasury, ex p. Smedley* [1985] 1 All E.R. 589 (*vires* of Treasury decision expressed in delegated legislation, even in draft, are justiciable, page 18) and Tribunals and Inquiries (F.C.C.) Order 1984, S.I. 1984 No. 1247 (Foreign Compensation Commission now under supervision of the Council on Tribunals, page 31) came too late to incorporate in the text.

Hull University
March 1985.

PREFACE TO THE SECOND EDITION

Since I completed the typescript for the first edition of this book, almost a decade ago, the subject of non-judicial redress of grievance has leapt to the forefront of legal and political attention. I claim no credit for that. The shape of the public sector and the philosophy of that sector have been revolutionised and the Citizen's Charter has impressed upon all in the public and privatised sectors the virtues of effective complaints procedures for those who have cause to complain when things go wrong in service delivery. Change and reform have been endemic. The consequence has been the need for a substantial re-write of all of the chapters and the addition of a concluding chapter. At times I felt a little like Karl Llewellyn who in contemplating a second edition of *The Bramble Bush* protested that the young man who wrote the original work was no longer there. I suppose in my case enough of him remained to complete the task. I have followed the original format. The subject matter is messy at times and complicated and as I once had occasion to remark in the Institute of Law and State in Moscow when giving a paper on Non Judicial Redress of Grievance in the UK, not all of the confusion is my fault! For detailed proposals for reform of our administrative justice system, readers might usefully consult *When Citizens Complain – Reforming Justice and Administration* by Norman Lewis and myself.

I am very grateful to Maurice Sunkin et al. and the Public Law Project for allowing me to use a table from *Judicial Remedies in Perspective* (1993). I am also extremely grateful to William Reid, the Parliamentary Commissioner, for allowing me to quote from his *Management Plan for 1992/3–1994/5* and more particularly for advising me on the contents of chapter two and the relevant parts of chapter five. I am sure he would still find many points on which to differ in the final content of those chapters but he was a very instructive and entertaining tutor. Under his stewardship the Parliamentary Commissioner has added notable vigour to his investigation and other reports, which is true also of his reports as Health Service Commissioner. As this preface is written, the Select Committee on the Parliamentary Commissioner is investigating the subject of Redress, Maladministration and the Citizen's

Charter and it should prove to be a very important report. I am also grateful to Gordon Adams and David Nice of the Commission for Local Administration for their advice. My thanks also to Norman Lewis, William Lucy and Mike Feintuck and to the editing staff at Sweet and Maxwell who assisted in the preparation of this edition. Ministerial responsibility may be waning but I must accept sole responsibility for all the errors, overstatements, gaucheness and juvenilia that remain.

On more particular points, the Police and Magistrates' Courts Act 1994 was published in its final form too late in the day to be incorporated, other than hastily and piecemeal, moments before going to press and reference should be made to the Parliamentary Commissioner Act 1994 which amends the jurisdiction of the Commissioner in relation to the staff of certain tribunals.

Patrick Birkinshaw
September 1994

CONTENTS

TABLE OF CASES

TABLE OF STATUTES

ABBREVIATIONS USED IN THE TEXT

AC	Audit Commission
ADR	Alternative Dispute Resolution
BA	Benefits Agency
C&E	Customs and Excise
CA	Complaints Adjudicator (prisons)
CAG	Comptroller and Auditor General
CBI	Confederation of British Industry
CC	Citizen's Charter
CICB	Criminal Injuries Compensation Board
CLA	Commission for Local Administration
CoT	Council on Tribunals
CPAG	Child Poverty Action Group
CRE	Commission for Racial Equality
CTC	Complaints Task Force
DES	Department for Education and Science (now Department for Education)
DGFT	Director General of Fair Trading
DoE	Department of the Environment
DTI	Department of Trade and Industry
EOC	Equal Opportunities Commission
ERA	Education Reform Act 1988
ESRC	Economic and Social Research Council
FHSA	Family Health Service Authority
HAT	Housing Action Trust
HC	Housing Corporation
HSC	Health Service Commissioner
I&N	Immigration and Nationality Department
IR	Inland Revenue
LEA	Local Education Authority
LGATIA	Local Government (Access To Information) Act 1985
LGFA	Local Government Finance Act
LGHA	Local Government and Housing Act 1989
LGO	Local Government Ombudsman
MAFF	Ministry of Agriculture, Fisheries and Food
MMC	Monopolies and Mergers Commission

Abbreviations

NAO	National Audit Office
NCC	National Consumer Council
NDPB	Non Departmental Public Body
NEDO	National Economic Development Office
NSA	Next Steps Agency
OFT	Office of Fair Trading
PAC	Public Accounts Committee
PCA	Parliamentary Commissioner for Administration
PMCA	Police and Magistrates' Courts Act 1994
POLCA	Police Complaints Authority
SIB	Securities and Investment Board
TUC	Trades Union Congress
VFM	Value for Money (audit)

Chapter 1

INTRODUCTION

Why Take Non-Judicial Redress of Grievance Seriously?

In the first edition of this book a good deal of space was devoted to a justification of why seeking redress of grievance against state institutions through non-judicial procedures was important for lawyers. Lawyers have tended to concentrate on judicial processes when thinking of redress and if they did contemplate other devices, the judicial was inevitably regarded as the superior mode; the ombudsman, for instance, "was a valuable adjunct to any system of administrative law".[1] Today the impact of the Alternative Dispute Resolution movement, as well as studies of non-judicial means of grievance redress, have ensured that many lawyers no longer think exclusively in terms of judicial redress. The Justice/All Souls Report of 1988 addressed the subject of non-judicial methods of obtaining relief and a more thorough survey of types of procedures was provided by Rawlings in his study for the ESRC.[2] The Citizen's Charter has made an impact upon people's thinking about redress, even if they tend to dismiss the Charter as a charade. Ombudsmen have spawned like the frogs of ancient Egypt. Competition in service delivery, the encouragement of consumerism, the re-invention of government to meet the people's needs rather than those of bureaucrats[3] and the growing importance of complaints as a source of information for managers about service delivery and system impact, effectiveness and efficiency have all promoted complaints and their resolution to the top of the political agenda. When a Cabinet seminar (February 1993) approves a statement that "complaints are jewels to be cherished", whether they believe it or not, something is stirring.

---

[1]   H.W.R. Wade, *Administrative Law*, 1988, at 90.
[2]   R. Rawlings, *The Complaints Industry: A Review of Sociolegal Research on Aspects of Administrative Justice* (London, ESRC, 1986). For a survey of 19th-century mechanisms see H.W. Arthurs, *Without the Law* (University of Toronto Press, 1985).
[3]   D. Osborne and T. Gaebler, *Reinventing Government* (New York, Addison Wesley, 1992).

One may agree that non-judicial means of redress have entered
into popular and even legal consciousness. But judicial redress is
superior, it may be said. This could mean one of a variety of
things. At the end of the day law counts; it has the final say.
True, but what if it is not being widely or effectively used? Sunkin
et al.[4] have shown how narrowly focused much judicial review is
in its targets, for instance, and anything up to 15 million people
are estimated to have fallen out of the Legal Aid net in the last
15 years. Conversely, the encouragement of non-judicial avenues
for redress may produce a two or three-tier system of justice; in
the Asylum and Immigration Appeals Act 1993 the introduction
of fast track procedures has been motivated more by a desire for
keeping asylum disputes out of the courts and easing the burden
on the executive than by any desire to achieve "justice". The
Child Support Agency, one of the new generation of Next Steps
Agencies, has brought into disrepute an administrative agency
seen in many quarters to be riding roughshod over judicial settlements on divorce.[5] Non-judicial justice is, the argument runs,
an inferior form of justice. Courts matter, make no mistake. But
their impact is problematical when there is limited access to them
or where they are seriously curtailed in what they can address. A
quote from the first edition is relevant to this latter point:

> "The role of our courts of law in public law matters is limited
> by two important factors. . . . The second . . . theoretically
> more important one [is] that our courts of law are inferior to
> Parliament, and the common law inferior as a form of law to
> parliamentary legislation to which the Crown has assented.
> This is not the place to develop the implications of this doc-
> trine, but our constitutional history has witnessed a rigid
> division between law and politics. There are realms within
> which judges may not operate. As one commentator has said,
> the language of law itself is noticeably remote from politics.
> 'On the one hand, the judiciary has a fierce independence;
> on the other law is not regarded as the great interpreter
> of the pattern of politics.'[6] Law may be successful, though
> not all would agree with the proposition, in presenting itself

---

4   M. Sunkin *et al.*, *Judicial Review in Perspective* (London, The Public Law
    Project, 1993).
5   See the Social Security Committee's *Operation of the Child Support Act*:
    HC 69 (1993/4). The Agency's first annual report was seen by some as an
    apologia for its existence.
6   K. Dyson, *The State Tradition in Western Europe*, (Oxford, Martin
    Robertson, 1980) at 41.

as an autonomous institution, but its autonomy has been bought at a price. Its narrow, technical and arid nature, especially . . . in the field of government, has helped to ensure a 'wholesome English contempt for legal technique'.[7]"

There are many, especially judges, who would deny the correctness of the above statement. After all, was it not a judicial decision which established that courts may disapply an Act of Parliament itself where the Act is in breach of Community law and that courts may award injunctions even against Ministers of the Crown acting in their official capacity?[8] Furthermore, there have been sensible suggestions from judges as to how judicial protection against public power may be made more effective.[9] The language of law and the culture of legal discourse, however, have not had an important role in informing the culture of government in Britain. Law has given government powers, enormous powers, and law limits those powers. But governments draft the laws and Parliament inevitably approves them. It is interesting, for instance, that two of the Government's flagships in its "citizen as consumer king" campaign, the Citizen's Charter and the White Paper and Code of Conduct on *Open Government*[10] are not even contained in legal instruments. Nor indeed is one of the most profound changes affecting central government organisation since the 1850s, the movement to executive agencies known as Next Steps Agencies (see chapter 2). White papers and framework documents are the progenitors of these initiatives. In fact law is seen as antipathetic to the Government's broad objectives. Government has shown its contempt for law,[11] and lawyers cannot apply the ideals of legality and constitutionality to politics and administration, or certainly not in a manner that would be familiar to North American and continental lawyers.

There is an important point that must not be overlooked.

---

7   *Per* F.W. Maitland, cited in Dyson (Note 6 above) at 42. See Maitland "The Crown as Corporation" (1901) 18 LQR 131.
8   *Factortame v Secretary of State* [1991] 1 AC 603; *M v Home Office* [1993] 3 All ER 537 (HL).
9   Sir H. Woolf, "Public Law – Private Law: Why the Divide?" *Public Law*, 1986, 220; *Protection of the Public: A New Challenge* (London, Stevens, 1991); "Judicial Review: A Possible Programme for Reform", *Public Law*, 1992, 221.
10 Cm. 2290, 1993.
11 *The Judge Over Your Shoulder*, Cabinet Office and Treasury Solicitor's Department, 1987; McAuslan and McEldowney *Law, Legitimacy and the Constitution* (London, Sweet & Maxwell, 1985 at 28–32) graphically list a catalogue of arrogant reaction by Government towards judicial decisions.

Justice is achieved through bodies other than courts. Where it is being achieved or where its achievement is attempted, then students and practitioners of law should be interested because they are witnessing the stuff of their craft. We should not be blinded by labels such as "judicial procedures are good" but should rather inquire into what they are good at doing and how the values which inform the idea of law such as fairness, equal protection, integrity, decency and deprecation of arbitrariness are given fuller expression. Courts are limited in what they can do for cultural reasons and financial factors limit access to the courts, certainly as the world is presently ordered. Our interest as lawyers should not end because courts are not making the decisions and nor should we abandon hopes that the role of our courts may develop, especially as prompted by European Community law and by the European Convention on Human Rights. The latter are influencing the mode of judicial discourse in the United Kingdom so that novel questions are being asked by the courts about the extent of governmental right.

Quite how this will affect the traditional position of courts in our constitution remains to be seen. Is it an exaggeration to state that courts have not until recently had a significant impact in influencing *a priori* the process of public decision-making with ideals such as fairness, impartiality or legitimacy? The battlefields of the 17th century ensured that decisons of constitutional significance and political importance are, in theory, the preserve of political institutions. "As the common law ceded pride of place to statute law . . . it was quite unable to provide a body of public law principles in terms of which legislation could be framed. Hence, the Rule of Law became a narrow, formal concept expressing a procedural philosophy and losing the substantive concerns that were apparent even in Dicey's later classic formulation"[12] (Dyson, 1980). It may well be, as a US jurist commented on the position in England, that this inculcated a reluctance among lawyers to ask, at least in courts, fundamental questions about governmental right as a consequence of such decisions being withdrawn from the courts.[13] The burden of the present work is not to suggest that there should be a shifting back to the courts of such a power. It is a more mundane, yet pervasive one that a lack of such legal involvement or concern has been detrimental to the creation of fair and open procedures in our governmental processes;

[12]   Dyson (Note 6 above), at 42.
[13]   R. Dworkin, "Philosophy and Politics", in B. Magee (ed.), *Men of Ideas*, (Oxford, Oxford University Press, 1978), at 209.

its absence has prevented the formulation of a critique against secrecy and arbitrary decision-making. Lawyers, in other words, were not troubled by problems of government legitimation. It legitimated itself.

The other side of this is that lawyers in any event would not be welcome outside legal fora, that is courts. As courts have been confined by technique and subject-matter, so the skills suited to those confined subjects and techniques are out of place outside courts. It has been said on many occasions that a narrow, rule-bound concept of law, a concept which is culturally dominant among politicians and their advisers and some jurists, is tied up with a 19th century image of law as an autonomous body of thought which is inherently individualistic and which is confined to the adjudication of clashes between individuals. The legacy of that concept still has a constraining hold on some aspects of judicial and certainly most political thinking. But in substance, like the 19th century, it has gone. Just as "knowledge of the rules alone never won any case worth winning", so that a winning argument is one that addresses context and flavour and the underlying *raison d'être* of a decision or series of decisions, so legal reasoning was never as formalistic or rule-bound as is often supposed. More crucial to our present purpose is the fact that while law is sometimes involved with the adjudication of disputes between individuals, one of whom might happen to be the state in one of its various bodily manifestations, law is often the medium through which the state organises and regulates activities collectively, that is, where primary reference is to the overall impact and utility of state policies, whatever their content – privatisation or nationalisation, regulation or deregulation. In 1911, the statute book for that year was 450 pages long. By 1929 it had reached 1,000 pages. In 1992, it numbered 13,000 pages.

Law, or legislation, has been the device through which a whole corpus of state activities has been created. In addition, an arabesque of public or quasi-public bodies has been established or co-opted to the state's enterprise, often without any legal foundation, covering all aspects of administration and management from executive decision-making, adjudicatory functions, resource allocation by licensing or franchising, legislative activity which includes statutory instruments and regulations, departmental rule-making, rule-making by non-departmental public bodies, self-regulatory bodies, professional and voluntary bodies, local authorities, the duties of overseeing contract performance and compliance and so on. The influence of the form of law which saw itself exclusively as technical rule-mongering in court

rooms and which saw legal skills as restricted to that task has
had a narrowing effect on the potential contribution that legal
skills have been able to make to government. This is the more
surprising when one considers the broad range of skills and
techniques involved in lawyering.[14] Summers,[15] for instance, has
outlined five basic techniques of law that a society may use. These
are the grievance remedial – and, one should add, through the
broad spectrum of remedial processes available; the penal; the
administrative-regulatory – now assuming more of a lead role in
privatisation programmes; the public benefit conferral technique
– which is not exhausted by social security or welfare programmes
but could involve conferral of public contracts for the performance by a private contractor of public tasks such as running
a prison, or a welfare programme where a strong public law
involvement will occur, for instance, ombudsman involvement;
lastly the private arranging technique most often seen in contract
law, property law or company law. There are more sophisticated
accounts of the functions of lawyering and the tasks of law[16] but
Summers' analysis clearly embraces techniques which transcend
the adjudication of collisions between individuals. To take the
administrative-regulatory and public benefit conferral techniques,
for instance, the point has been argued forcefully that the skills
of legal technique are alien to the broad discretionary basis upon
which public or private administration operates. Lawyers, it has
been argued, would introduce excessive formalism or legalism
into, for example, the tribunals administering the social security
programme.[17] Even tribunals are too lawyer-like and expensive,
and in these times of executive domination too unpredictably
independent, hence their removal from areas of social security
and prison discipline and their non-introduction into many areas
of citizen/state dispute concerning new statutory programmes.

On the other hand one cannot guarantee, and much of our
public administration does not support the belief, that politicians
bureaucrats and regulators, when left to themselves, will devise
procedures or decision-making processes which will ensure fairness in interest representation, fairness in procedure, avoidance of
arbitrariness, accessibility and meaningful participation for interested members of the public or effective accountability where the

---

14   N. Lewis, "Towards a Sociology of Lawyering in Public Administration",
      Northern Ireland Legal Quarterly, 1981, 89.
15   R. Summers, "The Technique Element in Law", 59 *Cal.L. Rev.* 733.
16   K. Llewellyn, "The Normative, the Legal and the Law Jobs: The Problem
      of Juristic Method", 49 *Yale Law Journal* (1940), 1355.
17   R. Titmus, "Welfare 'Rights', Law and Discretion", (1971) 42 PQ 113.

exercise of power and broad discretionary decision-making are involved. Inherent in the craft of "lawyering" is an awareness of the strength of procedural forms in protecting fairness, indifferent though many lawyers may be to extending this awareness beyond the dignity of our "high courts of law". We are put to shame in our country by those lawyers who have been in the vanguard of reform in the common law influenced world and who have been responsible for introducing freedom of information legislation, open government laws, institutions for the monitoring, overseeing and reforming of administrative systems of justice and who have built machinery to ensure that the task is undertaken regularly, professionally and independently of government. The reforms have been informed by a desire to enhance fairness, efficiency and accountability and not by a desire to line lawyers' pockets in new subject areas as more traditional areas of legal activity evaporate.

As stated in the first edition, a narrow approach to law and legal techniques would have been open to valid criticism even had the state not developed from its 19th century image of being equal with its subjects under the law while simultaneously possessing the authority of government and providing the framework within which free individuals allocated their resources. How much more open to criticism therefore is it when this image of state and law has not kept pace with changes in social and economic development. Poggi[18] and others have written of the progressive "compenetration" of state and society, of public and private. Government of the "official" kind syphoned off many of its tasks and functions to intermediaries, both of a public and non-public nature. It engaged in activities hitherto the preserve of the private sector; institutions and corporations in the private sector emerged as powers, almost, if not actually, equal with the state, though obviously not accountable in any political democratic manner. In short, the form of government associated with the 19th century state has long disappeared in practice, though whether this was, as Middlemas suggested, because it could not accommodate the antagonisms of industrial society is beyond the scope of this book.[19]

The legacy of the 19th century is still very much with us however, not only in its sketch of imagined constitutional

[18]   G. Poggi, *The Development of the Modern State* (London, Hutchinson, 1978).
[19]   K. Middlemas, *Politics in Industrial Society* (London, Macmillan, 1979); *Industry, Unions and Government* (London, Macmillan, 1983).

power, Parliamentary supremacy, for instance or appeals to Victorian values, but ironically in presenting us with the results of the "centralising tendency" of the 19th century state, a process which has not abated. Witness the diminution of local government and the accretion of central government; the recently announced reforms centralising controls over the police, the all-mighty Treasury and the locust-like spread of government-appointed non-departmental bodies and public/private hybrids.[20] While the state has become more powerful and more centralised, Parliament and the courts have exercised less control. Secrecy laws, now less scattergun in their scope but more focused and as potentially Draconian in effect,[21] and judicial deference to departmental sensitivities and ministerial etiquette set a sad precedent for the accountability of the modern British state. Law should not be exclusively involved with legitimating state activity; it should inform state activity and those whom the state sponsors with standards of fair procedure and openness.

Behind the procedures lies the substance, and behind the substance lie the ideals: ideals of legality, fairness, accountability and responsiveness, ideals of constitutionality. The task is to find devices to best express the ideals in a changing state structure.[22] These ideals may have been hijacked by an accountant's calculator or an economist's bludgeon or even an ideologue's passion, but their importance has not been denied, merely, as the notorious events surrounding the Matrix Churchill episode throughout the early 1990s testify, conveniently ignored by governors.[23] On the ideals which predicate a legal order, I would like to use a quote from the first edition, taken from comments by Norman Lewis on work by David Trubeck:

> "It has been argued elsewhere that the fundamental justification for a legal order in an open society related to its ability to contribute to equality, individuality and community, the latter implying sharing and participating in the larger enterprise.[24] We would not argue an ontological foundation for these values but at least we feel entitled to claim that

20 P. Birkinshaw, I. Harden and N. Lewis, *Government by Moonlight: The Hybrid Parts of the State* (London, Unwin Hyman, 1990).
21 P. Birkinshaw, *Reforming the Secret State* (Buckingham, Open University Press, 1991).
22 I. Harden and N. Lewis, *The Noble Lie: The British Constitution and the Rule of Law* (London, Hutchinson, 1986).
23 See p. 206 Note 58 below.
24 See D. Trubeck, "Complexity and Contradiction in the Legal Order", (1977) 11 *Law and Society* 529.

the liberal notion of the rule of law (formal rationality, autonomy, equal treatment, rational discourse) together with the idea of participation by the ruled in the process of rule connects the expectation of the modern state with the 'moral heritage of the west'."[25]

Grievances and Remedies

The term "grievances" is used here in a broad sense to mean a claim which concerns the righting of a perceived wrong whether ultimately justified or not.[26] Anyone who has worked in a free representation unit will know how difficult it is to locate somebody to whom it is possible to address a grievance on behalf of an individual who would not usually obtain representation; at least at this level things had improved even before the Citizen's Charter (CC) gave added impetus to complaints procedures. Where we still have a long way to go is in the creation of suitable procedures whereby those affected by decisions may have an opportunity to express their views before a decision is made. People may well know about the broad thrust of the CC, but do they know that the Ministry of Agriculture, Fisheries and Food has a quarterly meeting of an advisory body for consumer representatives involving, for example, the National Food Alliance and the Consumer Association? Or that the Benefits Agency has a Disability Forum and Ethnic Minority Forum or that the Employment Service has special consultation groups on which to bounce ideas, as does the Office of Telecommunications? Throughout the book, I will address opportunities for citizens to participate in the decision-making process in order to avoid or minimise grievances. Here, I remain in no doubt that our record is a poor one. "Remedies" refers to opportunities to put something right and, following on from what has just been said, the discussion will cover prophylactic measures aimed at preventing things going wrong.

The State

The term "state" has no precise meaning or separate legal identity in our domestic law, although somewhat strangely, the House of

---

25   See Note 18 above.

26   R. Rawlings, "The Parliamentary Redress of Grievance", in C. Harlow (ed.) *Public Law and Politics* (London, Sweet & Maxwell, 1986); N. Lewis *et al., Complaints procedures in Local Government* (University of Sheffield, 1987); N. Lewis and P. Birkinshaw, *When Citizens Complain: Reforming Justice and Administration* (Buckingham, Open University Press, 1993).

Lords has held that property may be held by the state.[27] It is a concept which is featuring more prominently under EC law.[28] The term is used loosely to refer to the *loci* of official power – the organs of central government, local government, police and the whole range of the hybrid quasi-governmental sector which has been chosen by government to carry out activities on its behalf, or onto which public functions have been devolved, off-loaded or contracted out. The Government may assert that its policies in the latter part of the 20th century have been aimed at reducing the state, getting it off people's backs and releasing initiative in an augmented and liberated private sector. In reality, much of what has taken place is not so much a removal as a reforming of the state. If government influence is not present in terms of ownership of the means of production for instance, it will be present in the regulation of those assets, especially in the privatised sector, or

[27] *Ross v Lord Advocate* [1986] 3 All ER 79 (HL). For a lucid account of the reasons behind the absence of a "state tradition" in England and Britain see K. Dyson, *The State Tradition in Western Europe*, 1980. On the use of the term "state" in English and British constitutional theory see G. Marshall, *Constitutional Theory*, 1971, especially chapter 2. In Britain, argues Dyson, "there is a disinclination to explore ideas about the distinctive character of public authority. Little or no attention is paid to state as a political concept which identifies the nation in its corporate and collectivist capacity; as a legal institution with an inherent responsibility for regulating matters of public concern; and as a socio-cultural phenomenon which expresses a new unique form of associative bond" (at 43). See F.W. Maitland, *Introduction to Otto Gierke: Political Theories of the Middle Ages* (Cambridge University Press, 1900). For an interesting judicial observation on the term "state" in British constitutional law, see Lord Simon of Glaisdale in *D v NSPCC* [1977] 1 All ER 589 (HL) at 609 to 610. On what are the "interests of the state" see *Chandler v DPP* [1962] 3 All ER 142 (HL). The term "state" occurs frequently in constitutional and administrative usage in the UK. We have Secretaries of State; Acts of State; State secrets; acts which are prejudicial to the safety or interests of the state; State Registered Nurses and "servant of the state", namely, a police officer who is not a servant of the Crown: *Fisher v Oldham Corp.* [1930] 2 KB 364. We also use an ambiguous variety of other epithets where other countries would be inclined to use the term "state". These include the "Crown", "government", "public", "civil", "national", "British" and so on; see Marshall, *op. cit.* On the separation of Minister from the Crown or the Crown as Monarch and the Crown as Executive see *M v Home Office* [1993] 3 All ER 537 (HL) and on the two Crowns, Maitland, "The Crown as Corporation" (1901) 18 LQR 131. For a broad brush treatment of the role of the state in Britain since 1945 see B. Jessop, "The Transformation of the state in Post-War Britain", in R. Scase (ed.), *The State in Western Europe*, and *The Capitalist State*, 1982; and P. Dunleavy and B. O'Leary, *Theories of the State* (2nd edn, 1992).

[28] For example, *Foster v British Gas* [1990] 3 All ER 897 (CJEC), *Marshall v Southampton etc AHA* [1986] 2 All ER 584 (CJEC), and in the burgeoning law covering public procurement and state aids.

in the way it shapes the decisions of influential actors in the market-place who occupy a *de facto* regulatory position of their own. "Power exercised behind the schemes is power exercised nonetheless", said Lloyd LJ in his judgment holding that the City Panel on Takeovers,[29] a private voluntary body in form, was subject to the supervisory public law jurisdiction of the High Court – a form of supervision until then exclusively restricted to bodies created by Parliament or by the Crown.

I believe Lloyd LJ puts the point beautifully. Government may privatise but it cannot abandon its responsibilities for appropriate regulation and grievance redress. Nor can it abandon its responsibilities for maintaining an appropriate justice system to meet the grievances of its citizens.[30] To put the matter bluntly, the state, as Stewart pointed out for the United States, simply cannot avoid delegating vast areas of executive, legislative and administrative activity to a multiplicity of permanent, *ad hoc* and varying institutions, whatever the ideology of the government.[31] This book deals with the means of redress that are provided where contact between official government and those to whom powers are delegated or contracted out on the one hand, and citizens on the other, generates grievance. What government may have to do is re-invent itself to carry out its responsibilities more responsively and efficiently and to organise the delivery of services in a manner which better meets public need, whether it provides the service itself or contracts for a private undertaker to provide the service under strict terms of compliance – "entrepreneurial government" is the phrase coined by Osborne and Gaebler.[32] As those influential authors have said, government cannot abandon its basic job, but it may not be the best person to do the job. Likewise, for most citizens, "exit" from public service, i.e. looking for service elsewhere, is not a real possibility;[33] unfortunately their "voice" is still not given sufficient consideration.

Citizen's Charter

Perhaps not unfairly described as John Major's "Big Idea", the CC was launched in July 1991 and its first annual report was

---

29 *R v Panel on Takeovers and Mergers ex parte Datafin* [1987] 1 All ER 564 (CA).
30 Lewis and Birkinshaw, Note 26 above.
31 R. Stewart *et al.*, "Vermont Yankee and the Evolution of Administrative Procedure", 91 *Harvard L.R.* (1978) 1804.
32 Note 3 above.
33 Hirschman, *Exit, Voice and Loyalty: Response to Decline in Firms, Organisations and States* (Cambridge, Cambridge University Press, 1970).

published in November 1992. Although the widespread publicity
attending the Charter and the litany of service-specific charters[34]
are hard to avoid, only one in ten people according to a survey in
February 1993 claimed to know anything about the Charter apart
from its existence and there was widespread public ignorance
about service providers and deep confusion about which bodies
were public and which private.[35] By August 1993, 71 per cent
claimed to know about the Charter. Described as a "programme
for a decade", there is clearly much that the CC has to achieve
in order to produce a better informed public and in this light
it is disappointing that the Minister responsible for the CC has
elected not to get onto the statute book freedom of information
legislation but rather a non-enforceable Code without any statutory
backing.[36] The attempts at defining a public service and public
sector ethos through the eyes of those who use the services should
not be denigrated although outside the privatised industries the
CC did not encompass any reforms in consumer laws in the private sector. Some of the ideas in the CC go back long before
1991 and could be found in operation in various local authorities
in the early 1980s. Of crucial significance were the internal drive
towards greater efficiency in public service going back to MINIS
and Financial Management Initiatives,[37] the movement towards
the Next Steps Agencies[38] for the delivery of government programmes (see chapter 2), and the Publication by the Cabinet
Office of *Service to the Public* (1988)[39] which accompanied the
Next Steps movement.

The basic point about the Charter is that it recognises that the
taxpayer pays for public services but often confronts a monopoly provider. In order to provide a surrogate for competition
which is not otherwise there, a series of incentives and market substitutes have to be produced to instil greater efficiency
in service delivery. These include creation of internal markets
where there is a separation between the purchaser of a service
and the provider, most graphically illustrated in the NHS where

---

34 By March, 1994 there were 38 charters. The Second Annual Report on the
     Charter is Cm 2540 (March 1994).
35 *The Independent*, 25 February 1993.
36 Cm 2290 (1993) and see Birkinshaw, (1993). Personal information held by
     public bodies and that concerning health and safety will be available under
     statutory provisions.
37 These were stepping-stones from a traditional bureaucratic model of admin-
     istration to a more managerial ethos in government.
38 Goldsworthy, *Setting Up Next Steps* (HMSO, 1991).
39 This was a talisman of consumer-led management techniques in the public
     service.

a purchaser, a health authority or fund-holding GP, can shop around a variety of providers to obtain the cheapest treatment for the patient. The theory states that a purchaser/provider split will mean that patients will get the best value for money. However, the director of the National Consumer Council has expressed the view that decisions concerning the purchase of services are based on information not available to the patient or public. Even the Health Minister has declared in Parliament that neither the patient nor the doctor needs information concerning waiting lists because it is available to his/her health authority – the patient's champion. Another example of a split is in the arrangements between government departments and agencies for the provision of public services according to terms of an agreement. Neither of the above arrangements[40] is a legally binding agreement although a special procedure exists to deal with disputes between purchasers and providers in the NHS (see chapter 5).

All public bodies involved in providing services to the public will have to state their objectives, the standards of service, their targets for service delivery and compensation schemes for failure to meet standards. A central feature will be an easily identified complaints procedure for dissatisfied clients/customers. Bodies will be expected to produce their own charters which will display all relevant information in a readily accessible form (and, one hopes, in languages other than English). Information from complaints will be used to improve service. Failure to meet specified standards, which feedback from customer surveys will influence, will be met with penalties and compensation. These could include reduction in grant, non-award of performance-related pay and the threat of awarding the service to a more efficient provider. In any event, no service will automatically be exempt from market testing to see whether it can be transferred to a private sector entity to provide a better service at better value for money and to enhance efficiency. Information about services and standards attained will have to be published – in the case of local authorities, schools and privatised industries, legislation has been passed imposing these features as a legal obligation (see chapters 3 and 5). The CC touches prisons with the result that prisoners are given an information pack at the start of their sentence, produced

---

[40] There is an extremely interesting agreement between the Secretary of State at the Department of Employment and the Secretary of State at the Department of Social Security whereby the former will administer benefits for unemployment on behalf of the latter. Constitutionally, Secretaries of State are one and indivisible.

by the Prison Service and Prison Reform Trust. This has details of complaints procedures, visits, letters, release arrangements and social security on release. Sentence planning has been introduced for longer-term prisoners covering employment, education and self-analysis. Compacts are produced in some prisons recalling Lord Justice Woolf's proposals[41] for a contract between the prisoner and the prison authorities, and an "independent" adjudicator has been introduced (see chapter 2). There will be constant monitoring of performance together with internal and, crucially, external audit and Ministers will be quizzed at Cabinet seminars on their achievements under the CC. The Government places much emphasis on the National Audit Office and the Audit Commission although very little was said in the original Charter about the Ombudsmen.[42]

Staff who have contact with the public are to wear name badges and Charter Marks are to be awarded to those bodies which achieve excellence in public service. Inspectorates are to be more widely used where appropriate and will display greater independence from the services they inspect. Greater lay involvement and more publicity for inspectors' reports will be expected and a requirement that those inspected, or those responsible for them, will respond to the reports. A new Office for Standards in Education has been established which with its Welsh equivalent will ensure regular inspection of schools. Crown immunities, especially from inspection, enforcement and regulatory control, will go in specific areas.[43] Performance tables may be used to compare service provision by different bodies – as in the case of health services in 1994. However, there has been widespread complaint that Charter information has not been as widely or effectively publicised as intended and some areas have been particularly resistant to its influence, most notably the courts.[44]

Two further features should be noted. The first is a Complaints Task Force (CTF). Originally, the CC envisaged that a lay adjudicator scheme would operate in public bodies but this idea was abandoned when it was realised that its introduction could be expensive, might unjustifiably cut across departmental priorities and it might be difficult to get those with appropriate skills to act as adjudicators. Each body was instead to come up

[41]   Sir H. Woolf, *Prison Disturbances*. Cm 1456 (London, HMSO, 1991).
[42]   The Parliamentary Commissioner for Administration complained that the CC did not adequately publicise his services especially re prisoners.
[43]   Planning, health and safety, health.
[44]   See F. Purchas, "The Constitution in the Market Place", (1993) *New L.J.* 1604.

with suggestions for its own complaints procedures. To assist their thinking, a CTF has been established which will set up a list of best practices in complaints procedures and existing procedures will be assessed against these principles. The Cabinet Office did not accept that there was a need for a statutory framework but an exhortatory stimulus might be required. The CTF will be a free agent without statutory powers with a mixed membership appointed by the Prime Minister. It formulates its own principles so there is no requirement upon it to pay especial regard to those who have spent years investigating complaints in the public sector although an interim report acknowledges their assistance (see the *Citizen's Charter Complaints Task Force*, Cabinet Office, 1994). The Local Government Ombudsman has, as we shall see in chapter 3, formulated very detailed guidance on complaints procedures for bodies within his jurisdiction.

The other development has been the introduction of "Charterline". Helplines have been a common feature in public sector bodies for some considerable time. Charterline, originally set up on a pilot basis in the East Midlands, aims to provide via a telephone call information on what standards people can expect from public services and utilities and what they have to do if they wish to complain. Price Waterhouse, who are managing the project for the CC Unit of the Cabinet Office, estimate that there will be 30,000 calls a month in the pilot area. Ultimately it is expected that up to 1,400 public bodies and utilities will be covered nationally. Information will cover: names, addresses, responsibilities, service standards, complaints procedures. The Unit will also have a means of establishing which services are creating the greatest number of complaints and where more attention to quality, improvement, training and realignment of existing resources must be given. Ninety per cent of calls must be answered within 10 seconds, 98 per cent within 20 seconds. To improve that rate would require a cost that could only be justified in a commercial environment according to Price Waterhouse. Even the cost of the original service proved beyond the Treasury's forbearance and the scheme was scrapped in May 1994.

The CC has been subjected to a great amount of criticism.[45] A common theme from the public – although the evidence suggests that people are more inclined to complain rather than simply "lump it", which may well be a sign of captiousness rather than enhanced citizenship – is posed by the question: what is the point in

---

[45] See A. Barron and C. Scott, "The Citizen's Charter Programme", (1992) *Modern L.R.* 526.

complaining if there is inadequate investment in a service? Or how can a service improve if it is paying out compensation from inadequate funding for not meeting standards? The Treasury has issued guidelines on service improvement and compensation (DAO/GEN 15/92 para. 2). The CC has as two of its objectives the more efficient delivery of public service and better value for money within existing resources or with reduced resources. Next Steps Agencies have to submit information on target achievement in their budget bid as part of the public expenditure process. Targets and standards are somewhat like contract specifications in the private sector. But in the private sector the cost of meeting the specifications is what the customer has agreed to pay and a wise customer will look to the lowest cost. In the public sector, the cost will be controlled by the Treasury who will take a very firm line on what can be afforded – as witness the Charterline experience. If complaints indicate that an improved service is required and an increase in taxes is not to be permitted, then economies will have to found somewhere. If the service cannot be provided within existing public sector constraints on, for example, salary levels, then it will have to be transferred to the private sector. The private sector has for many years sought to introduce enhanced efficiency at reduced cost and improved quality. To help ensure quality the British Standards Institute has formulated a quality assurance standard BS 5750, which has been used by local authorities in competitive tendering to help provide specifications or terms for the contract.[46] "Outsourcing" or buying in management specialists is becoming a widespread practice in the public sector, spreading private sector skills into delivery of public programmes; indeed, the Charterline experience is a good example (see above).

It is easy to criticise these developments as distinctly right-of-centre market ideology, with the citizen as consumer as contractor seeking to promote his or her self-interest at an inevitable detriment to someone else, invariably the poorer, less well-connected and less articulate, and the consequential dismantling of welfare provision as we know it. However, not all analyses run this way. For instance, it has been suggested that these developments might produce smaller units of service delivery which are more responsive to citizens and which allow for citizen participation. The evidence of NHS Trusts (see chapter 3) would not support this, but it should not be discounted. Furthermore, as I argued above,

---

[46]   Although the BSI employed decorating contractors who did not have the BS 5750 kitemark (*Financial Times*, 23 November 1993). They were obviously better value!

the state cannot simply withdraw. If it is not always to be the direct provider – to develop Wolfgang Friedmann's model[47] – it will be the contractor arranging for the provision. A government will want to ensure its own survival by ensuring quality and performance and grievance procedures will be a central feature of that arrangement; one has only to look at the contract specifications for the running of prisons.[48] Where I think the difficulties emerge are in the absence of an appropriate constitutional dimension to these developments: what are to be the standards of public ethics in the new shape of government or the public/private interface? As I write, the Treasury and Civil Service Committee are investigating the impact that a changing state structure will have on the civil service, and the Public Accounts Committee is to report on what it considers to be a worrying trend towards lowering of standards and fraud and incompetence in public services.[49] What of the representation of the disadvantaged and dispossessed? How is their voice to be heard? Even in the United States, government has encouraged the private sector to meet the credit needs of local depressed communities. The Community Reinvestment Act 1977 put the policy onto the statute book but it is intended that it will be replaced by a more effective piece of legislation. It is common, for instance, that when banks merge, community groups often participate in the public hearings (*public*, it should be noted), to get more favourable banking arrangements for their community. In the United Kingdom, banking is a service which is not touched by the CC because it is a private sector service. In a survey on the effects of the CC in 1993, banks rated very poorly in terms of service, far below public bodies (three private sector services used for comparators) and the Banking Ombudsman has been highly critical of service and practices by banks (see chapter 5).

Other criticisms centre around the argument that the CC debases the whole concept of citizenship. It does not enrich the concept, it impoverishes it. Nowhere does it refer to enhancing democratic rights or improving the nature of government

---

47   W. Friedmann, *The Rule of Law in a Mixed Economy* (London, Stevens, 1971); see chapter 4 p. 142 *et seq*.

48   These have detailed specifications on discipline and complaints processes and treatment of prisoners.

49   *The Proper Conduct of Public Business* HC 154 (1993/4). It is interesting that as the NAO and CAG are taking an ever more pivotal role in accountability of government, the CAG officers are being subjected to more "slagging off" by Whitehall officials. *Public Finance* 15 October (1993) had details of a confidential report by Sir Brian Cubbon, formerly of the Home Office, criticising the quality of the NAO's work.

decision-making affecting policy; and who, after all, has been responsible for the enormous budget deficit, the pursuit of good money after bad following the ERM debacle in 1992? There is no mention of a Bill of Rights, very few legal rights, no Freedom of Information Act but merely a code (see chapter 2), no open meetings or open advisory committee laws – even access to the papers relating to the development of the CC has been refused. The image is of a government maximising its discretion in government while creating a market for self-interested individuals to complain about others' shortcomings while successfully cocooning themselves from effective censure. In their response to such criticisms the Government stated that in consumer surveys "accountability" scored low in consumer preferences. The Government reported that consumers want responsiveness, quality and cost-effectiveness. As I have argued with others elsewhere, these are forms of accountability.[50] Furthermore, how responsive would the Government be to claims that a service should be improved and that it can only be improved by more expenditure? This may be an argument which can only be supported by political change from the ballot box because it is an approach which the CC has not countenanced.

William Waldegrave has said that the CC has improved standards and that is what Joe Consumer wants. "By leaving our reforms half-finished and diverting our energies for years to come to legal constitution mongering, designed to close a non-existent democratic deficit, we would be helping neither the public service itself, nor those long-suffering residents of Cleveland or anywhere else".[51] It is not simply a question of tinkering with the constitution; there is the question of removing its safeguards, as in the removal of legal aid from an estimated 14 to 15 million people, making legal protection through the courts less than likely in their cases. In the name of greater efficiency, the Government has removed independent adjudication in a series of "service areas", including most controversially immigration. Visitors to this country who require visas had rights of appeal removed by the Asylum and Immigration Appeals Act. Rights of appeal in such circumstances are rare among our EC neighbours, it must be said, but it is nothing less than stunning to realise that up to 20 per cent of the 10,000 cases appealed under the old system were found to have been wrongly decided. Efficiency demands

---

50   Birkinshaw *et al.*, Note 20 above.
51   W. Waldegrave, *The Reality of Reform and Accountability in Today's Public Service* (London, CIPFA, 1993).

that such mistakes are not exposed. Efficiency and justice are not incompatible virtues;[52] it is a poor form of efficiency that is allowed to defeat justice, or rather it is no form of efficiency at all but expediency.

If there is something of benefit in the CC proposals, how far should they extend? In relation to the police, the CC's first annual report[53] sets out the usual list of Charter elements involved in providing a public service and does also refer to accountability and consultation between the police and local communities. In a much publicised announcement the Home Secretary reported that the recommendations of the Sheehy Report on *Police Responsibilities and Rewards*,[54] which sought to introduce greater efficiency and incentive into police operations and activities, were to be substantially modified in their implementation (see chapter 5). Police Associations and even the Metropolitan Police Commissioner had argued that introduction of market forces was not the way to get better value for money in policing; such an approach was described by the Police Commissioner as "superficial":[55] "Policing was more than a mere business". Where does this specific public sector quality which is more than mere business end? If policing, why not apply a special case for prisons, immigration, social security? What are the criteria beyond the clout of a particular labour force and special pleading of a particular occupation?

An Audit Commission report of October 1993[56] has reported that the police will have to develop more coherent strategies to make the fight against crime more effective. The Audit Commission (AC) and the National Audit Office (NAO) feature prominently in the process of audit under the CC and about these bodies a little will now be said.

Audit

A crucial feature of audit under the NAO and AC, in addition to their auditing of the accounts, is their value for money audit. This involves a study of the economy, efficiency and effectiveness of the use of public resources by the bodies under their jurisdiction. The AC especially has been promoted to the fore in government campaigns to make public services more efficient (see chapter 3).

---

52 Lewis and Birkinshaw, Note 26 above, chapter 3.
53 Cm 2101, 1992.
54 Cm 2280, 1993.
55 *Guardian*, 14 October 1993.
56 *Helping with Inquiries: Tackling Crime Effectively*, 1993.

Crucially, surcharge provisions on individuals who have spent public money unlawfully or unreasonably only exist in local government, in spite of well catalogued and culpable waste in central and quasi government. Unlike the Ombudsman, the NAO, whose head is the Comptroller and Auditor General (CAG), is not concerned with individual grievances, although complaints he receives may well inform which services or sections of a service he is going to investigate. Like the Parliamentary Commissioner, the CAG reports to a Parliamentary Committee – the Public Accounts Committee. This Committee itself may receive complaints from members of the public which again may inform its investigations but it is not a grievance resolution mechanism. The CAG's powers and the Committee's remit prevent it investigating the merits of government policies[57] and it is also prevented from investigating commercial bodies in the public sector which are outside its jurisdiction.

Behind the scenes there is informal liaison between the CAG and the Parliamentary Commissioner for Administration (PCA). Indeed, since 1991 the CAG and NAO have handed unpublished papers from their investigations to the departmental select committees of the House of Commons (see chapter 2 on select committees) where they are relevant to a committee's inquiries.[58] These inquiries may well be triggered by a complaint but they will not be investigating the details of an individual grievance but examining the policy, administration and expenditure implications of departmental or agency action. Some subjects have triggered many complaints to committee chairs or members; the Child Support Agency was the subject of over 400 complaints to the Social Services Committee Chair which launched an inquiry into its operations. Select Committees are pressing for the right to ask the CAG to investigate subjects on a reference from the committee. Select Committees have asked Treasury officials to appear before them but the Treasury and Civil Service Committee has objected to evidence being given by Civil Servants to the Committee on the impact of Government changes on the morale and attitudes of the Civil Service. The possibility of joint investigations has been suggested. New powers were given to Committees in 1991, including the power of the Home Affairs Committee to investigate the Lord Chancellor's Department, the Attorney

---

57　　National Audit Act 1983, section 6(2).
58　　*Government Response to Second Report of House of Commons Select Committee on Procedure* (1989/90) 1 May 1991; "Scrutiny", BBC 2, 27 February 1993.

General's Department, the Treasury Solicitor's Department, the Serious Fraud Office and the Crown Prosecution Service. Individual cases will not be investigated.

The Audit Commission appoints auditors for the local authorities and NHS bodies under its jurisdiction and their close involvement in the hearing of objections concerning the accounts of local authorities[59] from local electors and so on (see chapter 3) doubtless instils a greater degree of complaints consciousness in their own investigations and reports than in the NAO. It is notable, for instance, how many of the AC reports have immediate implications for grievance redress and complaint handling and offer advice on practices over which the Commission for Local Administration has jurisdiction. No doubt there will be considerable effort to avoid duplication and contradiction but it does bring home the point that improved systems, complaint handling and redress are part of a continuum and not separate subjects.

Increasing resort is made to internal audit, that is, self-certification, which is subject to outside appraisal – as in the case of universities and standards of teaching – or by committees appointed by departmental heads to identify weaknesses in departmental administration. Such a committee is the one which will investigate complaints in deportation cases to "audit" standards but not provide redress. Internal financial audit in departments is a long-standing practice in central government, in addition to CAG audit and self audit is present in some EC Directives to help ensure compliance.

Complaints and the EC

Within four days of the commencement of the Single Market in the EC, complaints were being made about border controls, non-transferability of professional qualifications and other internal market-related subjects.[60] There may be complaints about the organs of the EC itself, including the much trumpeted "democratic deficit" of its institutions. The Maastricht Treaty makes provision for an EC Ombudsman (see below) and agreed a declaration on rights of access to information, and it has to be said that the operations of the Council and Commission are surrounded by a great degree of confidentiality, although John Major has highlighted the impact of his presidency of the EC in introducing greater openness

---

59 But not NHS bodies; see pp. 95 *et seq.* below.
60 *Financial Times*, 5 January 1993.

in its proceedings.[61] However, to take one example, information on the safety of consumer products including pharmaceuticals is seriously deficient at the EC and national level.[62]

The role of the EC Commission in law enforcement of EC provisions is well known. Much of its necessary information concerning alleged infringements of Treaty provisions comes from complaints. Under Article 169 EC, these will typically involve equal treatment, restrictions on freedoms established under the Treaty, state aids, the environment or public procurement. In 1990, the Commission commenced 283 cases after its own investigations and 1,252 after complaints. Snyder estimates that 85 per cent of the complaints came from companies and 5 per cent each from private individuals, Member States and the European Parliament.[63] The Commission has in fact prepared its own standard complaint form which it prefers complainants to follow.[64] This requests certain details about the complainant and about what action has been taken before national or Community institutions of an administrative or legal nature. The complaint may be lodged with the Commission in Brussels or with any of its information offices in any Member State. The complainant is kept fully informed of the action the Commission takes as a response to the complaint, including any infringement proceedings against a Member State or any legal action against an undertaking.

Procedure under Article 169 is split into two stages: first the administrative stage when a formal request is made for the observations of the Member State on the allegations, followed by the reasoned opinion (the hidden jurisprudence of EC law) of the Commission on the merits of the case; the second stage is reference to the Court where a settlement cannot be reached. However, the first stage is preceded by an informal request for better particulars. In 1980, from a total of 208 complaints, 19 (9.1 per cent) went to judgment of the Court. In 1990, of 1,535 complaints, 38 went to judgment (2.4 per cent). In fact Snyder believes that the pre-court procedure has moved back in time as it were from the reasoned opinion, to the formal letter and now to the informal request for particulars so that many cases are settled at this early stage. In other words the informal request is playing an increasingly important part in settlement of cases.

[61] *Open Government*, Cm 2290 (1993).
[62] *Access to Information in the EC*, Consumers in the European Community Group, 1993.
[63] F. Snyder, "The Effectiveness of European Community Law: Institutions, Processes, Tools and Techniques", (1993) *Modern Law Review* 19.
[64] OJ EC 1989 C26/6.

This stage usually takes place via the Committee of Permanent Representatives of the Member States or in meetings between the Commission and national administrative authorities; "in both settings, a specific legal obligation may be one element among many in a particular negotiation".[65] Put simply, the courts are an adjunct to negotiation and litigation is used as one element to develop the Commission's long-term strategies and establish its basic principles. "It is in a position to use litigation in a continuous, proactive as well as reactive way . . . it can convert litigation into a resource for structured bargaining".[66] Various Articles of the Treaty of Rome ensure that the Commission has far more experience of EC litigation than any other entity[67] – and it should not be forgotten that we are here dealing with governments. The Commission's role seems likely to be enforced by the revisions of the Maastricht Treaty to Articles 169 and 171 providing for fines or penalties where EC law is broken. Negotiation in the shadow of the courts is a well known phenomenon, but the status of the players and the size of the stakes give it added piquancy in this setting.

In competition cases, the Commission in the shape of DGIV has very wide powers of investigation which enhance its negotiating strength. Where these cases are litigated they go before the Court of First Instance. It has been acknowledged by a Director-General of DGIV that complaints may be extremely useful in deciding the types of conditions the Commission may impose on agreements or on modifications to an agreement, even if they do not alter the end decision on an infringement of Article 85.[68]

The EC Ombudsman was created under Article 138e EC Treaty and will be appointed by the European Parliament (EP). The details of the ombudsman are in a draft EP Decision (DOC A3-0298/92, adopted by the EP on 17 December 1992). Complainants may approach the EC Ombudsman directly; there are fewer restrictions on his jurisdiction than is the case with public sector ombudsmen in the UK (see chapter 5). Complaints relate to EC institutions but as well as being entitled to demand information from such bodies, the EC Ombudsman may, under the draft Decision, require national authorities to provide information upon request. Reports of maladministration must be sent to

---

65 Snyder, Note 63 above, at 30.
66 *Ibid.*, at 31.
67 For example, Articles, 169, 170, 171, 173, 177.
68 Which concerns agreements restricting, preventing or distorting competition. Temple Lang, *Lawyers' Europe*, 1993, at p. 2.

the EP. The EC Ombudsman may well become an effective aid supplementing lobbying of the EP (Hedemann-Robinson, 1994).

A Preview

As stated in the first edition, "a public lawyer's interest in the process of accountability and complaint resolution is not diminished simply because there is an absence of a judge or counsel, prerogative orders or writs. The pursuit of effective procedures for accountability and resolution of grievances is what counts". This book largely follows the pattern of the first edition. I begin with central government, its departments and agencies, particularly the Next Steps Agencies. Local government follows in chapter three. The diminution of local government has been one of the persistent themes of Conservative governments since 1979. It is still the tier of government with which most people have contact – indeed in the case of "quasi government" (chapter 4), most would not be aware that they were dealing with a form of government. The replacement of elected government with non-elected quasi-governmental institutions, the "new magistracy" as one commentator has described the trend,[69] poses particular problems from the perspective of accountability and grievance redress. This forms the subject of chapter four. In chapter five I examine the work of the various Ombudsmen schemes. There has been a certain defensive feel about Ombudsmen in relation to the Citizen's Charter; should they be doing more to advance redress of grievance and to achieve system improvement? Chapter six concerns the courts and I hope the chapter will explain why their role in grievance redress is extremely limited, in spite of protestations to the contrary, including a claim by the Minister responsible for the CC that the "re-interpretation" of administrative law by the courts was one reason why there was no need for fundamental legal and constitutional safeguards.[70] I have set out elsewhere suggestions for reform of the court structure in public law litigation.[71] Finally, I conclude with an attempt to bring together various points concerning optimum procedures, different modes of grievance redress, the strengths of different processes, problems facing those who wish to complain and some concluding thoughts on a justice overseer to watch over the state and the manifold forms that the state may take.

---

[69] J.D. Stewart, *Accountability to the Public* (London, European Policy Forum, 1992).
[70] Note 51 above.
[71] Note 26 above.

Chapter 2

CENTRAL GOVERNMENT

In this chapter we begin to unravel a form of power that was never effectively colonised by the imperatives of legal order as interpreted by the courts. The discussion highlights the collective nature of power and organisation arranged around central government, its departments and agencies and Ministers of State.

There will be an introductory discussion on government departments and agencies, their structure, organisation and administration. The discussion will assess the methods adopted by departments and agencies to process complaints and will include a discussion on appeals to tribunals – these are prevalent throughout government institutions but are particularly noticeable in central government administration. Indeed, one of the most interesting developments in the last ten years has been the resort by government to forms of internal review to replace "independent" tribunals, for example, in the social fund, and the development of an internal force of officials acting as adjudicators between departments and those aggrieved by departmental decisions. The chapter will also analyse the role of inquiries or other opportunities to be heard before a person appointed by a Minister, as well as the informal processing of complaints whether attending statutory or other procedures. The Parliamentary Commissioner for Administration will be examined in chapter five.

Government Departments and Agencies

First of all we have to have a clear idea about what constitutes a department or an executive agency of central government. Different sources give different answers. For instance, in the past after a general election, *The Times* and Hansard both described the government as comprising the Cabinet, Departments of State and Ministers. Notable omissions have included the Inland Revenue, Customs and Excise and even the Cabinet Office. In the case of the former two bodies, which are headed by senior civil servants, HM Treasury is described as exercising a "general oversight" over the Departments' administration. Other sources and statutes list

25

as governmental bodies and departments institutions which are really independent investigatory and/or regulatory agencies such as the Commission for Racial Equality, or the bodies regulating the privatised utilities such as the Office of Telecommunications – strictly speaking a non-ministerial Department of State – and "other bodies" such as the Data Protection Registrar, the Advisory, Conciliation and Arbitration Service and the Housing Corporation. In a way, of course, identifying what is central government may well depend upon the reason for making the identification, for example, in order to choose a defendant under the Crown Proceedings Act 1947 or to establish whether a body is within the jurisdiction of the Parliamentary Commissioner for Administration.[1]

Many of the bodies falling loosely within the rubric of central government are in fact non-departmental public bodies or quangos (see chapter 4). The present chapter is primarily concerned with two types of beasts: those departments which have a Minister at their head who is notionally responsible to Parliament for policy and administration (and here we include the Inland Revenue and Customs and Excise, for which the Chancellor of the Exchequer has such a responsibility); second, those agencies which are hived off from departments under the Next Steps Agencies programme or which form a part of the integral structure of a department, for example, the Immigration and Nationality Department of the Home Office, or the Prison Service. Bodies which are given "independence" from government departments, though this should not be taken at face value, are treated as non-departmental bodies (NDPBs) and are examined in chapter four.

The Next Steps Agencies are children of departments and are given a degree of operational "independence"[2] subject to certain financial, policy and performance restraints which are agreed between the Minister and Permanent Secretary and the agency chief. Their appearance on the map of central government has been one of the most dramatic and revolutionary developments in government apparatus this century. They demand further comment.

Next Steps Agencies (NSAs)

NSAs in their current form originated with the Ibbs proposals

---

[1]   Who now has jurisdiction over numerous non-departmental bodies and not simply Crown bodies and departments, see chapter 5.

[2]   A. Davies and J. Willman, *What Next? Agencies, Departments and the Civil Service* (London, Institute for Public Policy Research, 1991).

of 1988[3] and are basically a means of separating out the policy-making functions of government from the service delivery functions. As such they continue the theme of dividing policy and administration, although unlike the Fulton Report of 1968,[4] which advocated a split along similar lines, privatisation and market testing have been prominent in the objectives of governments since the introduction of the programme. Where appropriate, those sections of departments delivering services to the public, as opposed to formulating policy, are hived off from the department as an executive agency with its own Chief Executive, budget and priorities established in a Framework Document (FD), which is basically a matter of administrative *fiat* not law. This document sets out the duties of the agency, its objectives and targets of performance, its stated quality of service, financial performance and levels of efficiency. These are set out in Agreements on Financial Arrangements between the Permanent Secretary and the Chief Executive and Agreements on Annual Performance. Ministers are advised on the performance and "outputs" of Agencies through, for example, departmental advisory boards which have access to relevant business expertise. Their performance is evaluated usually every three years. By August 1993, 91 agencies had been established, with plans for a further 20. Over 348,000 civil servants are now working in Next Steps Agencies or bodies working on similar lines.

Following on from *Service to the Public*[5] and the Citizen's Charter (CC), enhancing customer service is a top priority of Next Steps. As we shall see, emphasis has been given to the creation of performance indicators, complaints procedures and customer surveys to gauge customer satisfaction and even the establishment of customers' committees. Target rates[6] will deal typically with the time taken to process a claim (for example, within six days of a claim being made to a local unemployment office it will be put into the unemployed benefits system) and the level of accurate payments. In the Inland Revenue, which operates on NSA lines, a new "performance management system" was introduced to link pay and performance and to enhance public service. Local tax offices will have "Tax Inquiry Centres" where visitors will be seen within 15 minutes and surveys of self-employed and

---

3 Cabinet Office, Efficiency Unit, 1988.
4 Cmnd 3638. Further changes in the Civil Service were announced in *Continuity and Change* 13 July 1994 Cm 2627.
5 Cabinet Office, 1988.
6 HM Treasury, 1992.

employees have been conducted to see what they want from an Inland Revenue service. The Planning Inspectorate has revised its complaints procedure. The Contributions Agency has engaged in customer market surveys, resulting in 113 recommendations including the speeding up of its service and the improvement of customer education about its operations. Perhaps one of the most interesting developments has taken place in the Benefits Agency which administers social security payments. We look at this Agency below.

The FDs of NSAs are published, as are their corporate plans, but their business plans are not usually published. They are subject to the jurisdiction of the Parliamentary Commissioner for Administration in his investigation of complaints[7] and Chief Executives may be summoned before the Public Accounts Committee as Accounting Officers of the Agencies and before Select Committees.[8] NSAs are not subject to the same degree of Parliamentary accountability as traditional departments because Chief Executives do not have to answer questions on the floor of the House, but following protests Parliamentary questions are given written answers in Hansard. All agencies publish detailed annual reports (like departments) and the accounts of some agencies are "accruals accounts" which, it is claimed, are far better for the "stewardship needs of Ministers and Parliament" and for the provision of information to the public.

NSAs are a tremendously important development in the organisation of central government. They do not fit easily into the traditional structure of government, which still exists alongside the NSAs. Ministerial Responsibility (MR), for instance has been truncated (although Ministers approve business plans and may issue directions and guidance[9]) because the agencies are given a degree of independence from their parent departments. The extent of MR and the degree of control of parent departments over NSAs are contested and controversial topics which take us outside our present brief.[10] The Civil Service (Management Functions) Act 1992 empowers the Treasury and Cabinet Office to

---

7   The Chief Executives have the duty of investigating and assisting the investigation of a complaint and reporting to the Permanent Secretary. See HC 652 1992/3.

8   A notorious case was the Child Support Agency and the Social Services Committee: HC (1993/4). The Agency received nearly 11,000 complaints in its first year of operation and 5,000 letters from MPs.

9   Ministers will have to answer for overall policy and for failures in their oversight of agencies.

10 HC Debs. Vol 217 col. 1287, 28 January 1993.

delegate the management functions which they perform to other Crown servants, that is, Chief Executives, especially the terms and conditions of employment. A lot more will be said about agencies, but now it is time to return to the mighty Departments of State.

Departments

It is trite constitutional knowledge, though like most trite knowledge tending to the naïve, that the Crown, or more accurately its Ministers on its behalf, governs through Cabinet decisions which are implemented through the Departments of State, usually following legislative approval. Our constitutional heritage has determined that "The Crown or its Ministers are restrained from ruling without a Parliament, since it is enacted that for the redress of all grievances and for the amending, strengthening and preserving of laws Parliaments ought to be held frequently".[11] Government departments owe their creation and organisation, along with their powers and duties, in part to the Royal Prerogative and in part to Parliament. The 17th century ensured that most ministerial powers were eventually to be derived from Parliament in the form of statute, and apart from loans and securities, Parliament alone provides Ministers with the finance for their expenditure. But a department's "internal arrangements . . . are hardly ever organised or interfered with by Parliament but have been a matter for the Royal Prerogative".[12] They are part of that mystery of central government which over one hundred years ago Maitland described as "extra legal organisation" – "the law does not condemn it; but it does not recognise it – knows nothing about it".[13]

It has been argued that it is inappropriate to describe what is basically an employment relationship under the rubric of Royal Prerogative, "that residue of arbitrary power" residing in the monarch.[14] However, not everyone employs in excess of 600,000 individuals – and this does not include military personnel, police and NHS employees – under terms of strict confidentiality enforced by the criminal law under the terms of the Official Secrets Acts, servants who are there to carry out the state's business without question, although there are safety valves for those stricken by conscience. There are quirkish and ostensibly eccentric qualities

11 Bill of Rights 1689, Article 13.
12 *Halsbury's Laws of England* (1974) Vol. 8, paragraphs 1156 to 1272.
13 F.W. Maitland, *The Constitutional History of England* (Cambridge University Press, 1955) at p. 387.
14 H.W.R. Wade, (1987) *Law Quarterly Review* 323.

attaching to the status, terms and conditions of civil service and Crown employment which are not repeated in other areas of employment and which the courts have repeatedly recognised and not eradicated.[15] It need only be pointed out that as many of a Minister's powers today are statutory, an increasing number of civil servants' employment responsibilities and duties are regulated under statutory authority. Nonetheless, the dramatic power of prerogative can be evidenced by the fact that two of the most important developments affecting central government administration since the Second World War, namely, the Next Steps Agencies and the Citizen's Charter, were not sanctioned by an enabling statute. Indeed, although several features of the latter have found their way into legislation, some of the most important aspects have not, for example, the complaints procedures in departments and agencies and the freedom of information provisions affecting central government.[16]

Since the 19th century it has become the usual practice to establish departments under statutory authority and to transfer functions between departments likewise.[17] As we saw above, a fundamental departure from this practice was witnessed with the creation of NSAs. Appointments of Secretaries of State and Ministers are effected under the Royal Prerogative and although most of their necessary powers are conferred upon them by statute, *qua* Secretary of State, they are not a statutory creation, but natural persons possessed of natural, prerogative (of the Crown) and statutory powers. This constitutional phenomenon is of fundamental importance especially, for instance, in relation to contractual powers.[18] Some Secretaries of State are corporations sole – although constitutionally the office of Secretary of State is one and indivisible – and finally the prerogatives of the Crown are usually exercised by Her Majesty's Ministers although some are exercised personally by the Monarch.

The bulk of departments have their headquarters in London;

---

15   See *R v Lord Chancellor's Department ex parte Nangle* (1991) IRLR 343 and *McClaren v Home Office* [1990] ICR 824.
16   Some duties relating to personal information and health and safety will be available as statutory rights, see p. 38.
17   Ministers of the Crown Act 1975 being the general authority for the latter.
18   Because they can exercise their power to contract on behalf of the Crown under natural and statutory power, *quaere* prerogative power? See Supply Powers Act 1975, Section 1(1); Daintith, "Regulation by Contract: The New Prerogative", (1979) 32 CLP 41; Turpin, (1989) and *R v Secretary of State for the Environment ex parte Greenwich LBC* (1989) *The Times* 17 May; McGougan, (1990) and *NSW v Bardolph* (1935) SL CLR 455.

Scotland, Northern Ireland and Wales are the homes of their respective Ministries, with offices also in England. There has been a policy of regionalisation of agencies so that some have been established in provincial cities. Many departments have a regional and even local presence. As I write, plans have been announced in outline to establish combinations of departments regionally. A regional presence is especially significant in Northern Ireland where it has been noted by the NI parliamentary Commissioner that the proximity of the NI departments to the local community has been a reason for the often close and accessible relationship between the departments and citizens in routine administration.[19] The Department of the Environment (DoE) has a strong regional presence. In other departments there are inspectorates to check on locally delivered services, for example, in prisons and the police. In some cases inspection is contracted out. Education has inspectorates and since 1993 the School Curriculum and Assessment Authority ensures quality in the curriculum and assessment and the Funding Agency oversees standards in grant-maintained (that is, non-local education authority provided) schools and also advises the Secretary of State on complaints about such schools.[20]

All departments and agencies have to establish policy aims and objectives, the realisation of which they have to report on in their annual reports – these are expenditure plans which are part of the financial reporting programme and the public expenditure survey. Under the Citizen's Charter, which was examined in chapter one, departments and agencies must establish their aims, objectives and priorities, establish grievance procedures as part of the management programme and be subject to internal and external audit in their programme delivery and output, all of which must be informed by public feedback via surveys and questionnaires.

Departments and agencies are split into sub-departments or units, divisions or sections which have specific responsibilities allocated to them. Quite obviously, the nature of departments differs enormously and they have been characterised as the functional, for example, environment, education and employment; the processual, which are concerned with financial and legal matters though obviously these involve functions also; and the territorial – the Home, Scottish, Welsh and Northern Ireland Offices which are multi-dimensional.[21] That basic division makes some sense but

---

[19] NIPCA Second Annual Report HC (NI) 2175 paragraph 9.
[20] Cm. 2021, 1992, paragraph 3.13.
[21] Jones, "Central–Local Relations, Finance and the Law", (1979) 2 *Urban Law and Policy* 25.

it must now be seen in the context of the CC which deliberately seeks to hive off the functional and service programmes of departments to agencies where they will be subject to market testing and privatisation.

When complaining to departments it is instructive to appreciate the sheer size of organisation that one may be contending with – even after a decade and a half of "cutting back the state". In 1782, the Home Office when it was established had a complement of 17 people including Ministers and shared 26 other staff with the Foreign Office. Its running costs amounted to £15,639 12s 9½d. In 1992, its running costs were estimated to be £1,282 million with an estimated outturn of £5,689 million. Its manpower was 48,373 rising to 53,680 by 1994/5. The responsibilities of the HO cover those not assigned to other government departments (*sic*), the administration of criminal justice, criminal law, treatment of offenders, the probation and prison service, immigration and nationality, passport policy matters, community relations, public safety, fire and civil defence services. It acts as the link between the Queen and the public and the Home Secretary exercises certain prerogative powers on her behalf such as the Royal Pardon.[22] The HO deals with electoral arrangements, addresses and petitions to the Queen, honours, extradition requests, scrutiny of local authority bye-laws, grants of licences for scientific experiments on animals, dangerous drugs and firearms, general policy on law relating to shops and liquor licences, gaming and lotteries, charitable collections, marriage, theatre and cinema licensing, co-ordination of government action in relation to voluntary social services, race relations and sex discrimination policy. Broadcasting and national heritage responsibilities were transferred to the Department of National Heritage in 1992. A plethora of NDPBs, quangos and specialist advisory bodies assist in many of these tasks, some of which we shall examine in chapter four.

Even with the process of hiving off of agencies and an apparent renewed vigour in the establishment of quangos, government departments are not simple, straightforward entities but are multi-purpose and complex organisations with protean dimensions. Some deal regularly and directly with the public: Ministry of Agriculture, Fisheries and Food (MAFF), Inland Revenue (IR), Customs and Excise (C&E), Immigration and Nationality Department (I&N), Department of Trade and Industry (DTI). Some departments which formerly dealt directly with the public

---

[22]   See *R v Secretary of State for the Home Department ex parte Bentley* [1993] 4 All ER 442.

on a large scale have been dramatically affected by the Next Steps revolution so that much of their former contact is now made by agencies, for example the DSS and the Benefits Agency, the Department of Employment and the Employment Service. Some do deal with citizens directly but in their capacity as overlookers, appellate bodies or complaint recipients about local authority administration or as regulators of aspects of the economy or industry. Some departments have responsibilities which feature daily in the lives of citizens yet they are reluctant to allow public contact to be made with them at HQ level. Neither the DES nor the Home Office encourage the public to make personal contact, although written complaints about schools and LEAs and prisoner correspondence[23] and requests for pardons, sometimes posthumously, are common.

Other departments remain aloof from the public. The Treasury is one such. However, within the Treasury is the Department for National Savings which has responsibility for over 50 million accounts and which, like the Treasury, has set target rates for correspondence and performance indicators. However, there is no surprise in knowing that the Treasury is subject to enormous special pleading as the Budget approaches. Nigel Lawson has described how his officials would keep a matrix which would signify support by way of respresentations on subjects received from outside groups and individuals. As the budget approached, particularly important groups identified on the matrix would be invited to the Treasury to discuss their objectives with the Chancellor and his advisers.[24] Nevertheless, the Government's preoccupation with value for money in public expenditure and the delivery of governmental programmes throughout the 1980s and 1990s and its emphasis upon monetarist policies, or at least those displaying tight fiscal and budgetary constraint, have projected the Treasury into even greater prominence than usual in the oversight and control of government programmes. Treasury policy is far removed from effective public, or legal, scrutiny and challenge – generally speaking its decisions on finance are not justiciable at the suit of ordinary individuals before courts of law; although *locus standi* may be established, the breadth and depth of the

---

23 Formal petitioning by prisoners has been removed although nothing in law prevents prisoners writing to the Secretary of State by way of complaint; indeed, a barrier would be contrary to the Bill of Rights. Petitioning the Home Secretary was infinitely more popular in simple numerical terms than complaining to the Ombudsman.
24 N. Lawson, *The View from No. 11*, 1992, chapter 26.

issues involved would render successful challenge on the grounds of *vires* or abuse of discretion less than likely.[25] Like all other departments, the Treasury has subjected itself to greater openness, especially following the withdrawal of the United Kingdom from the ERM,[26] but this remains incomplete and in spite of reforms in financial reporting to Parliament, the latter still lacks the appropriate information to make an informed analysis of service delivery and the quality of service. Here the Citizen's Charter may well assist in providing valuable information on service delivery, but the views of many are to the effect that the primary objective of the Charter is to put on a good front and a good sell – indeed to deflect criticism away from policy and financial decisions which lie behind service delivery. Effective scrutiny by Parliament of a government's expenditure plans and the matching of those plans to service delivery has not been a primary objective of the reforms, although it may be a consequence.

The most important decisions in our constitution are not to be subject to individual complaints procedures; they may well be subject to mass demonstration or vehement lobbying. In terms of economic management a government's record will speak for itself; citizens are left with the ballot box. It is the ballot box which has legitimated political power and which has justified the absence of fundamental reform in our system of administrative justice and civil rights.[27] Throughout the 1980s and 90s governments have been able to secure either overwhelming or commanding domination of the Commons – and have certainly been able to perpetuate a culture of executive domination in Westminster[28]

---

[25]   *Locus standi* was established in *R v HM Treasury ex parte Smedley* [1985] 1 All ER 589, where the *vires* of a draft statutory instrument authorising payments to the EEC was unsuccessfully challenged.

[26]   There is a committee of seven lay economic advisers to advise the Treasury, a written justification for changes in interest rates and a quarterly inflation report from the Bank of England. Initially the results of the monthly meetings between the Governor of the Bank of England and the Chancellor of the Exchequer were not published but this changed in April 1994 and minutes are published six weeks after the meetings. A commentary to accompany the publication of the Treasury's Monthly Monetary Report providing an assessment of the economy is not published. See section 3 European Communities (Amendment) Act 1993 requiring the Governor of the Bank of England to report annually to Parliament.

[27]   Englishmen are only free, according to Rousseau, at the moment they cast their ballots!

[28]   In 1903, 10 per cent of the Tory Parliamentary party was on the government pay-roll. In 1993, the figure was almost 40 per cent. A further crucial factor has been the lack of effective scrutiny of EC legislation in the Commons.

with less than a third of the electorate supporting them at general elections. In 1983, for instance, support was 31.6 per cent of the electorate and the majority was 144. In 1992, the figures were 32.5 per cent and 21. These figures, the former dramatically so, provide a chastening reminder of the frailty of the legitimation basis for the exercise of governmental power while also highlighting the unfairness of an electoral system which makes no concession to proportional representation.

Ministerial Responsibility

All constitutions are ultimately political affairs but in most modern democracies political pluralism has meant that a balance of power between state and citizen and between organs of the state *inter se* has been guaranteed by legally binding procedures independent of the executive. In Britain, ultimate responsibility for the exercise of power is owed by Ministers to Parliament; to bodies subject to political domination by the very forces they are seeking to restrain. Along with legislative supremacy and omnicompetence this is what Parliamentary Supremacy means. It was the accountability of Ministers to Parliament which made MPs "An Assembly of Kings" according to Enoch Powell. Such a statement has always been an exaggeration; it now represents simply hyperbole. Why should this be so?

In popular terms, if individual ministerial responsibility means anything, it means resignation after events have gone wrong in a department for which the Minister is responsible, whether the shortcomings have been caused by his own default or that of his civil servants.[29] The traditional doctrine of ministerial responsibility has been weakened by the movement to Next Steps Agencies, where no Minister presides over an Agency but a civil servant designated as a Chief Executive; by the increased tendency to designate responsibilities to named officials thereby removing anonymity of civil servants and holding them out as responsible for programme delivery;[30] and by the projection of civil servants into the public limelight. This point has been acknowledged by Sir Robin Butler, the Cabinet Secretary, who believed that the

---

[29] Resignations have seemed to follow most readily after personal scandal in the last 30 years, as opposed to managerial shortcomings. The resignations of Michael Heseltine, Nigel Lawson, Geoffrey Howe and Norman Lamont all raise interesting points of constitutional propriety: see further Turpin in Jowell and Oliver (1989).

[30] Civil servants were identified as blameworthy in the *Westland* case in 1986 and in the furore over the pit closure announcement in 1992.

traditional doctrine of MR would need recasting to accommodate the changes in central government administration brought about by these developments and the off-loading or contracting out to private contractors of hitherto centrally administered services.[31]

There is an interesting historical parallel here. MR would not have developed into such a central feature of our constitution had the movement toward the appointment of boards in the 1840s and 1850s and their autonomous development under the law not been hindered by the Parliamentary elite who were jealous of their own position and who were fretful of the power accompanying such a development in a burgeoning industrial economy. The new powers, usually statutory, were concentrated increasingly in the hands of Ministers at the head of departments who were to be responsible to Parliament and the courts for their exercise. As a method of achieving accountability for policy, let alone the redress of individual grievances, the doctrine and practice were always symbolic rather than effective and have become increasingly so.[32]

Nevil Johnson believes[33] that the convention of ministerial responsibility is not really about accountability and responsibility at all but "is fundamentally a doctrine about the manner in which public powers are to be established and located; it defines who is responsible for what rather than who is responsible for whom". It is not a grievance remedial device of a collective or individual nature, but allows us to know rather in whom powers are reposed and who answers the questions. Johnson has gone so far as to say that "if the British have any notion of the State, then it is to be found in the doctrine of Ministerial Responsibility"[34] – though one would surely wish to add Parliamentary Supremacy. And George II was probably more astute and insightful than Enoch Powell when he allegedly opined, "Ministers are Kings in this country" long before the 19th and 20th centuries accumulated vast additional power and patronage in their hands. We confront a dilemma: Ministers still possess the key powers – changes in

---

31   *The Independent*, 21 October 1991.
32   There is an increasingly marked reluctance to resign. The ERM debacle in October 1992 was catastrophic, costing the country an estimated £5 billion to keep Sterling within its ERM bands. If ever there was a resigning issue this was it! The Chancellor hung on for nine months; by the time he did resign, the Prime Minister effectively withdrawing his support, there was an arguable case for saying he should have stayed as economic indicators were improving considerably.
33   *In Search of the Constitution*, 1977 (London, Methuen).
34   *Ibid.*, at 84.

administration have weakened the traditional means of rendering an account for the exercise of that power.

Furthermore, the primary position given to political forms of accountability in our constitution nipped in the bud the development of any wider ranging and specific public law accountability. Again and again, for instance, judges, when faced by disputes that were clearly justiciable and which concerned individual grievances against a department or government board, would justify non-interference by declaring that the issue touched upon a matter of administration over which a department or board had authority or jurisdiction and for which a Minister was ultimately responsible to Parliament.[35] If the convention does not provide an effective method for resolving grievances, then judicial resort to the convention has merely helped to set back, and is still setting back, the development of a coherent system of administrative justice. There are signs that the convention is losing its paralysing grip at the centre of governmental organisation, and the judiciary have, very often at the prompting of EC law or the European Convention on Human Rights, but sometimes perhaps independently of European influence,[36] removed some of the barriers that prevented any serious inroads into ministerial misrule. Nonetheless, it is interesting to note how frequently the government of the day has argued that efforts to ensure greater accountability of departments by increasing the powers of the Parliamentary Commissioner for Administration (PCA) or Comptroller and Auditor General would unduly interfere with ministerial responsibility. An example from 1993 concerns the White Paper on *Open Government* where the Government refused to countenance the resolution of disputes over access to government documents by independent judicial bodies with powers of enforcement where departments were wrongly refusing access. The Ombudsman was selected as the grievance mechanism because this would enhance ministerial accountability to Parliament. Unlike countries with freedom of information laws, in the UK the Minister would retain ultimate control over release of information, although the Ombudsman and Select Committee have promised that they will play a "robust role" (see chapter 5).

However, if developments since the early 1980s have diminished the functional importance of the doctrine,[37] the question becomes

---

[35] *Local Government Board v Arlidge* [1915] AC 120; *Bushell v Secretary of State for the Environment* [1981] AC 75.

[36] *M v Home Office* [1993] 3 All ER 537 (HL) is the leading example.

[37] *Personnel Management Review*, MINIS and Next Steps.

what replaces MR as a legitimating symbol of state power. In fact is this not another example of Ministers evading any appropriate form of answerability for the exercise of their power? An evasion assisted by secrecy.

Secrecy

In 1989 the infamous section 2 of the Official Secrets Act 1911 (OSA) was replaced by the OSA of that year. A notoriously broad catch-all offence was replaced by a statute which concentrated its attention upon six areas of information[38] where there was a damaging and unauthorised leak of information. Crucially, the Government did not allow a defence of public interest to protect a person who leaks information for such a reason, as in the common law of confidentiality, nor was a defence of "prior publication" allowed. Reform was necessary because of the uncertainties introduced by unsuccessful prosecutions under section 2 and because the law of confidentiality which binds civil servants had proved unreliable.[39] Control over civil servants is far more likely to be achieved through internal disciplinary procedures whereby a career can effectively be concluded by internal proceedings. Where civil servants feel a "crisis of conscience" in their work, guidelines exist on the internal ventilation of grievances. These were drafted by Sir Robert Armstrong when Head of the Home Civil Service and Cabinet Secretary.[40] Much controversy has been caused in the NHS where it is claimed that employees are bound by secrecy clauses so that revealing an abuse involving, for example, patient care or waste is a serious disciplinary offence (see, however, chapter 5, page 214). The Government produced a code of conduct on statements to the press by employees which they claimed mitigated the situation, although not all were convinced.[41]

The Government in its White Paper, *Open Government*,[42] has

---

[38] Information relating to security and intelligence, defence, international relations, crime, information obtained under special investigations powers, that is, Interception of Communications Act 1985, Security Service Act 1989 and Intelligence Services Act 1994; and information entrusted in confidence to foreign states.

[39] Most famously in the Spycatcher saga: *AG v Guardian Newspapers (No. 2)* [1988] 3 All ER 545 (Ch. D, CA and HL); *Observer and Guardian Newspapers v UK* [1991] 14 EHRR 220; cf *Lord Advocate v Scotsman Publishing Ltd* [1989] 2 All ER 852 (HL).

[40] Sir R. Armstrong, *The Duties and Responsibilities of Civil Servants in Relation to Ministers* (London, Cabinet Office, 1987).

[41] EL (93) 51, Department of Health and NHS ME.

[42] Cm. 2290 (1993).

proposed that citizens should have access to information but not specific documents under a Code which is to be supervised by the Parliamentary Commissioner for Administration. The draft code has numerous exemptions including policy information, national security, where information is "unreliable", or where its release would be untimely or unduly burdensome for government. Information on immigration and nationality is given a complete exemption. This is a limp proposal when compared with those access provisions contained in laws in, for example, the USA, Canada, Australia and New Zealand. The PCA will not be able to enforce his decision against a reluctant department or agency and the Code operates under the terms of the PCA Act which is examined in chapter five. The PCA's own jurisdiction is subject to numerous exemptions in terms of subjects, functions and bodies which he cannot investigate. The PCA has indicated that he will modify the operation of the legislation to favour applicants for information (*quaere* the legality of this concession) even though they have not suffered injury, but the fact remains that this is a fiendishly complex arrangement. The Government announced that it will allow access to personal documents by the "subjects" of those documents with a legally enforceable right before a judicial body – not the PCA. It promises to give great attention to the procedures through which complaints may be made to departments and bodies holding information before outside bodies are resorted to.

Resolution of Grievances

It is surprising, perhaps, that in spite of many statutory appeal or complaints procedures, departments make widespread resort to informal methods for the resolution of grievances. What is more surprising, perhaps, is that until quite recently there was little in the way of recorded research into such practices. The ESRC initiative of 1987 did commission research into immigration and customs and excise complaints but in the case of the latter the initiative was overtaken by a new complaints procedure which was introduced in 1992.

There have been publications on ministerial correspondence, including a published study by the Cabinet Office.[43] In spite of the then Prime Minister's, Mrs Thatcher's, exhortations for departments to settle disputes as locally and as swiftly as possible, such

[43] *Scrutiny of Ministerial Correspondence* (London, Cabinet Office Efficiency Unit, HMSO, 1990).

exhortations were not accompanied by any uniform instructions on grievance handling for departments, although the development of NSAs brought forth advice that MPs should correspond with Agencies and not Ministers (see below). Internal unpublished guidelines existed. Departments were left largely to devise their own procedures, which of course they would invariably introduce, although it was not uncommon for senior officials in departments not to know about them. Now, of course, the Citizen's Charter has propelled the subject into prominence and a Complaints Task Force has been established by the CC Unit (see p. 14 above). Amongst its responsibilities will be offering advice to public bodies on the best method for dealing with grievances. In spite of criticisms, the consumer consciousness associated with the Charter has had its impact on departments so that the Management and Personnel Offices' strictures to civil servants in the early 1980s – "Is too much attention given to the wishes of individuals and to equity, and not enough to the needs of the department?"[44] – would not today be received as politically correct. I shall examine the internal practices of departments and agencies in a moment. The role of courts we can examine in chapter six although we should note that even Dicey observed that the Revolution Settlement in England was not a victory for immanent rights of man, but a defence of proprietary interests interpreted by inherently conservative common lawyers.[45] What other possibilities for redress exist?

Political Redress

A second avenue was to offer – or concede – political redress of grievances.[46] Parliament after all was to be a vehicle for the redress of all grievances, according to the Bill of Rights, as well as being the motor behind legislative amendment and reform. I have referred to the pressure that may be applied in the Commons through the convention of ministerial responsibility. Many regard MPs first and foremost as trouble-shooters on behalf of constituents and virtually all departments invariably identified their intervention as the first method or stage in

---

[44] *The Guardian* 26 August 1982.
[45] Dicey, *Law and Public Opinion*, 1914 (2nd edn), at 82. For Dicey, this was its strength. "A revolution, not made, but prevented" opined Burke on the events of 1688 to 1689.
[46] Gregory and Pearson, 1992, at 477 to 478.

complaint resolution.[47] When the NHS issued guidelines on disclosures to the press by employees, a further letter was sent out explaining that the guidelines had not sought to inhibit communication with MPs. Having stated that, the NSA development has placed a certain tension upon the MP/Minister correspondence. MPs are advised to contact the Agency Chief Executive directly and that this will be a far quicker route to reply and redress than will an approach to the Ministry. However, MPs are reluctant to release Ministers from their constitutional responsibilities. In certain areas, for example, immigration, social security, social welfare, health and prisons, MP intervention has been vital to prevent deportation or to obtain special or emergency treatment. MPs have complained of buck-passing by Ministers, thereby causing a further attenuation of the doctrine of MR, a point made particularly forcefully in March 1993 when Gerald Kaufman criticised a Home Office circular to MPs which said that prisoner representations were no longer to be made to HO Ministers.[48] One of the reasons behind the establishment of the NSAs was the fact that Ministers were being swamped by MP and other complaints correspondence. Ministers' correspondence was the subject of an Efficiency Unit study published in 1990.[49] This contains valuable information on departmental practice.

We are informed that Ministers answer personally 250,000 letters per annum and officials answer 600,000 letters at a total cost of £17.5 million or an average of £70 per letter. Target rates for reply were set although the success rate was poor. Annual reports of departments publish amounts of correspondence received and success in meeting targets. MPs and others should be advised on whom best to contact apart from a Minister and advice is given on best departmental practice. The study recommended that a publication should be available with names of officials whom MPs could contact in agencies and departments instead of Ministers and that MPs should receive training in official correspondence after their election. In immigration, guidelines have been produced for MPs on representations (see below). The Benefits Agency produced figures showing that from March 1992 until September 1993 only 25 per cent of complaints were sent directly to the Chief Executive (1,814), the rest went to

---

[47] P. Norton, "'Dear Minister . . .' The Importance of MP to Minister Correspondence", *Parliamentary Affairs* (1982) 59; J.A.G. Griffith and M. Ryle, *Parliament* (London, Sweet & Maxwell, 1989) at 71 to 74 for figures on correspondence.

[48] *The Independent*, 31 March 1993.

[49] Cabinet Office, Efficiency Unit, 1990.

Ministers and were generally from MPs. The total number of complaints was much larger (see below).

As long ago as 1977, a study of an MP's correspondence placed a question mark beside the efficacy of an MP acting as a trouble-shooter when s/he operated without appropriate back-up staff.[50] Various sources reveal that constituents' knowledge of the identity of MPs, even in marginal constituencies, is surprisingly low.[51] A close connection has been identified between an MP's personal status, knowledge of the system and connections and his/her effectiveness as a citizen's representative. Status as a Privy Councillor has been mentioned as a ground for special treatment. MPs can, of course, be very effective in raising the profile or stakes or a particular issue and allying it with a press campaign. Contrariwise, and this has been volunteered by several departments, a high profile intervention by MPs involving PQs,[52] Adjournment Debates, Early Day Motions and media may well have the effect of battening down the hatches within a department; civil servants may become even more cautious in dealing with a complainant or group.[53] But departments, and also agencies, do have fast track procedures for MPs, ensuring that their correspondence is processed through to the appropriate part of a department or section for a response which is then sent to the Minister's private office for reply.

Further intervention by MPs on behalf of complainants can take place at proceedings concerned with collective or policy issues. Officials acknowledged that individual grievances are raised under the cover of a policy relating to department or agency administration. This has happened at Select Committees and although in the early 1980s it was possible to identify an occasion when a Select Committee had been used to settle an industrial dispute, in correspondence between the author and the Chairs of Committees in 1990, there was no similar example. The activities concerning the Child Support Agency after its launch have been widely catalogued and the Chair of the Social Services Committee had received in excess of 400 letters of complaint about the Agency alone at the time of the Agency's investigation by the Committee. The Agency is an intriguing

---

50   F. Morrell, *From the Electors of Bristol.* Spokesman Pamphlet no. 57 (1977).
51   See Lewis and Birkinshaw, (1993, at pp. 142–44) and figures cited.
52   M. Franklin and P. Norton (eds), *Parliamentary Questions* (Oxford, Clarendon Press, 1993).
53   See the comments of Lord Keith in *Lonrho v Secretary of State* [1989] 2 All ER 609 at 617a (HL).

example of an administrative body set up for apparently good objectives but whose formula-fed and Treasury-led mandate soon brought it into disrepute. Further opportunities to air complaints may well arise in the legislative process through lobbying, especially at the Standing Committee stage when MPs will advance the interests of their sponsors. It has to be said that an authoritative study, albeit now a little dated, has shown the general impact of MPs at this level not to be substantial.[54] The power or influence of collective or institutional interests outside Parliament, and the pressure or persuasive force which they can bring to bear on a government, is the important feature and is never more richly demonstrated than when such an interest manages to prevent legislation being passed or takes a crucial role in shaping the legislation. Such might be achieved to maintain self-regulation, statutory or otherwise, as opposed to governmental control for example in the financial services, the professions, even the press – albeit precariously in the latter case with some elements determined to force legislation upon the Government[55] – or to facilitate as cosy a relationship as possible in what might otherwise be irksome regulation, such as health and safety at work or environmental pollution.[56] Consultation before making regulations or decisions of wide application provides the possibility of influence and courts have shown a growing maturity in dealing with more subtle and complex issues.[57] More overt are the private and local bill procedures which offer opportunity for legal representation of grievances from affected interests at Committee stage: this was the procedure used in the Channel Tunnel Act 1987. We have in this process moved from *ex post facto* redress of grievances by political arrangements and persona to *a priori* moulding of decisions to suit particular interests and to reduce the possibility of grievance felt by those interests. "Because the process of bargaining and compromise has gone on largely within departments and has been sheltered by confidentiality, we know relatively little about how alternatives are

---

54 Griffith, *Parliamentary Scrutiny of Government Bills* (London, Allen and Unwin, 1974); Hansard Society, 1992.
55 Calcutt (Cm. 1102, 1990 and Cm. 2135, 1993); National Heritage Committee HC 294 (1992/3) and the Lord Chancellor's Department on which see (1993) *Public Law* 518 to 519.
56 W.G. Carson, *The Other Price of Britain's Oil* (Oxford, Martin Robertson, 1981); K. Hawkins, *Environment and Enforcement* (Oxford, Oxford University Press, 1984).
57 For example, *R v Secretary of State for Health ex parte USTII* [1992] 1 All ER 212 (QBD).

weighed and how consequences are mapped out",[58] a position which the Code of Practice on *Open Government* is unlikely to alter.

I do not think there can be any doubt that MP intervention can be crucial in obtaining redress for the more routine of grievances or in those cases where no procedures are set down or where all else has failed,[59] and this is true whether the complaints are against central, local or quasi government (chapters 3 and 4). Furthermore, it has been suggested by Rawlings that MPs can play an important role in monitoring the response to PCA reports on behalf of their constituents. He has further suggested that much better use should be made of information obtained from grievance redress by MPs, which should be employed to enhance an oversight of the executive administrative process[60] so that it could be fed systematically into Select Committees, especially that on the PCA (see chapter 5). Where we move up the scale of importance as it were, from routine grievances – and here it is well to remember that indifferent performance on constituents' behalf could well affect election results and a government's future – to grievances touching more important and sensitive concerns of government, the role of MPs is generally symbolic rather than efficacious. If it were otherwise, we would have a very different style of government and very different governments. Too frequent a back bench revolt, for instance, from the governing party would produce government by Parliament, not government through Parliament.[61] Others can decide upon the desirability of this.

Tribunals

I have already made the point that tribunals are invariably bodies which are ostensibly independent of departments and it might appear a little strange to refer to them in this chapter and an explanation is required. In public law, the greatest resort to tribunals occurs in central government administration, although there has been an increased use of tribunals in local government administration and some of the most frequently used tribunals concern relationships which have nothing to do with the state, for example, employment, land valuation, rent assessment and patents and

58   Ashford, *Policy and Politics in Britain*, 1981.
59   R. Rawlings, "The MPs' Complaints Service". (1990) *Modern L.R.* 22 and 149.
60   Rawlings (1986b), at 137 and onward.
61   See the report relating to the Maastricht vote, which became an issue of confidence in the Government, a vote which the Government won (Marshall, 1993).

copyright. However, tribunals are so tied up historically with dispute resolution involving central government and individuals that it is appropriate to deal with them at this juncture. The word "historically" is important in this context because there are many indications that the traditional tribunal structure is coming under scrutiny insofar as government has opted for forms of internal review of officials' decisions or various hybrids of ombudsmen and adjudicator to deal with appeals/challenges in a widening variety of programmes. Furthermore, in the spring of 1994, it was reported that active consideration was being given to the contracting to private companies of the management and organisation of tribunal administration. Conversely, tribunals have been urged to deal with cases of miscarriage of justice where the appeal process has been exhausted and to act, after the Whyatt proposals of 1961, as checkers of ministerial discretion where there is no other avenue of redress.[62] What are the motives behind the establishment of tribunals?

First of all, they aim to provide an apparently autonomous form of dispute settlement by adjudicatory devices following adversarial procedure in government or governmentally approved programmes, originally in the field of industrial expansion and then social welfare.[63] Their primary objective is dispute resolution; but they also help to fulfil important legitimating functions for the exercise of public power. They constitute an independent forum of appeal when an individual is locked in conflict with the state. The famous Franks Report on Tribunals and Inquiries states that "Our terms of reference involve the consideration of an important part of the relationship between the individual and authority" and the seeking of a balance between "private right and public advantage, between fair play for the individual and efficiency of administration".[64] The emphasis is upon individual manifestation of conflict which could be subjected to a justiciable process less formal than a court of law. Tribunals apply, impartially and even-handedly, rules which have been made by departments and usually approved by Parliament.

It has been argued that the classification adopted by Franks does not embrace all tribunals. A substantial majority may fall under its spread, but a significant minority are not "court

62 Lewis and Birkinshaw, 1993.
63 Though as Wraith and Hutchesson show, the "administrative tribunal as a judicial phenomenon" has its origins deep in antiquity (*Administrative Tribunals*, 1973).
64 Sir O. Franks, *Report of the Committee on Administrative Tribunals and Enquiries*. Cmnd 218 (London, HMSO, 1957), at paragraph 5.

substitutes" but "policy oriented tribunals".[65] Franks' recommendations were of direct relevance to the former type of body,
namely, that decision-making before such tribunals should be
conducted with "openness, fairness and impartiality". A judicial body of any sort which did not possess these qualities would
lack credibility. In the case of many of the tribunals falling
under the court substitute heading, the department can tolerate
impartiality in determination of disputes between it and an individual claimant. The jurisdiction of the tribunal and the subject-
matter it adjudicates upon are restricted so that decisions are
unlikely to upset the policy of the Minister or government. There
may well be serious expenditure implications where benefits are
demand led which would introduce different considerations.

Membership of tribunals is carefully regulated. Chairmen are
usually appointed by the Lord Chancellor; other members may
be appointed from approved lists by the Lord Chancellor or the
relevant departmental Minister. The encouragement of a presi-
dential system in some tribunals has been a notable development
whereby a President is responsible for the overall administration
of the tribunals in a subject area and is *de facto* the chief adjudicator. That position should not be confused with departmental
adjudicators, who are civil servants in the case of social security
and unemployment benefit and are appointed as such, but in
immigration, adjudicators are appointed by the Lord Chancellor
to convey a sense of independence and are a sort of one-man
tribunal.[66] Those operating within departments are nonetheless
meant to function independently of the department in reviewing
a claim in social security or unemployment, though the same officials will also deal with the original claim. Standards and training
are the responsibility of the Chief Adjudicator.[67]

For the individuals in dispute with departments, their claims or
grievances are matters of supreme importance; in the wider context of public/constitutional decision-making, such tribunals inevitably adjudicate on relatively small claims and comparatively humble concerns. Impartiality in such decisions is permissible, though

---

[65]   B. Abel-Smith and R. Stevens, *Lawyers and the Courts* (London, Heine-
       mann, 1968); Farmer, *Tribunals and Government* (London, Weidenfeld and
       Nicolson, 1974).
[66]   See *R v IAT ex parte Secretary of State* (1992) *The Times* 7 September.
       Jones v Department of Employment [1989] QB 1 held that an adjudication
       officer acts quasi judicially and does not owe a duty of care to a claimant
       when determining a claim.
[67]   N. Wikeley and R. Young. "The Administration of Benefits in Britain"
       (1992) *Public Law* 238.

the DHSS and latterly the DSS have frequently resorted to legislation, regulations and other high-handed practices to reverse the effects of unfavourable decisions. Immigration is an area where the number of appellants will put strain on an appellate process so that in all but clearly defined cases appeals must be made from overseas and not in person from within the jurisdiction – a restriction which has led to the use of MPs and judicial review to try and circumvent the restrictions and attempts by the government and courts to limit the opportunities of challenge when in the UK. The Asylum and Immigration Act 1993 allows those seeking asylum (refugee status) rights of appeal to an adjudicator against removal from the UK and an appeal against refusal of a variation of conditions of leave to stay in the UK where events have occurred which would lead to their removal. However, certain rights of appeal to adjudicators have been removed for visitors and short-term (under six months) and prospective students and their dependants unless they hold a current entry clearance at the time of appeal. Rights of appeal are also removed from those not possessing relevant documentation. In 1992, 3,845 decisions refusing a visitor's visa were reversed on appeal so the numbers involved are considerable.[68] The Government has appointed a monitor to report on a random sample of cases where visas are refused as a substitute for appeal rights. Schedule 2 paragraph 4 of the 1993 Act introduces a special appeal procedure for "claims [to asylum] which are without foundation". This will be an expedited procedure to a special adjudicator (SA) and if the SA agrees that the claim is without foundation there is no further right of appeal to the Immigration Appeal Tribunal[69]. The procedure will be contained in regulations made under section 22 Immigration Act 1971.[70]

Even informal adjudicatory techniques have their costs. Nonetheless there are still about 2,000 tribunals under the Council on Tribunals, hearing about 250,000 cases per year. Plausible arguments have been advanced that by judicialising the administration to this extent, government is able to depoliticise such decision-making.[71] A concentration upon technicalities concerning the amount of individual entitlement to social security, income support, unemployment benefit or whether a dismissal was fair or

---

68   HC Debs, Col. 62, 7 June 1993.
69   Paragraph 4(5).
70   SI 1993/1661 and see *R v Secretary of State for the Home Department ex parte Mehari* [1994] 2 All ER 494 (QBD).
71   A.J. Prosser, "Poverty, Ideology, and Legality . . .", (1977) 4 BJLS 539.

unfair or caused by redundancy directs attention away from political choices lying behind such decisions. The extent, for instance, of state assistance to the impoverished, the infirm, the unemployed or the exercise of managerial prerogative or movement of capital is effectively ignored. The fact that it might be legitimating does not deprive these procedures of legitimacy. This point is particularly true given the movement away from tribunals by government to forms of internal departmental review, usually subject to a departmental inspectorate notionally independent of the department. Very often ministerial guidance exists in these latter cases to colour the way a discretion is exercised. The resort to such practices is necessitated, from government's point of view, by the need to cap public spending or to place limits on a scarce commodity. We have looked at the asylum provisions above. It is felt that these tensions have been particularly acute in the operation of the Social Fund and the movement towards these sorts of internal review and away from judicial procedures have met with vociferous criticism from the Council on Tribunals (CoT) in particular.[72]

Part III of the Social Security Act 1986 introduced the Social Fund. It is a system of discretionary payments and loans replacing the "special needs" payments of previous legislation. Instead of a right of appeal to an independent tribunal, there is an internal review of a cash limited payment by DSS Social Fund Officers with a further review by a Social Fund Inspector. Decisions of the SFOs and SFI are monitored by the SF Commissioner who is meant to operate independently of the department. Her reports have been constructive and critical of standards of decision-making. SFOs have to operate in accordance with guidance from the Secretary of State in exercising their discretion – as do SFOs and the SFI when exercising their review powers.[73]

When we consider policy-oriented bodies, the impact of Franks' recommendations rings less persuasively. Tribunals which license or which regulate economic activity, monopolies and mergers, trading practices and trade relationships and transport activities to name a few, can, if not subjected to ministerial control, quite easily wield power and make decisions upsetting the policy of a government. Very often Ministers have power to issue directions and supervise by direct intervention or by reserving

[72] Council on Tribunals *Annual Report 1989/90*, HMSO, 1990, paragraphs 1.1–1.14.
[73] *R v Secretary of State for Social Security ex parte Stitt* (1990) *The Times* 23 February.

appellate powers over such bodies. What makes the bodies regulating the privatised industries so interesting is that the usual means of control by Ministers is not there (see chapter 4) unless it concerns a merger or matter over which the Secretary of State has ultimate control. The problems policy-oriented bodies pose for government are: how can they appear autonomous and expert and be controlled or influenced without being seen to be controlled or influenced? how can they be controlled without a Minister having to account to Parliament for that control? how can they assist in the formulation of policy without upsetting the overall aim and strategy of a department? Even if policy-oriented bodies operate within policy parameters established in Whitehall, and this also applies to court substitute bodies, there is no guarantee that the judiciary will abstain from intervention in such bodies' decision-making processes at the suit of complainants. *Anisminic v Foreign Compensation Commission*[74] extended considerably the power of the High Court to review the decisions of tribunals when the House of Lords decided that virtually all errors of law made by inferior tribunals took them outside their jurisdictional competence.[75]

Who could doubt that the ideals identified by Franks of openness, fairness and impartiality in decision-making are desirable? But many tribunals which are listed in the Schedule to the Tribunal and Inquiries Act (now 1992 consolidation) and subject to the supervision of the Council on Tribunals are susceptible to a degree of ministerial control or influence which will bring into question their impartiality. Or, where the decision may be of crucial significance, the body in question does not make a formal determination but only a recommendation.[76] Because of their intimate involvement in the policy-making process, the relationship of such bodies with departments and Ministers is not characterised by openness and public candour.

A second reason for the increasing utilisation of tribunals by government was the requirement of expertise and/or technical

---

74 [1969] 2 AC 147.
75 See, however, *Page v Hull University* [1993] 1 All ER 97 (HL); *R v Visitor to the Inns of Court ex parte Calder* [1993] 2 All ER 876 (CA).
76 For example, as in the case of the Parole Board, Office of Fair Trading, Monopolies and Mergers Commission – although the latter acts as an appeal body in TV networking decisions under the Broadcasting Act. None of these bodies is under the supervision of the Council on Tribunals. Sometimes the formal powers of the Secretary of State are not exercisable unless a recommendation is made to that effect, for example, to release a prisoner on parole or stop a takeover.

knowledge which it was felt had to be applied in a judicial manner in the resolution of grievances. One does not have to be a lawyer to act judicially, but the inclusion of a lawyer whether as chairman or member has been common. In the field of social welfare, increasing resort has been made to the use of lawyers as chairmen of social security and medical tribunals. When Social Security Appeal Tribunals (SSATs) were formed by amalgamating national insurance and supplementary benefit tribunals, part of these "rationalising tendencies" included directions for full-time chairmen of SSATs to be lawyers. The TUC objected and initially won a concession that "work peoples" representatives' would automatically sit as one of the wing persons. This concession was ended by section 16 of the Health and Social Security Act 1984.

A third reason for resort to tribunals was their relative speed and informality of procedure. It need only be said that speed and procedure vary enormously as is to be expected for bodies created on an "*ad hoc* and pragmatic" fashion owing their *raison d'être* to the exigencies of political legitimation and administrative convenience as the industrial revolution metamorphosed into the welfare state and now, arguably, into the post-welfare state. Speed and informality are relative terms and it has been suggested that legal representation is an essential requirement to improve a participant's chances of success; that justice does not simply "out" as it were. We can pick up this theme in a moment but we should note successive governments' reluctance to extend legal aid to tribunals.

The legacy of Franks was the Tribunal and Inquiries Act 1958 (now 1992) described at the time by Lord Denning as "a first chapter in a new Bill of Rights".[77] The legislation provided in essence that for tribunals listed in the Schedule to the Act, procedural rules under statutory instrument were not to be effective until after departments had consulted with the Council on Tribunals, a body created by the legislation. As well as acting in an advisory and consultative capacity with government and its departments, the Council also supervises tribunals listed in Schedule 1 of the Act. It enjoys no executive powers. Listed tribunals had to provide a statement of reasons for decisions when requested, either written or oral, save in exceptional circumstances such as national security or unless specifically exempted. Reasons given were to be considered part of the record of proceedings, thereby extending the possibility of review for error of

[77]   HL Debs. vol. 208 col. 605.

law within, or post *Anisminic*, without jurisdiction. The requirement facilitated judicial control of tribunals. Governments of very
different persuasions had resorted to tribunals in order to keep the
courts out of their administration – Labour its programmes for
social reform, Conservative its schemes for financial regulation
and regulation of the privatised utilities (see Chapter 4), nationality and security and intelligence decisions. Under the legislation,
rights of appeal on a point of law to the High Court or Court of
Session were to be available generally and there were limitations
on the scope of statutory clauses restricting or otherwise ousting
the jurisdiction of the High Court to review tribunal decisions.[78]
The presumption was that tribunals exercising judicial functions
would sit in public unless exempted.[79] Where necessary, statutory
tribunals may take evidence on oath and cross-examination may
be allowed. Tribunals are masters of their own procedure and
although the rules of evidence do not apply, proceedings must
be conducted fairly so that hearsay evidence ought not to be
heard without appropriate safeguards.[80] Tribunals, not being a
"part of the judicial arm of the state," have no power to punish
for contempt although it has been held that the Mental Health
Review Tribunal does possess such power.[81]

One of the thorniest issues concerns legal aid. At a time when
the state has sought to reduce its legal aid bill now approaching
£1.1 million *per annum* it is hardly surprising that no advances
have been made in extending legal aid to tribunals. The Government refused to accept a recommendation of the Council on
Tribunals to the Royal Commission on Legal Services that legal
aid should be extended to all tribunals supervised by the Council.
At present, legal aid is available before the Lands Tribunal, the
Commons Commissioners, the Employment Appeal Tribunal and
the Mental Health Review Tribunal. Assistance by Way of Representation was made available for hearings before the Parole Board
Panels considering cases of parole for discretionary life prisoners.
These were set up under the Criminal Justice Act 1991.[82] It is also
available to prisoners on disciplinary charges heard by governors

---

78 With reference to tribunals created under statute prior to 1 August 1958.
79 For example, Mental Health Tribunals and Tax Commissioners although
    the position of the latter has been modified.
80 *R v Hull Prison Board of Visitors ex parte St Germain (No. 2)* [1979] 1
    WLR 1401; *R v Deputy Industrial Injuries Commissioner ex parte Moore*
    [1965] 1 All ER 81; *Mahon v Air NZ* [1984] 3 All ER 201 (PC).
81 *Pickering v Liverpool Daily Post etc* [1990] 1 All ER 335 (CA).
82 These provisions under section 4 of the CJA 1991 introduce a tribunal to
    deal with such cases and followed criticism of existing procedures by the
    European Court of Human Rights in *Thynne v UK* [1991] 13 EHRR 616.

where they have given permission for legal representation. There is also a considerable amount of empirical evidence to show that the presence of a trained representative to assist a party before tribunals has a decisive impact on increasing the chances of success. For unrepresented participants, "informal" procedures may still be very complex and there will often be a total failure to appreciate what has to be established and how, or indeed why. This will have an obvious impact on a decision-maker, who will not have all relevant information before him/her, through no fault of their own, and whose impressions cannot help but be coloured by the picture that is presented. Furthermore, studies have shown that although a procedure may be informal, the *decision-making process itself* will be very formal so that weight will be given to the coherence of a case against, say, a claimant, to what the rules require and even to possible technicalities in construction of a relevant rule. Justice will not "out"; its achievement is skill-dependent.[83] Further suggestions for specialist representation from sources other than private practitioners have not met with official approval.[84]

The Council on Tribunals publishes informative annual reports and has produced Model Rules of Procedure for tribunals,[85] but there is much evidence to suggest that its proposals on more contentious matters are not taken seriously by government.[86] As is too familiar in the British way of doing things, government is under no legal duty to take a "hard look" or to consider seriously the arguments of the Council after a process of consultation. The Council is assuming a more campaigning role instead of responding to individual complaints as in its early years of existence. It has been denied the statutory powers which Franks recommended and it is still true to say, as did its Chairman in 1970, that "The Council's principal difficulty is that they have no effective means of securing attention for the tribunal system as a whole". This is not the Council's fault. In recent years the Council has taken a more active role in encouraging research and it has been vociferous in its criticism of what it regards as a weakening of the independent tribunal system in favour of one-man investigatory procedures and internal government review. It has also expressed in very forceful

83   See H. Genn, "Tribunals and Informal Justice" (1993) *Modern L.R.* 393 for details.
84   H. Genn and Y. Genn, *The Effectiveness of Representation at Tribunals* (London, Lord Chancellor's Department, 1989). See chapter 5 below for developments in FHSA service committees.
85   Cm. 1434, 1991.
86   Lewis and Birkinshaw, Note 51 above, chapter 4.

terms its annoyance at government failure to consider its views.[87] However, as I indicate elsewhere,[88] it does not provide systematic oversight of the complete system of administrative justice as occurs through the Australian Administrative Review Council or the Administrative Conference of the US (see chapter 7).

These shortcomings were inevitable given the limited terms of reference of the Franks Report. The Report and subsequent legislation only covered statutory tribunals. Hundreds of tribunals are outside its supervisory remit. This can encourage haphazard activity on the part of the body in question. A leading example was the Criminal Injuries Compensation Board.[89] When the appropriate rules are made, this body will be under the supervision of the CoT, which has expressed surprise that the CICB may be subject to NSA principles (examined above) – how could these apply to a tribunal operating *judicially*, queried the CoT?[90] The Government's latest response has been the replacement of the CICB by a fixed tariff administered by officials in the Criminal Injuries Compensation Authority (see Cm. 2434, 1993). This change was blocked in the House of Lords by an amendment to the Criminal Justice and Public Order Bill 1994 from Lord Ackner and awaits further developments.

Secondly, some bodies established under statute, for example, Housing Benefit Appeal Committees, are not within the schedule of the CoT; the operation of these bodies has also been subject to severe criticism (see chapter 3). There are in fact many statutory bodies performing the tasks or some of the tasks of tribunals which are excluded from the Act. Leading examples would include the Foreign Compensation Commission, the Gaming Board, Legal Aid Committees, the Parole Board and prison Boards of Visitors when they exercise disciplinary and grievance remedial functions in HM prisons. Disciplinary hearings will now be conducted by governors and assistant governors. Grievance remedial functions will now be handed over to a prisoner's Ombudsman or Adjudicator, who will also deal with complaints generally from prisoners as well as those relating to discipline, although it is envisaged that s/he will remit "appropriate" complaints back to Boards. The disciplinary powers of prison authorities are enormous and

---

[87] Especially over the reform of Family Health Service Committees. See further, CoT *Annual Report* (1993), at 4 to 11.

[88] Lewis and Birkinshaw, Note 51 above.

[89] Section 108 Criminal Justice Act 1988 provided for this to become a statutory body. See the text for the latest developments.

[90] CoT *Annual Report* 1991/2, paragraph 1.47 onward.

although the creation of an "in house" Ombudsman is welcome, the Government may justifiably be accused of confusing discipline and grievance redress, a criticism previously levelled successfully against Boards. In fact, the new procedures seem geared as much to reducing the incidence of judicial review as anything else. During the 1980s prison administration was one of the most "successful" areas for judicial review in areas limited to discipline, access to legal advice and increasingly the provision to prisoners of reasons for decisions.

As a general point, it is not always clear why some bodies are included and some are excluded from the provisions of the legislation, though it doubtless relates to unarticulated assumptions concerning national security (security tribunal, intelligence tribunal, interceptions tribunal), public policy and the appropriate extent to which the ideals of legality should operate in public administration. A coherent system of administrative justice demands that these points are addressed and that they should not remain unarticulated.

A third weakness of the Franks Report was its failure to examine the *ad hoc* methods of raising objections about departmental decisions. This is all the more curious given that the widely regarded reason for establishing the Committee in the first place was that it was a reaction to the *ad hoc* inquiries into the Crichel Down fiasco in the early 1950s. For many years after the Whyatt Report of 1961[91] in which this issue was touched upon, it received scant official treatment although it has come into prominence in the last decade. Indeed this book bears witness to that.

A fourth point is that Franks' brief did not cover those instances where a department, instead of handing an appeal to a tribunal or inquiry (see below, p. 62), deals with a complaint itself. On many occasions, decisions on appeal or arising from a statutory opportunity to register a complaint or simply as an *ad hoc* response to informal appeals are dealt with by departmental officials internally. Examples are complaints under sections 68 and 99 of the Education Act 1944, now modified by subsequent legislation (see p. 84); various licensing and approval functions, for example, in insurance, activities concerned with inner city rejuvenation or public procurement. Under pressure, the practices tend to become more formalised. However, these practices frequently

---

[91]　Sir J. Whyatt, *The Citizen and the Administration: The Redress of Grievances* (London, Stevens, 1961).

spawn "internal law" known only to departmental officials.[92] Why are some decision-making processes handed over to "independent" bodies and others not, when the security or political aspects would not seem to necessitate any distinction? Sometimes it might be possible to discern a rational distinction in the choice of forum or method adopted.[93] At other times one is left with the distinct impression that it is simply the result of "muddling through" which gives to much of our public administration the appearance of an "unsystematic hotch-potch". The thought might be prompted that behind the facade lies a malevolent *primum mobile* deliberately seeking to impede the rational exposition of decision-making and accountability in the division of powers in contemporary government. Although we can take some comfort from the fact that governments are rarely efficient enough to effect such a conspiracy, there is no doubt that recent years have seen numerous examples whereby government has sought to minimise the opportunity for independent challenge to the pursuit and implementation of its policies and programmes. In government contract disputes internal "appeals" to a Director of Contracts are common and may even end up at Cabinet level. A fear expressed in some quarters is that the Citizen's Charter's concentration upon internal review procedures may help to encourage this absence of independence. There is no reason why this should necessarily follow, but one must pay attention to the safeguards which are incorporated in Charter procedures (chapters one, five and seven).

There are merits in internal review procedures, which I address below, but departments have made serious errors of judgment in the past when instead of handing over a grievance to an independent tribunal to deal with the issue, they attempted to resolve the matter internally. In *Sachsenhausen*[94] an early and important investigation of the Parliamentary Commissioner, the Foreign Office was distributing compensation from the then West German Government to victims of Nazi atrocities. There was an expert body on hand to deal with such a distribution, the Foreign Compensation Commission. The Foreign Office instead chose to deal with the cases itself informally and dragged itself

[92] Gower, *Review of Investor Protection*. Cmnd 9125 (London, HMSO, 1984). C. Turpin, *Government Contracts* (London, Penguin Books, 1972), and *Government Procurement and Contracts* (Harlow, Longman, 1989).

[93] Ganz, "The Allocation of Decision-Making Functions", (1972) PL 215 at 219; Lewis and Birkinshaw, Note 51 above.

[94] HC 54 (1967–8); and see the *slaughtered chickens* case HC 947 (1992–3), the *DLA* case HC 65 (1992–3) and the *DVLA* case HC 13 (1993–4), and chapter 5 below.

into heavy-handed administration after drawing up pettifogging distinctions between classes of victims.

The final weakness in Franks' Report in terms of its setting the framework in which "openness, fairness and impartiality" may be achieved in the administrative process was glanced at when we looked at policy-oriented tribunals. It also concerns all those bodies which are part of, or connected with, the formulation of government policy. At issue here are the overtly collective dimensions to public or governmental decision-making. Since the late 1970s, it has been claimed that the state has a limited role in economic and industrial development and even in the provision of welfare programmes. Such claims owe much to political rhetoric. The economic structure of advanced capitalism requires state support through the provision of a system of law and legal institutions, the creation of regulatory and self-regulatory bodies and other institutions whose task is the achievement of a fair market system, competitive markets and the establishment of economic direction through government decisions on fiscal and expenditure policy. This overlooks the activities of local government, the expenditure of health authorities and trusts, the public sector at large and the profusion of public/private hybrids which are engaged in economic activity of one kind or another, for example, Training and Enterprise Councils, the City Panel on Takeovers, 3is[95] and its role in commercial investment or English Estates (Urban Regeneration Agency). Neither Franks, nor anyone else for that matter, explored what was required in the interests of administrative justice in decision-making involving collective and policy choices. It is well to remember that a proliferation of multipurpose, protean advisory agencies will remain a fixture of governmental apparatus for the foreseeable future (see chapter 4).

Although the decisions of policy-oriented bodies often impinge on individuals directly, such as in the case of Monopoly and Mergers Commission investigations, their primary focus is on the collective weal: competitiveness, a fair market, consumer choice and protection of the public interest in large-scale mergers. Through the achievement of economic collective aims, governments hope to create a climate in which economic success will help to minimise individual grievances, although new grievances will be precipitated by the very pursuit of those policies. The pursuit of sound economic policy through economic expansion and growth has been the objective of every British government since the Second World

---

[95] 3is is the UK's largest investment capital provider; a principal shareholder is the Bank of England.

War, hard though this may be to reconcile with the evidence, particularly in the early 1990s. In pursuit of this objective there has been and will be persistent resort to policy-oriented bodies operating informally to assist departmental officials and their political overlords in the preparation of "appropriate strategies". Sometimes such bodies operate by making rules which might define a policy of regulation (in the field of financial regulation, self regulatory organisations (SROs) under the Financial Services Act 1986 are a clear example and their form of self-regulation has been heavily criticised, especially in relation to personal pensions and sharp sales practices), sometimes they do not. Monetarist, free-market and non-interventionist governmental policies since 1979 have fostered a climate where the use of specialist bodies to advise government of interventionist or regulatory policies is officially regarded as anathema, whereas nothing is too arduous, or too expensive, for private consultants. However, in reality one of the pivotal agencies in economic policy in this period has been the Office of Fair Trading (OFT) for much of the period operating under Sir Gordon Borrie QC. Its importance merits closer attention.

The Director-General of Fair Trading (DGFT) has executive powers and wide-ranging advisory powers in the field of competition policy and consumer affairs. The DGFT's powers are judicial (some of them are supervised by the CoT, though not those under the Restrictive Trade Practices legislation[96]) regulatory and prosecutorial. He often, particularly in competition, proceeds by way of negotiation and confidential guidance with the regulated or those within his field of competence. The Fair Trading Act 1973, the Competition Act 1980, the Companies Act 1988 and proposals for further powers[97] are replete with examples. The DGFT advises the Secretary of State and is an advocate for the consumer interest. He has to co-ordinate activities with other agencies regulating utilities as well as DGIV of the EC Commission – the Competition Directorate. The invariable method of proceeding is informal in the case of the DGFT, far less so in the case of the Monopolies and Mergers Commission (MMC) and the latter has faced a series of judicial review challenges which may well cause it to proceed with ever greater degrees of formality. Their recommendations are publishable at the

---

96   Those relating to consumer credit and estate agents.
97   *Abuse of Market Power*, Cm 2100; on restrictive practices Cm 331 and 727. Individual challenge by "victims" is increasingly being introduced and a general alignment with EC competition law.

Secretary of State's discretion[98] and may remain confidential, although the MMC's reports are published automatically with necessary protection for confidential information. The details behind these processes will inevitably remain a mystery and opportunities to participate and be informed remain oblique.[99] The OFT lacks a large investigatory staff and wide investigatory powers, particularly when compared with the Competition Division of the European Commission (DGIV) and so it has to rely upon receipt of complaints for a good deal of its information. Of the 1,690 complaints received in 1991 many are somewhat trivial and the more important information comes from OFT investigations into cartels and monopolies. An interesting development in 1993 saw the DGFT conducting public hearings at various sites around the country on the reform of consumer credit law.

Informal control over such bodies has been achieved in the past, and doubtless will be in the future, by two basic devices: firstly, by the Secretary of State retaining final power of decision. In 14 cases since 1979 the Secretary of State has rejected the advice of the DGFT over referral of a merger to the MMC, including twice in two weeks in 1993. Secondly, and more generally, by a Minister's power of appointment and the role of the Public Appointments Unit.[100] It is more widely known as patronage. Moving beyond the bodies which are our present concern, control over appointment is of crucial importance throughout the public and extended public/private interface; in regional and district Health Authorities, Hospital Trusts, city institutions. A further form of creeping control has been achieved by increasing statutory regulation of professional bodies starting with the Medicines Act 1858 concerning doctors, and more latterly evidenced by government intervention in engineering, auditing and teaching. Furthermore, commercial organisations such as building societies, banks, financial institutions and insurance companies have found themselves under increasing legislative regulation and more pervasive governmental prompting to pursue government policies on mortgage repayments, levels of lending, reporting of financial irregularities and good practice for consumers. Even the legal

---

98   *Lonrho v Secretary of State* [1989] 2 All ER 609 (HL).
99   Especially in the absence of freedom of information laws, government in the sunshine (open meetings) and open advisory committee laws (Birkinshaw, (1991b).
100 Lists of eligible candidates are not published by the Public Appointments Unit. In the US, membership of advisory committees must be "balanced" as between different interests.

profession has felt the "state's all intrusive grasp" in the form of the Courts and Legal Services Act 1989 (see chapter 5).

What is common throughout the modes of organisation outlined in the preceding paragraphs is that the necessity for social and economic survival has impelled successive governments to organise collectively and often by informal means the processes necessary for the continuation and reproduction of social life. On these points Franks, or for that matter the 1988 Justice/All Souls Report on administrative justice, has little relevance. The individualistic outlook of the Franks Report owes much to that *gesellschaft* notion of justice and law perfected by the law and legal profession in the 19th and first half of the 20th centuries – namely atomic individual versus atomic individual, one of whom happens to be the state. Such an outlook overlooks the fact that the problems which tribunals were to address were not simple manifestations of unfair practices in the individualisation of disputes, but were themselves inherently caused by increasing collective processes of production, consumption, centralisation of authority and a secretive state which had not been forced to come to terms with the requirements of constitutionality in a modern democratic state. The Franks Committee did not understand many relevant decision-making processes of this state or they were excluded from its terms of reference.

One may argue "But wait! Surely the policies of governments since the late seventies have been aimed at minimising the state's presence, rolling back its frontiers and releasing initiative in private or privatised markets." As I explain elsewhere with others, the state never withdraws; it merely reforms.[101] This is part of a thesis to which I cannot allot sufficient time at the present but the central question of justice against the state is probably more confused and difficult now than when Franks wrote. The state takes myriad forms and operates through countless processes; many of these have a direct bearing on justice and raise items about which individuals or groups will wish to complain; they have rarely been the subject of any appropriate comment.

In many areas of contemporary government and its organisation, opportunities for individual or group challenge, complaint or redress are not present – this in spite of the growing influence of the Citizen's Charter. In economic policy, the expenditure and taxation decisions of the Government (apart from the challenge of personal assessment in the latter) are inevitably beyond legal or

---

[101] P. Birkinshaw, I. Harden and N. Lewis, *Government by Moonlight: The Hybrid Parts of the State* (London, Unwin Hyman, 1990).

effective administrative challenge, and many would still maintain also beyond effective political challenge in representative bodies in spite of reforms from the 1980s onwards.[102] Successful challenge through demonstration is rare but may be graphically illustrated, as in the demonstrations in 1990 which finally convinced the Government that the poll tax had to go – along, one may add, with the Prime Minister responsible for its introduction. Of course influence from the powerful is frequently brought to bear *a priori* on financial and taxation decisions but it is rarely a matter of public record. Informal economic pressure has often been used by government to influence the money supply, the level of wages and prices and employment, as in the case of the coal industry when the privatised and supposedly independent electricity industry continued, initially under ministerial pressure, to purchase British coal instead of cheaper foreign coal. Statutory mechanisms exist for the investigation of abuses or potential abuses of market domination, yet the most common *modus operandi* is by informal deals off the record between the authorities and the companies concerned, a process facilitated by the 1988 Companies Act in the case of mergers.[103] Naturally enough, were government to provide open and impartial grievance procedures to complain about such policy-making, the opportunity would be presented to upset government policy. This could not be tolerated. All governments will want to get their way; the opacity of the British system prevents "outsiders" having an effective say.

What we find then, even under a government which has espoused the philosophy of individualism and free choice for almost a decade and a half, is a series of devices the collective governmental nature of which render individual challenge largely nugatory when the object of challenge is the policy of central government.[104]

[102] The most recent of which have been a unified budget in November and a new committee (EDX Committee) to settle priorities and make final adjustments to departmental bids.

[103] See Note 97 above. There is an opportunity for individual redress after ministerial orders have been approved, however.

[104] ACAS is a body charged with powers to settle and conciliate in industrial disputes – its provenance is collectivist. In 1992 it received 1,207 cases for conciliation and 60 per cent related to pay and terms and conditions of employment and redundancy. In 1992 it dealt with almost 500,000 inquiries. ACAS was to be a central agent in the extension of collective bargaining to avoid disruptive disputes; the TU Reform and Employment Rights Acts 1993 section 43 removes the general duty from ACAS of "encouraging the extension of collective bargaining and the development and, where necessary, reform of collective bargaining machinery". Under section 44 those using ACAS may be charged for the service. The Minister may *direct* that fees be charged.

Arbitration

Arbitration is a commonly employed method to resolve commercial disputes. The essential features usually involve a degree of choice by those in dispute over the decision-maker and the presentation to that decision-maker of a body of rules or "law" agreed upon by the disputants. One would imagine that following commercial practice, arbitrations would be resorted to frequently by central government to resolve their contractual disputes. In fact this is not the case. Government contracts in the UK which involve central government show a remarkable resistance to either litigation or arbitration to resolve disputes and such litigation as there is has been disappointing in refusing to acknowledge a public law dimension to public procureent.[105] There are disputes between departments or agencies and other parties; orthodox explanations suggest that the ordinary law of contract applies to these disputes. In fact, an enormous body of internal law developed by the Public Accounts Committee, the Treasury and departments, and known largely only by them, is applied to resolve disputes, generally by informal processes. In local government, arbitration is more common – much of it concerning building contracts before the Joint Contracts Tribunal in fact – and the Local Government Act 1988 encourages contractors to take authorities to court where the provisions of the Act which cover the award of contracts for non-commercial considerations are not complied with.

EC Directives which have been implemented into domestic law by statutory instrument have made considerable changes to the requirements of publicity, advertising and open tendering in public procurement, and Directives also set out legal requirements for their enforcement.[106] Interestingly, for disputes which emerge from the pre-contractual requirements contained in the Directives, the UK Government opted for a court of law to deal with alleged breaches of the legal duties contained in the implementing provisions and not, as might be expected, for a specialised tribunal. Directives concerning the works and supplies contracts of public authorities have been in existence since 1971 and 1977 (and amended) but recent additions have extended the operation of the Directives to the award of contracts by utilities – in both the public and private sectors – and to the award of services by public authorities. This will have crucial significance for contracting out policies.

---

[105] *R v Lord Chancellor ex parte Hibbit* (1993) *The Times*, 12 March.
[106] SIs 1991/80 and 1992/3279.

In two crucial areas of contracting carried out by central government, namely, defence and pharmaceuticals, special arrangements
have been made between the Government and the industries
concerned to establish rule-making and price-setting bodies for
contracts where there is no competition. The relevant bodies: the
Review Board for Government Contracts and the Pharmaceutical Price Regulation Scheme also provide a procedure to deal
with disputes between the industries and goverent over contract
prices and profit levels.[107]

Public Inquiries

The second term of reference of Franks concerned public
inquiries, about which Wraith and Lamb have written that it would
be "pointless to try to apply any coherent system to the use of the
term inquiry, public inquiry, local inquiry, public local inquiry and
'opportunity to be heard'; it is safe to say that none exists".[108] The
Government has come to accept that the procedure suitable as an
appeal mechanism to the Secretary of State against a local authority's planning decision affecting an individual's proprietary rights
may not be appropriate for discussion of proposals affecting a wide
range of local, regional or national interests such as the siting of
a nuclear reprocessing plant; whether a pressurised water nuclear
reactor plant should be established; where a major international
airport should be positioned; or what approach should be taken
by trains to the Channel Tunnel. The statutory details for the
procedure in the first three of the above examples are virtually
identical;[109] administrative concession has brought considerable
variation in practice. In the case of the Chunnel the Government
resorted to hearings before a Parliamentary Select Committee to
hear objections by those affected by the proposals.

---

[107] Birkinshaw *et al.*, Note 101 above.
[108] Wraith and Lamb, *Public Inquiries as an Instrument of Government*, 1971.
       This section does not address a tribunal of inquiry under statute or other-
       wise to establish facts, for example, Scott LJ and the Matrix Churchill
       inquiry.
[109] Planning inquiries fall under three main heads: statutory inquiries which
       are mandatory and for which the Lord Chancellor has power to make
       regulations detailing procedure. These are under the supervision of the
       CoT and the Tribunals and Inquiries Act 1992 applies to them. Second,
       statutory inquiries which are discretionary, though if "designated" they are
       subject to similar controls as those above. Lastly, non-statutory inquiries
       operating without supervision apart from the common law. See Planning
       Inquiries (Attendance of Public) Act 1980 – inquiries usually in public.
       Inspectors' reports are generally published.

In planning appeals, for instance, the appeal may be disposed of by a written representation (WR) procedure supplemented by a site visit, and regulations in 1987 improved the position of third parties, i.e. those without a "legal interest", to some extent.[110] The appeal may also be dealt with through an "informal hearing" for which detailed guidance is now provided by the Department of the Environment.[111] The hearing is a "round-table discussion" led by the inspector, and the code requires the appellant and local authority to provide written statements of their cases. Legal representation is discouraged and the procedure is not suitable if members of the public are likely to be present. Questioning is encouraged but not formal cross-examination. Unlike the WR procedure, informal hearings may use site visits as a forum for *inter partes* discussions.[112]

In 1992/93, the Planning Inspectorate, now a Next Steps Agency, reported that there were 17,832 appeals of which 98 per cent were determined by the inspector, 2 per cent by the Secretary of State. Of the inspector decisions, 82 per cent followed a WR procedure, 8 per cent a formal inquiry and 10 per cent an informal hearing. Of the Secretary of State's decisions, 56 per cent were after a formal inquiry – s/he does not conduct informal hearings, at least not under the code. As the Inspectorate acknowledges,[113] this has transformed the planning appeal process from a local public inquiry to a "one-man" tribunal system. Interestingly, the figures show a greater chance of success after a formal inquiry than after the WR procedure.[114]

For inquiries into projects of major significance, departments have invariably relied upon the usual statutory procedure for the holding of an inquiry, supplemented by pre-inquiry hearings and appointing as an inspector (who reports to the Secretary of State) an eminent person, often a lawyer, assisted if necessary by a panel of lay experts.[115] At the Sizewell inquiry into the proposed siting

---

[110] See DoE Circ. 11/87.
[111] Annex 2, DoE Circ. 10/88.
[112] See *South Bucks DC v Secretary of State for the Environment* (1992) JPL 921.
[113] 1992/3 Annual Report.
[114] Purdue, 1991.
[115] Planning Inquiry Commissions, which provided a statutory procedure under the Town and Country Planning Act 1968 – now under the 1990 TCP Act – for investigation into major proposals, have never been used. The refusal to hold a public inquiry into the proposal to build a nuclear reprocessing plant at Thorp, Cumbria was challenged unsuccessfully by judicial review: *R v Secretary of State for the Environment ex p. Greenpeace.* (1994) *The Independent* 8 March (QBD) and Radioactive Substances Act 1993.

of a pressurised water nuclear reactor when an application was made for the Minister's consent under section 2 of the Electric Lighting Act 1909 for the placing of high voltage lines, the then Department of Energy utilised powers under section 34 of the Electricity Act 1957 to hold an inquiry.[116] The Chairman was an eminent QC, Sir Frank Layfield. The frequent choice of a lawyer chairman is not without significance, Patrick McAuslan believes. A panel with a broad range of talents is less likely to confine itself to the "official line" and more likely to challenge officially sponsored plans. Discussion of highly technical and inherently controversial issues is more easily kept within a narrow rein by a figure who is, by virtue of his legal training and public position, sympathetically disposed to the prevailing orthodoxy.[117] To many this would sound a little too neat and convenient. However, since 1968 the government has been able to resort to a statutory Planning Inquiry Commission to investigate major proposals of the kind under discussion. It would sit under a panel of experts and would carry out a wide-ranging investigation into the proposal; its procedure has never been invoked by the Government in spite of its obvious advantages as a procedure of investigation.[118]

There is a problem concerning the appropriateness of a procedure whereby the Secretary of State acts as an appellate authority on a dispute between a local or public authority and an individual where he can act on the hearing inspector's recommendations impartially, and those inquiries which touch upon a subject of wide public concern and in the outcome of which a department has a very keen interest. In the latter case the inquiry is not aimed at resolving, or at least assuaging, an individual grievance or complaint. These latter inquiries are primarily concerned with the provision of information to the Minister, better to inform his decision, and raising objections is subordinate to this function. The information obtained from these inquiries and the recommendations of the inspector form but one part, probably a substantial part, of the total information which the Minister will consider when s/he determines what conclusions are in the public interest. This point is set in relief when one considers that *officially* the range of discussion at inquiries is usually restricted to matters which do not touch upon the merits or policy dimension underlying

---

[116] See CoT Annual Report 1991/2, Part II on the Hinkley Point inquiry, and see sections 36 and 37 Electricity Act 1989 and SI 528/1990 on procedural rules.
[117] McAuslan, *The Ideologies of Planning Law*, 1980.
[118] See Note 115.

a proposal in question, though as a matter of *practice* discussion of policy or merits invariably finds its way into the proceedings. Indeed changes in the most commonly resorted to procedural rules for major inquiries have allowed cross-examination of the government's case on the merits where the official representative is willing for this to happen, although the inspector cannot force the representative to answer questions.[119] Furthermore, the government may draw the terms of reference to include wider issues.

The range of discussion is further restricted by placing third parties, that is, those who are not statutory bodies and who have no direct legal (proprietary) interests, at a disadvantage to those with such interests. At major inquiries, third parties are invariably the major protestors; they represent interest groups. They have no individual legal right to insist on being present or on being heard at the inquiry or to challenge the ultimate decision of the Minister as "persons aggrieved",[120] although those conducting the inquiry must act fairly and not abuse their discretion. General administrative practice has been to allow them to participate in proceedings and to present their own case, though as major inquiries have shown, their participation and its effectiveness is at the total discretion of the inspector. At the Sizewell inquiry, for instance, the inspector informed one pressure group that discussion of safety aspects of the proposed construction of Britain's first nuclear pressurised water reactor could not be adjourned, even though the review on safety by the Nuclear Installation Inspectorate (NII) had been delayed and was not available. One of the reasons given by the Secretary of State for not funding objectors from the public purse was that safety aspects were to be investigated by the NII.[121] It is extremely unlikely that third parties will be awarded costs, although there has been an increased tendency to award costs against local authorities at the suit of appellants.[122]

"Policy" has been taken to include the "merits" of a proposal and even the need for a proposal. The inspector would be correct to stop examination of these matters by objectors, unless, as

---

[119] SI 1992/2038 r. 12(3).

[120] Though see: *Turner v Secretary of State* (1973) 28 P&CR 123; *Wilson v Secretary of State* [1974] 1 All ER 428; and in particular *R v Hammersmith LBC ex parte "People Before Profit"* (1982) 80 LGR 322.

[121] The Inspector became very critical of the delay by the CEGB and NII: *The Guardian*, 14 January 1984.

[122] M. Purdue, *Planning Appeals: A Critique* (Buckingham, Open University Press, 1991) chapter 5; *R v Secretary of State ex parte Chichester DC* (1992) JPL 140, and see DoE Circ. 1993/8.

at Sizewell, need and economics are written into the terms of reference, the government representative is willing to be examined on these subjects or the inspector believes the objectors are questioning the specific application of a policy and not the policy itself. However, a decision of the Court of Appeal has given cold comfort to the last of these propositions when it was decided that non-inclusion in his report by the inspector of the discussion at the inquiry of the local impact of a policy to increase user charges for a toll bridge was justified because it related to a government policy and would not assist the Minister in his decision.[123] The Court was satisfied that all relevant items had in any event been fully considered by the department, a sentiment, it must be said, not supported by many notorious episodes. Nor was the Court swayed by a very vigorous first instance judgment in support of the objectors' claim that no proper consideration of the objectors' case had been considered by the Minister (see below). Government is accountable to Parliament for policy, not to objectors. The importance of the expression "policy" and judicial interpretation of the term require further elaboration.

The basic procedure for planning and development, highway and compulsory purchase schemes where an inquiry takes place is publicaion of the proposal, receipt of objections thereto and, where bargains cannot be struck to satisfy objectors, pre-inquiry hearings where necessary and the holding of an inquiry before an inspector. At the conclusion of the inquiry, the inspector sends his report and recommendations to the Secretary of State, who may accept or reject them, though if s/he disagrees on a point of fact or considers new evidence, s/he has to provide the opportunity for a reopening of the inquiry if s/he thereby is minded to disagree with the inspector's recommendations. Judicial interpretation on what constitutes a disagreement to activate this safeguard has been very circumscribed.[124] The House of Lords has held that where the Minister accepts the recommendations but takes into consideration new evidence which constitutes part of the *factual* evidence behind the proposal – namely, statistical analysis supporting a proposal – there is no breach of natural justice where s/he refuses to reopen the inquiry. The Secretary of State is also entitled to receive new evidence and advice from within his/her own department (which will inevitably come from outside sources) after the inquiry, which may result in a change in the

---

123   *R v Secretary of State for Transport ex parte Gwent CC* [1987] 1 All ER 161.
124   *R v Secretary of State etc ex parte GLC* (1986) JPL 32.

proposal or supporting argument without an obligation to put this new evidence before the objectors.[125] The Minister and the officials are constitutionally one and the same, and the Minister is not therefore taking new evidence into account but talking to himself, as it were.[126] The feeling of unfair treatment among the objectors was provoked largely by the refusal of the inspector to allow cross-examination of the factual basis supporting the policy, which involved the prediction of future traffic flows along particular routes and which was employed as a justification for building a motorway. This refusal, the majority held, did not constitute a breach of natural justice because the factual basis was an inherent part of the policy. This Lord Edmund Davis found too much to accept and he even cited Franks in support of his dissent. Subsequently, the factual basis of the proposal was amended without any opportunity of challenge from the objectors.

Certain key points call for comment. Lord Diplock, who decided in favour of the Secretary of State, insisted that an inquiry is not a proceeding in a civil court of law and it should not be attended by overlong procedural niceties. Too many challenges to public decision-making would seize up the operations of government. This is not an idle point. The judgment affirms a belief in the division of labour in government – policy is for the executive to be overseen by the legislature, it is not to be made by the judiciary or public at large. Again this is basically a widely accepted implication of government under a representative democracy, although a written constitution would give the judiciary a greater say in the setting of the parameters of political action. However, ought not a valid constructive and possibly valuable improvement on policy be welcome after a public hearing, especially where a policy is to have a constraining influence on our future development, public resources and style of life and environment? Does this not apply *a fortiori* when we are talking about the facts and statistics upon which a policy is based and not an overt appraisal of the policy itself? The majority decision

---

125   *Bushell v Secretary of State for the Environment* [1981] AC 75. No inquiries procedure rules were in operation which specifically covered the inquiry (into major roads) in *Bushell*. For Government plans to produce streamlined highways inquiries see CoT *Annual Report* 1992/3 2.37–38.

126   See the comments of Tudor Evans J on whether the Minister could have imputed to him statements by senior civil servants on the punitive nature of the control unit in Wakefield Prison: *Williams v Home Office (No. 2)* [1981] 1 All ER 1211. See *Carltona v Commissioners of Works* [1943] 2 All ER 560 and *R v Secretary of State for Home Department ex parte Oladehinde* [1990] All ER 393.

in *Bushell* encourages officialdom to maintain its preserve on *all* features of decision-making, thereby encouraging the widespread feeling that participatory exercises are irrelevant and tokenism. It must be said that the view that the public inquiry is a prolix and time-wasting process is widespread, especially when in all likelihood the inquiry is unlikely to change anything, merely delay the implementation of a proposal. Many who believe in the virtues of effective public participation would argue that the appropriate forum is Parliament so that elected representatives could, with no expense to private individuals, beyond the expense of maintaining Parliament, examine all the implications. The difficulty here is that Parliament alone could not adequately represent the objections and apprehensions of regional and local areas; furthermore, for MPs outside those regions or localities the subject will be of little interest and carry no votes.

It seems to me that one of the most useful contributions in this area in trying to balance in a fair procedure the often conflicting interests involved in the clash of national, regional and local priorities still remains the recommendations put forward by the Outer Circle Policy Unit in its study *The Big Public Inquiry*.[127] The inquiry emerges after the real decision has effectively been made as in *Bushell*; a department has usually a very close interest or commitment in the outcome; the procedural rules do not ensure that enough time is provided to study such information as is provided by the authorities; traditional inquiries encourage a "yes/no" solution to a highly complex proposal which is not susceptible to such a straightforward response. In spite of Lord Diplock's warnings, the inquiry is modelled on legal/adversarial lines and a looser, more flexible procedure might allow fuller examination of the wider dimensions involved.

The OCPU's suggested balance in procedure to accommodate the legitimate requirements of the administration and fair treatment for the interested parties is a "Project Inquiry". This would operate as the inquiry into major proposals and would investigate impartially, thoroughly and in public the *need* for a project, its costs, risks and benefits: "in short all the foreseeable economic, social and environmental implications and repercussions of the project" – all the material facts would be brought out and tested. The Project Inquiry (PI) – which OCPU envisaged would be non-statutory for reasons which I believe are dubious, and which would not be chaired by a lawyer – would precede a Standing Commission (which have long been out of fashion) or Select

127   OCPU, 1979.

Committee of Parliament. These latter bodies would scrutinise general policy before traditional local inquiries examined specific planning applications. The PI would proceed in two stages: a stage of investigation followed by a stage of argument taking a maximum of 30 months. Commissioners to sit on the PI would be chosen according to two broad criteria: "a sufficient degree of expertise and the maximum degree of impartiality", although they would be appointed by the Secretary of State after "very wide consultation". These recommendations have not been acted upon by government[128] and nor have the recommendations for a pool of public money to fund objectors. Conviction politics has little place for enfranchising the basis of policy formulation.

The majority judgment of their Lordships in the *Bushell* case operates under a paradigm of governmental decision-making which is symptomatic of representative democracy in the 19th century. There was a signal failure to acknowledge a point emphasised by the OCPU: the democratic implications of the fact that policy formulation is a cumulative process, developed at various stages and by various bodies of a governmental, quasi-governmental and private character meshing in often confidential debate or dialogue long before any parliamentary appraisal, let alone any programme of public participation, is countenanced. In the USA this realisation was partly responsible for federal judges insisting that policy, when developed by the regulatory agencies, should take the form of rule-making, that is, delegated legislation. Under the Administrative Procedure Act 1946 a formal procedure with interested parties participating in the making of the rules will sometimes be followed. At the other end of the statutory spectrum was a "Notice and Comment" procedure, whereby interested parties would be informed of proposed rule-making and asked for their comments; the proposals are also published in the Federal Register and comments invited. This latter process was supplemented by decisions of federal courts which insisted on a "hybrid" procedure – not quite a full judicial hearing but a substantial fleshing out of the "Notice and Comment" procedure. The hybrid procedure, though still in existence, has been subject to attack in the Supreme Court[129] and rule-making as a whole was

---

128 See the report of the Select Committee on the Environment, HC 181 (1986) and Purdue (1991). For new arrangements replacing the Private Bill procedure authorising transport projects, see Part 1 Transport and Works Act 1992.
129 *Vermont Yankee Nuclear Power Corp. v NRDC Inc.* 519 US 435 (1978); R.B. Stewart *et al.*, (1977–78) 91 *Harvard LR* 1805.

subject to opposition in the deregulatory drives under the Reagan and Bush administrations and Clinton's re-invention of government.[130] A more recent development has been the encouragement of negotiated rule-making whereby an authority will negotiate with interested parties the form and detail of rules encapsulating various policies. It remains true to say that opportunities to participate in policy formulation by regulatory bodies in the USA far surpass any British analogue (and see utility regulators, chapter 4) apart from the planning process in land use and inquiries. Even here, the growing resort to calling in procedures where the decision is taken by the Secretary of State, use classes orders, informal inquiries (above), and removal of planning restrictions in Enterprise Zones, Restricted Planning Zones and the replacement of local authority planning controls by Urban Development Corporations and the Urban Regeneration Agency have all made substantial inroads into opportunities to object before an environmental decision is taken.

In the case of the "Big Inquiries" it remains as true today as it did when the OCPU wrote:

> "[T]he institutions and procedures which make and carry out national policies for the planning of our industries, and decisions about their associated 'works' should [adapt themselves to maintain government by consent] . . . . There are today mounting calls for more open government. These include proposals for new procedures for submitting central policy-making in general to more profound, critical and expert scrutiny than is provided by existing arrangements."[131]

The Citizen's Charter has turned a deaf ear and a blind eye to these concerns. The White Paper on *Open Government* has virtually eliminated the policy-making process from its provisions covering greater openness.

Formal and Informal Internal Resolution of Grievances

The last category of practices for processing complaints concerns the methods adopted *within* departments and agencies to resolve grievances. Clearly this is Citizen's Charter territory. I have already spoken about the major features of the Charter and

---

[130] See *Motor Vehicle Manufacturers' Ass. v State Farm Mutual Auto. Insurance Co.* 51 USLW 4953 (1983), where the Supreme Court held that deregulation may well be subject to rule-making procedures requiring a "thorough, probing and in-depth" review. See chapter 6 below.

[131] OCPU, Note 127 above.

need not repeat them specifically but only need to state that at the level of individual grievance, increased efficiency, speedier turnover of processing of complaints, obtaining customer feedback on standards of service and consulting customers on the content of a service, monitoring of performance and the provision of an effective grievance procedure are all making their impact upon public services. It remains to be seen whether the Treasury will countenance such developments if enhanced consumer consciousness threatens to place an increasing demand upon the Exchequer.

As well as being provided under Citizen's Charter exhortations, processes for dealing with complaints can accompany a statutory opportunity to appeal or make complaint to the Secretary of State or they may attend another statutory procedure. Prior to the operation of the NHS and Community Care Act 1990, local authorities were under a range of duties to make arrangements for one or more classes of services for disabled persons. A default power existed in the Secretary of State. These provisions have now been replaced by the 1990 Act under which local authorities have to draw up a plan for community care services in their area and assess needs for such services where an individual requires them. Section 50 empowers the Secretary of State to give directions to authorities regarding the exercise of their social service functions. The Secretary of State is given powers to declare by order that an authority has failed in its social services functions, and he is given specific power of inquiry. His decision is ultimately enforceable through the High Court by mandamus. Complaints or representations from individuals or representative bodies such as The Royal Association for Disability and Rehabilitation are processed within the Department of Health by staff of at least Principal level and may involve deliberations with a Minister and even the Secretary of State.

The previous relevant provision, namely, section 2 of the Chronically Sick and Disabled Persons Act 1970, did not appear to have given the impetus to local authorities to devise adequate complaints procedures for members of the public.[132] Section 50 of the 1990 Act now contains a power for the Secretary of State to require local authorities to provide and publicise complaints procedures which I examine in chapter 3 while observing at this stage that much criticism has been heaped upon central government because it has, the allegation suggests, attempted to

---

[132]   *R v Kent CC ex parte Bruce* (1986) *The Times* 8 February.

appear virtuous while not supplying adequate funding to carry out statutory responsibilities and it has failed to give clear guidance to authorities on what to do in the case of assessing individuals' needs where there is inadequate funding. In notorious circumstances in 1994, the Government "talked out" a Bill giving greater positive rights to the disabled, and subsequently promised its own more "realistic", i.e. Treasury approved, reforms.

When, however, a department maintains ultimate control over grievance procedures, it and no-one else has the ultimate power to control policy. There are some quite dramatic examples where the provision of an appeal mechanism will give the department control over what may become a central feature of policy. For example, free competition in transport policies could flourish by the simple incorporation of a right of appeal to a Minister as in section 35 of the Transport Act 1980. This allowed an application for permission by a private concern to compete with public transport in the metropolis and appeal was against the decision of the London Transport Executive. Under section 20 Education Act 1993, the Secretary of State determines disputes between funding authorities established by that Act and local education authorities, the former of which the Secretary of State was instrumental in establishing.

Many departments have licensing responsibilities. It was common to find that these were not confined by any procedural requirements, let alone by any appeal to an independent tribunal. Inevitably, however, the department would develop a procedure to deal with what was often a mixture of grievance/complaint/appeal against an initial decision. This is still the situation in the case of insurance companies which have to be licensed by the Secretary of State under the Insurance Companies Act 1974 from which decision there is no appeal.[133] Companies incorporated by law have to be registered with Companies House but complaints about companies find their way to the Department of Trade and Industry where they have developed internal procedures to deal with them. Indeed, one of the major consequences of the revolution in the regulation of financial markets and financial advisers under the Financial Services Act 1986 was that many of the informal practices of the DTI were formalised in that Act and were delegated by the Secretary of State to the Securities and Investment Board (SIB), which in turn has delegated the responsibility of licensing actors in the market to self-regulatory

133 See *Kaplan v UK* [1980] 4 EHRR 64.

organisations, of which there are four as of writing. Each of these is responsible for regulating its particular aspect of the market. From their decisions and those of the SIB there are very wide grounds of appeal provided for firms to the Financial Services Tribunal. What was hitherto "internal law" to the department and its officials, rather like the erstwhile "A" Code in social security administration, is now formalised in the statute and in the rule books which the SIB and the SROs have to produce and which have to be approved by the Secretary of State who is advised by the DGFT.[134]

In the absence of any statutory provisions or guidelines, departments and agencies will develop their own practices. These often will only be known to those officials who deal with them as part of their responsibilities. One senior legal adviser whose department had regular contact with the public informed me that he was sure there were established practices to deal with grievances from the public but he did not know what they were! Very few complainants make their complaints by personal appearance at headquarters – although the practice is far from unknown. Before the Benefits Agency was established, the DSS informed me of the following practice. Designated customer service personnel were appointed at local offices and regional offices. These were the local manager and regional director respectively. However, above the regional director was a national director who would deal with a complaint at national level and who would even interview complainants, although the practice was not advertised or encouraged. Generally speaking, appearances at departmental local or regional offices are far more common and the more local the office, the more likely that a complaint will be made personally. This was graphically illustrated in the case of Northern Ireland Departments where the Northern Ireland Parliamentary Commissioner for Administration described a tradition of visits by complainants to departments in Northern Ireland because of their proximity to the departments (see p. 31 above). It is far more common in the case of departments for the complaint to be in writing and for it then to be dealt with at the most local level as appropriate. In the case of agencies, where many of them deal with large numbers of the public, MPs and complainants are urged to deal with the Agency itself and not the department (see above).

---

134 The SROs are subject to judicial review: *R v LAUTRO ex parte Ross* [1993] 1 All ER 545 (CA) but not the Insurance Ombudsman who deals with LAUTRO complaints *R v IOB ex parte Aegon Life Ass.* (1994) *The Times* 7 January.

While there is still evidence of "ad hocery" in the way departments deal with disputes, the Citizen's Charter, ombudsman investigations and government emphasis upon consumerism have all served to heighten official recognition of the necessity to establish to outsiders, for example, the PCA, the NAO on value for money (VFM) audits and the Citizen's Charter Unit that their house is in order. Of course, the pressure points only emerge where there is frequent contact with the public, something which most departments are likely to experience less with the advent of the NSAs. Even where there were departmental claims to ad hocery in resolving disputes, regularised practices have been noted by the PCA and this was reinforced by my own examination.

A former PCA, Sir Cecil Clothier, informed the author of the following types of complaint as the kind which recurred frequently in his work:

(a) Against the conduct of a particular member of staff. Here the PCA identified regular, internal and rather formal procedures involving trade union representatives.

(b) About a department's general handling of a specific case. Here complaints are invariably in writing and where there is a local network, letters received by the centre are handed to the local level. It was the PCA's impression that interviews were seldom refused if requested "or if the department felt that it was a sensible way of progressing"; the presence of a complainant can often have a beneficial effect on a positive outcome in the complainant's favour.

(c) Those made by MPs on constituents' behalf. We have looked at these above.

(d) About government or department policy. Complaints about policy are dealt with by specialist sections. In the DSS, for instance, policy complaints go to central policy units which also deal with systemic complaints raised by groups such as the Child Poverty Action Group.

The Home Office still maintains, of all the departments, an antipathy towards interviewing complainants, although it should be borne in mind that there is a wide range of institutions which act as grievance remedial devices, *inter alia*, in areas over which the Home Office assumes ultimate responsibility. These include the Police Complaints Authority; the Commission for Racial Equality; Boards of Visitors and newly introduced grievance procedures for prisoners and formerly the Broadcasting Complaints Commission, Broadcasting Standards Council and Independent Television Commission; the latter three are now under the aegis of the Department of National Heritage. In spite of a statutory appeal process, the Immigration and Nationality Department (I&N) receives about 240,000 to 250,000 general letters each year from the public and its "ministerial correspondence" section in 1990 opened 9,294 files; discretionary decisions on naturalisation and citizenship under the British Nationality Act 1981 are dealt with by *written* application.[135] Furthermore, about 170,000 callers come to I&N HQ's Public Enquiry Office annually. However, the number of complaints is officially estimated at 300–400 per annum, a figure which seems surprisingly small and which may not adequately account for various inhibiting factors such as lack of information, fear of reprisal or scepticism about impartial treatment. PCA reports refer frequently to other departments conducting interviews if requested and it is not uncommon for complainants to be accompanied by friends, representatives from claimants' unions or relatives. His reports also refer to departments possessing internal standing procedures for complaint handling. However, departments have claimed to possess grievance procedures which in fact no-one knew about and which were never resorted to or which were certainly not publicised.[136] The I&N publishes guidance for MP representations and has guidelines for complaint handling.

The I&N in fact identified the following types of complaint handled through their complaints section at HQ or which might be syphoned off to a relevant section:

(1) Against an adverse decision. Many representations were made directly to the relevant Minister in early 1991. Minister involvement would occur where there was sensitive media coverage. It was not the practice in 1991 to refuse representations from an MP who was not a constituent's MP in spite of the Code of Guidance on MP representations indicating otherwise. Compassionate grounds are cited as the major consideration which may change a decision at this level. After the Immigration Act 1988 section 5, Adjudication Officers and the Immigration Appeal Tribunal are more restricted in the grounds of appeal they may

---

135 More difficult cases will be dealt with by interview, Standing Committee F, British Nationality Bill, cols. 691 to 696.
136 On the lack of knowledge of procedures by the public – and officials – see HC 158 (1991–2) Qus. 6 and 7.

apply to reverse a decision, so dispensing powers in the Minister are all the more crucial.[137]

(2) Against an individual, for example, rudeness or racism. Detailed guidance is available on the steps to pursue.

(3) Complaints against what were referred to as "systemic shortcomings" such as delay or confusion, which were seen as ombudsman territory.

Along with many other departments, I&N has centralised the oversight of complaints handling and a separate Complaints Section was set up in 1987 following a critical report by the Commission for Racial Equality (CRE) which recommended an independent complaints system. This was originally rejected by the Home Office. The Section deals only with immigration complaints. Local staff are asked to send a resumé of all complaints they deal with and their reply, and the Inspector may take action if unhappy with the response. Since 1991, complaints against officers are to be reported to the Section within 24 hours and a decision is made on who will investigate: a local District Inspector, a Manager from another area or the Complaints Inspector himself. Complaints coming directly to the Section or from other internal sources are treated in a similar fashion. Guidelines refer to the desirability of set turn-around times to deal with complaints (30 days); the involvement of inspectors who have no connection with the file; and a right to further review. Better monitoring and recording of complaints is advocated, along with consideration of complaints patterns by policy-makers. However, I&N papers are not to be available to subjects under the provisions of the White Paper on *Open Government*, it should be noted.

HM Prison Service is a NSA of the Home Office. Early in 1993, the Home Secretary announced that an independent prisoners' Ombudsman or Complaints' Adjudicator (CA) is to be created to deal with prisoners' complaints relating to procedures and merits. He will have access to all relevant files, subject to the maintenance of confidentiality by the CA on certain grounds. He will deal with complaints concerning disciplinary matters as well as other subjects. The CA will have power to recommend remedies. He will have jurisdiction over private prisons whose officers have to be certified by the Home Secretary. Interestingly, the possibility of the CA examining the clinical judgment of prison medical

---

[137] There was no appeal but only review from the IAT: see now section 9 Asylum and Immigration Appeals Act 1993, which provides for an appeal to the Court of Appeal. See *R v Secretary of State ex parte Mundowa* [1992] 3 All ER 606 (CA).

staff was under consideration. Certain limits to the CA's jurisdiction are set out and include the release of mandatory life prisoners, decisions and actions of the Parole Board and local review committees,[138] and the actions of the courts. The CA will be responsible for screening complaints, not the Prison Service. Time limits for response and reporting are set out and an annual report will be published. The CA is expected to maintain good liaison with HM Inspector of Prisons, whose reports have been severely damning of conditions in prison, and the Parliamentary Commissioner for Administration, who received surprisingly few prisoner complaints but who retains this jurisdiction.[139] Appointing a CA has proved rather difficult. Internal complaints procedures were modified in 1990.[140] These involve complaints to prison officers, governors, Boards of Visitors[141] and area managers. Complaints are meant to be confidential, a claim about which Lord Justice Woolf was sceptical.[142] In private prisons the Home Secretary appoints a Controller, a Crown servant, who is responsible for disciplinary adjudications and complaints against staff.

Customs and Excise, which has frequent contact with the public, has defined a complaint to include a "finding" (*sic*) of fault by a member of the public, either oral or in writing and made by the complainant or on their behalf. It further categorised "complaint against an officer" and "complaint against a system". In fact, this department had introduced a comprehensive-looking complaints procedure. It sets out the tiers at which complaints may be made, the sorts of things people commonly complain about, the importance of information from complaints to assist management improve service level, response times and so on. However, the absence of an independent element from outside the department is a ground for criticism in an otherwise interesting complaints procedure.

The Inland Revenue has 33 executive units operating on Next Steps lines. In 1992 a taxpayer's charter was published (there had been previous charters in the 1980s) and a new "independent"

---

138 Who examine the cases of prisoners with a view to release.
139 The PCA in fact will be able to investigate the CA, who is for these purposes part of the Prison Service.
140 SI 1990/1762.
141 BoVs will no longer have any role in discipline although they will advise on R43 removals; the legal aid ABWOR scheme applies to disciplinary hearings although it is intended that criminal matters will be brought before the courts.
142 Sir H. Woolf, *Protection of the Public: A New Challenge* (London, Stevens, 1990).

adjudicator was appointed by the Board of IR in July 1993 to whom complainants may turn when they have a complaint about IR's handling of their affairs. This is in addition to tribunals which deal with appeals over assessments and the PCA. As we have seen with adjudicators elsewhere in departmental administration, they are often a curious mixture of quasi-independent one-person tribunal, one-person semi-autonomous internal reviewer and part civil servant administrator. Between July and September 1993, the adjudicator received 758 complaints but only 85 of these could be dealt with straight away because the other cases had not been referred to local offices for attempted resolution as requested. Like the PO above, the adjudicator will have access to all relevant files and will be able to interview staff, recommend relief and publish an annual report. The IR declares, intriguingly, that it will accept, the adjudicator's decisions "in the vast majority of cases". There would have to be "very strong reasons" for disputing a decision, for example, it would set a precedent that the IR could not follow. A detailed leaflet outlines procedures for complaining but it does not deal with complaints about tax liability where appeal provisions exist and for which separate advice is given. IR is also developing Codes of Practice on, for example, *Mistakes by the Inland Revenue*, which sets out what action the IR will take where it makes a mistake. Every year there are about 15,000 recorded complaints which get through to the various regional offices.[143]

With the Benefits Agency – which produced its second charter in December 1993 – it is interesting to note that, in spite of the pressure to get complaints treated as locally as possible, as with the former supplementary benefits system successful complaints often emerged after the intervention of pressure groups such as CPAG or MENCAP, and it was acknowledged that the best recourse was for a pressure group to take up the issue with a Minister which countered the official exhortation to deal with grievances at as low a level as possible – a point seemingly not lost on MPs. In 1992, it was estimated that 40 per cent of MPs were writing directly to the Chief Executive rather than to the Minister. Direct communication with the Chief Executive has been encouraged by the BA, as has communication with a local manager.

There is no doubt that a great deal of BA time and effort has gone into "customer care", although the NAO has criticised

---

[143] Interestingly there is an HMI *internal* document on "spotting dodges", "Dispatches" 14 April 1993, Channel 4. Some internal guidance documents are to be published: *Financial Times* 27 August 1994.

certain features of BA service, especially towards the self-employed, late disability payments to 500,000 claimants and errors in the award of income support in 1992/3 to the level of £825 million – criticism which provoked a lively riposte from the Chief Executive (see chapter 7). The Parliamentary Commission has produced a scathing report on late payments of Disability Allowance (see chapter 5 p. 203). The desire to provide a service in which complaints will be minimised seemed genuine enough although the BA's customer charter nevertheless spells out the complaints procedure for complainants. Customer care packages have been produced and interest groups were contacted in their preparation and all 159 local managers were exhorted to sound out local client opinion on what was required in service delivery. Client surveys had been conducted on what was being delivered. A document about complaining has been produced: *Have Your Say* (1991). Opportunity to Improve Service (OTIS) provides a chance for customers by way of questionnaire to express their views on service. These comments are fed into relevant operational sections where they and responses to them are analysed. Detailed advice is given on the appropriate level at which to deal with a complaint and on whether an Adjudication Officer needs to be involved and the various stages through which a dispute is processed. Information from customers and complaints is also fed into the Territorial Director's Customer Service Unit. Clear emphasis is given to the central role of complaints and information received from them to enhance procedures and to improve performance.[144]

The Employment Service, an NSA of the Department of Employment, offers interesting examples of an agency approach to complaints handling. There are 1,300 offices dealing with 5 million "contacts" per week. ES emphasises the role of complaint redress as a function of all officials and, unlike BA, has no specially designated "Complaints Officer". Responsibility for complaints is considered the duty of all staff. Out of 8,863 complaints received in local offices between April 1992 and March 1993, 4,946 were resolved at local office level, 331 by the Regional Manager and 48 by the Chief Executive. The nine Regional Managers give a three-monthly breakdown of complaints to the Chief Executive and these are categorised according to subject-matter – there are nine specified headings and one described as "other". The former include: benefit procedures, adjudications, advisory service, TEC programmes. There was a

---

[144] The Social Security Fraud Squad's *Fraud Investigator's Guide* is not published.

lack of detailed knowledge of how information on complaints handling in local offices was fed back to the manager; how, in other words, procedures for self-knowledge and improvement were formalised. Each month one region will have to give a detailed assessment of its client handling procedures, including complaints. All letters of complaint at the local offices were requested by HQ for analysis by someone specifically employed for the task. A considerable amount of publicly available material has been produced, including complaints/comments forms. 348 suggestions for improvement were made in the 12-month period mentioned above. In spite of all this rather impressive work, only one concrete example came to mind of significant changes in service leading from complaints – the travel to interview scheme whereby payment would be made for an unemployed person to travel to a job interview.

Until recently, departments rarely possessed a central procedural point where complaints were made to headquarters. Regional offices of the DoE had regular experience of complaints of a group or collective nature on, for example, inner city funding, housing or planning which were made by representative groups, or compulsory purchase. Regional offices had previously set up special units to deal with subjects that generated numerous complaints against local authorities. This involved the sale of council houses where authorities were proving to be too dilatory or were imposing unduly restrictive covenants on the public. Complaints about local authorities and other public bodies such as UDCs were still made to the DoE, as well as complaints about the functions of other departments, in which case the DoE acts as "a sieve and a co-ordinator". Interviews with complainants did not take place as a matter of course in the DoE, though there was a readiness to see organisations with a grievance. The announcement of a combined departmental regional presence in the autumn of 1993 to tackle urban regeneration will doubtless bring with it interesting practices for regional dispute settlement.

In the Department of Transport, regional offices deal with complaints about road schemes and "surprisingly on road schemes we find that the actual volume of complaints as distinct from negotiations with those affected during the progress of road schemes is quite small". This is important because, if after negotiations between public authorities and the department, the authority subsequently withdraws objection to the road scheme, any duty to hold an inquiry under the appropriate legislation evaporates.[145]

---

[145]   Highways Act 1980, Schedule 1 paragraphs 7(2) and 14(2).

It has been claimed that these general procedures represent a regress from public debate to enable "a reduction in procedural delays in the construction and improvement of highways".[146] A decision by a Secretary of State not to hold a public inquiry is extremely difficult to upset in a court of law.[147] Any "deals" negotiated privately are unlikely in the vast majority of cases to be set aside.

Most departments could cite instances of individual complaints on administrative and more routine topics changing the outcome of a decision. Although some departments mentioned that policy reviews had taken place as a consequence of an individual or group complaint, only the Department of Employment offered a specific example of this. In the past, that Department was the frequent recipient of complaints from employers' associations, trade unions or public corporations about policy concerns. Quite clearly, trade unions had not enjoyed intimate involvement in the deliberations and evolution of government plans for almost a decade and a half. However, complaints of a policy nature were frequently made to the Department by employers' groups about, for example, the Vredeling Directive on worker participation or the Social Chapter and employment implications of the Maastricht Treaty. The point has been made by these representative bodies that changes in working conditions could only be as a response to improvements in market conditions and should be brought about by changes in custom and practice. Changes in employee and trade union organisation and rights which involved a reduction in their rights and privileges had, on the contrary, to be achieved by legislation.[148]

A department may not receive direct complaints, or receive very few, but it may be subject to representations which become the basis of interviews. The former Department of Energy (many of whose responsibilities were transferred to the DTI) interviewed commercial interests along with their representatives where the former were affected by the regulatory activities of the Department. Very often the interviews were geared towards establishing the precise nature of the companies' obligations under legislation, for example, Health and Safety at Work etc. Act 1974.

---

[146] McAuslan, *The Ideologies of Planning Law*, 1980.

[147] *Shorman v Secretary of State for the Environment* (1977) JPL 98; though see *R v Secretary of State for the Environment ex parte Binney* (1983) *The Times* 8 October.

[148] There have been nine separate statutes covering employment and trade unions and their reform since 1980.

One study in the 1980s identified how the regulated can have a decisive influence not only upon the attitudes of the regulators and upon their statutory duties, but upon the very framework of legislation that is adopted. The particular study concerned regulation of health and safety in the North Sea oil-fields.[149] Such a relationship has many analogues in governmental regulatory programmes in areas as diverse as the environment and pollution, financial and investment regulation, professional associations and their ability to persuade governments to allow them to regulate, or to continue to regulate, themselves. Planning agreements were a familiar example of negotiated outcomes between private companies and government departments whereby the former would trade their technical knowledge and expertise in return for permission to exploit resources and "sympathetic" regulation by government or its agencies. Similar developments have been anticipated and identified in government/privatised industry relationships.

All departments will maintain confidentiality in their treatment of complaints, unless the complainant chooses to adopt a "high profile" strategy. The Department of Trade and Industry is responsible for oversight of industrial and commercial development in England and Wales and under its umbrella are various non-departmental bodies such as English Estates and the Development Corporation and the Urban Regeneration Agency. It is also the body which has ultimate responsibility for protection of the consumer and regulation of competition policy, a task which it performs by ever-growing liaison with the European Commission. Under regional programmes, funding exists to assist businesses, a policy which has existed since the 1960s and even earlier, although since 1988 the policy of the department has been more selective in provision of assistance, a policy which reflected the inclinations of a series of Secretaries of State. The point was made that the Development Agencies of Scotland and Wales, by adopting more active partnership with the private sector and a more interventionist approach, had been far more successful in attracting industry and encouraging development in their respective areas than had the DTI, although the Welsh DA had attracted a great deal of criticism over the controversial appointment and action of a senior official and the absence of appropriate controls over a non-departmental body.[150]

For regional development, the details are still in the Industrial Development Act 1982. The details of the 1982 scheme are

149   Carson, Note 56 above.
150   HC 353 (1992/3).

complex, and they also tie in with other schemes to encourage regional development, including those funded by the EC. The Department has maintained total control over the disbursement of funds or grants under the legislation,[151] and this has been supported by judicial deference, leaving the exercise of discretion almost totally within the Department and offering limited scope even for ombudsman intervention.[152]

There is no appeal from refusal or revocation of an award, though the Department does engage in early discussion between applicants and the relevant office. Selective Financial Assistance is made under sections 7 and 8, the former being restricted to Assisted Areas. Powers to award are couched in extremely broad discretionary terms, applications are considered by various officials and the great majority are then referred to the Regional Industrial Development Board. Larger and more complex cases are referred to the Industrial Development Advisory Board and where Ministers decide not to follow its advice they must inform Parliament before a final decision is made by the Secretary of State. There is no formal appeal mechanism, so unsuccessful applicants will contact Ministers for a possible review, with or without MP representations. Any form of progressing may be used, for example, meetings, interviews, legal representation and so on. Views from trade competitors on grants are not sought and most information is treated as highly confidential because it falls within the designation "trade secret" or "commercial" – in confidence". For Regional Enterprise Grants complaint may be made to regional offices of the DTI.

As we saw above, departments will have general guidelines on complaints procedures and guidance is available from the Office of Public Service and Science. In the Foreign and Commonwealth Office (FCO) instructions are available on how to deal with complaints, although these are not available to the public. It is standard practice to have internal guidelines and brief explanatory material for the public, the latter only of which is published. Those in the FCO specify that relevant departments are responsible for investigating complaints. As is common, special units will deal with MP and PCA complaints – the Ministerial Private Office and the Parliamentary Relations Unit. Deadlines will be set for

---

151 Industrial Development Act 1982 and see HC 911 (1992–3) *Industrial Development Act Annual Review 1992.*
152 *British Oxygen v Board of Trade* [1971] AC 610. See *R v Secretary of State for Transport ex parte Sherriff & Sons Ltd* (1986) *The Times* 18 December, and grants under section 8 Railways Act 1974 as amended.

investigation and replies, checking of responses by senior officials and so on. No formal uniform guidelines are available.

The Department for Education has long been taciturn about its treatment of complaints relating to school education. Since the mid-1980s the major thrust in government policy in education has been the reduction in the role of Local Education Authorities (LEAs), the increase of opted-out schools (that is, those paid by direct grant), the introduction of the national curriculum and the promotion of City Technology Colleges. Consumerism has been rampant and the period has witnessed ever-increasing duties upon schools to publish details of performance under the Citizen's Charter, now in the Education (Schools) Act 1992; the diminution in the importance of local catchment areas following the 1980 legislation, which conferred rights of appeal against school admission and subsequently expulsion decisions, and rights of access to students' records by children and by their parents; and a reformed system of inspection carried out by a private inspectorate which is licensed by the relevant authorities. The Education Act 1993, to which we have made brief reference, is designed to reduce the role of LEAs even further. This is a far cry from the period prior to the 1980s when parents and consumers possessed certain legal rights after the 1944 Education Act, difficult though these were and still are to realise in the courts. The proper recourse was to complain to the Secretary of State under section 68 or 99 Education Act 1944 – the unreasonable behaviour etc. provisions. Judicial decisions have interpreted section 68 as offering extremely limited scope for intervention by the Secretary of State in the affairs of an LEA.[153] The Secretary of State does not have to give reasons for refusing a complaint under the sections, and surprisingly records of complaints received are not maintained, or at least not in an accessible manner because, I was informed, complainants do not refer to the section.[154] The Department has been reluctant to reveal the manner in which it processes complaints, although an informed guess has speculated that as well as interviewing officers in the relevant LEA or the governors, the Department will study the advice of the schools' inspectors and examine the written statement of the complainant who will, however, rarely be interviewed.[154] There are some PCA reports which shed some light on the process. Complaints on school admissions and Special Educational Needs we can examine

---

[153] *Secretary of State for Education and Science v Tameside MBC* [1977] AC 1014.
[154] Letter from Department for Education, January 1993.

in chapter 3, noting at this stage the establishment of a new tribunal. Under the 1981 Education Act sections 5(6) and 8(6) there were a total of 255 and 200 appeals to the Secretary of State from 1990/92. The establishment of a "dedicated appeals team" (*sic*) in April 1992 allowed reliable statistics to be collected for the first time and allowed the Department to assess parental "success rate" at approximately 61:39.

Since the Education Reform Act, and earlier legislation in fact, central government has placed a greater onus on LEAs and schools to provide effective grievance procedures and appeals procedures and this is more appropriately dealt with in chapter three. However, we find here, as elsewhere, although it is particularly notable in education, an emphasis upon consumer choice, competition and enhanced rights for parents and children. However, it has come at a time when education policies have become increasingly polarised and strident, alienating many parents and teachers, and when expenditure on the vast majority of schools has decreased because of government cutbacks. Effective grievance procedures to address these dimensions have not been forthcoming.

Conclusion

The wide variety of options open to departments and citizens, now consumers, confronted by, or wishing to articulate a grievance represent a rich if confused and confusing tapestry. Even with the exhortations of the Citizen's Charter in mind, the following still seem apt: the enactment of a statutory code of good administrative practice and open government – the exhortations of the Charter and the White Paper on *Open Government* remain non-statutory exhortations; the giving of reasoned decisions as a matter of course and not simply exiguous and *pro forma* statements of reasons, although the White Paper states that reasons will be given – unless there is a clear tradition not to; full publication of *internal* grievance procedures and processes which affect interested parties; a clearer articulation of when independent tribunals or internal review of decisions is to be preferred and why, and when tribunals are to be preferred to courts; how the policy-making process itself may be made more open to rational scrutiny, starting with the item at the heart of the agenda, the planning of the expenditure programme and budget. Much has been made of departmental and agency efforts to sound out public opinion in service delivery; what, however, of effective feed-back of public opinion in policy-making and serious response to that opinion?

Finally, it has recently come to light that there is a wide variation between departments and agencies and their approaches towards making *ex gratia* compensatory awards to individuals and on the award of interest. There were also dramatic differences between the power delegated to departments by the Treasury in respect of the size of award that could be made and the level of official who could make the award. Surely clear and uniform guidance should be issued by the Cabinet Office to replace existing Treasury guidelines (DAO/GEN 15/92). The Office of Public Service and Science has promised to issue guidance on payments under the Citizen's Charter.

Chapter 3

LOCAL GOVERNMENT

Local Government Organisation and Administration

Local government has been witness to enormous changes in its structure in recent years. The widely criticised reorganisation of local government by the Local Government Act 1972 was a response to the growth of activity and bureaucratic development of local government. The changes have not solved the problem of rational organisation – on what basis are authorities to be organised to carry out their functions efficiently? – nor concomitant problems for citizens caused by authorities becoming repositories of vast amounts of information, expertise and resources. As I write, further changes in organisation and structure which may introduce some unitary or single tier authorities appear imminent. While much has been made of the diminution of local government, authorities employed 1,890,750 individuals (full time equivalents) in 1991.[1]

The 1972 legislation introduced a system of metropolitan and non-metropolitan counties, subdivided into metropolitan and non-metropolitan districts respectively. Non-metropolitan districts are further subdivided into parish councils.[2] Various recommendations to establish local "neighbourhood councils" for urban areas on a statutory basis have not been pursued as far as the statute book. London has its own local government structure. A cursory

---

[1] DoE, Cm. 1908, at 127.

[2] England and Wales are divided into 47 counties, 36 metropolitan districts and 333 non-metropolitan districts. There are about 10,000 parish councils, mainly in rural areas. Scotland is divided into a two-tier system of regional and district authorities, with three island authorities and various community authorities. Single-tier all-purpose authorities seem likely to be created north and south of the border. Northern Ireland has 26 district councils, though local government lost many of its more important functions in 1973 in the effort to counter political and religious discrimination. London is divided into the City and 32 boroughs (12 inner and 20 outer), with some minor authorities and a plethora of nominated and appointed quangos. As I describe in the text, a variety of major reforms involving organisation appear imminent. See *R v Secretary of State for the Environment ex parte Lancashire CC* (1994) *The Times* 3 February.

glance at Part IX of the 1972 legislation indicates the enormous variety of functions performed by local authorities in England and Wales, which are divided between the various tiers of authorities.[3] Local authority administration is further characterised by the presence and combination of elected councillors (members) and paid officials.

In 1985 the Government abolished, by virtue of the Local Government Act of that year, the six metropolitan counties and the Greater London Council, replacing them for administrative purposes by joint nominated boards and non-elected public bodies.[4] Together with the reformulation of local authority taxation, the introduction of a new system for paying government grants to local authorities, powers for rate-capping and tax-capping by central government, that is, controlling the amount of tax raised by authorities,[5] this development represents the culmination of bitter relationships between central and local government as the former has sought to control the expenditure and effective independence of the latter.[6] A further onslaught has seen the removal of responsibilities from authorities[7] and the compulsory tendering out of publicly provided services.[8] The Government sees the future in terms of tight financial control over local expenditure and increased marketisation in the delivery of local services. More effective control by the centre does not augur well for local accountability and democracy. Consumers who can vote with their feet have no need to vote with their ballot. It is true to say that the record of local government has often left much to be desired. Too frequently unresponsive elements have persisted in controlling local government in spite of the strenuous efforts made by many authorities to improve their image and practices in relation to local communities and the services they provide, efforts which predate the Citizen's Charter by more than a decade. In the Sheffield report on local authority complaints procedures of 1987, there was ample evidence of an absence of effective complaints procedures in the majority of local authorities, although there

---

3   A further complicating factor has been the change of names of departments, for example, public health, environmental and so on.
4   See, for example, M. Hebbert and T. Travers (eds), *The London Government Handbook*, 1988.
5   Rates Act 1984, Local Government Finance Act 1988 (LGFA) and LGFA 1992.
6   M. Loughlin, *Local Government in the Modern State* (London, Sweet & Maxwell, 1986).
7   Particularly in housing, education and planning.
8   Local Government Acts 1988 and 1992.

were many in existence that were exemplary.[9] Reports from the local government Ombudsman consistently refer to authorities which refuse to accept their recommendations.

The New Local Authorities, Management and Structure[10] was an influential report upon local government organisation in the 1970s and 1980s. The report presented "an attempt to secure unity of purpose in the affairs of a local authority through adjusting activities to changing needs and problems. This involves making assumptions explicit, methodically reviewing policy, and attempting to measure outputs".[11] The report was claimed to have had an "astonishing impact" in introducing what Bains referred to as a "corporate approach" to local authority management and planning.[12] A departmental approach to administration, lacking appropriate co-ordination, was no longer adequate for the brave new world facing local authority administration. McAuslan, amongst others, has supported the point that the corporate management approach pays too little regard to the democratic basis of local government. The role of the public and councillors is decreased as emphasis is placed upon a Policy and Resources Committee (with only a few "heavy weight" councillors present) shaping major decisions. This committee's meetings are commonly preceded by the Chief Executive's Principal Chief Officers' Management Team Committee "filtering out that which it is, for one reason or another, impolitic to put before the councillors".[13] Criticisms have been made suggesting that the corporate approach has reduced the effective role of many councillors, is mechanistic, developed further the hiatus between the council and local people and local organisations and that it depoliticised policy-making. This last aspect has various causes, chief among them being a stress on the managerial and technical aspects of policy-making and an overdue reverence for professionalisation in political decision-making. In the early 1980s Lewis and Harden expressed the view that a disenchantment with the reduction

---

9   N. Lewis *et al. Complaints Procedures in Local Government* (University of Sheffield, 1987), hereafter "Sheffield".
10 M. Bains, *The New Local Authorities: Management and Structure* (London, HMSO, 1972).
11 Lewis and Harden, "Law and the Local State", (1982) 5 *Urban Law and Policy* 65.
12 Hambleton, *Policy, Planning and Local Government*, 1978; D. Widdicombe, *The Conduct of Local Authority Business*, Cmnd 9797 (London, HMSO, 1986) at 61.
13 McAuslan, *The Ideologies of Planning Law*, 1980 and see "The Widdicombe Report: Local Government Business or Politics?" *Public Law* (1987) 154.

of overt political discussion in policy formulation and the common concentration upon professional/bureaucratic values had become discernible in local authority administration. The authors described how such developments were accompanied by attempts to politicise the local population into defending their services against attack from the centre (central government).[14] Be that as it may, the Government's response was not to redemocratise but to "downsize" local government. We have seen the removal of local authorities from many spheres of activity; among the Government's plans for executive local authorities was the removal of statutory rights of access to information from all members who were not members of the executive council.[15]

The problem of "alienated local government" and the barriers this presents against the airing and effective resolution of grievances, as well as participation in decision-making, is particularly acute in the urban and especially inner urban areas. These latter areas often display a concentration of poverty, lack of opportunity, poor housing and racial tension. The problems caused by "alienated local government" are not, however, confined to urban areas. Various attempts have been made to deal with the causes and consequences of inner urban decay ranging from the Community Development Project – a government sponsored attempt to involve the community in local affairs which ultimately proved to be unpopular with the government – to "total approaches" as advised by consultant planning and management specialists employed by the Department of the Environment (DoE). Their urban studies sought to "formulate guidelines to help local authorities in developing a 'total approach' to the urban environment and to propose advice which the DoE could commend to local authorities." More recent attempts to rejuvenate inner urban areas include various private/public partnership schemes such as City Challenge, City Grant, City Action Teams and Urban Programmes along with Urban Development Corporations and Enterprise Zones and the Urban Regeneration Agency (see pp. 130 *et seq.* below) together with regional offices of co-ordinated central government departments.

Even before the 1980s, central government initiated partnerships between itself and local authorities for urban rejuvenation in which the opportunities for public involvement were limited if not non-existent. Government stoutly resisted attempts to place

---

[14] Lewis and Harden, Note 11 above.
[15] DoE, *The Internal Management of Local Authorities in England*, 1991, paragraphs 38 to 39.

consultation with voluntary groups on a statutory basis (Inner Urban Areas Act 1978) and the 1978 Act, as well as the Local Government Grants (Social Need) Act 1968, under which grants are made by the DoE to areas of special need, are both silent as regards consultation and participation from affected communities. Indeed DoE pressure prevented meetings of partnership committees being open to the public. Lord Scarman in his report on the Brixton riots in 1981 made the following observations *à propos* of the partnerships:

> "In the result, there emerges lack of co-ordinated policy for the control of services which must be central to any strategy designed to tackle the related, but not identical, problems of inner city decline and minority disadvantage."[16]

On greater community involvement in urban programmes, he said:

> "[L]ocal communities should be more fully involved in the decisions which affect them. A 'top down' approach to regeneration does not seem to have worked. Local communities must be fully and effectively involved in the management and financing of specific projects. I should like to see, for example, greater consultation than exists at present between local authorities and community groups about the allocation of resources to projects under the Urban Programme."[17]

The last official attempt at involving the community in such decision-making, a "bottom-up" approach as opposed to a "top-down" one, met with scepticism and eventual disapproval from a Labour government. The Community Development Project, which was the scheme in question, had become too successful in getting local communities *involved* in decision-making rather than merely being *informed* about decision-making.[18] The spirit of the times has moved on and the Government has little time for participation or consultation with local communities in urban renewal;[19] the solution, they believe, lies elsewhere, as we shall see. Local government exists largely for one purpose: to administer and to provide services that cannot be provided more cheaply

---

16 Scarman, *The Brixton Disorders, April 10–12, 1981*, Cmnd 8427 (1981), paragraph 6.6.
17 *Ibid*.
18 The Community Development Project was disbanded in 1977. See their *Limits of the Law*, 1977 and McAuslan, 1980, Note 13 above, chapter 9. See also Gyfford, J., *Local Government and the Public*, 1991.
19 *The Docklands Experiment*, Docklands Consultative Committee, 1990.

by other means. Where local authorities are to carry out provision of services, the Citizen's Charter has placed maximum emphasis upon the role of effective grievance procedures to assist in monitoring performance and to act as accountability devices where there is no competitor, that is, no market.

A selection from the statutory duties, circular guidelines and current practices for participation in decision-making will be examined briefly later in the chapter. Our attention now turns to current practices, some statutory, some not, for the reception, resolution and airing of complaints by the public about local government activities.

Complaints: The Background

In the late 1970s, a chief executive of one authority replied to a question about the availability of grievance procedures for members of the public in his authority "that the seventeenth century had established his accountability in legal terms to the courts, and his political accountability to Parliament." The Sheffield (1987) study found a predilection among authorities for remedying complaints via the elected representative or through the local authority committee structure, and this instilled a certain complacency.[20] Many authorities pointed out that this did not mean indifference as there was the Commission for Local Administration (CLA) – the local Ombudsman (see chapter 5) – in the background. With the CLA, housing and planning complaints have been numerically dominant – in spite of, in the case of planning, a statutory procedure for appeals to the Secretary of State, planning inquiries, and resort to the courts, although the DoE has asked authorities to settle planning complaints informally and locally.[21] Some of the statutory prohibitions on what the CLA can investigate contain their own mysteries. They are not allowed, for instance, to investigate complaints about commercial activities which have included the allocation of market stalls and alleged mishandling of concessionary bus passes,[22] though they can investigate complaints about council house allocation (see chapter 5).

In one respect, of course, what the chief executive asserted is correct. For over a century, various statutory rights of appeal, and more recently of statutory review have existed to a range of courts against local authority decisions and actions. The law of contract

[20]   Sheffield, 1987, Note 9 above. See Crawford (1988).
[21]   DoE Circ. No. 38/81, *Planning and Enforcement Appeals.*
[22]   See CLA Annual Report, 1991/2.

and tort and, it would appear, restitution[23] applies to them. In addition, there is opportunity for judicial review under Rules of the Supreme Court, Ord. 53 (see chapter 6) – local authorities constitute by far the largest number of defendants among public bodies. Several points call for comment, however. Resort to the courts can be time-consuming, expensive and fraught with uncertainty. The law of judicial review can be complex to the point of being almost unpredictable. More pertinent perhaps is the claim that litigation best serves the interests of those owning private property, or those representing the "public interest" as identified by public officials. Courts do not show themselves being particularly sympathetic to larger community claims or to group interests relating to "public participation" which cannot be easily attached to legal right or political influence.[24] Judicial interference in local authority administration has frequently been accused of being motivated by a conservative dislike of forward planning exercises involving broad social purposes or by a desire to curtail their powers to those appropriate for bodies which are not subject to the discipline of the market-place.[25] Whether or not this is so, the influence of judicial decision-making upon the internal procedures and processes of local government administration has been, until recently, minimal. Generally, there is an enhanced awareness of procedural fairness which might include the giving of reasons for decisions and on some subjects, for example elected members' access to information, the common law principles have moved on (see below pp. 107 *et seq.*). Some areas of administration from the point of view of the consumer may be more procedurally aware than others; matters relating to licensing might fall under this category. The practice of some authorities is to allow a complainant to be present at a committee accompanied by a legal representative. This has been noted especially in the field of planning and hackney-cab licences.[26] This apparent forbearance on the part of authorities could be a recognition of the obvious complexity which

---

[23] *WLG v Islington LBC* (1993) 91 LGR 323 and on appeal: (1994) *The Independent* 5 January (CA). For an interesting case on the application of public law *vires* and reasonableness to local authority contracts see: *R v Newcastle Upon Tyne City Council ex parte Dixon* (1993) *The Times* 20 October.

[24] See *R v Secretary of State for the Environment ex parte Rose Theatre Trust* [1990] 1 All ER 714 (QBD) and note Lord Diplock's views in *Bushell v Secretary of State*, see chapter 6, p. 257 below, though see also Woolf, 1986, 1990, 1992.

[25] *Hazell v Hammersmith etc LBC* [1991] 1 All ER 545 (HL), the Rates Swap litigation (Loughlin, 1991).

[26] See Transport Act 1985 section 17 and appeals for taxi drivers in London.

traditionally attends these subject-matters. But such committees would rarely deal with manifest issues of law but rather with facts and/or interpretation of terms such as "reasonableness". This procedural awareness could owe something to the impact of judicial decisions,[27] but as a general proposition the statement on judicial influence appears to be correct. Courts are only a long-stop. At a fundamental level, complaints should be dealt with effectively by the authorities themselves. Since the 1980s the Government has provided for numerous statutory appeal/complaints mechanisms in particular local authority services. Where appropriate complaints procedures for the public are lacking, authorities should be prompted to put their own house in order.

As to the chief executive's statement that political responsibility is owed to Parliament, this is not functionally correct. His political overlords are the Secretary of State in the DoE, Department for Education and other relevant departments, and the leader of the council. This is not the place to discuss these extremely complex relationships.[28] Suffice it to say, the relationship between central government and local government centres around finance, and more pronounced centripetal tendencies in this relationship have confused the issue of accountability of local government.[29] Is accountability owed to the local electorate, the local taxpayers and ratepayers, central government or the national taxpayer? The rhetoric would have us believe that it is owed to all. The reality is not so clear-cut. From the point of view of a complainant on the street, all this might appear a little confusing and it would be of little comfort to answer their problem: "Vote differently at the

---

[27] *R v Liverpool Corporation ex parte Liverpool Taxi Fleet Operators' Association* [1972] 2 QB 299 in relation to taxi cab licensing; but see *R v Reading BC ex parte Quietlynn* (1987) 85 LGR 357. More generally see *R v Lancashire CC ex parte Huddleston* [1986] 2 All ER 941 (CA) and on section 159 LGA 1972 (now LGFA 1982 section 17): *Hillingdon LBC v Paulssen* (1977) JPL 518.

[28] See Griffith, *Central Departments and Local Authorities*, 1966; Layfield, *Local Government Finance*, Cmnd 6813 (1976); Jones, "Central–Local Relationships, Finance and the Law", (1979) 2 *Urban Law and Policy* 25 (1979); Widdicombe, Note 12 above; J.D. Stewart and G. Stoker, *The Future of Local Government* (1989); S. Leach *et al.*, *The Changing Organisation and Management of Local Government* (1993). The PCA Select Committee have in the past suggested that authorities which refused to accept the decisions of local ombudsmen should be examined by the Select Committee.

[29] Layfield, Note 28 above, is a particularly useful analysis. The centripetal tendencies of "reforming" legislation have not abated since the Local Government Planning and Land Act 1980.

next local or central election or frame your complaint into a legal issue for the courts."

Taxpayers, Ratepayers, Electors and Expenditure

It would be difficult to over-emphasise the importance placed by central government, and indeed judicial decisions, upon the duties owed by local authorities to their local taxpayers, formerly rate-payers.[30] The emphasis is upon "value for money" for local tax-payers in local government administration – a message hammered home with a vengeance in the Citizen's Charter and in numerous reports of the Audit Commission (see below). In law the position which local authorities occupy, *vis-à-vis* the ratepayer, and one presumes the local taxpayer, has been compared with that of trustees (though not *actually* trustees) owing fiduciary duties, duties of special good faith, to ratepayers within their respective areas.[31] This legal relationship, which is the creature of judicial decision, was given dramatic reaffirmation in the widely debated and hotly disputed judgment of the House of Lords in *Bromley London Borough Council v Greater London Council*[32] and to some extent lies behind the almost as notorious "Interest rates swaps" litigation in the early 1990s.[33] In *Bromley*, The House of Lords held that the GLC's statutory power to award grants to the London Transport Executive supplementing revenue from the fare-paying public was restricted by various factors. The most important for present purposes was the fiduciary duty to rate-payers and the Council's obligation to balance that duty against its duty to transport users when making a grant. The decision by the GLC to reduce fares by 25 per cent transferred the cost of doing so (about £69 million) from transport users to ratepayers. This was held to be unfair. It also incurred a loss of £50 million from the rate support grant (from central government) to the GLC which the ratepayers would have to make good "without any compensating improvement in transport services". Because the last aspect was a "thriftless use of ratepayers' money", it amounted to a breach of the fiduciary relationship. It is true that courts have shown a disinclination to follow the logic of this constricting ruling in later decisions, but this has been more than offset by the tightening of the financial noose around local government by central government. Because many complaints

---

[30] Businesses still pay a "business rate" (see below).
[31] *Per* Jenkins LJ: *Prescott v Birmingham Corp.* [1955] Ch. 210.
[32] [1983] 1 AC 768.
[33] *Hazell v Hammersmith etc LBC*, Note 25 above.

relating to local government services will arise from inadequate funding – the Government would allege inefficient provision of services by authorities – it is necessary to say a few words about allocating grant and controlling local taxes and the Local Government (Finance) Act 1992.

Basically, local authorities have to send information to central government from which the latter can assess the Standard Spending Assessment (SSA) of each authority. This figure represents an amount which central government calculates will provide adequate services at a local level for each authority. It is expected that the aggregate of all SSAs will coincide in approximate terms with the Government's overall calculation for local government expenditure, the Total Standard Spending, although each service block within an SSA (there are seven) will be calculated according to local physical, social and demographic features. From its SSA, the Government will determine what a local authority's grant entitlement, that is, its share of central financial support, will be. There will also be an allocation of non-domestic rates whose rate is set by central government, collected by local government and which is then handed over to and pooled by central government for reallocation.[34] In very crude terms[35] the remainder of a local authority's expenditure will be made up by local taxation. Where an authority sets a rate of council tax which government believes is in excess of that required to make up the authority's SSA, government may cap, that is, limit the amount, which may be taxed by setting the local tax rate. All authorities may be capped and the power may be exercised in the current financial year and not simply prospectively as under the 1984 Rates Act. There are "appeal" provisions through which an authority may make representations to the Secretary of State;[36] challenge through the courts of the latter's use of his powers is unlikely ever to be successful.[37] Central control is complete.

[34] This is allocated on a *per capita* basis although definition of the relevant population is at the Secretary of State's discretion.

[35] There are in addition various subject-specific grants.

[36] LGFA 1992 sections 56 and 57.

[37] The House of Lords seems to have made the power of the Secretary of State to issue guidance to authorities on expenditure and to designate authorities as overspenders virtually inviolable; the Secretary of State would have to be outside his powers in the narrow sense, acting in the "extremes of bad faith or manifest absurdity" or would have to have misled Parliament. A great deal was made of the fact that parliamentary approval of the Secretary of State's decision on "national economic policy" had been given: *Nottinghamshire CC v Secretary of State for the Environment* [1986] AC 240; *Hammersmith LBC v Secretary of State for the Environment* [1990] 3 All ER 589 (QBD, CA and HL).

Audit and Publicity

It is interesting to note that in relation to the public inspection of local authority accounts and so on, at each audit, the opportunity for inspection is open to "any person interested". It is, however, a "local government elector" for the area, or his representative who has "an opportunity to question the auditor about the accounts" or "attend before the auditor and make objections" on various related matters. The auditor must receive written notice of the proposed objection and the grounds on which it is to be made, and the notice must be sent to the authority. The right is not restricted to a ratepayer/local taxpayer.[38] Opportunities exist to take the matter to the courts.[39] These provisions are supplemented by regulations and a code of guidance.[40] The Code specifies that the auditor is under no statutory duty to hold an oral hearing with all parties to determine an objection, although the auditor must consider whether oral hearings ought to be conducted and, if so, whether the public should be given the right to attend. The 1988 LGA and the 1992 LGA have both extended the powers of the auditor and Audit Commission considerably in terms of opportunities to seek orders from the courts to prevent unlawful expenditure by an authority and to give directions to authorities on the publication of information and indicators on standards of performance and other matters[41] – the latter as a direct consequence of the "Citizen's Charter" provisions.

The Audit Commission has published its views on performance indicators in *Charting a Course*. It saw the development of performance indicators as the "start of a process which could help to strengthen local democracy, by empowering people with information and increasing their interests in local affairs".[42] Under the Act the AC is required to determine a set of indicators, which it believes should address citizens' key concerns for local authority services and against which authorities would have to measure their performances and publish the results in the local press. The point has been made by local authority associations that national comparisons will skew local priorities and that such statistics may

---

38 Local Government (Finance) Act 1982 section 17, and see section 24.
39 Sections 19(4) and 20(3).
40 SI 1983/1761 and 1990/435 and SI 1991/724 and *Code of Local Government Audit Practice for England and Wales* (1990, amended 1992); see *Lloyd v McMahon* [1987] 1 All ER 1118 (HL).
41 LGA 1988 section 30 and Schedule 4; LGA 1992 sections 1 to 7.
42 Audit Commission, *Charting a Course*, 1993, at 2.

be used to set SSAs, although the statistics may be misleading, points with which the AC had some sympathy although it felt that some national comparisons were unavoidable. SSAs are not hypothecated, that is, earmarked, so that the amount set for an authority's service may not be the amount actually spent on that service, which will therefore render unreliable any judgment based upon the SSA about economy, efficiency and effectiveness. It may prompt questions, naturally enough, of why money notionally allocated to a service was not spent on that service.[43] The advice to authorities was that they should set their own targets on performance and assess local user satisfaction with services to provide additional evidence to the national comparisons. The AC offered to help authorities by establishing a "help-line", a good practice guide on additional information beyond the LGA 1992 requirements which authorities could publish in an annual report, and advice on carrying out local surveys to stimulate citizens' feedback.

The indicators would contain information on the following items, setting out, where relevant, targets, monitoring and performance; for example, under "Dealing with the Public":

- A1 How quickly is the telephone answered?
- A2 How quickly are letters answered?
- A3 How many complaints are made to the local Ombudsman?
- A4 How good is the complaints system?
- A5 How easy is it for disabled persons to use council buildings?

Under A4, a series of criteria are set out which seek information on authorities' definitions of complaints and the following:

- Does the authority have a written policy and procedure for dealing with complaints which covers all services and which is up to date and available to members of the public?
- Does the written policy contain information on the procedure for making a complaint?
- Does it contain a clear allocation of responsibility for receiving and investigating complaints and of overall responsibility for managing arrangements for dealing with complaints?

---

[43] Though it may facilitate questions about why a budget was underspent; in the autumn of 1993 Birmingham was claimed to have significantly underspent on its education budget and to have directed much of the relevant money towards attracting business and tourism.

- Does it contain time limits and targets for dealing with complaints?
- Does it specify that when time limits and targets are not met, complainants must be informed of the reasons for delays and revised targets?
- Does it specify that those complaining in writing must receive a written explanation of the outcome of the investigation (and, one may add, why not for oral complaints)?
- Is there a follow-up procedure if the complainant is not satisfied with the response from the department to which the complaint relates?
- Does the authority have a written policy on remedies?
- Is there a system for reviewing the cause of complaints to ensure that avoidable problems do not recur?
- Does the authority publish a report of the complaint which is available to the public?

The AC has been given a central role in improving quality of service as well as overseeing financial regularity of local authorities, and latterly health authorities and NHS Trusts and fund-holding practices – with important modifications.[44] Some of its work seems to be bringing it closer to the Commission for Local Administration; the work on complaints procedures is a striking example. It displays how efficiency in overall system performance is dependent upon effective complaints procedures.

Complaining to Local Government

The Commission for Local Administration (CLA) Code of Practice

The Redcliffe-Maud Committee (1974) strongly recommended that authorities should develop clear arrangements for receiving and investigating complaints from members of the public. In 1978, the CLA, its representative body and the Local Authority Associations produced *A Code of Practice for Handling Complaints by Local Authorities and Water Authorities*. This gave the appearance of being essentially a checklist for action and provided an outline model procedure for handling complaints. The Code tended to be "defensive" in tone, to ensure greater management efficiency, the

---

[44] NHS and Community Care Act 1990, section 20 and Schedule 4. Unlike local government, items of unlawful expenditure are not subject to individual challenge under sections 19 and 20, but are referred to the Secretary of State.

monitoring of overall performance and corporate responsibility but in a manner which ensured that authorities were not "caught out". Its eyes seemed more firmly set on internal processes rather than external devices to deal with complaints or receive the views of the public. The 1982 supplement showed more awareness of the consumer dimension. The available evidence, particularly the Sheffield study, would suggest that the influence of the Code has been, if not negligible, then certainly not significant.

Under the Local Government and Housing Act 1989 the CLA is given power to issue codes of practice and guidance for authorities and to date, three have been issued, the first of which is *Devising a Complaints System* (1992). This reiterates the point that the local government Ombudsmen expect an authority to have had a chance to have used their own procedures to achieve a local resolution. It is described as advisory and not prescriptive and builds upon best existing practice. The CLA may publish the advice. The Code is merely a recommendation and authorities have shown themselves to be unwilling to comply with non-statutory standards from outside agencies. This point was supported in the findings of the *Justice* Report on the first five years of the local Ombudsmen[45] and the Sheffield study.[46] Although some authorities have complained in the past that such codes, if implemented, would produce too much centralisation of complaints handling, and that this is a matter best left to departments themselves, one must question whether such procedures ought not to be based in statute, with opportunities for them to be tailored to an individual authority's particular needs. This is equally applicable to central government departments and agencies (see chapter 2).

What is interesting to note is that the *raison d'être* for the succession of codes was the unsatisfactory nature of local authority voluntary procedures. This was confirmed by the Sheffield study. Many chief executives said in response to research questions that the persistent and obstreperous tend to achieve more in the way of redress than the meek and mild. As one North American commentator noted, "The squeaky wheel gets the grease."[47] More specifically, a chief executive of a large district council declared: "In my experience the manner in which people take up and pursue their complaints varies enormously and depends often on their knowledge of the local government system, the complexity and

---

[45]　*Justice, The Local Ombudsman, The First Five Years*, 1980.
[46]　Sheffield, 1987, Note 9 above.
[47]　Friedmann, *Comparative Aspects of Complaint and Attitudes Towards Complaining in Canada and the U.K.*, 1974.

seriousness of the issue and indeed on their personality." This was a view shared implicitly by the CLA, both in reports of investigations and surveys. As of September 1993 there had been no available research on the 1992 Code to see what impact it had had on establishing complaints procedures. However, the Local Government Ombudsman (LGO) has stated that authorities are expected to deal with complaints before they are taken up by the LGO and the absence of an internal complaints procedure may well be evidence of maladministration.

Looking at the Code itself, it defines a complaint as: "an expression of dissatisfaction, however made, about the standard of service, actions or lack of action by the Council or their staff affecting an individual customer or group of customers."[48] It states encouragingly that complaints systems need not be defensive responses to the identification of a fault of deficiency, but can be a positive means of promoting customer satisfaction and identifying opportunities to improve services. It identifies the aims of an effective complaints system: provision of a straightforward means of complaining, procedures for investigating, keeping complainants informed of progress, appropriate redress, preventing problems recurring and feedback to departments and elected members so that the pattern and frequency of complaints can be considered in decision-making on resource allocation, prioritisation, planning and quality assurance. A culture of "consumer consciousness" will have to be fostered and a senior officer appointed to be responsible for oversight of the system and reporting to the relevant committee. That officer should solicit assistance from within the council and its departments and from outside bodies such as user groups and those representing ethnic minorities, those with disabilities and those with special needs. Resource implications will have to be taken on board, including those necessary for training and publicity.

The Code identifies the principles of a good complaints system:

- accessible and conspicuous;
- easy to invoke and use;
- quick action and speedy resolution with predetermined time limits;
- objective, with possibility of independent investigation from outside the department concerned, although there is no mention of participation of by non-council employees and members;

[48]   Paragraph 7.

- confidential;
- comprehensive although possibly tailored to individual departments.

The Code advises that there should be as few stages as possible and its own example contains three: initial approaches and attempted resolution; investigation by named officer within the department; further investigation by someone outside the department where necessary, with member involvement where desirable. No specific form for complaining should be necessary but the Code advises that from the second stage on, complaints should be in writing. It does not refer to the provision of assistance to an individual in writing down the details, that is, explaining what the complaint is about, what s/he would like the council to do and so on, although elsewhere the Code spells out the desiderata for a good complaints procedure. It offers further advice on the steps to be taken to set up a procedure and to ensure its monitoring and review; on publicity for the procedure and training arrangements; on recording, analysing and feedback of information to help identify trouble spots and improve service; finally, the Code offers advice on good investigative practice and what action is necessary if a complaint is considered justified. Particularly useful would be the "guidance on compensation".

There is much that is impressive in the Code and it avoids the rather vulgar consumerism that so many charters are prey to. It is clearly the result of much careful thought and experience and not simply the sloganising of a bright idea. However, on a couple of points a little more thought could be given. I have mentioned the absence of a reference to assistance being given to complainants; for most but the obstreperous the initial barrier is psychological and any help here with written complaints is essential. The CLA does not envisage any commitment to writing until the second stage but it is silent on the question of assistance. Secondly, although the use of parties outside the department is mentioned and even, in special cases, the use of outside agencies, the Code is perhaps a little tame on the position of the Council and its role in settling the most resistant of complaints. Along with colleagues I have suggested that there should ideally be an authority-wide procedure operating from the Chief Executive's office which should comprise elected members including those from outside the ruling party and membership from outside the authority itself. The Code suggests the appointment of a senior officer to oversee and report on the procedures but it stops short of a full-blooded authority-wide procedure. Thirdly, the Code does not refer to the publication of the complaint in anonymous terms to inform the public of what the council is doing in relation to particular kinds of complaints. It will help to let the public know that the Council means business.

That said, the Code is welcome and mention should be made of another Guidance Note, *Good Administrative Practice* (1993). This provides advice on policy-making and decision-making and what is required by the tenets of good administrative practice and, increasingly, the law, although it is certainly not a legal treatise. It also bears the influence of the *Principles of Good Administrative Practice* of the Committee of Ministers of the Council of Europe (see p. 249 below).

Ad Hoc Inquiries in Local Government

The position of more formal inquiries into local government conduct has been appraised from time to time. A report, *Ad Hoc Inquiries in Local Government* (1978) by the Society of Local Authority Chief Executives (SOLACE) dealt with the more serious extra-statutory inquiry into local authority misadventures. The document cited the range of opportunities open to local authorities to conduct such inquiries and noted: "they do not operate within any framework of procedural rules and there have been occasional shortcomings".[49]

This point was supported by the Local Authority Associations (LAA) in their reply in 1980, and they also believed that local inquiries under the *aegis* of the authority were to be preferred to ministerial inquiries. The use of inquiries in government has been studied in the previous chapter but they are often resorted to by local authorities either under statute or on a non-statutory and *ad hoc* basis. In this latter class, the Council on Tribunals will have no supervisory powers, nor will there be an inspector appointed by central government. The response of the LAA is interesting as it preferred the inquiries discussed by SOLACE to be non-statutory. In fact, their response shows quite clearly that they prefer discretion and vagueness both for the setting up of such inquiries and the procedures which they should adopt; in other words greater local authority control. Although it was difficult to lay down ground rules as to when a local inquiry was justified, they placed greater emphasis upon "serious internal investigations", feeling that "political sensitivity to local feelings

---

[49] Paragraph 1.2.

of the authority concerned can be relied upon to ensure that the right approach is adopted".[50]

The Code of Practice drafted by the LAA for "Formal Local Inquiries" is not of course binding and it would be at the authority's discretion whether or not the Code was adopted for "the more serious internal investigations". In some cases a statutory inquiry may be unavoidable. The Code recommends a lawyer chairman and an independent panel with a "lay member". Interestingly, complainants and those complained against shall have a right to call their own witnesses, subject to the panel's agreement, and it is at the panel's discretion to allow bodies representing "the public interest" to address it, either directly or through a legal representative.

The opinion was commonly held by chief executives in reply to queries that the committee system and the role of the elected representative rendered superfluous further procedural devices for complainants, a view which survived previous codes from the CLA. It was notable that committees did not play that significant role in the 1992 Guidance.

Committee, Sub-Committee, Members and Complainants

Authorities are given wide powers to "arrange for the discharge of their functions" by allocating them to committees, sub-committees and officers, as well as joint committees. Some form of "appeal" to a committee or sub-committee from an officer's decision is common among English local authorities. The public have, since April 1986, a general right to be admitted to committees and sub-committees, along with a variety of other rights under an amendment to the Local Government Act 1972, section 100.[51] The provisions include a right to agendas, officer reports relating to items and background papers insofar as these are deemed relevant by the "responsible officer". There are excluded items of information and exempted information. My own research shows these provisions to be scantily used and no specific enforcement mechanism is provided. The rights do not cover bodies such as officer groups or working parties although the papers may belong to "background documents" covered by the

---

50 LAA, *Ad Hoc Inquiries in Local Government*, 1980, paragraph 9. See Butler Sloss, *Child Abuse in Cleveland*, Cm. 412 (1988) and Child Care Act 1980 section 76 and Children Act 1989 section 81; note LGA 1972 section 250.
51 Local Government (Access to Information) Act 1985 (Birkinshaw, 1990).

Act. They are important, however, because until this legislation was passed there was no right to reports and background papers in local government which may well contain vital information which could be used to support a complaint. There is a wide exemption under the legislation for legal advice and opinion it should be noted. The existence of the legislation has not deterred the Government from recommending in its White Paper on Open Government a code of practice for information possessed by local authorities similar to that recommended for central government without explaining its relationship to the 1985 Local Government (Access to Information) Act (LGATIA).

Where sub-committees are used as informal appeal mechanisms, research in the past has shown that there is a general division between those which allow the complainant to state his or her case in writing and those which allow a personal appearance,[52] the former being much more common practice and written appeals are a regular feature, for instance in the field of housing. For more than a decade there have been examples of such authorities resorting to different forms of procedure, other than the committee, for allocation of council tenancies. Allocations were made by an officer "conference" involving the transfer officer, clearance officer, lettings officer and senior allocation officer.[53] Certainly at appeal level member involvement is common and Widdicombe noted a desire for members to be involved at policy implementation stage at all levels of decision.[54] Too much councillor involvement in council house allocation has been criticised by the LGO.[55]

LGO reports have also highlighted egregious abuses in committee and sub-committee procedure. The LGO has also commended a council's practice of permitting citizens to attend a committee and state their case and has encouraged the giving of reasons for decisions.[56] A *locus classicus* for public lawyers must be an investigation and further report at Slough,[57] where there were substantial abuses of procedural regularity where hearsay evidence of a particularly damning kind was admitted by a councillor against a homeless applicant for housing, and in the absence of

52 Lewis and Birkinshaw, "Taking Complaints Seriously", in *Welfare Law and Policy* (Partington and Jowell, eds), 1979.
53 Lewis and Livock, "Council House Allocation Procedures", (1979) 2 *Urban Law and Policy* 133.
54 See Widdicombe, Note 13 above, at 103.
55 Inv. 88/A/2329.
56 *Ibid.*
57 Inv. 387/H/77.

the applicant. There was no opportunity for this evidence to be challenged. In previous and subsequent field research a lack of basic safeguards was found to be common.[58] On further investigation Slough replied: "It is permissible and indeed common for local authority committees of this nature to receive and act upon uncorroborated statements which appear to them to come from a reliable source."[59]

Where committees act in a less than even-handed manner, the courts have not always been vigilant to protect the rights of those affected by committee deliberations. More generally, rights of the general public to attend meetings have been overridden with little ceremony by courts.[60] The courts have given wide dispensation for breaches of the 1960 Public Bodies (Access to Meetings) Act which still applies to a wide range of public bodies, for example, parish councils, consumer committees under the Water Act, although not to bodies covered by the amended section 100 of the 1972 Act, that is, "Principal Councils" (see above). In the *Liverpool City Council* litigation, it was accepted that the public had been excluded from a meeting in breach of legal requirements insofar as the reasons for excluding the public had not been mentioned in the resolution nor minuted as required by section 1(2) of the 1960 Act. The Court held nevertheless that the exclusion only involved directory and not mandatory provisions and did not vitiate the committee's decision. It may be that a more sophisticated approach to fair procedure would be expected from the courts today but the precedents have not always been helpful.

Officers are sometimes hopelessly confused by the oblique dealings of their putative political overlords – the councillors. In the Slough investigation (above), the commissioner stated:

> "[I]t was clear that there was a divergence between the attitudes of councillors and officers towards homelessness, and that it was common for the officers' recommendations not to be accepted. The officers confirmed this and said that they found it difficult to understand the Sub-committee's decisions

---

58	Lewis and Birkinshaw, "Local Authorities and the Resolution of Grievances – Some Second Thoughts", (1979) *Local Government Studies* 7; Sheffield, 1987, Note 9 above.

59	Cf *R v Southampton City Council ex parte Ward* [1984] 14 HLR 114.

60	*R v Liverpool City Council ex parte Liverpool Taxi Fleet Operators' Association* [1975] 1 WLR 701; *R v Brent Health Authority ex parte Francis* [1985] 1 All ER 74.

when no reasons were given for them or because of their inconsistency."[61]

Research has shown that too much member involvement in the minutiae of administration can detract from their role as tribunes,[62] although this was not a common occurrence since the widespread delegation of powers to officers in the LGA 1972 – and details of such delegations must be published under LGATIA 1985.

The role of the member in representing citizens has revealed serious shortcomings. According to the Maud Report,[63] a councillor required the capacity to "understand sympathetically the problems of constituents and to (be able) to convey them to the authority". However, a councillor, unlike an MP, has two roles. S/he is a representative of the electors and a member of the body delivering the services. It will be recalled that many authorities suggested that problems were best resolved through the intercession of the member: "this authority has 50 local ombudsmen – its members", the Sheffield study reported on the comments of one chief executive. Reference has already been made to the belief, held in various quarters,[64] that the role of the councillor has been diminishing in local government. Doubtless, this may not be a universal reflection of developments in local government, but the frequency with which it has allegedly come to pass is sufficient to raise questions about the utility of the member as the "people's champion". Can they get to the right people? Can they make their presence felt at influential places? Can they obtain the necessary information? – for it is a trite observation that without this, their utility for a complainant will be severely limited.

Research carried out for the Widdicombe Committee and its report, *The Conduct of Local Authority Business*, found that on average councillors spent 74 hours each month on council business, 13 hours of which were spent on electors' problems, surgeries and pressure group activity. Labour and Liberal members spent more time on such matters than did Conservatives (16, 17 and 10 hours respectively).[65]

Throughout the 1980s, litigation tested the rights of Council

---

61 Inv. 387/H/77.
62 Widdicombe, Note 54 above; Sheffield, (1987) Note 9 above, Seneviratne, 1991.
63 *Committee on Management of Local Government*, 1967, Vol. 2 at 143.
64 Cockburn, 1977; McAuslan, Note 13 above.
65 Widdicombe, 1986, Vol. II at 42.

members to obtain documents and attend meetings of committees of which they were not members. These are rights which are often crucial for the effective representation of those with a grievance. The Court of Appeal has maintained that councillors do not have a roving commission to go through council documents and that they are only entitled to such documents as are reasonably necessary for them to perform their duties.[66] An "improper or indirect" motive has been held to disbar their entitlement to documents. Such a motive has been held to exist where a member wanted documents to assist an elector in litigation against an authority, that is, where from the elector's point of view the member might require the information most urgently.[67] What if the member was assisting a complainant and not a litigant? Such an approach has equated a local authority with an individual litigant or commercial corporation with secrets to be kept and protected by law, even against those whom they purport to serve. Yet preventing a member from looking at the books destroys their utility where it could be required most. The implications for practice are enormous. A subsequent decision of the House of Lords has emphasised that the decision on whether to disclose documents to a councillor is essentially for the council itself, or for the relevant committee where there has been delegation of authority.[68] If a request by a councillor is interpreted as being hostile to the council, or is seen as motivated by an ulterior motive and refused, the councillor will face an onerous task when challenging such a decision upon judicial review. The chances of success are in reality minimal if s/he is not a member of the committee whose documents s/he wishes to see or a member of the parent committee of a sub-committee to which business has been delegated.[69] In other cases, a councillor will have to establish a need to know on the particular facts of the case. Councillors have litigated and have been successful, especially at seeing the papers going before sub-committees where they are members of the parent committee; indeed it was held that the member would

---

[66] *R v Lancashire CC Police Committee ex parte Hook* [1980] QB 603.

[67] *R v Hampstead BC ex parte Woodward* (1917) 116 LT 213 and *R v Barnes BC ex parte Conlan* [1938] 3 All ER 226; in *R v Southwold Corp. ex parte Wrightson* (1907) 97 LT 431 it was suggested that the fact that a member was critical of a council's policy was not sufficient in itself to prevent his access to documents.

[68] *R v Birmingham City DC ex parte 'O'* [1983] AC 578, where access was allowed.

[69] *R v Hackney LBC ex parte Gamper* [1985] 3 All ER 275 (QBD).

have a right to attend the sub-committee.[70] However, courts have been reluctant to allow rights of access to papers going before working parties or to allow rights to be in attendance if not designated as a member of the working party.[71] The LGATIA 1985 gave statutory rights to councillors to obtain information, and although these are wider than those enjoyed by members of the public, they are still subject to wide exemptions. The LGHA 1989 also amended legal requirements relating to membership of committees and members' interests. Basically, appointment to committees and sub-committees has to be effected proportionate with the political parties' membership of the Council.

This was seen as an effective way of getting around a problem which had grown throughout the 1980s: the problem of councillors' access to information had become embroiled in local party political feuding, reflecting to some extent political feuding in the national arena. In *Hook*'s case there were suspicions of party political feuding. Such feuding has, not surprisingly, been reported by LGO investigation reports. In Inv. 4862/C, opposition members of the city council were not allowed to appear at the housing sub-committee at which allocations and disputes were dealt with. It was noted that the authority complained against had replied to a questionnaire that the usual method by which a complaint was taken up was via the ward member. Indeed, Lord Denning dissenting in *Hook* said that lack of information for members, if taken too far, could lead to rule by caucus. The implications for an individual complainant are obvious. Comments such as "too interested in policy-making and not in individual grievances" were fairly typical. One executive stated that complaining through a councillor was useful "as long as the authority had a clear practice about what it did to put the matter right at local level."

> "Even where such procedures existed, they did not always seem to work satisfactorily, either because councillors thought they could make political capital out of a reference to the [LGO] or because they were alarmed at the prospect of becoming involved in a complaint against the authority or because they had simply forgotten what the correct procedures were."[72]

---

70 *Gamper* and see *R v Sheffield City C ex parte Chadwick* (1985) 84 LGR 563. An allegation that the council or committee was motivated by improper or irrelevant considerations in the exercise of a discretion would have to be proved by the councillor.
71 Birkinshaw, Note 51 above, at 144 to 145.
72 R. Rawlings, "The MPs Complaints Service", (1990) Modern Law Review 22 and 149.

The *Justice* report found that complainants in its survey were largely negative about the role of councillors.[73] The Sheffield study reported that officers felt that councillors were more interested in vote catching than in equity and fairness, so that councillors were very active before elections. It was also felt that members were too interested in getting around policies which they had created. Research has found that the lower socio-economic groups were more likely to contact the councillor than any other groups. Not surprisingly the report noted: "What is clear from the surveys is that the ability of complainants to obtain a positive response from the responsible authority is in part related to factors such as social class and length of education", those higher up the social scale invariably being more successful in finding redress.

MPs of course feature in local authority complaints although the Sheffield study did not find their intervention very widespread. Rawlings found MPs taking up a considerable number of local authority complaints and they were particularly useful for those "non routine cases with no obvious haven".[74] MP complaints and member complaints often followed set procedures to the chief officer of a service and then to the Chief Executive.

Statutory Requirements

Quite apart from a range of appeals procedures from the decisions of local authorities to courts or the Secretary of State, who possesses various default powers, there are numerous statutory duties on authorities to provide individuals with an opportunity of presenting a case against them in less formal surroundings than courts of law or central government offices. There are also statutory obligations upon authorities to produce information and/or reasons in writing for their decisions, a recent example coming with the competitive tendering provisions and related procedures under the LGA 1988.[75] Reference has already been made to the right to inspect accounts at audit, make representations thereon and challenge related items. The legislation which unified rent and rate rebate schemes and rent allowance schemes, making them the responsibility of local authorities and not the former DHSS, was widely criticised for its over-hasty implementation causing

---

73 Though the survey concerned those who had complained to the Commission and were therefore not satisfied with local treatment.

74 Rawlings, 1990, at 40.

75 See *R v Secretary of State for the Environment ex parte Knowsley MBC* (1991) *The Independent* 29 September.

administrative chaos and individual hardship. It is ironical to note that regulations have introduced detailed procedures for claimants to make representations in writing; for an officer review; to apply for further review before a review board appointed by the authority at which s/he can be legally represented; to call witnesses; to cross-examine, and so forth. Claimants receive a statement of reasons for a decision in writing and the board's findings on material questions of fact. There has been criticism of these boards as their membership comprises councillors of the appointing authority although they act as a "quasi judicial" body and not as a committee of the authority. Recent work has shown that the procedures are characterised by a considerable degree of confusion. For instance there is too much scope for officer manipulation of the review procedures in so much as they persuade people not to seek review or give in too easily on cases which merit a challenge. Internal review procedures were not clearly defined, poor statistics were kept and training for review board members was poor with too little knowledge of regulations and judicial procedures, poor standards of decision-making and record keeping and inappropriate participation by local authority legal officers acting as advisers.[76] More generally, the Audit Commission has reported that it is difficult to determine when an individual is complaining and asking for an internal review and when s/he is making a complaint about the regulations generally. In surveys on claimants' views on quality of service the uppermost request was for "clear information on entitlement".[77] In addition, the LGO has criticised the rather wooden exercise of discretion by authorities in always asking for repayments of overpayments rather than treating cases on their merits. DSS guidance has attempted to address some of these shortcomings.[78]

General Provisions

Some statutory obligations have a tendency to produce additional administrative practices which result in increased procedural protection, or at least increased opportunity to present one's case to a decision-maker, a practice noted by the Court of Appeal and encouraged by the High Court.[79] For example, an appeal lay to

[76] Housing Benefits Review, HMSO, (1991); Sainsbury and Eardley, 1992, at 551.
[77] Audit Commission, *Management and Administration of Housing Benefit Audit Guide*, 1992. See *Housing Benefit Review* (1991) HMSO.
[78] For example, HB/CCB (92)20, DSS.
[79] *R v Secretary of State for the Environment ex parte Powis* [1981] 1 WLR 584; *Steeples v Derbyshire CC* [1984] 3 All ER 468 at 495.

the Secretary of State against a local authority which refused or revoked a disposal licence for controlled waste,[80] yet authorities often displayed a willingness to conduct informal meetings with applicants for licences as a matter of course. Legislation and regulations now cover environmental pollution and provide for consultation and objections but these are no less likely to generate similar practices. Research has found supplementation of even quite detailed statutory procedures by informal negotiation to be common.[81] Such informal practices are not made public knowledge and quite easily gravitate towards the interests of the obstreperous, the knowledgeable, the powerful. Although licensing is an area notoriously lacking in procedural coherence, there are many statutory provisions extending procedural protection to individuals,[82] for example, control and licensing of sex establishments and refreshment premises and environmental pollution.[83] The Rent (Agriculture) Act 1976 and the activities of the Agriculture Dwelling-House Advisory Committee (ADHAC) caused particular interest. Briefly, the Act places upon local authorities a duty to "do their utmost" to rehouse farmworkers where a farmer can establish "agricultural need" for the premises in question. Any of the parties concerned can call upon the advice of an ADHAC which is tendered in writing to all participants. In fact, hearings before these bodies, and representations of farmer or tenant have been numerous.

Looked at as a whole these provisions seem to do much to advance the argument that whether or not a procedural protection exists has often been largely fortuitous and that a statutory provision once produced tends to bring in its wake supplementary safeguards and devices. Whether this is always the case is open to empirical examination. MENCAP, for instance, have suggested that the default powers of the Secretary of State under the

---

80 Control of Pollution Act 1974, section 10; see chapter 6 p. 277 below.
81 Sheffield 1987, Note 9 above; see also for previous practice Lewis and Birkinshaw, (1979b).
82 In education, housing management, social services, residential homes and so on.
83 Local Government (Misc Provs) Act 1982, section 2, Schedule 3 and section 5 respectively. With reference to public entertainment licensing under section 1 and Schedule 1 of the 1982 legislation and a strong judicial statement of procedural fairness extending well beyond the statutory langauge, see *R v Huntingdon DC ex parte Cowan* [1984] 1 All ER 58. On water pollution see sections 118 and 119 Water Industry Act 1991; sections 85 and 89 Water Resources Act 1991 and SI 1989/1151, and on pollution registers see Water Resources Act 1991 section 190 (1).

Chronically Sick and Disabled Persons Act 1970 have proved "largely ineffective" in prompting such procedural protection. MENCAP argued for a statutory regional appeals procedure against an authority's assessment of the needs of an individual who is chronically sick or disabled. Under the Children Act 1989 and NHS and Community Care Act 1990, authorities have to provide complaints review panels. Five authorities have been assessed by the Social Services Inspectorate and their procedures compared with a list of 16 desiderata. Of these, about half were "met or partly met", a quarter were well met and a quarter were "not met". Authorities seemed to be facing difficulties with the same areas: there was a lack of comprehensive distribution of complaints leaflets (although the quality was generally good); establishing "user friendly" (that is, no need for written complaint) procedures seemed to be an excuse for not recording or collating complaints centrally; information from complaints was not being used to inform policy-making; difficulties were encountered by investigating officers who felt uneasy challenging their peers in reports or who could not devote enough time to their role; provision of procedures to some sectors of the clientele was inadequate, for example, foster care children and home care recipients and occupants of residential homes concerning complaints of lack of privacy; and too often only English was used for publicity purposes; generally the authorities were not resolving complaints anywhere near quickly enough.[84]

Education

Education has been one of the most bitterly divisive policies of the Conservative governments in the 1980s and 1990s. Nowhere, not even in health care, are the battles so fierce over the collective philosophy that dominated the post Second World War political consensus on the role of the state and the provision of essential services and the assault on that philosophy by free-marketeers and guardians of the "new right". The ultimate objective of the Government has been the creation of a market in schools to provide parents with "greater choice" in the types of school open to their children. As in all markets, there are winners and losers and some of the winners have been made so by deliberately interventionist policies of government, for example, the creation

---

[84] *Inspection of Complaints Procedures in LA Social Service Departments*, SSI/DH, 1993.

of City Technology Colleges and opted-out schools.[85] A definite
loser has been local government, as the Government hoped that
local management of schools and then opting out of LEA control
under the Education Reform Act 1988 (ERA) and the operation of the 1993 legislation would remove the necessity of an
intermediary authority between central and local government.
The 1993 Act has established a Funding Agency to take over
responsibility for funding schools, opted-out schools and bodies
to run under-performing schools (see chapter 4). In this area we
have seen a spate of appeals/grievance procedures, more geared
towards advancing government policy many feel than towards
equity and justice - but justice has a limited interpretation in the
market and equity connotes a sense of conscience born of responsibility, not competition.

For a statutory complaints or appeals procedure, that provided
by the Education Act 1980 is of outstanding interest. Before
spelling out the more interesting procedural features of the statute
it should be noted that it was normal for education authorities to
provide some form of appeals structure to challenge education
decisions before the 1980 Act. As opposed to the examples in
the next section, the regularity of these structures was striking. It
would, perhaps, be explained to a certain extent by the requirements of the Education Act 1944. Sections 37 and 76 provide for
a degree of parental choice in the matter of secondary schooling.
These particular provisions were not heavily utilised, but section
68 has been frequently invoked (see chapter 2).

The Education Act 1980 (as amended) section 6 provides that
arrangements shall be made by every local education authority to
enable the parents of a child in the area of the authority to express
a preference of school(s) for his or her child and to give reasons
for this preference. The procedure is also used to hear appeals
against exclusions from schools. This duty is hedged in with exceptions in section 6(3). Of present interest is section 7, which states
that all education authorities shall make arrangements to enable
the parent of a child to appeal against decisions of local education
authorities or governors of voluntary schools. Local education
authorities shall establish appeal committees. The decisions of
committees are binding on local authorities or governors. They

---

[85] Detailed provisions are contained in ERA 1988 for the procedures to
be followed in establishing opted-out schools, sections 60–72. Feintuck
believes that very often parents are not the prime movers in opting out,
but governors or head teachers, M. Feintuck, *Accountability and Choice in
Schooling* (Buckingham, Open University Press, 1994).

are subject to the supervision of the Council on Tribunals, and the jurisdiction of the Local Government Ombudsman, both of which have been extremely critical of the procedures. Schedule 2 Part I to the Act sets out the constitution of the committees in a manner which seeks to avoid suspicion of bias or partiality, though the members are appointed by the authority or governors from persons nominated by the authority or governors. Part II details the procedure. The appellant, who must set out grounds of appeal in writing, has the right to be afforded the opportunity of appearing and making oral representations and to be accompanied by a friend or to be represented. The decision, by simple majority if necessary, shall be communicated to the appellant in writing. The appeals are heard in private. Codes of guidance on the operation of the procedures have been drafted by relevant local authority associations which emphasise the desirability of informality in proceedings, and the Act has been the subject of considerable judicial interpretation, one of the major consequences of which appeared to be the virtual elimination of catchment areas.[86]

The Education Act 1981 contained considerable detail on procedures to be followed by an authority in assessing "special educational needs" (SEN) of a child and the same appeal procedure as under the 1980 Act was used. The Education Act 1993 now provides for a right of appeal to a SEN Tribunal where the authority refuses to make a statement of SEN or where the parents wish to challenge its contents.[87] Regulations will provide for the Tribunal's procedure and will include discovery rights, sitting in private, power to review or vary its own decisions and orders and representation of parties, *inter alia*. SEN has been one of the most heavily criticised aspects of education provision, not necessarily because of any procedural shortcomings but because of the complexity and number of cases involved and the fact that decisions were resource led rather than need led. Complaints on this area formed the largest number of education complaints to the LGO, and the Audit Commission had been highly critical of delays and inequitable and inconsistent treatment; the existence of a specific tribunal will now limit the scope for local ombudsman

---

[86] *R v Shadow Education Com. Greenwich LBC ex parte Governors of J. Ball School* (1989) 88 LGR 589; see, for a possible qualification, *R v Bradford MBC ex parte S. Ali* (1993) *The Times* 21 October.

[87] See section 167 on the procedure for making an initial assessment; note also the procedure to make an assessment at the request of the parent, section 173, is not as copious.

intervention.[88] The Warnock Committee of 1978 believed that 16 per cent of children at any one time had SEN – in 1991, 168,000 children had formal statements, 2 per cent of the total number of schoolchildren in England.[89]

Under section 23 ERA, every LEA is responsible for operating a complaints procedure relating to the performance by schools or LEAs of their considerable legal responsibilities for the national curriculum and the provision of information to parents. For relevant complaints, complainants must use this procedure before complaining to the Secretary of State under the Education Act 1944 (section 68). However, research conducted for the NCC[90] reported that there was considerable ignorance among parents of the responsibilities of governing bodies and LEAs and there was widespread uncertainty and varying interpretations among LEAs and governing bodies of the scope of section 23. The DES guidance was considered inadequate and a large number of those LEAs investigated had based their procedure on models drafted by representative bodies.[91] On some vital aspects, for example, naming LEA designated complaints officers, practices differed and while most were user friendly, there were some which were "confusing, over-legalistic and poorly drafted".[92] Again one encounters the criticism of little training for complaints staff. Publicity for the procedures in both schools and LEAs was poor and the number of formal complaints, in writing and to the governing body (stage 2) or LEA (stage 3), recorded by LEAs for 1989/90 and 1990/91 was under one hundred. Only a minority were upheld, although many stage 2 complaints are probably not reported. Neither governing bodies nor LEAs record or monitor complaints made informally (stage 1). One worrying aspect was that the views of children were rarely sought. On the subject of the views of children, it might be worth mentioning that 18,000 calls concerning bullying were made by children to Childline in 1990/91.

Although these provisions may appear akin to taking a sledge-hammer to crack a nut, it is not surprising that relatively copious procedures should be provided for such an area as education.

---

[88] See chapter 5 and *R v CLA ex parte Croydon LBC* [1989] 1 All ER 1033 (DC).

[89] The Council on Tribunals (AR 1991/2 paragraph 1.18) and the Commission for Local Administration have criticised the operation of the 1980 and 1981 procedures; see also NCC (1992).

[90] Harris, 1992.

[91] See AMA and ACC *Education Appeals* (revised 1992).

[92] Harris, Note 90 above, at 3.

Education generally has been a focal point for Conservative governments' attacks on the evils of socialist dirigisme in welfare and the economy. School allocations frequently exercise vociferous and articulate members of the community, and their heavy utilisation of non-statutory procedures ultimately led to government support for a statutory procedural form, which is still nonetheless monopolised by the same groups. Consumer-led reforms, including the provision of complaints procedures and publication of information relating to performance, would appear to pander to traditional Conservative values such as freedom, but they soon became valuable tools in helping to dismantle many of its traditional enemies, namely Labour-controlled authorities, public sector and teaching unions and education "specialists" whose advanced views, the Government claimed, had taken education from the people.

Housing

The Housing Act 1980 (now the Housing Act 1985), as well as introducing a right for public sector tenants to buy their council houses, produced important changes in the legal position between landlords and tenants in the public sector, providing security of tenure for what the Act defines as "secure tenants". More important for our present purposes are the provisions relating to housing management, especially consultation with secure tenants under section 43 (section 105 of the 1985 Act; hereafter references will be to the 1985 legislation). Successful housing management enterprises *involving* the residents were applauded as long ago as 1981 by the Scarman Report into the Brixton riots.[93] Prior to the changes introduced by the Housing Act, constant criticism had been made about the frequent arbitrary, almost feudal presumptions operating behind allocation and transfer of council tenancies.

The post-1979 transformation in welfare provision has been as profound here as elsewhere. A right to buy was followed by provision for the privatising of council estates, greater reliance upon the Housing Corporation, a non-departmental public body (see chapter 4), to provide publicly funded housing and the introduction of Housing Action Trusts (public corporations) to manage publicly owned estates. As I write, the Government is discussing the feasibility of converting local authority housing departments into private sector companies so that they may borrow from the

93 Cmnd 8427 (1981), paragraph 6.14.

money markets without distorting the PSBR figures. What does the 1985 Act require? We should note that to all intents and purposes, the following details apply to housing associations (see chapter 4).

If the "landlord authority" is one within section 105(1) – essentially all public landlords – and relates to "housing management" as defined in section 105(2), then the landlord authority shall, within 12 months of commencement of that part of the Act, make and thereafter maintain such arrangements as it considers appropriate to enable those of its secure tenants who are likely to be substantially affected by a matter of housing management to be informed of the proposals and to make their views known. The landlord authority is under the familiar duty to consider any representations made to it in accordance with arrangements made by the authority under this section. The landlord authority must publish details of the arrangements, to be made available at the authority's principal office for inspection and to be furnished on payment of a reasonable fee, to any member of the public who requests them. Similar provisions apply to housing associations. It should be made plain that these provisions are not directly comparable with the appeal provisions contained in the Education Act 1980. Those latter provisions provide, on paper at least, firmer procedural opportunities to complain and appeal.

It is to be noted that the provisions are expressed in vague and subjective terms, and in general will not be easy to upset, for example, "appropriate arrangements", "likely to be substantially affected". Also "housing management" does not include matters relating to rent payable under the secure tenancy and any charge for services and facilities provided by the landlord authority.[94] The Court of Appeal ruled that the consultation provisions do not apply to pre-privatisation disposals, although subsequent legislation gave stronger procedural rights in proposed sales only for the law to state that any defects in procedure would not vitiate a sale.[95] So often in the past the feeling has been present that exercises aimed at involving tenants in management schemes have amounted to no more than mere "tokenism" on the authority's part. Such gestures from authorities lead to disillusion and cynicism though there is no doubting that effective and participatory schemes involving tenants may have much to offer.[96] That said, it

---

[94] HA 1985 section 105(2).
[95] Housing and Planning Act 1986 section 6 and Schedule 1 and Housing Act 1988 sections 97, 102 and 103, SI 1990/367 and DoE Circ 11/89.
[96] See DoE, 1993.

should be noted that there are qualifications to be made about the Housing Act. Although the authority must consider representations from the tenants, nowhere is there any machinery to ensure that authorities take the representations seriously. The statute sets out a bare framework, the rest will be left to the good will, no doubt, of authorities. It will also be interesting to note what forms possible legal challenge may take if, or when, there is an alleged failure to comply with these provisions, as their vagueness appears to offer little that could be encashed in terms of hard legal rights in the courts.[97]

Section 106 deals with provisions of information about housing allocation: every landlord authority shall publish a summary of its rules as regards priority between applicants and transfer of tenancies; a set of these rules together with procedural rules must be made available for inspection – separate provisions for publicity apply for housing associations. A summary of the rules is available without charge, and a set of rules furnished on payment of a reasonable fee. Provisions in the 1985 Act relating to access to personal information by tenants were subsumed within the much more substantial Access to Personal Files (Housing) Regulations which also stipulate that an authority must make provision to review an adverse decision concerning a "subject's" access to documents. The review will be by members who were uninvolved in the original decision or by the full authority. The tenant may make oral or written representations.

These provisions, though incomplete, are welcome in themselves, as it has been noted in the past that a statutory duty to provide information and give reasons may supply the ammunition to launch an attack on unjustified or questionable public decision-making. Absence of any duty to provide reasons for an adverse decision has proved fatal on more than one occasion. In *Cannock Chase District Council* v *Kelly*[98] a mother and five children were evicted from a council house, though it was accepted by the authority that there were no blemishes or arrears of rent on her part. The Court of Appeal held that it was up to her to prove abuse of power or unreasonable behaviour and in the absence of a duty to supply reasons for the eviction, this would be virtually impossible for her to establish, as indeed it proved in the particular case. Be that as it may, the statutory framework offers what at first glance is an improvement on the previous fragmented

---

97 P. Birkinshaw, *Open Government, Freedom of Information and Local Government* (Local Government Legal Society Trust, 1986).
98 [1978] 1 All ER 152 (CA).

and haphazard practices of housing authorities. But it has not been without its critics.[99] As a common method of processing complaints about allocation and transfer of tenancies is via the Housing, etc. Committee, or rather Sub-committee, readers are reminded of the discussion on committees above.

There is only space to mention briefly that under the Housing and Urban Development Act 1993 management agreements have been extended whereby authorities may delegate their management responsibilities to other bodies and tenants' rights to be consulted have been developed. Provision is also made for such responsibilities to be delegated to tenants' management organisations.

Homeless Cases

We have seen in this section a series of statutory procedures whereby complainants or individuals with a grievance may make contact with agencies or persons independent of the authority complained against and how such possibilities can assist in the more obvious presence of informal practices among authorities dealing with complaints to reduce the risk of outside intervention. We have noted specific statutory procedures aimed at local resolution of grievances, before the LGO is involved. It might be convenient at this juncture to describe the development of one piece of legislation, the controversial Housing (Homeless Persons) Act 1977, (now under the Housing Act 1985, Part III) which imposed various duties upon housing authorities in 1978 towards the homeless. A major review of the homeless law was promised by the Government in the autumn of 1993. Those receiving the full benefit of the Act have to be "non-intentionally" homeless and in "priority need," for example, with children.[100]

The interest in the legislation lies in the fact that it does not establish a particular procedure for applications, or complaints/appeals, nor does the statute allow for appeal, either to the Secretary of State or to the courts. The statute does say that applications, where the authority believes homelessness or the threat of homelessness to exist, will be subject to inquiries as are necessary to satisfy itself that the applicant is homeless or threatened with homelessness. By section 62(2), the authority conducts such inquiries to satisfy itself on: first, whether there is a "priority

[99]   Birkinshaw, Note 97 above; Lewis and Harden, Note 11 above.
[100] The butt of government criticism was single mothers allegedly using the legislation to queue-jump housing waiting lists.

need"; second, whether the homelessness was intentional and lastly, whether there is a local connection with another housing authority in the UK. Given the importance of these inquiries on the first two points, for if the findings are adverse to the applicants the authority will not be under a duty "to secure that accommodation becomes available," how fair are these inquiries when set against the legal paradigm of due process? If the decision is adverse in any wise to the applicant, reasons must be made available for collection for a reasonable time at the council offices. The decisions are reviewable in the courts. Indeed, the legislation has spawned an enormous progeny of litigation,[101] and local authority associations mooted for a time establishing their own domestic appeal forum to deal with applicants' complaints. The litigation has also been one of the major reasons behind the suggestion for a housing court/tribunal to relieve the pressure on the High Court and judicial review applications.

The Code of Guidance (DoE 1991) issued under section 71 of the Act advises that interviews should be kept to a minimum and that those under stress should be accompanied or there may be a need for an intermediary or an interpreter. The Code has come a long way since the original version which spoke of all issues under section 3 being conducted *in the course of a single interview*. What, however, about being informed of impressions or conclusions and being able to disabuse the interviewer or examiner of such impressions? The possibility of hearsay evidence being taken into consideration in the absence of the applicant when deciding homelessness cases has been witnessed again and again.[102] What safeguards exist to prevent this taking place if the decision-maker is under no positive structural constraint to comply with basic principles of natural justice or the less wooden test of fair procedure?[103] Is there an opportunity for an appeal against a decision of an authority to a higher domestic appeal body? On one point, assessing people from outside the UK, the Court of Appeal has ruled that the Code is unlawful insofar as authorities are not constrained to consider the case if they believe that the

---

[101] M. Sunkin *et al.*, *Judicial Review in Perspective* (London, The Public Law Project, 1993).

[102] See Local Ombudsman Inv. 387/H/77 and *R v Southampton City Council ex parte Ward* (1984) *The Times* 24 February.

[103] *Re HK* [1967] 2 QB 617; *R v Liverpool Corporation ex parte Liverpool Taxi Fleet Operators' Association* [1972] 2 QB 299; *Att. Gen. of Hong Kong v Ng Yuen Shiu* [1983] 2 AC 629 (PC); *R v Great Yarmouth BC ex parte Botton Bros. Arcades Ltd* (1987) 56 P & CR 99; see *NJ Stoop v Royal Borough of Kensington and Chelsea* (1991) JPL 1129.

applicant has entered the UK illegally; the consequences of this are that authorities are deemed appropriate bodies to decide on the legality of the applicant's presence in the jurisdiction, a duty usually confined to the immigration authorities. Given that the courts have stated on other occasions that authorities are not expected to carry out CID-type investigations into applications, are they encouraged to make judgments on legality on a perfunctory basis?[104]

Work carried out on the operation of the legislation in the early and mid-1980s would suggest that the procedural safeguards operated by authorities were generally jejune; an approach it must be said encouraged by many review cases including decisions of the House of Lords.[105] For instance, it was common for the initial interviewer not to be the person making the final decision.[106] Only six authorities made decisions via the appropriate sub-committee, therefore offering at least the basic appearance of formal constraint in decision-making. In most other cases, the decision was taken by a more senior officer in the housing authority. A minority of authorities allowed the applicant and a friend or representative to be present after interview, but none of these authorities invited or encouraged their presence. A majority did not allow their presence after interview, either alone or with a friend. Only one authority provided a set procedure for an internal appeal against its own decision, and this appeal was a written appeal. The procedural side, in other words, appeared undeveloped from the point of view of obvious safeguards and the duty to give reasons where the decision was adverse was carried out in a rather desultory fashion. In the absence of an insistence by the courts that full and proper reasons be given, exiguous reasons afford sparse opportunity to challenge an authority's decision. The Code speaks of full and clear explanation for a decision and provision of information on any appeals procedures operated by the authority and it advises that such procedures should be established. The first stage would be a review at senior officer level with the possibility of an appeal panel at member level with a Chair who is independent of the decision process (paragraph 9.2).

---

[104] *R v Secretary of State for the Environment ex parte Tower Hamlets LBC* [1993] 3 All ER 439.
[105] Birkinshaw (1982); *Pulhofer v Hillingdon LBC* [1986] AC 484.
[106] See *R v Harrow LBC ex parte Hobbs* [1992] *The Times* 13 October.

Non-Statutory Procedures

The Sheffield (1987) study, building upon earlier research, found the following forms of grievance redress to be operative in local authorities. Formal procedures other than the committee system existed and included an executive Ombudsman (see below) or a centralised and institutionalised method of dealing with disputes, usually operating out of the Chief Executive's office; use of committee and sub-committee, especially for housing; informal procedures where the processing of complaints tended to follow a set pattern, generally internal in nature inasmuch as the complainant was not invited to be present at any stage, for example, complaint sent to the chief executive who would refer the issue to the head of the department concerned. Many authorities claimed to possess no procedures, which obviously cannot be taken at face value, or they resorted to *ad hoc* methods which revealed little consistency, for example, complaint to the Chief Executive's office, ward councillor, MP, and so on. In a small proportion of authorities there was provision for a complainant to be interviewed, or for public participation, that is, members of the public were actively invited to attend committee meetings, public information meetings or, for example, area tenants' sub-committees or residents' sub-committees were encouraged. Opportunities were given to address the council at the end of a meeting on a sort of "any complaints" basis and topics included house improvement, area rejuvenation, rent assessment, Sunday trading or the introduction of taxi meters. At the more structured end it included invitations to attend the various bodies hearing the complaints or complainants were given "a formal interview". Some authorities had complaints postcards which had been pre-addressed. No doubt such deliberations might prove extremely satisfactory but their unsystematic nature is unlikely to excite the general public to unsolicited action.

More recent examples include departments which had institutionalised internal administrative review involving either senior officer review or a case conference between officers and members. The Sheffield study found institutionalised negotiation in planning departments, which was more concerned with grievance avoidance than redress, whereby developers' plans were modified to make them acceptable rather than rejected out of hand. "Tribunal type" hearings were also held in a range of different departments although allowing persons to present their case orally and to receive reasons for decisions was something which happened "from time to time".[107] Executive Ombudsmen had grown in popularity, an expression that the LGO has criticised because it may lead to confusion about the role of the LGO.

Over the years we have noted that the best practices of authorities have all anticipated the list of best practice suggested by the LGO in its guidance (p. 100 above). This included registering and monitoring of complaints, much of the anonymised information being available for councillors and the public; identifying complaints officers; setting time limits; feeding relevant information back into policy-making agendas; and providing freedom of information about council policies, administration and services in a way which went beyond the duties and powers laid out in the LGATIA 1985.

A fairly typical response where it was claimed that procedures existed was as follows:

(1) complaint to departmental head
(2) to chief executive
(3) to elected representative
(4) to committee/sub-committee via ward members
(5) to full council
(6) to Local Ombudsman

Too often procedures which it was claimed existed had in fact lain fallow since their acceptance and the minuted instruction to publicise the procedure appeared to have been overlooked. What is perhaps of even greater interest is that one recorded procedure appeared very similar to internal procedures which were frequently noted in other authorities, but which in fact were simply defensive mechanisms operating against the background of a possible investigation by the Local Ombudsman.

We have referred on several occasions to "Executive Ombudsmen", in-house Ombudsmen appointed by the authority.[108] The Sheffield study supported the view formed in earlier years that their presence considerably reduced resort to outside agencies such as courts, the Ombudsman or elsewhere. This fitted in with a theme which must be constantly stressed: local authorities themselves are the bodies who could and should deal effectively and efficiently with disputes and complaints at a local level. This is not, however, to deny the residuary role which external agencies

---

[107]   Sheffield, Note 9 above, at 226.
[108]   As far as I am aware the term originated with A.S. Wyner (ed.) *Executive Ombudsmen in the U.S.A.*, 1973.

must naturally be expected to perform on the occasions when domestic decision-making proves partial or unfair.

In September 1993 the CLA informed the author that as at that date no studies had been conducted on the impact of the Citizen's Charter (CC) on local authority procedures although we have looked at relevant legislation, and the 1992 annual report on the progress of the CC pointed out good practices. The CLA collect local authority complaints documents but not all authorities send them, although it has reported an enormous growth of interest in complaints procedures and substantial progress in their implementation.

Local Authority Decision-Making and Public Participation

Some of the procedures discussed so far, for example, the committee and sub-committee, may well be utilised by individuals or groups who wish to participate in the process of decision-making itself – to influence a policy or decision with a group interest *a priori* rather than complain about administrative practices as individuals *a posteriori*. We shall bear in mind that admission of the public to committees is an observation device not a participation process. The tenants' management schemes under the Housing Act 1985 constitute legislative encouragement for participation.[109] It will be recalled that misgivings were voiced about the procedure and the half-hearted efforts behind the intention of actually *involving* tenants. In local authority practice, we do not have to look too far to discern planning or policy-making exercises where involvement of the community may be not only desirable from the perspective of legitimation, but beneficial inasmuch as their contribution may assist in better policy-making. This subject has, however, generated a tremendous amount of conflict from bureaucracy, both central and local, as the programmes we are about to discuss initially frequently involved a close working relationship between the centre and localities. More latterly, paying lipservice to participatory democracy has not been as fashionable as in the 1970s and government has sought to achieve policies locally by excluding local authorities and by transferring their powers to executive appointed bodies and by giving a special voice in favour of special interest groups, for example, local

---

[109]   DoE, Note 96 above.

businesses,[110] in the development of local policies or making of local decisions. Where the Government was anxious to bring about a significant change in policy in the field of education, that is, to get more schools to opt out of LEA control, it encouraged participatory exercises involving consultation and public inquiries. Where schools or LEAs are failing in their duties to improve standards in "at risk" schools, Education Associations have been recommended whose members will be appointed by the Secretary of State. These will set up procedures to consult with and benefit from local advice – parents, business, industry and others, the sort of "community involvement" which will be essential for the future success of the schools concerned, as the Government believed.

The kinds of participatory programmes which are encountered[111] have included the structure plan exercises – a "broad brush treatment of future policies on land use and the allocation of public resources in respect of public development",[112] now superseded by Unitary Development Plans in urban areas.[113] Local plans filling in details of the structure plans were made by district and sometimes county authorities and have to follow various inquiry procedures involving the public.[114]

The subject of urban renewal, rejuvenation and redevelopment has generated a vast array of statutory schemes aimed at urban and inner urban areas. Reference has been made to the introduction of the urban partnerships and other urban programmes. Other schemes, having as their central concern the conservation and restoration of areas within particular authorities, are general improvement areas and housing action areas under Part VIII of the 1985 Housing Act. Where areas were declared "general improvement areas" or "housing action areas" by authorities, they engaged in renewal and repair of dwellings rather than slum clearance. In an attempt to develop commercial expansion, private enterprise and urban renewal, we have seen the creation of Urban Development Corporations and Enterprise Zones.[115] Schemes introduced subsequently have involved central/local

---

110 Under the Rates Act 1984, LGFAs 1988 and 1992, in the joint financing of City Technology Colleges and co-opting governors onto school governing bodies.

111 And see J. Gyford, Local Government and the Public (Macmillan, 1991).

112 McAuslan, The Ideologies of Planning Law, 1980.

113 Under the Town and Country Planning Act (TCPA) 1990.

114 The Planning Inspectorate reported that in 1992/3, inquiries and plans were becoming more complex and longer. See Cm. 569, Future of Development Plans, (1989) and TCPA 1990 Part I chapter II.

115 Local Government, Planning and Land Act 1980 sections 135 to 172 and Schedules 26 to 31, and section 179 and Schedule 32 respectively.

government negotiation or competitive applications by local authorities determined by central government and have placed little priority on local views, although local chambers of commerce may take an important role in sifting through applications.

Local authorities differ significantly in their styles of administration – some being more user friendly than others. Many of the Government's reforms since 1980 have had as their objective the reduction in the role of rigid party political control of the "old style" of local government; generally this was anti-participatory and in metropolitan areas Labour dominated. Other styles of government include the "representative mechanistic" model which the LGHA 1989 sought to foster; other styles place greater emphasis upon citizen involvement and participation,[116] though even here the structures for active involvement were invariably lacking – and the latest model in which the expression "local government" is a contradiction in terms insofar as there is little in the way of government, merely service delivery contracted out to contractors and citizen's charter exercises, for example, monitoring of performance, consumer surveys, published standards, complaints procedures and compensation for breach of standards. It has to be said that even in the participatory-conscious authorities, officials were often surprised at "tepid" responses from those invited to participate. What opportunities have existed for the public to participate in the schemes outlined above? Have opportunities which exist been laid down in statute, in circular, or are they left to the unstructured discretion of authorities? It is instructive to note the practice of "planning cells" in some German cities and Länder. These produce citizens' reports which are based upon provision of information, time off work and remuneration for participants selected randomly in areas and whose selection is supervised by a judge. The aim is to avoid grievances emerging rather than grievance resolution and maximum emphasis is placed upon citizen involvement, a process allowing the "silent majority to participate in making decisions that affect everyone".[117]

Strategic Planning

Since the introduction of structure plans in the 1970s, strategic planning has presented, on paper at least, interesting procedures

---

[116] Chamberlayne, "The Politics of Participation", (1978) 4 *The London Journal* 47.

[117] P. Dienel, "The Citizen as Assessor: Planning Public Services" in J. Epstein, ed., *Providing Public Services that Serve the Public* (London, Anglo-German Foundation, 1989).

through which the public could, if not exert influence, at least register their views. The latest exercises involve the preparation of county planning policies and for districts, comprehensive development plans (UDPs). Metropolitan areas and London will produce unitary development plans as stated above. The participatory procedures build upon those which covered pre-existing schemes. In structure (county) and local plans first, before they were submitted to the Secretary of State, the local planning authority was required to "take such steps as will in their own opinion secure" adequate publicity for their survey in connection with the plan and their proposals, that the public is informed of opportunities to make representations and that there are suitable opportunities for such. These have to be considered by the authority. The grave procedural deficiencies in these steps from the point of view of effective participation have been detailed by McAuslan.[118] The "Examination in Public" which takes place in relation to structure plans and UDPs after they have been submitted to the Secretary of State has also attracted much criticism. Local plans can be dealt with at a local inquiry before an inspector appointed on behalf of the authority, though inquiries are not obligatory if there are no objections. McAuslan has claimed that a vague and relatively unstructured procedure such as the Examination in Public would not allow the opportunity to challenge the details of a structure plan in the way that the Greater London Development Plan, for instance, was criticised at a special inquiry held to examine that plan.[119] Procedures at inquiries tend to be more formalised, as noted in the previous chapter. The subject-matter and procedure at an Examination is left, ultimately, up to the virtually unfettered discretion of the Secretary of State, who appoints a person or persons to conduct an examination in public "of such matters affecting his consideration of the plan *as he* considers *ought to be so examined.*" Nobody has a right to be present. Research on Examinations has described the overbearing influence of officials, both central and local, and powerful industrial or commercial interests.[120]

The Government in fact removed in the 1980s many of the provisions concerning participation and publicity relating to alteration of structure plans and local plans and even removed the requirement to hold inquiries into local plans which effectively

118   McAuslan, Note 112 above.
119   McAuslan, *Land, Law and Planning*, chs 2 and 3 1975.
120   Reade, "Town and Country Planning", in M.L. Harrison, *Corporatism and the Welfare State*, 1984.

superseded structure plans where they covered, literally, the same ground. These are not issues which seize the popular imagination as cutting to the quick of democratic ideals; their intricacy would prevent that. But the whole process reveals a considerable diminution of the possibility for public involvement, considerable bureaucratic sensitivity (central government's) to outside (citizen) interference and complete reversal of the tenor of the now far distant Skeffington report advocating greater participation in the planning process by the public.[121] The Government summed up its view on participation after these changes, ironically or cynically, depending on your point of view: "The contribution of the individual citizen and of interest groups to the preparation of structure and local plans remains one of the central features of the development plan system."[122]

General Improvement Areas and Housing Action Areas

The general improvement areas and housing action areas are not new schemes but they are instructive in illustrating the administrator's approach to public involvement. Neither scheme contained details for public participation in the statutes. Instead, details on participation were covered in circulars which are not binding in law. *Public Participation and Information* urged that "authorities should not only develop new channels of communication between themselves and the residents of housing action areas" (which were more run-down areas than general improvement areas) "but should also use local organisations and groups by whom information already passes within communities",[123] though authorities are reminded that the "Act leaves the *manner and amount of publicity to the discretion* of the local authority".[124] *Renewal Strategies* states: "In considering areas suitable for declaration, authorities have the opportunity to see how, in the areas they select, they can, in a practical way, involve neighbourhood councils, associations of residents and tenants, voluntary bodies and the community generally".[125] Details of these two schemes and differences between them have been noted elsewhere.[126]

---

121 Skeffington Report, *People and Planning*, 1968. Royal Town Planning Institute, *The Public and Planning: Means to Better Participation*, 1982, and see Purdue, 1991.
122 DoE Circular 23/81, paragraph 15.
123 DoE Circular 14/75, paragraph 32.
124 *Ibid.*, paragraph 31.
125 DoE Circular 13/75, paragraph 28.
126 McAuslan, Note 112 above.

While of course the details of particular exercises in participation depend upon the attitudes of individual authorities, the record being somewhat mixed,[127] the failure to provide hard statutory machinery to achieve participation has allowed bureaucracy to ride high on the rhetorical wagon of good intent, but to produce little in the way of effective goods where real motivation is absent.

The circulars did no more than encourage what the more aware authorities would have done in any event.

Urban Partnerships, Urban Programmes and Urban Rejuvenation

Lack of formal statutory opportunity for consultation and participation by voluntary and local groups in the urban partnerships, which have gone out of favour with government, and other urban programmes has been referred to earlier, though the DoE has emphasised the importance of consultation with private business in inner city programmes.[128] Earlier studies[129] have detailed the efforts of one city authority in its attempts to involve the community in its urban programme and planning in relation to housing investment programmes. While the study showed what can be achieved if the spirit of democratic involvement is present in town halls, it brought home yet again the anaemic and indifferent quality of our present devices for involving the public in our local state.

The Government's preferred policies now involve Urban Partnership Funds, which use local authority capital receipts and private finance, and City Challenge, which involves conferral of grant on a competitive basis to local authorities in partnership with local businesses and voluntary groups. There is no procedure to challenge non-conferral other than through ministerial correspondence via MPs.[130] "Task Forces" involve civil servants and secondees operating in deprived urban areas aiming to generate local employment and enterprise, and City Action Teams

---

[127] Lambert, Blackaby and Paris, *Housing Policy and the State* 1978; Paris and Blackaby, in Kantor (ed.), "Not much Improvement" *The Governable City*, 1979.

[128] Chambers of Commerce have been used to advise on the channelling of urban grants; see N. Lewis, *Inner City Regeneration* (Buckingham, Open University Press, 1992).

[129] Lewis and Harden, "Law and the Local State", (1982) 5 *Urban Law and Policy* 65.

[130] Letter from the DoE.

bring together civil servants, local authorities, voluntary groups and local communities promoting maximum support for private sector involvement in urban regeneration. The official literature is noticeably quiet on public participation. In the autumn of 1993 the Government announced plans to appoint a series of senior Whitehall officials to co-ordinate urban regeneration policy throughout England, involving several Ministries. The regional director of each office may well report directly to a Cabinet Committee; there are obvious implications for the DoE.

Urban Development Corporations (UDCs) and Enterprise Zones (EZs)

UDCs and EZs are one political response and interpretation as to the best way of resurrecting moribund urban areas. Briefly, the urban development corporation is a public corporation given a large array of statutory powers in relation to housing, planning, and so on and it has a limited life span. It has assumed many local authority functions and is the creature of central government. It presents us with some of the classic issues of accountability of "quangos" (see chapter 4). Enterprise zones are specific zones within authorities where fiscal and administrative controls are relaxed to encourage commercial development.

Urban development corporations (UDCs) are under a duty to prepare a code of practice for consultation with local authorities, with no enforcement provision to ensure urban development corporations comply with their own code. The creation of an enterprise zone scheme can be challenged in the High Court and proposals for such schemes have to be published. Yet nowhere do the statutes refer to consultation, let alone participation with a broader community of interests within the respective areas. In a way it is naive to expect such provisions, as these schemes are seen by their progenitors as exercises in economic and managerial efficiency in which the ideal of public participation is ill placed, if not counter-productive. The London Docklands Development Corporation (LDDC) opened its planning committee to the public but much of its information is commercially sensitive. Board papers and minutes are confidential but public meetings were held in residential areas every six months. All complaints are answered by the Chief Executive or a director, and local councillors and MPs receive a reply within 24 hours. The LDDC was widely criticised for not consulting local interests which were not of a non-commercial nature.[131]

---

[131]   Docklands Consultative Committee 1990.

The two schemes make explicit what has been implicit in the development of local administration for more than a decade and a half. The movement towards more centralised management reflected in the corporate tendencies within local administration, along with greater control over local government by the centre, would be hampered by increased participation, or duties to consult local communities in a meaningful manner. While it is perfectly safe to encourage an aggressive posture in local citizens in terms of shortcomings in service delivery, encouraging citizens to become active in the process of decision-making relating to policy is not afforded a high priority by political overlords in Westminster, unless it is to the latter's advantage. UDCs have been extended to 11 areas.

Under the Leasing Reform and Housing and Urban Development Act 1993, UDCs may act as agents of the Urban Regeneration Agency established under Part III of the Act. This is a non-departmental public body in the form of a public corporation. It will assume responsibility for a variety of grants and take over the work of English Estates – the publicly owned and largest commercial landlord in the UK. It will promote the reclamation and development of derelict, vacant and under-used land and buildings in the UK, especially in urban areas. It will be answerable to the Secretary of State, publish its accounts and annual report and operate on Citizen's Charter lines. It will have considerable powers of compulsory purchase and public land acquisition as well as development control powers and highway connection powers where designated by the Secretary of State. It will operate under guidance from the Secretary of State who will have reserve powers of direction. It is envisaged that the URA will facilitate the development of land within its responsibility, if necessary in partnership with private developers; it will only perform such development or manage estates itself as a last resort.

Rhetoric, even goodwill, is one thing. Achieving meaningful results is another. In a report for the National Council of Voluntary Organisations in November 1992 on the operation of City Challenge it was stated that:

> "Community involvement in City Challenge could lead to the empowerment of local citizens, a better targeting of resources, the development of more appropriate solutions for local problems . . . . However, this cannot be achieved unless there is a shift of resources to enable local communities to participate effectively, and a willingness to change their conventional organisational cultures by local authorities, plcs and the government institutions involved."

Publicity and Information

Information about the existence of complaints procedures is vital. Information for voluntary bodies in participatory exercises is essential – discussion is useless without it. Many of the developments looked at in our local administration have had the effect not of extending discussion and information, but it is claimed, of limiting it. The Official Secrets Act 1989 does not automatically protect local authority information; it is only protected where it happens to fall within one or other of the protected categories under that Act (see p. 38 above). Outside police authorities and forces the application of the Act to local government will be extremely limited; it is concerned with central government information. However, prohibitions on the publication of information have been imposed by central government to prevent political campaigning by authorities.[132]

Without publicly available information, complaints will clearly be harder to pursue. Some good practices do exist among local authorities: pre-franked, pre-addressed postcards for the registration of grievances, information on complaints centres, an information and public relations officer responsible to a Public Information Committee which encourages public participation exercises; detailed public documents and detailed free newspapers were also commonly found which advertise the functions and procedures of the authority.

More generally, the position and roles of local government have become complex and multifarious and remain so, even after a decade and a half of the onslaught of central government. Its role is part judicial, part provider, part entrepreneur, part contract allocator and supervisor. Its developing role has obviously enough increased bureaucratisation and the attendant inevitable information gathering. As local government has become more of an opponent and antagonist and not a universal protector and protagonist, the information which it amasses has assumed a more and more critical role. Central government has exploited these tensions to the full.[133]

Local authorities are big operators requiring highly professionalised and often bureaucratised interpretations of the public

---

[132] LGA 1986 section 2(1) as amended.

[133] In the White Paper on *Open Government*, the Government spoke of a code of guidance for local government, seeming to forget, or at least not adverting to the fact that a detailed statute was passed covering local government in 1985.

interest on an array of issues: personal, commercial, regulatory and strategic. Any body whose responsibilities include such functions will develop sensitivities about and practices to informalise the exercise of its powers – including secreting information. Many commentators and official reports have referred to the practice of "planning agreements" between authorities and developers whereby the authorities hope to achieve a planning "gain" in return for grant of development permission upon certain conditions.[134] Short of the agreement being *ultra vires* or illegal in some other respect, there is little that a third party can do, or little that he is likely to know about if the authority and developer find the agreement mutually beneficial.

It was noted above how legislation has provided public access to local authority officers' reports, to background papers and has further opened up the committee and sub-committee process. The LGHA has created the post of monitoring officer to report on maladministration or breaches of law within the authority and the LGFA 1988 established the post of "Responsible Officer" to report on actual or anticipated financial misconduct within the authority. The LGA 1992 has created legal duties on authorities to publish details of their performance according to nationally determined indicators (see above p. 98) and we have observed some of the provisions in education.[135] Previous duties under the Local Government, Planning and Land Act 1980 to enjoin local authorities to publish information about performance were regarded as a dead letter by authorities and, it seemed, by the Government.[136] Present intentions seem far more serious on the part of government. However, they occur when local government has been downgraded. It is ironic that local government is opened up and made more transparent when central government

---

[134] J. Jowell (1977) 30 CLP 63; Property Advisory Group, *Planning Gains*, 1981; DoE Circ. 22/83 and *Richmond Upon Thames LBC v Secretary of State for the Environment* (1983) *The Times* 16 May. The agreements are made by undertaking, contractual or otherwise, or under section 106 of the Town and Country Planning Act 1990.

[135] Previous provisions which have been concerned with the "establishment, discontinuance and alterations of schools" by LEAs under sections 12 to 16 Education Act 1980 have afforded the opportunity, Meredith argues (1984), for the then Department of Education and Science to achieve a "deeper direct involvement" in the restructuring of schools against LEA wishes and have allowed very little real opportunity for parents to participate in reorganisation. Parental governors are now mandatory by law in the case of state schools. On opting out provisions and participation, see Note 85 above.

[136] See Note 97 above.

no longer sees it as a major player in contemporary government and has transferred many of its responsibilities to what are commonly called "quangos".

Conclusions

Too many authorities had relied upon a representative mechanistic form of government to justify their existence and had not taken the necessary steps to involve local communities in decision-making or to provide responsive grievance procedures. Consequently, they became an easy victim of a centralising onslaught. When the attack came they were often wanting in popular support and goodwill. There is a bigger story of fiscal and expenditure crisis of the state, of the draining effect of the redistributive tendencies of local government on public enterprise.[137] Parliamentary supremacy has been put to a ruthless job; the redistribution of power to central government and its quasi-governmental companions has considerably weakened the democratic base of this country. Without a strong local government, that precarious balance of power so necessary in our unwritten constitution lies enfeebled. But local government, like central government, must realise that precious though the ballot box is, it must be supplemented by more developed accountability devices.

---

[137] But one should bear in mind that the cost to the taxpayer of the poll tax and its compensation provisions and the cost of introducing the council tax was £14.75 billion and £6.25 billion respectively – the direct responsibility of central government. No equivalent of sections 19 and 20 LGFA 1982 – the surcharge provisions covering local government members and officials – exist for central government and its employees.

Chapter 4

NON-DEPARTMENTAL BODIES, PUBLIC CORPORATIONS AND QUASI-GOVERNMENT

As government intervened more pervasively into the affairs of civil society, it found it increasingly convenient to effect its intervention indirectly; that is, not by establishing a government department with a Minister at its head who was responsible to Parliament, but by creating or using non-departmental bodies operating locally, as well as local government, to assist in government and regulation. The 19th and 20th centuries saw a centralisation of power in central government and also witnessed a proliferation of non-departmental bodies, the latter constituting one of the chief causes and effects of what has been termed the "compenetration of state and civil society". This describes that stage of social organisation in advanced capitalist societies where the division between the realm of the public and the official, and the private spheres becomes impossible to discern.[1] "Quasi-government" refers to the process whereby a government resorts to non-departmental and non-elected bodies to implement its policies, regulate activities on its behalf, to help deliver essential services, or to manage its, or regulate others', commercial interests. Contracting out and marketisation are variations on a theme rather than a whole-hearted transfer of state responsibilities to the "pure" private realm. Even privatisation involves significant state oversight and regulation of privatised concerns.

After various introductory comments, I will look specifically at the institutions which the Government has provided to act as watchdogs for the consumer interest and as complaints mechanisms for the consumer against privatised industries. The argument will be advanced that, as in the case of the nationalised industries, the Government has not made satisfactory provision of procedures through which individuals may make complaint about the services or activities of the industries although these latter have a fundamental impact upon our lives. The Competition and Services (Utilities) Act 1992, following the Citizen's Charter

---

[1] Poggi, *The Development of the Modern State*, 1978.

initiative, has made some contribution to consumer protection, but even after this legislation such protection is still largely seen as a feature of regulation which may have objectives which are at odds with consumer protection. I will move on to make some general points about the range of institutions discussed in the next section and I will pick a representative sample of bodies to illustrate particular points to conclude the chapter. This is a selective approach as the range of institutions is beguiling in its enormity, variety and resistance to classification.[2]

Definition of Terms

In 1981, the now defunct Civil Service Department (see now Office of Public Service and Science) drew up guidelines for government departments on the creation and control by a Minister of non-departmental public bodies (NDPBs). These were updated in 1985 and 1992. The 1992 guidelines state that "justification for all public functions, and the resources committed to them, should be reviewed on a regular basis".[3] We have to be clear that the concern of these guidelines is with those bodies created by the state, making them emanations of the state, as opposed to those "private" bodies used by the state to achieve policies or service delivery. There is, therefore, a concern with delegation of power and independence and ministerial accountability for the bodies' actions, together with the appropriateness of choosing an NDPB or whether the task should be privatised or contracted out. Further concerns relate to the need for regular comprehensive review of NDPBs to see whether their continuation or winding up is necessary. The guidelines exclude certain kinds of NDPB from their purview, especially commercial bodies, although NDPBs perform the following functions: commercial, executive and administrative; judicial, namely tribunals (see chapter 2); and advisory.

Bodies, both within and outside the guidelines, are established by:

(1) Act of Parliament where constitutionally necessary, for example, public corporations for nationalised industries or commercial regulators (Independent TV Commission) – the privatised industry regulators it should be emphasised are non-Ministerial Departments of State – or, for example,

---

2   P. Birkinshaw, I. Harden and N. Lewis, *Government by Moonlight: The Hybrid Parts of the State* (London, Unwin Hyman, 1990).
3   Cabinet Office, HM Treasury, 1992, paragraph 1.1.2.

to transfer the assets of the Bank of England into public ownership, Bank of England Act 1946;

(2) Incorporation under the Companies Acts (either directly or by share acquisitions or by a company limited by guarantee);[4]

(3) Royal Charter, which is a "prestigious" way of acquiring legal personality reflecting the "high status" of the body concerned: BBC; Arts Council; British Council; Research and Sports Councils; the Bank of England is a corporation under Royal Charter, though appointments to it are effected by statute, and see 1 above; "old", as opposed to new statutory universities;

and by various other exercises of the Royal Prerogative:

(4) Royal Warrant – for example, for standing Royal Commissions – but not favoured for executive bodies;

(5) Treasury Minute (University Grants Committee, now replaced by the statutory Higher Education Funding Council, Review Board for Government Contracts);

(6) Informal creation of "shadow organisations" by the Minister before a proposed statutory body has been given official statutory authorisation (the PCA was established on this basis and a more recent example is the Broadcasting Standards Council);

(7) Pure administrative *fiat* (for example, for advisory or *ad hoc* bodies); Ministers should consider whether an answer to a Parliamentary Question should announce the body's creation.

As we shall see in chapter six, the status of a body may help to determine whether its decisions or actions are subject to judicial review under RSC Order 53, although the position has become more flexible in this regard since the *Datafin* decision.[5] The guidelines advised that new members of such non-departmental bodies ought not to be civil servants of the Crown, although they may be served by civil servants in the case of tribunals and advisory bodies, and that these bodies should not usually be Crown bodies. There is detailed guidance on Next Steps provisions and the Citizen's Charter applies to NDPBs (see chapters 1 and 2) as well as the role of the Parliamentary Commissioner where there are complaints against an NDPB. Many NDPBs were and are added

4 *Ibid.*, paragraphs 3.2.11 and onward.
5 [1987] 1 All ER 564.

to the PCA's "scheduled bodies"[6] which he may investigate (see chapter 5) where they satisfy certain criteria:

(1) the body must have administrative functions directly affecting an individual or group;
(2) the body must have been created
 (a) by statute directly;
 (b) by Crown Prerogative instrument;
 (c) by a Minister of the Crown pursuant to an express statutory power;
 (d) by or on behalf of a Minister of the Crown;
(3) it must be financed wholly or mainly by revenues voted directly by Parliament;
(4) some or all of its members must be appointed by Her Majesty or any Minister of the Crown or government department.

We should also note that our range of discussion is not confined to bodies established by any of the methods above, which make them in some sense "*official*". The official discussion is merely the starting point in our tour of quasi government.

In 1979, the new Conservative Government was intent on reducing the number of NDPBs and with that aim in mind it established a review under Sir Leo Pliatzky.[7] The review did not cover all public sector bodies – "a single comprehensive review of this whole field" was "impracticable". Many of the more obvious candidates were excluded, including nationalised industries, other public corporations, NHS bodies, universities, the judiciary and certain professional registration bodies. Even so, the bodies listed covered 48 pages of small print! Sir Leo Pliatzky's suggestions for winding up were minimal – a decimation would present problems for governability. Nonetheless, a significant number of NDPBs have been culled from an estimated 2,167 in 1981 (including the White Fish Authority) to 1,412 by 1993. However, 1992 saw an increase in such bodies over 1991 and even more significantly, many new bodies have been created in crucial and strategic positions for the delivery of governmental programmes, for example, hospital trusts in the NHS, Training and Enterprise Councils, Housing Action Trusts, the Funding Agency and education associations in education and Urban Development Corporations and

---

6 In the first year of the extended jurisdiction of the PCA over NDPBs, 18 complaints were referred from such bodies (Harlow and Drewry, 1990, at 753).
7 Cmnd. 7797, 1980.

the Urban Regeneration Agency to name but a few. It has been pointed out that there is no local democratic control over such bodies and safeguards such as Access to Information legislation, let alone elections or public meetings, do not apply to them. Appointments are by the Secretary of State, and declarations of interest do not always have to be made, and ministerial responsibility is unlikely to extend to the actions, policies and shortcomings of such bodies – in short, quasi-government should be a supplement to democratic control, not a replacement for it.[8] It has been estimated that by 1996, between 20 and 25 per cent of public expenditure will be spent by such bodies. Other reports put the number of NDPBs at over 5,500 spending up to one-third of public expenditure (Charter 88, 1994).

Non-departmental bodies are often referred to as QUAN-GOS, an acronym for quasi-autonomous non-governmental or-ganisations, or QUAGOS which *are* governmental yet quasi-autonomous institutions. A variation for local government called QUALGO has not caught the popular imagination as have the former two. The point has been made that these widely used acronyms are virtually meaningless. Barker[9] has provided the following gradations which are useful, though contestable:

(1) *Government departments* as described in chapter two; Next Steps Agencies (NSAs) are an emanation of classic depart-ments.

(2) *Governmental bodies* – established by one of the devices outlined in the 1992 guidelines; membership appointments made by the government inevitably on the advice of the Public Appointments Unit of the Cabinet Office; Excheq-uer funding; varying levels of civil service or Parliamen-tary supervision, control or accountability. These include bodies hived off by government departments and depart-mental agencies where responsibility to Ministers for man-agement is intended to be different from the department itself. Although NSAs (see chapter 2) would tend to fall within this categorisation, they are best treated under (1) though that raises more questions than it resolves. It is not difficult to imagine other awkward cases; for instance the regulatory agencies regulating privatised industries are non-ministerial government departments.

8   Stewart, 1992.
9   A. Barker (ed.), *Quangos in Britain: Governments and the Networks of Public Policy Making*, 1982.

(3) *Semi-private bodies* – a body not established by or dependent on the state for its existence but in a significant relation to it for the making and application of government policy or provision of services (Building Societies Association (not to be confused with the Building Societies' Commission); housing associations; National House-Building Council; National Federation of Housing Societies; the CBI; Institute of Directors, or, in former years, the TUC; or the London Forum, promoting inward investment in the capital.

(4) *Private organisations* or "the surrounding society as a whole". About these, I will have little to say.[10]

This is a categorisation which offers a useful starting point, albeit a somewhat simplistic taxonomy which would require detailed qualifications in a more extended paper.[11] It will provide a working guide for present purposes. The questions we are concerned with are: What kinds of accountability exist and should exist?[12] Are the procedures and processes adopted by such a wide variety of bodies as fair and open as is desirable in all the circumstances? Are there effective means for gaining redress of grievances? The general point will be made that the array of devices which operate is woefully inadequate for forms of redress or for participation by interests apart from the most powerful or influential, a theme emphasised by the fact that the bodies in question are not elected, but appointed, selected or approved, usually by Ministers. Where, in addition, the PCA has jurisdiction over a NDPB or other body, it will be under the access provisions of the White Paper on *Open Government*.[13] The vast majority of the bodies constituting quasi government are not so covered.

---

10 Birkinshaw *et al.*, Note 2 above. See Cawson (1985) and Streeck and Schmitter (1985).

11 I. Harden, "A Constitution for Quangos", (1988) Public Law 27; N. Lewis, "Regulating Non-Governmental Bodies: Privatization, Accountability and the Public-Private Divide" in J. Jowell and D. Oliver (eds), *The Changing Constitution* (Oxford, Oxford University Press, 1989).

12 Barker, citing Hague *et al.* (1975), mentioned vertical accountability (upward accountability to government); downward to clienteles by, for example, participation or grievance redress; horizontal to peer groups. Accountability may be *ex ante*, *ex post* and "process accountability" (monitoring of work and performance). See Law Reform Commission of Canada, *Independent Administrative Agencies*, 1980 and 1985 and *Parliament and Administrative Agencies*, 1982.

13 Cm. 2290, 1993.

Why Are Non-Departmental Bodies Resorted To?

Non-departmental bodies can be useful ways of facilitating government by utilising experts and advisers without employing them as civil servants. They can operate in highly politically charged areas over which a government department might assume responsibility but which are felt to be too contentious or sensitive to be under the aegis of politicians and party politics – such might be race relations, arts subsidies, university financing or funding an industry. This use is described as the buffer theory. They can be established to placate demands of pressure groups in a particular area, so that the government can appear to be doing something although the body in question will be starved of appropriate resources, powers or procedures to achieve its statutory aims effectively – many claim the Commission for Racial Equality and Equal Opportunities Commission, or the Health and Safety at Work Executive illustrate this practice. A particular activity may require sensitive and independent judgment which it may be inappropriate to hand over to courts or specialised tribunals. A body may have to perform a variety of regulatory, supervisory, advisory or adjudicatory functions in a particular field of administration, requiring a high degree of expertise and a broad range of skills. Using non-departmental bodies may be a convenient device to avoid control and accountability for decision-making or to achieve irreconcilable political ideologies;[14] or to spread more broadly the base of power. They can be used as an effective means to "get the business done" without labouring under the constraints which are imposed on departments of state. They can be used as surrogates for the state, particularly attractive to a government anxious to "return" to the private sector those tasks which are ill-suited to the public sector and for which an NDPB may be a convenient stepping stone.

The State in a Modern Economy

Over 20 years ago Wolfgang Friedmann[15] described the tasks of the state in a mixed economy where there is a mixture of

---

14 To achieve state intervention or to withdraw from state intervention; Davies, *What's Wrong with Quangos?* 1979, says that the ambivalence derives from the "quasi-governmental" nature; see also Hague, McKenzie and Barker (eds), *Public Policy and Private Interests: the Institutions of Compromise*, (1975); or to achieve party hegemony, see – in a polemical spirit – the Labour Party's: *Quangos & Political Donations to the Tory Party*, 1993.

15 W. Friedmann, *The Rule of Law in a Mixed Economy*, 1971.

private and public enterprise – and it is worthwhile remember-
ing that, although as I write we have witnessed over a decade
of privatisation so that state holding by way of ownership and
enterprise has been diminished substantially, state influence and
activity in the market place is still crucial in employment and
public contracts, in strategic support and regulation, in guarantees
and business promotion. Friedmann described the functions as
the regulation of the economy and industrial relations, allocation of scarce and collective resources, regulation of potentially
dangerous activities, and regulation of race relations and equal
opportunities, to name but a few. One would add environmental regulation. Regulation can be achieved by a department directly or via an agency or quasi-independent body appointed by
Ministers or by central government, allowing a degree of autonomy and self-regulation to particular institutions such as financial markets, the Press, professional bodies and, to a decreas-
ing extent, Trade Unions.[16] The state is further identified by
Friedmann as a provider through its social welfare, health and
educational programmes. The state is also an entrepreneur. It
seeks to maximise profits in its provision of essential and basic
services, or to minimise cost by enhancing competition even if
it no longer actively seeks ownership of business and commercial
interests and nationalisation of strategic industries.

The state is an umpire. It establishes the bodies to adjudicate in
disputes, to regulate and arbitrate according to a body of precepts,
principles, rules or exigencies to settle disputes. Limitation upon
what the courts could achieve led to the widespread creation of
tribunals. General statutory complaints mechanisms might also
fall under this head.

We might also add that the state is a protector through its
provision of armed services and police forces and a prison regime,
and in its control over immigration. In fact, these latter roles of
the state are given pre-eminence in the political philosophy of
the right in the Conservative Party which espouses the notion of
"The Strong State" to protect property interests or to reassert
basic values, hand in hand, ambivalently, with "The Minimal
State" which purports not to intervene in economic affairs. Such
an ambivalence has survived the post "Cold War" world.

To a greater or lesser extent, the contemporary state is involved
in making effective the above tasks, either directly or through
encouragement of others whether as a partner or a contractor.

---

[16]   Although Trade Union representatives were invited to No. 10 Downing St.
in November 1993 for the first time in over a decade.

As a fact of our political existence, successive governments have found it convenient to rely upon bodies shortly to be described to assist in the various tasks just outlined. This has been problematical for a variety of reasons.

First, there is an increased and increasing risk of internal conflict within the state apparatus when the state engages in such a variety of roles. The state as umpire, for instance, may clash, unsurprisingly, with the state as entrepreneur, or the state as regulator may clash with the state as provider or protector.[17]

Secondly, the above processes assisted and accompanied "corporatism" – a system of government organisation and control which brought with it particular problems for legitimation of public authority and power. I must briefly describe why this concept is still important even though it has faced official condemnation in the UK since 1979. Indeed one of the worst things Mrs Thatcher could call Mr Heseltine in their uneasy relationship was a "corporatist".

Corporatism

Corporatism is characterised by, *inter alia*, mutual agreement between interest groups in the private sphere such as employers, the professions, consumers or suppliers of services, business associations, banking, insurance and commercial groups, charitable groups and the government. Formerly, trade unions would have been accorded a central position of influence in what was often a three-way dialogue between government, representatives of capital and labour. The government bargains not to regulate the affairs of the particular interest groups directly, but to allow a degree of self-regulation in return for mutual accommodation and support. It can involve an effective delegation of public power to private groups.

Corporatism takes many forms, but along with the basic features outlined above may be increasing state direction of

---

[17] The confusion over energy policy is a case in point; in water the National Rivers Authority has clashed with the Office of Water Supply over "highly misleading" statements concerning water prices being driven up by water quality standards, *The Guardian* 7 April 1993; C. Veljanovski, *The Future of Industry Regulation in the UK* (London, European Policy Forum, 1993); see Veljanovski, 1993 at 74 on the confusion between the OFT and OFGAS and the Secretary of State over the regulation of British Gas. As I write, the Secretary of State has rejected MMC proposals for the restructuring of BG, *Financial Times* 22 December 1993.

the economy to avoid the vicissitudes of unregulated market competition. Corporatism as a form of social organisation differs markedly from competitive market capitalism. In the latter mode of production, the central features are, in theory, a limited state, a clear separation between the public and private sectors – sectors which corporatism helps to confuse – a neutral and autonomous body of law and a free and open market in which private individuals exchange their privately produced goods or commodities or services. It has been persuasively argued that throughout 20th century Britain – and this merely built upon previous developments – corporatism effected a movement from government by law to government by administration.[18] The extent of state control and exercise of power was not made explicit in law, but had to be located in Circulars, Codes of Guidance, Planning Agreements,[19] informal bargained relationships and consultative processes, ministerial letters and internal departmental rules. Law has long since undergone a transformation so that it is no longer an autonomous device to control government, where that is possible in our constitutional theory, and help establish along with universal franchise and market mechanisms the basis of state legitimation claims. It became a tool to achieve specific ends; to be used increasingly instrumentally, that is, for partial purposes, to such an extent that the Rule of Law ideal itself, the control of political power by an independent body of law, became undermined. Law became a tool of government, not a means of controlling government. There is a movement away from the formal institutions of law and politics to informal and administrative *fora* for the making of important governmental decisions. Very often, what *is* happening is not open to public scrutiny or debate and therefore escapes orthodox political or legal forms of accountability.[20] The resort to non-departmental and privately based interest groups/bodies offers further opportunities

---

[18] A little dated but very useful is Winkler, "Law, State and the Economy: The Industry Act 1975 in Perspective", (1975) BJLS 103; see Birkinshaw *et al.*, Note 2 above, for a detailed institutional analysis and reading list.

[19] These took the form of non-legal guarantees by a department – first the Department of Trade and Industry and then Energy – for assistance to a company in return for extensive disclosure to government and, for example, unions on corporate development and activities.

[20] Although not involving an NDPB, for a lack of effective Parliamentary scrutiny of delegated legislation and judicial impotence, see *R v Secretary of State for Social Security ex parte Stitt* (1990) *The Times* 23 February and Feldman, (1991) LQR 40.

for governments to control without being seen to control – hospital trusts have been a striking example of this.[21]

It needs to be emphasised that there are good and legitimate reasons why resort has been made to non-departmental bodies. Outright hostility, from whatever direction, is often ill-informed and tendentious.[22] The present chapter will detail pressing concern about the use of non-departmental bodies in a governmental framework which considers itself democratic. Many of the declared aims of the present Government are directly opposed to corporatist tendencies and seek a reversion to pure market capitalism by privatisation of state assets and deregulation of administrative control. Be that as it may, the structure and types of institutions which were the product of the 19th and 20th centuries still remain, and the problems associated with their development, particularly the movement to wholesale delegation of public power and widespread discretion, will still confront those who wish to see democratic ideals given greater realisation. Indeed, the policies of the present Government have exacerbated the problem, as the confusion of public and private power has become more complicated and questions of accountability more difficult to unravel.

While the model of corporatism which saw the trade unions as an incorporated group of central significance in governmental policies relating to industrial peace, wage settlements, health and safety at work, and so on, has been considerably dismantled, we should be far from complacent that corporatism has disappeared. Recent work has detailed how different interests have moved into prominence within the charmed circle, especially finance capital and, to a lesser extent, advisors and philosophers of a free-market, right-wing disposition,[23] and how a different form of corporatism had replaced one in which organised labour had a prominent role and which centred around close relationships between government and leaders of specific commercial, industrial, financial and professional interest groups.[24] More subliminal has been the emergence of "welfare corporatism", whereby interests and interest groups such as the insurance world, private health organisations, building societies and professional groups

---

[21] Insofar as they are dominated by Secretary of State appointments.
[22] See Fulton *Report of the Committee on the Civil Service*, Cmnd 3638 (1968); Holland and Fallon, *The Quango Explosion*, 1978; Stewart, Note 8 above.
[23] Lewis and Wiles, "The Post-Corporatist State", (1984) 11 JLS 65.
[24] Birkinshaw *et al.*, Note 2 above.

attain fiscal and welfare advantages denied to poorer groups, not as a result of *direct* state hand-out, but after informal and sometimes protracted negotiation.[25] Their resultant advantages are not seen as the consequence of public welfare, but as the product of private wealth and private negotiation and thus in some sense apolitical and uncontroversial. Voluntary organisations have often featured in corporatist analyses of contemporary government and late in 1993 a think-tank publication by the Home Office recommended that in future charities should be split into two types: those carrying out services for the state which would retain fiscal advantages and those which would act as campaigners for change, very often responding to grievances from the disadvantaged and disabled, and which would lose the advantages. Regulation through the Charities Commission would go. Dual capacity would not be tolerated.[26] Interestingly, the Government quickly distanced itself from these proposals but a warning signal has been sent.

Privatisation and Deregulation

Privatisation of state assets[27] has included the widespread selling-off of publicly owned industries and shares and de-nationalisation, as well as selling off public sector housing. Deregulation has included the movement towards enterprise zones (see chapter 3), relaxation of planning controls, "free ports", increased opportunity for entry to markets by relaxing licensing in, for example, bus services, and generally encouraging greater competition. Liberalisation has allowed competitors to enter monopoly markets.

The aims of privatisation and deregulation are cumulatively

---

[25] M.L. Harrison, *Corporatism and the Welfare State* (Aldershot, Gower, 1984); A. Cawson (ed.), *Organised Interests and the State: Studies in Meso Corporatism* (London, Sage, 1985); C. Crouch and R. Dore, *Corporatism and Accountability* (Oxford, Oxford University Press, 1990). Corporatist work had shown how special relationships had developed between water authorities and major user groups pre-privatisation; a recent study has shown how the water industry and regulator have made domestic users pay to clean up pollution caused by industry and farmers to comply with EC regulations: *Water Pollution from Agricultural Pesticides*, Centre for Rural Economy, University of Newcastle upon Tyne, 1993.

[26] *Voluntary Action*, Home Office, 1993. In June 1994, the Duke of Edinburgh expressed similar views to those in the Home Office paper.

[27] C. Graham and A. Prosser, *Privatising Public Enterprises* (Oxford, Clarendon Press, 1991).

the contraction of the public sector, the expansion of the private sector, decrease of the public sector borrowing requirement, widening of the number of individual shareholders, removing inhibitions to enterprise and the jettisoning of as many public bodies as possible to enhance private enterprise. One of the objectives is the hope that the private and the public sectors will become more easily distinguishable, the latter diminishing in size and significance. It has been plausibly argued that such developments will not unequivocally separate the two sectors, but may well increase the opportunity for informal networks and relationships to develop between them, even in the absence of formal regulatory mechanisms.[28] The methods, for instance, which governments have employed in the past to achieve policies which have relied upon the power of the public purse and placing of government contracts without appropriate scrutiny from Parliament have been well documented.[29] In the United States a great deal of attention has been devoted to the methods whereby large private corporations render the government favourable to the interests of the former and whereby the United States government and its agencies effectively delegate to private interests policy-making of a public nature.[30] Where the federal government relies upon regulatory agencies to regulate the private sector, there are well-catalogued studies of the agencies being "captured" by the interests they are supposed to be regulating. The Administrative Procedure Act (1946) of the United States and judicial interpretation of that Act, and the Freedom of Information and open government laws have sought to protect procedurally and fairly all interests within these informal and *ex parte*[31] developments. Many of the bodies I am going to examine in the United Kingdom are involved in management or regulation on behalf of

---

[28] Lewis and Harden, "Privatisation, De-regulation, etc.", (1983) 34 NILQ 207.

[29] Ganz, *Government and Industry*, 1977; Daintith, "Legal Analysis of Economic Policy", (1983) JLS 191; It is interesting to note the emergence of "planning agreements" in local government whereby authorities are offering financial assistance to firms who sign such agreements. See Local Government and Housing Act 1989 Parts III and V on local authority companies. See Lewis (1992). On quasi-government in local government see Cousins in Barker (ed.), Note 9 above.

[30] Smith and Hague (eds), *The Dilemma of Accountability in Modern Government: Independence versus Control*, 1971; Smith (ed.), *The New Political Economy: the Public Use of the Private Sector*, 1975; Hague *et al.*, *Public Policy and Private Interests: The Institutions of Compromise*, 1975.

[31] Which means with only the party pressing a point or special pleading being present in discussions with the government representative.

the government and therefore in some respect on behalf of the "public interest". This chapter will attempt to show how they have inevitably performed their duties in an undemocratic and unaccountable manner – the consequence being the subjugation of politics and a resultant "failure to identify and to facilitate public goals".[32] It is idle to suppose that terminating the life of non-departmental bodies which perform regulatory or managerial tasks, or privatising industries or utilities and returning them to a "neutral" framework of an open competitive market will reduce the degree of state influence in the private sector. Not to regulate private utility monopolies would be political suicide – the question is the appropriate form of regulation. The private/public interface will continue but under circumstances which will become more covert and secretive, more informal and negotiated than what they replaced.

The Public Corporation and Quasi-Government

The public corporation device has been a remarkably useful mechanism by which governments have been able to pursue diametrically opposed policies, for example, public monopoly ownership (Nationalised Industry boards) and marketisation; privatisation and de-regulation (urban development corporations and the Urban Regeneration Agency) and regulation (Civil Aviation Authority, Independent Television Commission and so on). The history of nationalisation offers some interesting insight into the use of a public corporation to achieve public ownership; and the problems created by governmental use of such bodies has outlived the demise of nationalisation as a government policy. The general pattern of public ownership in the United Kingdom has been to vest the assets of an industry or utility in a public corporation. This is not an agency of the Crown,[33] although various statutory powers and duties are attached to it. Power of appointment to the boards of public corporations tended to reside in ministers, and exclusively so in the case of nationalised industries. Herbert Morrison, whose influence on the programme of nationalisation was crucial in the UK, emphasised not only the board's commercial responsibilities but also its wider social responsibilities. The board was not merely engaged in "capitalist business"; the board and its officers must regard themselves as

32   N. Lewis, Note 11 above.
33   See *Pfizer v Ministry of Health* [1963] 3 WLR 999.

the high custodians of the public interest.[34] There were serious
ambivalences in these dual approaches which were never resolved
and which related to the lack of an appropriate public law framework to capture the relationship between a minister and the board
of a nationalised industry[35] and, for example, protection for the
consumer.[36]

More to the point for present purposes, the public corporation
is an empty vessel into whose shell may be poured any legal
content; given the history of the use of the public corporation
this is usually with a view to enhancing the opacity of governmental activity. This does not facilitate the effective resolution of
grievances or participation by those on the "receiving end" of the
boards' activities.

Boards' Duties and Relationships with Ministers

However, points of wider significance than those concerning
nationalised industries are exemplified by the boards' relationships with Ministers. The duties of each corporation are set out
in separate statutes, though there were, in the case of nationalised
industries, plans to unify these in one statute. The 1976 NEDO
report on NIs stated, "They are usually described in general terms
with little guidance on relative priorities or means of reconcilia-
tion when conflicts arise", for example, whether to be profitable
or simply "break even" in the case of nationalised industries or
whether there should be strong governmental control or influence
over the activities of a board of a public corporation when it is a
regulatory authority, as in the case of the Civil Aviation Authority (also a nationalised industry) or National Rivers Authority
– ambiguity is a feature which exists in fact in the case of the
regulators of the privatised industries (see pp. 153 *et seq.* below).
The ambiguity of the statutes reflects much of the inherent conflict
in the purposes of nationalisation (and, it has been argued from
the right, subsequent programmes such as privatisation[37]) and

---

34   Morrison, *Socialisation and Transport*, 1933.
35   A.J. Prosser, *Nationalised Industries and Public Control* (Oxford, Blackwell, 1986).
36   P. Birkinshaw, *Grievances, Remedies and the State (1st edn)* (London, Sweet & Maxwell, 1985), ch. 4.
37   *But Who will Regulate the Regulators?* Adam Smith Institute, 1993.

often renders the statutes for all practical purposes non-justiciable before a court of law.[38]

The Morrisonian concept was widely seen as representing an "arms length" relationship between the corporation and the government which characterises relationships in other Board/Minister associations. Ministers were given power to issue general directions, but the day to day management was to be the concern of the board. Ministers, however, have preferred not to direct NIs formally to comply with wider political objectives, but to impose influence by informal means: "government by nudge and fudge", according to Sir Peter Parker, former board chairman of British Rail, although there are examples of formal ministerial direction.[39] Litigation and practice would suggest that the degree of ministerial intervention has been really quite substantial in the case of public corporations running industries,[40] in the case of the Bank of England and its regulation of finance[41] and in the case of a privatised industry which was forced to take British Coal on terms which amounted to it subsidising a nationalised industry.[42] Ministerial interference may occasionally be dramatically illustrated,

---

[38]   *Charles Roberts and Co. v British Railways Board* [1965] 1 WLR 396; though see *British Oxygen Co. v South of Scotland Electricity Board* [1959] 1 WLR 587 (HL). Note also *Booth and Co. Ltd v National Enterprise Board* [1978] 3 All ER 624. Statutory duties have been expressly excluded from judicial review in some cases, and because they are couched in exhortatory language are not usually susceptible to judicial review in others. In *Booth* the plaintiff had an interest which was specific enough to test by litigation where there was an alleged breach of duty. There will doubtless be more chance of judicial review of such duties under the revised Order 53. See chapter 6. The London Electricity Consumer Consultative Committee has argued that the Government's use of Financial Targets and External Financing Limits to achieve wider economic objectives, namely, the increase of the price of electricity by 2 per cent to achieve a reduction in the public sector borrowing requirement was outside the powers of the Electricity Acts 1947 and 1957; (1983–84; HC 215. ii, at 57 to 59). In July 1993, the POUNC (see below) accused the Treasury of financing the losses accruing to Parcelforce through excessive charges and profits elsewhere in its services.

[39]   *Brind v Secretary of State for the Home Department* [1991] 1 All ER 720 (HL).

[40]   *BSC v Granada TV* [1982] AC 1096; *Air Canada v Secretary of State for Trade (No. 2)* [1983] 1 All ER 910 (HL).

[41]   The Bingham Report on the BCCI collapse (HC 198 1992/3) found no evidence of ministerial involvement in the bank's supervision; on recommendations for greater independence for the Bank from political interference, see the Treasury and Civil Service Committee's *Role of the Bank of England*, HC 666 (1992/3).

[42]   The end of the "subsidy" precipitated the collapse of the coal industry.

as in the summer of 1994 when the Government intervened to prevent Railtrack settling a pay dispute with signalmen.

Powers of Secretaries of State in relation to the regulators of privatised industries have increased chronologically in the first three major privatisations. Under the Telecommunications legislation, directions to the DG do not have to be published, and in electricity he can veto any licence modification agreement made between the DG and a company. Needless to say, Parliamentary oversight was grossly deficient and in the case of the NIs and commercial bodies (BBC, ITVC) the Comptroller and Auditor General does not have powers of audit. The "arms length" relationship between Ministers and boards posed obvious problems in relation to effective Parliamentary oversight, and government limits on borrowing – or indeed financial targets – had crucial importance for prices which were beyond effective consumer challenge, a position which many regard as little changed in the case of privatised utilities (see below). Generally, the statutory duties of public corporations are couched in exhortatory language and do not create legal rights for individuals, although the development of judicial review may well facilitate opportunities for legal challenge.[43]

The creation of an Ombudsman for NIs was consistently denied by government, though the introduction of such was supported by Justice.[44] A frequent complaint has been that the monopoly or near monopoly position of NIs has created both a power akin to taxation by the state in the provision of essential services and unfair competition for competitors. For the latter, domestic law offers little by way of redress, though the impact of European law offers various possibilities.[45] The Competition Act 1980 contains a power for the Secretary of State to refer to the Monopolies and Mergers Commission activities of NIs on questions relating to efficiency and monopoly position, and the anti-competitive practices provisions of that Act apply to public and private bodies.

The government White Paper on *Abuse of Market Power*[46] has made a variety of suggestions for law reform which will affect

---

43　　*R v ITVC ex parte TSW Broadcasting Ltd* (1992) *The Times* 30 March; *locus standi* will present difficulties in many cases; compare the position of the CRE (below) and procedural challenges where there is a feeling of unfairness.

44　　*The Citizen and the Public Agencies* (London, Justice, 1976).

45　　Articles 85, 86 and 90 EC Treaty; *Garden Cottage Foods v Milk Marketing Board* [1983] 2 All ER 770 (HL).

46　　Cm. 2100, 1992.

the remaining NIs. The Government saw the panacea for the consumer and private businessman in privatisation, and a free competitive market. The pursuit of those policies meant that the objectives of the 1976 NEDO Report on *Nationalised Industries* – which had made very interesting recommendations to open up and democratise the running of nationalised industries, albeit along traditional corporatist lines – and the provision of more effective redress procedures for consumers by way of giving greater powers to Nationalised Industry Consultative Consumer Councils (NICCs)[47] were rendered otiose.

Privatisation and the Consumer

Even though the world we face today has changed irrevocably from that of the post-war era when nationalisation was introduced, and the philosophy of the Government could not be more diametrically opposed to that which introduced the welfare state, nonetheless a tradition is being perpetuated in which government seeks to protect its activities and sphere of influence from appropriate forms of public law control. I do not simply refer to control through judicial review, which has made considerable advances since 1977, but to the absence of appropriate procedures to make complaint and introduce the voice of those who remain disorganised and without effective representation against state-created monopolies. The NICCs which represented consumers' interests *vis-à-vis* NIs, which still exist in relation to post and rail and which were developed in the case of British Telecom, were sorry affairs. Cumbersome in organisation, devoid of any powers or influence and largely unknown to the public they were meant to serve, they are a serious indictment of a philosophy that believed once the state bought the industry, the inequities of the market would be removed – if they were, they were only replaced by other inequities. In electricity, for instance, a statutory procedure which existed from 1947 to deal with defects in an area board's general plans and arrangements was not used by consumer bodies until 1978 – largely because the consumer councils were unsure as to its scope and to what extent it could cover grievances. Even where representations were made, the follow-up procedures were anodyne and vacuous. In the case of rail closures covering passenger lines, the economic case for

---

[47] Birkinshaw, Note 36 above.

closure could not be examined.[48] However, a 1982 paper from
the National Consumer Council (NCC) suggested reforms which
would have made consumer representation far more effective,
and recommended developments which anticipated the Citizen's
Charter by almost a decade, for example, setting published standards of performance with a substantial consumer input as well
as performance targets; monitoring the effectiveness with which
industries meet the needs of consumers in terms of both standards
of service and value for money. The NCC also set out recommendations for effective grievance procedures. These were never
realised in relation to industries which remained within the public
sector until the appearance of the Citizen's Charter.

Much of the attention that has been paid to privatised industries
has concerned the mode of regulation and the clashes between
regulators and industries. The regulators are one-person non-
ministerial departments with powers of appointment and as such
they would be more comfortable in chapter two than here. I
apologise for the constitutional solecism, but thematically they are
more at home here. In an industry with a combined pre-tax profit
of £5.3 billion (1990/91), a market capitalisation of £65 billion
(November 1992) and employing half a million people,[49] it is
hardly surprising that major clashes would occur between the
industries and the regulators. Furthermore, in spite of regulatory
regimes which seem to achieve enhanced efficiency and to ensure
the financial security of the industry,[50] competition did not feature
prominently in the privatisation of the industries although the
legislation does refer to the promotion and facilitation of competition and the regulators have emphasised its virtue. Competition
featured prominently in the report of Professor Littlechild on the
privatisation of British Telecommunications.[51] He recommended
a price-capping formula and a system of licensing which would
operate as a temporary measure until competition emerged. In
fact, these temporary measures have become established practice in all the utility privatisations although each one possessed
its own modifications. "The progress of the British privatisation

---

48   Transport Users' Consultative Committees can only make recommendations
     on whether the closure of a passenger-carrying railway line would cause
     hardship or not. They lost the right to consider the financial case for
     closure in 1962. The Government has rejected the case for a Transport
     Users' Consultative Committee for the bus industry. On the position
     post-privatisation see Note 69 below.
49   Veljanovski, Note 17 above, at 2.
50   *Ibid.*, at 15.
51   *Regulation of BT's Profitability*, London, HMSO, 1983.

programme was *ad hoc*, bereft of any coherent plan".[52] This typically pragmatic approach was in fact prompted by political exigencies, negotiation between the NIs to be privatised and Ministers concerning industry structure, and too often an absence of outside independent reports or any attempt to assist or encourage informed public debate. The whole process was characterised by the obsessive secrecy which cloaks our public life.[53]

The consumer was to be protected by a price-capping formula which would control prices for a set interval of not less than five years and which would contain an inbuilt efficiency factor "X". A price increase would allow for the increase in the annual price retail index minus the efficiency factor. Unavoidable costs, the "Y" factor, might be passed on to the consumer and corrections or investment incentives might be incorporated. This would constitute, it was hoped, a non-discretionary control. The formulae are far more simple than their operation in practice and the regulators have had to modify their operation to make them more comprehensive – from the industries' point of view more stringent. The statutes would also provide for a universal service or variations thereon, for example, in the case of gas, BG would "ensure all reasonable demands were met where 'economical'". The statutes also laid out in the barest of terms provisions designed to protect the consumer in terms of supply, price, variety and so on. Details of regulation are contained in the licence (authorisation, interconnection agreements), which may be modified by the agreement of the regulator and industry or, failing agreement, it may be referred to the MMC whose decision on modification is binding but "solutions" are a discretionary matter for the regulator. In the case of airports (all three in London, and Manchester) – which are the responsibility of the CAA – and water, prices may be modified after MMC reference.

Before looking directly at the position of the consumer, I must say a few words about criticisms of the regulatory regimes. First of all the DGs operate largely by negotiation and compromise rather than by formal powers. There are no public hearings on modifications or changes to licences although there are "notice and comment" provisions. Where modification is achieved by negotiation between the industry and regulator, discussions are not made public and other affected parties are not involved. Secondly, the regulators are not co-ordinated to conduct overall investigations

---

52 Veljanovski, Note 17 above, at 9.
53 See, however, Foster, *Privatisation, Public Ownership and the Regulation of Natural Monopoly*, 1992.

into industry operations. This is particularly acute in the field of energy policy where there are still, as of writing, NIs in operation.[54] Furthermore, many powers of the DGs are exercised concurrently with the DGFT and on reference to the MMC. Thirdly, the regulators have been accused of abusing their powers in a variety of ways. For instance, they have promoted competition from a secondary consideration under the Acts (apart from electricity) to an issue of primary importance; they have employed "reasonable rate of return" on capital as a means of limiting profits in addition to the pricing formulae. Last of all, they have been accused of adopting deliberately confrontational tactics and of over-personalising their mode of regulation in a way that goes beyond their personal duty to enforce the law and regulate the industry.[55] On the other hand the formative years of regulators' existence displayed their lack of appropriate powers to obtain information from the industries on vital subjects, and their resources when compared with industries were infinitesimal. Industries were initially very slow to develop, indeed resisted developing published standards of service and performance indicators, a subject now dealt with by the Competition and Service (Utilities) Act 1992 (CASU).

Consumer bodies have also claimed that there are particular problems relating to the representation of consumer interests apropos of the regulators. In the case of representative bodies, there has been a varied arrangement whereby there are bodies separate from the regulator to deal with grievances, the regulator had been given primary responsibility to deal with them or the bodies in question are part of the regulatory office (see below). The division of responsibility between the regulators and the consumer bodies over complaints has caused difficult questions of jurisdiction and the fact that regulators do have to look after a variety of interests of the industries has caused the NCC to question how disinterested the regulators can be in advancing the interests of consumers. Even between consumers there is well-documented evidence to show that domestic consumers have been prejudiced to the advantage of commercial and contract consumers in price modifications.[56]

In relation to the regulators and their pursuit of competition, consumer groups have expressed the concern that while the

---

54   British Coal and the nuclear industry.
55   Veljanovski, Note 17 above. Adam Smith Institute, *But Who will Regulate the Regulators?* 1993.
56   National Consumer Council, *The Gas Industry*, 1991.

regulators have argued that there is a clear community of interest between increased competition and consumer protection, a theme made articulately by a former DGFT,[57] there are other sides to the argument. Competition may advantage large commercial and industrial users because of their ability to pick and choose; this will not be the case with domestic users and small businesses. While competition may move towards improved quality of service, there will be trade-offs prejudicing safety and domestic consumers especially if utilities are broken up: "This feeling is in part created, at least in the minds of consumer groups, by the lack of analysis by regulators as to the distributional consequences of greater competition and what they feel to be the weaker voice that domestic consumers have in the regulatory process."[58] However, it must be remembered that the industries were not restructured prior to privatisation (two electricity generating companies were created along with the state-held nuclear energy industry which has been given permission to compete in the market for the sale of electricity) and that there had been considerable abuse of monopoly position by, for example, the Central Electricity Generating Board in its pricing of electricity. The utilities today still represent either national or regional monopolies on a mammoth scale and the concern of the DGs is understandable. But there is another side to the story.

Looking more closely at the methods for dealing with complaints, the DG is the licence enforcer; this may be implemented through court order but only after becoming a "final" order which requires consultation and procedural safeguards. In telecommunications OFTEL is the body to deal with grievances although we have seen how the DG relies upon the POUNCs and also advisory bodies, some of which he must establish (for the disabled and for small businesses). In the case of gas, the DG investigates enforcement matters which are either the subject of representations or which are referred to him by the Gas Consumer Council. The GCC investigates in its turn matters of a non-enforcement nature and certain complaints not relating to tariff customers which may be within the DGFT's jurisdiction under the Fair Trading Act although it may refer complaints back to the DG where "appropriate". The GCC is established as a separate body under the Gas Act 1986 and it has 12 regional offices. It has to advise the DG on certain matters.

---

57 OFT AR HC 502 1989/90.
58 Veljanovski, Note 17 above, at 45.

In Electricity, consumer committees were established as a part of the DG's office although there is a National Consumers' Consultative Committee. It likewise advises the DG, and the consumer committees deal with non-enforcement complaints. The division of responsibilities, which to an outsider would appear calculated to confuse the consumer, is not adequately explained in the literature of the regulator. Committees have no jurisdiction over prices and the NCC described the scope of consumer representation in the electricity market as "grossly unsatisfactory" given that the committees are appointed by the DG and they may well have conflicting interests, especially between commercial and domestic users where the pricing of electricity differs. Committees are under the Public Bodies (Admission to Meetings) Act 1960 which means that the public may be admitted, but excluded where a confidential item is taken. The past treatment of this provision by the courts has given Chairs the widest of scope to exclude the public even on terms that were in breach of the Act.[59]

Before saying a few words about water, it should be noted that the electricity industry has performance standards set out in a statutory instrument.[60] The regulator has said that the standards are comprehensive but this does not appear to be the case; there is an escape for the industry from performance standards where failure has been caused by external factors. As the NCC has expressed it: the risk is thrown onto the consumer when the industry is best positioned to calculate and insure against the risk. The Competition and Services (Utilities) Act 1992 (CASU) extends the use of statutory PIs to telecommunications and gas. On one further point, disquiet has been expressed by the NCC over electricity disconnections. While numbers had in fact decreased between the years 1986 and 1991, the NCC found a good deal of opacity over the procedures adopted by the industry insofar as they seemed to provide little or no information on distinguishing between those who "won't pay" and those who "can't pay". Duties and details of services are laid out in codes which usually have to be produced after consultation with consumer bodies. However, the record here has been far from constructive and even bodies such as the NCC have been treated somewhat haughtily by the regulators themselves. It should be noted that water and gas consumer bodies have both produced excellent computerised systems for monitoring complaints and assessing their treatment.

---

59 *R v Liverpool City Council ex parte Liverpool Taxi Fleet Operators' Association* [1975] 1 All ER 379, and chapter 3, p. 106 above.
60 SI 1991 1344.

In fact in the case of gas the industry uses the GCC's system to extract information to assist in its enhancement of efficiency in management.

In water, the DG uses the example of service provided by the best water company – there were 39 on privatisation – to act as an incentive to the rest. The National Rivers Authority[61] regulates the environmental pollution caused by industry and agriculture. Consumer affairs are dealt with by customer service committees (CSC). Complaints have increased dramatically in 1990/91 and the DG has been instrumental in achieving better procedures and safeguards in guidance on non-payment of bills. A county court order is required before there can be a disconnection; in 1990/91, 900,000 customers were served with summonses for non-payment of bills. Under the terms of its licence, a company is required to provide detailed information on a variety of levels of service indicators[62] and this information is used by the DG to draw up comparative information on companies' performances. Guidelines are sent out to directors of companies and have included guidance on establishing grievance procedures. As in all the industries, companies are expected to have an opportunity to resolve a grievance before it is handed to the CSC; this requirement for an internal grievance procedure is now placed on industries as a statutory duty following CASU (below). Where they are not resolved by this means, they are usually handed to CSCs unless they contain an alleged breach of statutory duty when they will be dealt with by the DG. From the complaints, CSCs draw information to advise on customers' priorities and on various aspects of policy. The DG has acknowledged that their small size and paucity of number, there are ten covering the areas of former water authorities, may prevent them adequately covering the water companies. Codes have been introduced covering such subjects as disconnections – up a staggering 177 per cent in 1991 – and other matters under the licence conditions. Compensation schemes have been set out in statutory instruments since 1989.

CASU 1992 represents the Prime Minister's commitment to

---

61 The NRA is a public corporation established by the Water Act 1989 Part I and it is under a duty to establish advisory committees for the different regions of England and Wales. The Minister may approve by statutory order a code of guidance for the NRA and water and sewerage undertakers, and under section 146 the Minister may issue directions to the NRA.

62 There are eight, for example, raw water availability; pressure of water mains; interruptions of water supplies; hose-pipe restrictions; response times to billing inquiries; response times to complaints and so on.

placing essential features of the Citizen's Charter affecting privatised utilities onto the statute book. It was considerably amended in its Parliamentary passage to provide greater impetus to consumer interests. Basically, the CASU allows the regulators in water and telecommunications to set compulsory standards of service in individual cases, and in the case of gas, in relation to certain customers. Disputes will be determined by the regulator or his appointee. Regulations for standards will be made after the regulator has engaged in consultation with affected parties, having undertaken research to establish the views of consumers. Overall standards may likewise be set. The means of enforcement differs but it involves legal compulsion. Failure to meet the individual standards of service will result in compensation. Information has to be provided by companies to customers on the operation of individual standards and on compliance with overall standards. There are legal duties to provide regulators with information on compensation and levels of overall service and the regulators must publish information collected by them at least once a year.

Companies must establish their own internal grievance procedures so that there will, in effect, be a three-tier system involving companies, consumer committees and the regulators. The procedures must be approved by the regulator and consultation may take place with committees or at the regulators' discretion on their form; where they are modified no consultation need take place. Anyone requesting a copy of the procedure must be supplied with one by the company. Regulators are given various powers to determine disputes over terms of supply in gas and telecommunications and in disputes over bills in those industries and in the water industry. Regulations will provide details of the disputes procedures. Consumers will be protected against disconnection where there is a dispute, although the position varies. Regulators are given enhanced powers of enforcement, rights to demand information from the industries and must give reasons for decisions in determining disputes. CASU gives the gas regulator powers to refer certain topics to the Gas Consumer Council for preliminary investigation and builds upon that already Byzantine and cumbersome structure.

CASU is a step in the right direction although many of its provisions will have to be implemented by regulations which, as of writing (November 1993), had not been made. Nonetheless, as there is a lack of a body or regulator to take an overall strategic view of the industries, so the absence of an overall independent body with responsibility for consumers is becoming increasingly felt. The Government in the past rejected the case for a NI Ombudsman and the variety and complexity of procedures currently on offer would tax the legal advisers in *Jarndyce v Jarndyce*.[63] This cannot be in the consumers' interests. Furthermore, there is an absence of effective ways to ensure that at the policy level the consumer voice is adequately protected, especially when many of the most important decisions fall outside the ambit of regulators and within the political arena, as in the Government's decision to impose VAT on fuel consumption in its 1993 spring Budget.

Complaints about Public Transport

In the early 1980s, public transport was one of the most frequently complained about areas of public service. Various reports noted widespread public disquiet and the indifferent quality of county council annual transport plans. Transport Users' organisations, *inter alia*, had to be consulted in the making of these plans under the Transport Act 1978 and consultation generally had been described as "disappointing". The plans were often badly produced, frequently changed, covered too large a geographical area, were often considered irrelevant and aroused little curiosity or interest, in spite of complaints about public transport being among the most frequently aired grievances of consumers. The plan-making exercise revealed the usual faults where there is an absence of a duty to report comments received and an inability to insist that councils produce adequate plans. Much criticised though these exercises have been, it is interesting to compare them with the Transport Act 1983 which increased government control over revenue grants paid by metropolitan counties to transport executives. The executives are under a duty to prepare annual plans covering a three-year period concerning proposals relating to the provision of transport services and fares. Nowhere in the statute is there reference to consultation with groups representing consumer interests when preparing plans.

With transport, information on performance criteria was generally poor, particularly in the bus industry, and a draft code of practice published by the DoE in 1981 for bus operators on the provision of information was not circulated to user or consumer representatives. London Transport had a better record than many operators. Transport Users' Consultative Committees only cover trains, and cannot deal with complaints about fares or charges (see above). Transport Commissioners can hear complaints from

---

[63] Charles Dickens, *Bleak House*. See P. Hain, *Regulating for the Common Good* (1994).

the public about bus operators, though this role is even more secluded from public knowledge than comparable functions of other NICCs.[64] There were complaints procedures in the London Transport system for Greater London, as well as for metropolitan county systems, and in fact these authorities featured better than average in NCC reports.

Legislation from 1980 onwards encouraged a greater degree of competition from private operators by easing or restricting regulation by licensing, particularly the abolition of road service licences outside London and the privatisation of the National Bus Company (Transport Act 1985). Deregulation and privatisation have not precipitated greater accountability to the extent that was predicted and have done little to obviate the anachronistic and Byzantine procedures for redress of grievances or to encourage constructive participation in decision-making. There is little publication of the details as to how public bodies spend subsidies and it is as well to remember that private operators are the recipients of public subsidies. Studies have shown that in bus services outside London, competition has not enhanced service information: "the instability and fragmentation of services associated with that competition have often inhibited the development of any up to date, comprehensive information to enable passengers to discover what services were currently available and make a real informed choice".[65] Competition had forced the sale of previously publicly owned common facilities, for example, bus stations, and had seen a significant decrease in facilities off the bus such as bus shelters and toilets and considerable uncertainty about the exact location of unofficial stops, as well as dirty and shabby buses en route. The public have difficulty appreciating which services are the responsibility of local authorities (tendered and subsidised) and which are not (commercial). Traffic commissioners, who under the Transport Act 1985 act under the direction of the Secretary of State, do respond to complaints about the latter, but the feeling was that they do not have adequate resources to keep a close eye on what is happening.[66] They receive few complaints – most people do not know of their existence and there is no clear or publicised channel of access to commissioners, nor are they under a duty to take passenger evidence into account. In London, prior to its abolition, the GLC lost its responsibility for London Transport to London Regional Transport, a non-departmental public body,

---

[64] See, for example, section 4 Transport Act 1985 and holding of inquiries.
[65] C. Cahm and J. Guiver, *Buswatch*, 1988, at 15.
[66] *Ibid.*, at 52.

amid plans to allow greater competition from private transport operators in the metropolis, but without any considered reference to consumer participation or complaints procedures.[67] LRT is a public corporation whose chair and members are appointed by the Secretary of State.[68] The London Regional Passengers' Committee has no power to investigate charges for services or facilities, and only limited powers in relation to railway closures.

The London Underground and British Rail are covered by TUCCs and by Citizen Charter provisions such as published targets, consultation with travellers about service requirements and compensation provisions for late arrival and cancellation. As of writing, privatisation of BR is well under way within a regulatory scheme involving two regulators.[69]

Non-Departmental Bodies and Regulatory Activity

I now intend looking at specific examples of regulation by particular bodies, and I will attempt to explain why, or why not, they offer examples of fair, efficient and open administration. The range extends from public corporations operating in a formal manner to the semi-official bodies in Barker's third category (see p. 141 above). The method of regulation adopted by government over particular bodies or activities will often reflect the degree of trust with which a body or institution is held by government. One political outlook will place faith in the ability of professional bodies, the City or the financial and commercial worlds to regulate themselves – though we should note significant statutory incursions since the 1980s, particularly in the form of grievance redress and the provision of governing rule books dealing with, for example, competition. The same outlook will often distrust forces of labour represented by trade unions, which are seen as posing a threat to national unity and stability without, it is argued, displaying any commensurate sense of responsibility. In this case direct and detailed regulation by legislation and judicial involvement is the order of the day. It serves to remind us that

---

[67] See London Regional Transport Act 1984 sections 40–41 and Schedule 3.
[68] *Ibid.*, Schedule 1 and see section 70(2).
[69] Railways Act 1993. There are the Rail Regulator and the Director of Passenger Rail Franchising. Rail Users' Consultative Committees (RUCCs) are to be established, and a Central Rail Users' Consultative Committee. Decisions on closure of passenger lines are to be made by the Regulator to whom objections may be made. RUCCs "may" hold public hearings. A "person aggrieved" (see chapter 6 p. 262 below) may "refer" the matter to the Secretary of State – there is no further provision for public hearings.

not only is the choice of those areas which require regulation often highly politically motivated, but the *method* adopted by the government is often equally political. A relatively successful mode of regulation will now be examined. It should be noted that the interests it regulates are often powerful and extremely influential.

Civil Aviation Authority (CAA)[70]

It would be hard to imagine aviation, national or international, being free of regulatory controls. Fitness of pilots, aeroplanes and operators; passenger safety; international implications of traffic rights' negotiations to name a few points dictate the necessity. In the United Kingdom the problem has been what kind of regulation, how much, and by whom? Baldwin has presented a convincing argument that the body charged with this task until 1971 – the Air Transport Licensing Board – operated in too judicial and inflexible a manner in its licensing and other functions. Its decisions were frequently overruled by the Board of Trade, thereby creating a good deal of uncertainty for flight operators. The Civil Aviation Authority,[71] which is in fact a nationalised industry, has a wide variety of statutory duties and powers to regulate the aviation industry, realising certain objectives, including securing that British airlines (so far as they reasonably can) provide air transport services satisfying "all substantial categories of public demand",[72] and securing "the reasonable interests of air transport users". It is an "independent" agency of the Department of Trade and Industry, responsible for economic and safety regulation.

It was envisaged that the CAA would regulate, make decisions in a judicial manner in trial-like proceedings and issue policy statements and guidance notes to operators and prospective operators under the ultimate policy guidance of the Minister, who can also issue directions on specific grounds.[73] This relationship envisaged independence for the CAA and exercise of its own expertise in technical matters, while the government retained the residuary power to shape policy after its own political objectives. It has

---

70 Baldwin (1978) 57; (1980) 287 and (1985). The CAA is financed by the aviation industry.
71 Established by the Civil Aviation Act 1971, now Civil Aviation Act 1982.
72 "[A]t the lowest charges consistent with a high standard of safety in operating the services and economic return to efficient operators . . . and with securing the sound development of the civil transport industry in the UK", section 4(1) Civil Aviation Act 1982.
73 In 1989–90, three directions were issued under section 6.

been plausibly argued that this relationship was misunderstood by the Court of Appeal, which saw the CAA as a totally independent judicial body, not a body exercising a subtle blend of administrative, judicial and executive functions under a residuary government direction.[74] Since 1971, the CAA has consistently moved away from judicial hearings to engage in "consultative proceedings in combination with public hearings", thereby producing guides for future licensing decisions. Formal hearings have been used in conjunction with other formal and informal proceedings, and by utilising its research knowledge it has frequently been able to set down its policy for future decisions in some detail, achieving a fair balance between the creation of policy and the exercise of its discretion. The CAA was distinctive because of its combination of functions and skills in a highly technical area – judicial, regulatory, executive and advisory. What was also distinctive was the wide variety of approaches it adopted to suit different decisional *milieux*.

The Civil Aviation Act 1980 abolished the powers of the Secretary of State to issue policy guidance to the CAA. There is still a right of appeal to the Secretary of State from CAA decisions; between 1989 and 1990 there were six appeals, in five of which the CAA's decision was upheld, though the CAA also lost one appeal in 1988/89. There were 32 public hearings related to air transport licensing in the same period. Procedures for the hearings and appeals are contained in the CAA Regulations 1983. The CAA also publishes an Official Record which describes classes of licences and the procedure for applying for a licence, making objections and representations, procedure at public hearings, and so on. Before granting, refusing, revoking, suspending or varying an air transport licence, bodies representing the views of users may be heard as well as environmental groups (if the latter have made objections or representations). The CAA can hear other parties, who have entered an objection, at their discretion. No person shall be heard where the Secretary of State has directed the CAA to grant or refuse *etc.* a licence. Legal representation is allowed; evidence may be presented orally or in writing. At hearings, mutual examination of cases of the interested parties is allowed. Appeals to the Secretary of State cannot be made by the user or environmental bodies, or by parties appearing at the hearing at the CAA's discretion, though all these parties will be served with transcripts of the appeal. Appeals are in writing,

[74]   *Laker Airways v Department of Trade* [1977] QB 643.

"though if heard orally, the other parties at the first hearing would presumably have the right to make oral representation", the CAA believed. New regulations allow for expedited hearings involving decisions and appeals where an anti-competitive practice is alleged under the Competition Act 1980. The trend generally is for shorter public hearings.

The 1980 Act preserved the power of the Secretary of State to issue directions upon specific grounds to the CAA but it also imposed a duty upon the CAA to publish the policies which it intends to adopt in relation to its duties. Prior to the Act, the CAA had published copious booklets outlining its policy intentions, and it engaged in detailed programmes of consultation and research with operators and users to produce such statements. These documents did not constitute "law", yet they helped applicants marshal their cases at the licence application hearings.

There can be little doubt that the record of the CAA is impressive and it has achieved much to provide predictability and consistency of standard in a flexible and dynamic field of administration. There were, however, two perceived problems associated with the removal of the Secretary of State's power to issue policy guidance to the CAA. How was the CAA to be made politically accountable for the exercise of public power? Secondly, if accountability was to be achieved by a right of appeal to the Secretary of State, would the lessons of the Air Transport Licensing Board experience be forgotten? Would there be a temptation for the Secretary of State to overrule the CAA more frequently, causing incoherence and inconsistency where such decisions went against policy statements and research by the CAA? Reversals of CAA decisions are not uncommon given the number of appeals, but certainly not frequent. The danger is that the government will be tempted to achieve its ends by informal pressures and private persuasion, without appropriate public and Parliamentary scrutiny.[75] A powerful committee, for instance, which included the Prime Minister, was established to decide on the outcome of a review by the CAA on the privatisation of British Airways and its impact upon the United Kingdom airline industry.[76]

[75] Especially when, for instance, the CAA was instructed by the Transport Secretary to review completely its airline routes policy after lobbying by private airline operators concerned about the "unfair competition" from British Airways on the latter's privatisation; HC Deb., Vol. 50, cols. 686 to 694, 12 December 1983.

[76] *Airline Competition Policy*, CAA 1984. This recommended divesting British Airways of various routes and the report was felt in many quarters to be below the standard of previous CAA reports.

The CAA in its early years established the Air Transport Users' Committee to deal with travellers' complaints. In recent years this has seen an increase in complaints (10 per cent up in 1992/93 over 1991/92). The increase, the Committee believed, was explained partly by the Citizen's Charter making people more complaint conscious.

The Commission for Racial Equality (CRE)

The CAA has generally been acknowledged as an efficient and effective regulatory body. The CRE has been perceived in some quarters as less successful, though of course it has attempted to regulate human relationships in an area which many still believe is best left to personal choice rather than public opinion or public regulation, and comparison is not really fair, for they are chalk and cheese. The CRE attempts to advance the interests of those groups, members of which have rarely attained standing or influence in public life, and it frequently runs counter to deeply ingrained prejudices, not least in government and governmental bodies.

The CRE is a "multi-faceted" statutory agency of government, combining grievance remedial, advisory, investigatory, promotional and regulatory functions in pursuit of its statutory objectives to eliminate racial discrimination and to promote equality of opportunity and good race relations. The Race Relations Act 1976 was the third legislative attempt since 1965 to tackle the problems of racial discrimination and division. Official publications and the CRE's own researches show that not only is racial discrimination still widespread, if in a more covert[77] form, but that public and government bodies at *all* levels had failed to respond adequately to discrimination and disadvantage of a racial nature.[78] "A major constraint has been a lack of support from government" failing to demonstrate "a firm commitment to equal opportunity", and the Home Office itself has been investigated for alleged discriminatory practice in its immigration control. Its administration and the

---

[77] Although racially motivated assaults are showing an alarming increase: *Racial Attacks and Harassment*, Home Affairs Committee HC 164 1993/4.

[78] For central and local government see the Memorandum of the Commission to the Home Affairs Committee (Race Relations and Immigration sub-committee) 1981–82, HC 46). Reports of the CRE cover the NHS and the Metropolitan Police and Racial Disadvantage (1890–81, HC 424). Also: *Immigration Control Procedures: Report of a Formal Investigation*, CRE, 1985. See CRE *Annual Report* 1992 at 43 and Note 80 below.

system of immigration control were criticised.[79] It is true to say that Central Government has made an effort to improve its position but complaints against departments and local authorities are common – which is not to say justified. There were 294 complaints against local authorities and 94 against departments in 1992.[80]

The CRE has power to conduct formal investigations for "any purpose connected with its statutory duties". These have been described as "general" investigations where there is no allegation of discrimination and "belief" investigations where an individual or organisation is suspected of discriminatory practices and is named.[81] In 1993 the CRE suspended a formal investigation into the Council of Legal Education concerning allegations of discrimination over Bar examinations pending an internal investigation by the Council (*Equal Opportunities at the Inns of Court School of Law*, April 1994, Barrow Committee of Inquiry). It possesses powers to issue non-discrimination notices; to give assistance to individuals seeking redress against unlawful discrimination; to provide grants to bodies promoting equality of opportunity and to conduct research to influence policy. It alone has power to investigate formally allegations of systematic indirect discrimination and to instigate certain proceedings. It also issues Codes of Guidance and has various subpoena powers.

All applications for assistance by individuals are considered by the complaints' committee; if the CRE does not bring the case to the industrial tribunal or county court but leaves it to the individual, the record of success is very poor. It frequently attempts to settle complaints informally, especially in advertising cases where there were 62 complaints in 1992. In the ten years from 1982 to 1992, applications for assistance had increased from 769 to 1,557 *per annum* and assistance by way of representation had been allowed in 345 cases in 1992. It noted that there was a disappointing increase in the number of assisted cases it was losing (17.5 per cent in 1991; 30 per cent in 1992). Where there is a complaint of pressure to discriminate and only in such a case

---

79   *Home Office v CRE* [1981] 1 All ER 865; though see *Amin v Entry Clearance Officer* [1983] 2 All ER 865 (HL). Note 78 above for the report.

80   Liverpool and housing, Cleveland and Bradford and education; *R v Cleveland CC and Sec. of State ex parte CRE* (1993) 91 LGR 193 (CA) section 6 Education Act 1980 and parental preferences; *R v Bradford MBC ex parte Sikander Ali* (1993) The Times 21 October.

81   See Griffiths LJ, *R v Commission for Racial Equality ex parte Hillingdon LBC* [1981] I QB 276.

the CRE may initiate proceedings under sections 30 and 31. Of 39 complaints in this area in 1992, three were proceeded with.

The powers of the CRE to conduct formal investigations have been the object of a great deal of judicial scrutiny. By the end of 1992 it had completed 56 formal investigations. The CRE's procedures are prolix – "So complicated that I will not attempt to explain it", said Lord Denning. Their proceedings are administrative, and though they must be conducted fairly,[82] witnesses cannot be compelled by respondents to undergo cross-examination.[83] The Court of Appeal has held that the whole of the investigatory proceedings can be reopened upon appeal to an industrial tribunal, involving a full rehearing of the facts – even though proceedings had taken four years and the respondent had two opportunities to submit his representations through counsel to the Commission.[84] The House of Lords has held that allegations of direct racial discrimination had to specify the acts in the notice where a person was named, and have insisted upon strict compliance with the preliminary hearing under section 49(4) before the investigation. Section 49(4), in fact, appears to have been the result of a Parliamentary misunderstanding.[85] The judges have inhibited quite drastically an already prolix procedure and have limited formal investigations to two types: "belief" investigations into named persons, and general investigations without such a belief (in 1992 there was one such latter investigation).

These decisions have made much of the "Draconian", "inquisitorial" and "criminal" nature of the allegations, and that accordingly it is only right that the respondent must have the protection of adversarial proceedings.[86] There can be no other expression for it: "judicial hostility" to the CRE has been widespread and not infrequently outspoken. Some of this hostility, no doubt, related to the existence of the CRE itself and its aims; other judges doubtless distrusted the novel framework of an agency created to tackle collective and systemic manifestations of prejudice: by word of mouth, employment opportunities or cultural attitudes,

---

[82] *Selvarajan v Race Relations Board* [1976] 1 All ER 12.
[83] *R v Commission for Racial Equality, ex parte Cottrell and Rothon* [1980] 3 All ER 265.
[84] *CRE v Amari Plastics* [1982] 2 All ER 499. This means an examination and re-examination of *all* the issues of fact on appeal before an industrial tribunal or county court.
[85] *CRE v Hillingdon LBC* [1982] AC 779; *R v CRE ex parte Prestige Group plc* [1984] 1 WLR 335.
[86] Non-discrimination notices can ultimately be enforced by an injunction. The former *per* Griffiths LJ, "condemn".

for instance, but whose procedures differ from those familiar to judges.

If there is a judicial hint that the CRE procedures should be more legalistic and technically precise, then this would seem to have the support of the Home Affairs Select Committee in its 1981/2 report on the CRE.[87] It recommended that the CRE employ more lawyers for complaints' handling and investigations and it placed an unjustifiably high premium on lawyers and legal processes, although the report was published without reference to the cases discussed above. The CRE, it argued, should concentrate on promoting its victories and investigations, rather than on general promotional work which should be the responsibility of the Home Office and local government.[88] The Committee was in fact highly critical of the CRE's commitment to law enforcement *and* promotional work. Judged by "victories", the CRE has not been a notable success.[89] The ambitions of the CRE have also been over-expansive and sometimes in the past incoherent. In its defence can be placed the fact that its weaponry has been ill-conceived and prolix, that there has been widespread antipathy to its existence and techniques and that there has been little attempt by government or Parliament to provide leadership on what is meant by "good race relations". Support from the Government has not generally been forthcoming – it refused to extend legal aid to industrial tribunals on discrimination cases in its reply to the Select Committee, and the Citizen's Charter

---

87   HC 46 (1981–2).
88   Readers are reminded of the number of complaints against these bodies. The CRE was not meant to be a shadow Race Relations Department, believed the Home Affairs Committee. The Home Office itself has been the subject of a CRE formal investigation, and for local government's record on race relations, see Young and Connelly, *Policy and Practice in the Multi-Racial City*, 1981.
89   In the first five years of the CRE's existence it had only completed 10 of its 45 formal investigations. By 1992 (that is, after a further eleven years) it had completed an additional 42. The Government ought on its own criteria to interpret that as enhanced efficiency. For a famous "victory" however, see *Mandla v Dowell Lee* [1983] 1 All ER 1062 (HL) and a wide interpretation of "ethnic". For an appraisal of the CRE and the Equal Opportunities Commission, see Appleby and Ellis, (1984) *Public Law* 236; C. McCrudden, "The Commission for Racial Equality: Formal Investigations in the Shadow of Judicial Review", in R. Baldwin and C. McCrudden, *Regulation and Public Law* (London, Weidenfeld & Nicolson, 1987). On a variety of issues concerning the Equal Opportunities Commission, a body very similar in power and structure to the CRE, see *R v Secretary of State for Employment ex parte EOC* [1994] 1 All ER 910 (HL).

takes little account of ethnic monitoring.[90] Community Relations Councils often had indifferent relationships with the CRE, and new bodies, Racial Equality Councils (RECs), took over from the former. A third of the CRE's funding goes to financing RECs who hand on by far the largest proportion of complaints to the CRE than any other bodies.

The CRE is clear as to how it would like to see its role being made more effective. In a 1983 consultative document, it recommended 10 changes which would, *inter alia*, shift the onus of proof onto the respondent once less favourable treatment has been established, which is a feature of the law in Northern Ireland which saw the introduction of the Fair Employment Commission, which deals with religious and political discrimination in employment in the province;[91] render "indirect discrimination" less technical; impose stronger obligations on *all* public authorities to combat racial prejudice; improve and shorten their investigatory procedures; and create a Discrimination Tribunal, which might prompt the demand for a discrimination commission such as exists in Canadian provincial and federal laws. The CRE has not supported such a development. The Canadian models deal with a far broader range of discriminatory practices, have wider powers than the British commission and exist alongside a Charter of Rights.[92] Reaction to the 1983 proposals from public bodies was generally hostile and the CRE's detailed review of the operation of the 1976 legislation in 1985 and its recommendations have largely gone ignored by government, a point noted in its second review in 1992. As well as repeated calls that the decision in the *Prestige* case limiting the scope of formal investigations be reversed, the 1992 review noted that the Government had refused

---

90 CRE, *Annual Report*, 1992, at 43.
91 Established by the Fair Employment (NI) Act 1989, the Commission replaced the Fair Employment Agency; the 1989 Act also established the FE Tribunal to exercise jurisdiction conferred by the fair employment legislation in Northern Ireland. Section 5 and regulations provide for procedural powers, including discovery and inspection equivalent to a county court – non-compliance with which amounts to a criminal offence – and power to sit in private.
92 Federal and provincial human rights laws, which deal with discrimination, enumerate an exclusive list of discriminatory practices, whereas the Charter is open-ended, and this has caused difficulties in terms of the relationship between the Charter and discrimination laws. The common model in the human rights procedures is for a commission with broad investigatory powers and powers to achieve conciliation and settlement, adjudication by a tribunal or board of inquiry where settlement cannot be achieved and appeal to the courts on points of law.

to hand over to the CRE information on implementation of "equal opportunities proofing", that is, assessment of all legislation and policy developments and vetting thereon. It is unlikely that its recommendations, especially that non-discrimination notices should prescribe changes in required practice from those against whom they are directed and that there should be greater powers to deal with future potential discrimination and enforcement proceedings on behalf of groups, as well as the recommendation that the county court should lose its jurisdiction to an industrial tribunal, will be accepted. It is also seeking a more appropriate definition of "indirect discrimination". The Home Secretary announced in July 1994 that legally binding undertakings would be introduced to remove the need for lengthy investigation, but the compulsory monitoring of workforce composition would not be introduced.

Opponents of the CRE argue that the Commission, in its present role and through its suggested reforms, is attempting to transmute into legal duties what are more appropriately left to moral aspiration. On the other hand, leading human rights lawyers believe that the CRE and EOC[93] are at the forefront of European laws combating discrimination. If that is the case then Europe has a long way to go to match the laws of Canada. One legal reform has been the removal of the limits placed on compensation awards by tribunals under section 56 Race Relations Act 1976 (Race Relations (Remedies) Act 1994).

The Housing Corporation (HC)

The CAA and the CRE both possess a degree of formality and openness in the manner in which they perform their duties. Formality and openness do not characterise the working of the next corporation, not because of any obvious specific intention that these should be absent, but rather because of the unstructured development of the body. The consequence has been a degree of informality which has invariably operated against the general interests of those whom the body regulates, namely, the 2,300 housing associations which provide rented housing and which the Government has resorted to increasingly to replace local authorities as providers of publicly financed housing.

The Housing Corporation (HC)[94] was created by the Housing Act 1964 and gradually emerged in preference to other bodies as

93 Both bodies have been the subject of reports in the 1992/3 session from the Employment Committee: HC 844 and 816 respectively.
94 See HC 466 (1992/3) and Cm. 2363 on the Corporation.

the overseer and registrar of housing associations. These latter bodies date from the 19th century. Finance for associations comes from central government and loans from the HC. Under the 1964 Act, the Corporation had statutory rulemaking powers which are exercised after consultation with the Housing Association Registration Advisory Committee (now HA Consultancy and Advisory Service Ltd). In fact, published criteria were largely ignored in favour of individual bargaining between the HC and associations. Details of the relationship between the Department of the Environment (DoE) and the HC were not spelled out in statute. Nor was the relationship between these two and the National Federation of Housing Associations (NFHA), a representative body of associations which in fact diminished in importance when the HC became the supervisory body of associations at the DoE's instigation. All three bodies have a regional presence. The relationship between the DoE and the HC has little by way of a public or open dimension.

The history of the HC from the early 1970s shows obvious shortcomings in its oversight of associations. There has been an emphasis upon informality of relationship between the DoE, HC and NFHA at central and regional levels. For tenants of shoddy housing, this often resulted in the absence of a forum through which to complain, especially about some repairs which are the responsibility of the DoE. Bad feeling has existed about the allocation of housing units to associations on a generally presumed "grace and favour" basis by regional offices of the HC. The NFHA has achieved some informal improvements at regional level and is pressing for procedural and substantive reforms covering unit allocations and the HC's disciplinary functions, open criteria for HC decision-making and reasoned justification for allocations. There has also been pressure for an internal appeals mechanism for aggrieved associations. The DoE has done little to encourage their development in the past.

The Housing Associations Act 1985 made new provisions for the HC. It acts as the agent of the Secretary of State in relation to grants to housing associations and it must act in accordance with directions which may be issued by the Secretary of State. The HC provides guidance to associations in the form of circulars and one such is the tenants' guarantee. Many of the basic provisions of the Housing Act 1985 which apply to local authority tenants also apply to association tenants (see chapter 3, pp. 117–120). Advice on complaints procedures is given for tenants of associations and the HC was developing an ombudsman role in relation to associations and their tenants. It has power to stop grant and has certain disciplinary powers after a statutory inquiry.

Housing Action Trusts

From the 1980s the Government has encouraged the privatisation of council housing, although in 1991 there were still 4 million houses/flats in council ownership. Housing Action Trusts (HATs) are statutory corporations empowered to take over responsibility for the management of an estate in public ownership. The details behind the setting up of a scheme are contained in the Housing Act 1988. One of the first to be set up was on the North Hull Estate and it provided a complaints procedure involving five stages from the filling in of two Resident Complaint Forms, a Complaints Appeal Form and a Final Complaint Form where the complaint went all the way to the Chairman of the Board. Attendance of the complainant may be requested at the Chairman's hearing or at the full Board although the descriptive material is silent about the right of a friend or representative to attend. On one hand the procedure has a lot to offer, including strict time limits, setting out clearly who makes the decisions and asking the complainant for their views, but conversely it does appear a little too formalistic at all levels and may appear somewhat officious. Others which have been examined emphasise the confidentiality of the complaint and its treatment and that it will be taken seriously. They also spell out what could form the subject of a complaint and that a friend could assist the complainant. They point out that complaints will be used for monitoring of performance. All of this deserves applause, but they are a little thin on detail on what processes would be involved (Waltham Forest).

Regulation of Commercial Broadcasting and Complaints about Broadcasters

Even when a formal statutory body is established to regulate a particular activity by licensing or disposing of franchises, there is often a relegation of wider interests apart from the contracting parties to the sidelines. It might be instructive to look at the ITV Commission, a statutory body charged with the task of regulating television services in the independent sector however delivered, for example, by satellite, terrestrial, cable or microwave technology. A separate authority, the Radio Authority, exists for radio transmission. Both these bodies had been established in "shadow" form before the Act of 1990 conferred statutory corporate status upon them and in fact both had made contributions to the legislation and had provided outline assurances about their operation in the course of the Broadcasting Bill.[95] The ITVC replaced the Independent Broadcasting Authority (IBA) and Cable Authority and administers a more market-oriented system, for licensing commercial broadcasters. Basically, once a quality threshold is established, licences will be allocated on a highest bid basis. Unlike the previous regime under the IBA, there are no duties to hold public hearings before licences are allocated in relation to Channel Three licences, although certain details are published and notice and comment provisions exist.[96] The House of Lords refused to do other than apply a "hands off" form of judicial review when the allocation of licences was made although in the Court of Appeal Lord Donaldson MR asked the ITVC to deliver to the court documents which were used to reject the highest bid. Finding these so seriously flawed, he felt that no regulator could have allowed themselves to be guided by them and gave them the benefit of the doubt![97]

Licences may be subject to general and specific conditions (section 4(6) for the latter) and the Commission may draw up codes on, for example, political impartiality in broadcasting, violence and standards particularly in relation to children, and advertising. By section 10, the Secretary of State is given power to require the Commission to direct licence holders on specified matters. The ITVC is given power of revocation over licences, to impose financial penalties and to shorten the licence period. Interestingly, the Commission is given power to direct a licensee to broadcast a correction or apology or not to repeat a programme. This is not aimed at resolving an individual grievance but at breaches of the licence condition where the service has fallen below standard.

Individual complaints are dealt with by the Broadcasting Complaints Commission (Part V of the Act) which was established under the 1981 Broadcasting Act. Its primary concern is with complaints about accuracy, impartiality and privacy although the principles involved have not been developed by the BCC. Section 144 sets out the procedure. Complaints must be in writing and special provisions apply as to who may make a complaint and the position concerning complaints on behalf of the deceased. The High Court has refused to intervene in a decision of the BCC

---

95   T. Gibbons, *Regulating the Media* (London, Sweet & Maxwell, 1991).
96   Broadcasting Act 1990 section 15(6)(b).
97   *R v ITC ex parte TSW Broadcasting* (1992) *The Times* 7 February (CA).

that it was an inappropriate body to determine a dispute of a party political nature.[98] Hearings are in private although rarely are parties allowed to cross-examine each other. A streamlined procedure allows an agreement on heads of complaint, exchanges of written statements and responses. The only sanction of the BCC is publication of its findings by the licensee; it cannot insist upon an apology, or a correction or financial compensation. It publishes an annual report.[99]

Part VI of the Act establishes on a statutory basis the Broadcasting Standards Council,[100] originally established in a non-statutory form. Its concern is with standards of decency and taste in portrayal of sex and violence and it must draw up a code on such matters. It has to monitor broadcasting standards and it may initiate *sua sponte* the complaints procedure in section 154. Complaints, which are dealt with by a complaints committee, must be in writing and not be frivolous or inappropriate for the Council to entertain. If legal proceedings are in progress or where a legal remedy is available, a complaint will not be processed. It should be borne in mind that the Obscene Publications Acts 1959 and 1964 now apply to broadcast programmes. Investigation may take place with or without a hearing and in the former case in private. Complaints have been upheld in about 20 per cent of cases. Like the BCC, its sanction is publicity although it may make observations on its findings which must be published. Broadcasting and regulatory bodies must publicise the existence and work of the BSC, as they must the BCC, and it also publishes an annual report.

The "Unofficial" End of Officialdom: University Governance

To recapitulate an earlier point, the nebulous constitutional position of many non-departmental bodies, even within Barker's second category (p. 140 above), and the denial by government that such bodies are really governmental, allow the government to avoid an appropriate level of responsibility for the bodies, be the responsibility constitutional, legal or political. The vagueness helps to conceal the range of "public" activity; it helps to conceal what the state is actually doing and through which instruments it operates, and *a fortiori* what it ought to be doing; that is, it clouds debate about what the responsibilities and objectives of

---

[98] *R v BCC ex parte Owen* [1985] 2 All ER 522 (QBD). See also *R v BCC ex parte BBC* (1994) *The Times* 26 May.

[99] See HC 806 (1992/3).

[100] Coleman, 1993.

the state are. The University Grants Committee (UGC), although now defunct, nevertheless provides some instructive illustrations. The UGC, a body replaced originally by the Universities Funding Council[101] and then in turn the Higher Education Funding Council, was a body established by Treasury Minute[102] to inquire into the financial needs of universities, to advise the Secretary of State on the allocation of public grants, to assist in the preparation and execution of plans for the development of universities and to collect, examine and make available information about university education. It is often claimed that the UGC acted as a "buffer" standing between the government and universities to maintain independence and academic freedom. When universities faced severe cuts in expenditure, Ministers responded in Parliament to questions about cuts by saying that this was a matter for the UGC alone. All the members of the UGC were appointed by the Secretary of State. When the UGC was questioned about certain of its recommendations by the Select Committee on Education or the Public Accounts Committee,[103] it has replied that its advice to the Secretary of State is confidential and must remain so. Universities which complained because they suffered financial penalties for not complying with what they felt to be unspecified criteria in general policies laid down by the UGC, had to engage in negotiations and a process akin to roulette to disengage themselves from the penalties. The end result was one of uncertainty, ambivalence and outright discretion. The criteria changed as government attitudes to expenditure on universities unfolded, requiring further cuts in expenditure. The universities, and indeed the UGC, were placed in a very uncertain position, the latter taking much of the criticism that may have been more appropriately directed towards the DES.

It must be said that even under the "buffer" theory not a few decisions of the UGC were baffling. Few tears were lost when a statutory body replaced the UGC, but unwittingly a statutory body has allowed the Secretary of State to take a far more directive role in relation to university administration and co-ordination – the Secretary of State may issue directions to the Council(s)

---

[101] Education Reform Act 1988 section 131.
[102] Are such bodies judicially reviewable? If they satisfy the *Datafin* principles as developed, the answer must be yes; recommendatory bodies have been held to be judicially reviewable: *R v Boundary Commission ex parte Foot* [1983] QB 600.
[103] The UGC had a "roasting" before the Public Accounts Committee in HC 136 (1989/90).

with which the Council(s) must comply[104] – while at the individual institutional level maintaining the semblance of university independence.[105] The point is that both arrangements – the former one based on Treasury Minute – allow the real exercise of public power to be obfuscated; at the end of the day that is the issue of constitutional significance.

Government Contracts, "Semi-Official" Relationships and the Review Board for Government Contracts and the Pharmaceutical Price Regulation Scheme

The degree of informality between government and those non-departmental bodies, which Barker placed in category 3, hinders even more completely the public knowledge of, and accountability for, such quasi-governmental decision-making processes. Hood has shown, for instance, how the relationship between government and football pools operators developed to protect a few of them "by carefully maintained loopholes in the gambling laws" (while they also became the Post Office's largest customer). Pools operators acquired a position akin to tax farmers, and further protection was afforded by tax legislation which made it impracticable for competitors to enter the market.[106] The most recent development has seen a national lottery which is to be regulated by the state[107] and operated by a private contractor. Hood argues further that the desire to avoid a "Ministry of Culture" resulted in a series of semi-official arrangements for censorship and "oblique methods of finance", for example, the Press Council, British Board of Film Censors, the Arts Council, local authorities, tourist promotion bodies, universities, and so on.

Government contracts in the field of armaments, drugs, telephones, computers, and microtechnology have helped to create giant "private building and engineering firms" within what is largely a public sector context.[108] Caution should be invoked before arguing that because a body contracts with the state, it should be considered quasi-governmental; when, however, the contract is a way of achieving government policy on unrelated

---

[104] Education Reform Act section 134(8) and Further and Higher Education Act 1992 section 81.
[105] See, for example, section 69 and section 79 Further and Higher Education Act 1992 and by control over student numbers and varying levels of fee.
[106] Hood, 1973.
[107] By a body similar in design to the regulators of the privatised utilities – "Oflot". Se CoT Annual Report 1992/3 at 2.64.
[108] Birkinshaw *et al.*, Note 2 above.

themes such as: extension of collective bargaining, health and safety at work or de-unionisation; price controls, wage controls or deregulation; the delivery of essential services, nationally or regionally directed employment training or provision of welfare services, a quasi-governmental framework is difficult to eschew.[109] In the case of employment training we have witnessed a movement away from schemes which involved a tripartite relationship between government, employers and trade unions through the Manpower Services Commission, to a Training Agency and latterly to a series of training and enterprise councils (TECs) which are contracted out to local businesses and a full-time secretariat to administer although they are supported by public finance. The Parliamentary Commissioner has spoken about the obscurity surrounding TECs and complaints procedures.[110] However, the initiative of some TECs has provided charters for those undertaking training and includes a published grievance procedure.[111]

Two further examples of government/private proximity may be cited largely because they present us with interesting procedural devices. Both concern the area of government procurement (contracting) in highly sensitive fields: armaments and pharmaceuticals. Both are strategic industries in the British economy. Contracts in defence procurement are extremely difficult to price because they are invariably negotiated and the Government finds it difficult to obtain all the information it would need in order to assess whether it has made a good bargain or been the victim of a dupe. To attempt to establish rules of the game the Government, through the Treasury (now the MoD) and the Confederation of British Industry established the Review Board for Government Contracts. This acts as a rule maker setting out acceptable rates of return on capital, as a complaint recipient for members of the industry which feel they have been harshly treated by the government, as an adjudicator in disputes between the industry and government in contracts and as a general promoter of the industry's interests. The activities of the RBGC are subject to scrutiny by the CAG and his reports are laid before the Public Accounts Committee. Invariably, the industry has achieved profit

---

[109] The implications of *R v Lord Chancellor* Note 112 below, are that the courts yet again will refuse to take on board the public law dimension to a governmental contract. See, however, *R v Enfield LBC ex parte Unwin Ltd* (1989) *The Times* 16 February and the Local Government Act 1988, ss. 17–23.

[110] PCA AR HC 299 1990/91, paragraph 38.

[111] *Financial Times* 2 February 1992.

levels beyond that envisaged in the agreed formula. In pharmaceuticals, a scheme has been devised which sets out the agreement
between the industry and government, and also provides for a system of arbitration which is not binding in the event of dispute.

While the Government has moved to policies to provide public
services on a contracted-out basis, wherever possible after competitive tender, it has in some cases increased the opportunities
for openness and the raising of grievance through the courts as
in the case of local government where a variety of procedural
safeguards are present under the Local Government Act 1988.
While in some instances there has been a reluctance in the courts
to open up what are closed tendering processes,[112] the movement
towards greater openness and accountability is in some quarters
irresistible; such is likely to be the case with the directives that
open up public procurement in services, supplies, works (buildings) and utilities within Member States. What these laws do
is to open up, or help to open up, to greater competition the
allocation of contracts and with that the enormous power and
patronage that accompanies such allocation.[113] However, we are
witnessing the emergence of a new type of contract; one which
is not justiciable through the private law courts. This public law
contract, Harden suggests,[114] throws up challenges to lawyers to
establish satisfactory procedures through which common interests
may be reconciled or harmonised in the event of dispute. Such
contracts are to be found in the NHS between service providers
and purchasers, both of which are public bodies but where resolution of dispute takes place through the Secretary of State, not
the courts.[115] Yet another example is the framework document
which sets out the relationship and duties of Next Steps Agencies. A particularly interesting example is found in the agreement
between the Secretaries of State for Social Security and Employment on the administration of benefits for unemployment which

---

[112] See *R v Lord Chancellor ex parte Hibbitt* (1993) *The Times* 12 March; note
       Blackpool and Fylde AC Ltd v Blackpool BC [1990] 3 All ER 25 (CA).
[113] Council Directive EEC 93/36.
[114] I. Harden, *The Contracting State* (Buckingham, Open University Press,
       1992).
[115] National Health Service Contracts (Dispute Resolution) Regulations SI
       1991/725 apply where the Secretary of State appoints an adjudicator to settle
       a dispute. Disputes not so referred are resolved by managers. Adjudicators
       must proceed fairly and give written decisions with reasons for their
       decisions.

is undertaken by the latter for the former.[116] It is quite clearly the desire of government that these contracts will not be subject to interpretation in the courts; in the case of NSAs they possess no legal identity to bring judicial review. Such an obstacle would not bar NHS bodies because trusts have a legal identity.

Self-Regulation

A greater trend towards self-regulation by trusted private bodies is unlikely to decrease the opportunities for such informal relationships between government and "private" concerns. The attraction for government to achieve its desired ends by "hidden persuasion" and the implications for democratic standards are obvious and insidious. Self-regulation means quite simply that the body is left to regulate itself, either in the absence of any statutory controls or under a loose statutory framework operated by an intermediary commission or appointed body which often is either dominated by interests which are regulated, as in the case of the four self-regulatory organisations (SROs) which regulate sections of the investment business although there may be outsiders appointed to give an appropriate sense of balance or there may be no outside membership. In financial regulation, membership of SROs must strike a balance between the interests of the SRO, its members and the general public and board membership must comprise those independent of the SRO in sufficient number to achieve such a balance. There is no detailed regulation or control under statutory power by a government department or mediating agency and very often the detail of conduct is contained in a code of guidance or rule-book. If any variant of governmentally approved or authorised self-regulation for such bodies becomes the norm, the exclusion of representation of interests apart from the government and the private body has undesirable and undemocratic consequences, especially where such interests stand to be vitally affected. Yet there is rarely any formal or informal opportunity for such interests to be heard in the private bartering processes, although since the mid-1980s we have witnessed a keener awareness of the need for grievance procedures and measures to reduce

---

[116] The agreement covers the provision of information for monitoring of performance and exchange of information collected by their Departments and Agencies relating to administration of benefits, including information on claims and claimants. This may cover information "not routinely collected" by the Employment Service.

conflicts of interest.[117] Under the Financial Services Act 1986, which governs the activity of the Securities and Investment Board (a limited company) and self-regulatory organisations (SROs) which regulate particular businesses, complaints procedures have to be established by each SRO which punishes breaches of the rules and which each SRO has to formulate in its "rule-book".[118] These procedures must be as efficient as those of the SIBs to which the Secretary of State's regulatory powers under the statute are delegated. Lord Ackner has recommended that if or when a single regulatory authority takes over from the four SROs, they should appoint a single Ombudsman to hear complaints and should end the process whereby the Insurance Ombudsman operates as the complaints mechanism on an agency basis for one of the SROs, the extension of which was suggested. Interestingly, while SROs are judicially reviewable under public law procedure, it has been held that the Insurance Ombudsman is not, even though he acts for Life Assurance and Unit Trust Regulatory Organisation, one of the SROs.[119]

Although professions largely regulate themselves and maintain control over discipline we shall see elsewhere how procedures exist to challenge clinical judgment and GP misdemeanours (chapter 5). Accountants have disciplinary procedures which are notable for their comparative openness although the most interesting development has been the Legal Services Ombudsman (LSO) created by the Courts and Legal Services Act 1990. Both legal professions are self-regulating although in the case of the solicitors there are certain statutory requirements. The Ombudsman deals with complaints made against the professions' own grievance procedures. Where such a complaint is made the LSO may also investigate the original complaint itself although there are strict time limits and the complaint must be made to the professional bodies initially. Complaints to the LSO number in the region of 1,250 *per annum*.

---

[117] Law Comm. Paper 124, 1992. However, in December 1993 there was a damning report by Peat Marwick on the sharp practices of pension salesmen selling products to those encouraged by the Government to purchase personal pensions, having traded in their occupational pension. The Personal Investment Authority will replace two SROs: LAUTRO and FIMBRA.

[118] Rule-books are examined by the DGFT who advises the Secretary of State but the Secretary of State does not have to follow that advice. The rules of competition and practice are controlled through the Secretary of State and not through the courts.

[119] *R v IOB ex p. Aegon Life Ass.* (1994) *The Times* 7 January.

In other areas the government may choose a representative body to regulate an industry or commercial activity. The Advertising Standards Authority[120] is a clear example and has now in fact been given recognition under EC law as the body which will regulate all non-broadcast media in the UK. It supervises the British Code of Advertising Practice and the British Code of Sales Promotion Practice, both of which are drawn up by the Committee of Advertising Practice. It investigates all complaints whether from industry or the public. CAP comprises trade and professional organisations within the advertising industry and also provides a free and confidential pre-publication advice service to ensure that advertisements conform with the codes. CAP further examines the implications of complaints and takes appropriate action. Where there are persistent breaches the DGFT may seek a court injunction. Along with financial services this is a particularly arresting example of self-regulation given statutory backing.[121] One of the ASA's most famous actions concerned the advertising campaign involving Benetton's clothing in 1990 – most famously the new-born and "blood smeared" baby with unsevered umbilical cord. It received 800 complaints. Its total number of complaints in 1991 was 10,610 of which 2,416 were upheld.

Elsewhere, banks and building societies have avoided statutory regulation for customer relations and have relied upon informal codes.[122] In the case of the press the issue has been looked at in great detail in two reports by David Calcutt QC, together with a report from the National Heritage Committee and Lord Chancellor's Department.[123] A non-statutory Press Complaints Commission has been established which has produced a code of practice on press behaviour and has a majority of lay members. The Calcutt report No. 2 was universally condemned by the press and although some of its recommendations may give cause for concern that there will be too wide a protection for the privacy of those, particularly politicians, who operate in the public arena, it does contain some constructive suggestions for a complaints

---

[120] Which is established as a company limited by guarantee and is subject to judicial review: *R v ASA ex parte Insurance Service plc* (1989) *The Times* 14 July, as is the Committee of Advertising Practice.

[121] On codes elsewhere see Lewis and Birkinshaw, 1993, chapter 9.

[122] Though obviously they operate within a general framework of statutory regulation: Banking Act 1987; Building Societies Act 1986.

[123] Cm. 1102 (1990) and Cm. 2135 (1993) for Calcutt; *Privacy and Media Intrusion*, 4th Report of the National Heritage Committee 1992/3; and Lord Chancellor's Department, *Infringement of Privacy* (1993).

procedure for victims of unprincipled investigative journalism.[124] If the non-statutory self-regulation fails to produce responsible behaviour in sections of the press, statutory regulation will be imposed along with laws protecting privacy.[125] However, one has to appreciate that many of the sections of the press who are guilty of the most serious abuses belong to newspapers whose owners are staunch supporters of the Government. In fact, it is surprising how many "last chances" have been given to the press and late in 1993 the Government were suggesting that self-regulation could continue under an effective voluntary Ombudsman scheme. In January 1994, an "in-house" Ombudsman was appointed by the Press Complaints Commission. The presence of an effective Ombudsman, statutory or voluntary, is seen as the price to pay for continuing self-regulation, as is the ability to enforce the self-created rules.

Conclusion

Ten years ago, it was possible to write that few non-departmental bodies had published grievance procedures for those aggrieved by their decisions. Throughout the whole spectrum of such bodies, the informal processing of complaints by the relevant bodies was repeatedly discovered to be a common event. There was little recorded about such processes. Today, the impact of the Citizen's Charter has been felt here as in other areas. On the surface, complaints procedures abound. There is, on the other hand, a frequent absence of provisions allowing public participation in decisions and means to ensure that that viewpoint is taken seriously – the CAA is in this company a striking exception. Where it is permitted in a structured manner, participation is invariably too late in the process to allow any opportunity to influence the nature of a decision.

Pursuit by government of policies of privatisation, contracting out and deregulation has, perhaps not surprisingly, produced new bodies under Barker's group 2 (see p. 140 above) as others have been disbanded. EC obligations are also creating EC-wide bodies

---

124 These include the establishment of a statutory Press Complaints Tribunal which would draw up and review a statutory code, receive complaints including those from third parties, have power to act on its own initiative, powers to conciliate and adjudicate and demand responses, to enforce publication of judgments, costs and fines, to review its own procedures and publish reports and to require the press to publish advertisements about complaints procedures.

125 Birkinshaw, 1993b.

responsible for regulation at the Community level on sensitive areas such as drug testing.[126] The pursuit has also generated a wide resort to the "semi-official" bodies in group 3, the status of many of which is indeterminate. Regulation will be achieved by co-operation built around mutual self-respect and informality, making it more difficult for public law techniques to foster the ideals which law, I would argue, is supposed to convey – openness, accountability, responsiveness, efficiency, participation by the governed in the process of government. Our public law has done little to advance the ideals through the wide range of networks which this chapter examined. At least in the United States the process of regulation, and de-regulation, is more open and allows greater procedural opportunity for participation of interested parties in rule-making, deregulation and other decisions having a substantial impact upon the public interest. And of course in the United States there is legislative provision for freedom of information and "government in the sunshine".[127] The legal problems associated with the enabling and regulating state were addressed in the US decades before they emerged as problematical for constitutional lawyers in the UK.

Privatisation has proceeded by conferring on Ministers the widest possible powers of sale. Sale of public assets has in many cases resulted in financial loss to the taxpayer, or has been detrimental to the interests of industries still remaining within the public sphere. The methods of regulation have attracted increasing criticism for their lack of transparency from all sides of the political spectrum. The methods of sale have been criticised by a non-partisan Public Accounts Committee. The Government initially accepted that the privatisation programme was not a long-term rational plan, it involved an "ideology": the private sector is *always* better, *always* more efficient. That theme has grown. There has, of course, to be Parliamentary sanction and approval of privatisation proposals enshrined in legislation. The details of these developments are left largely to non-departmental bodies and informal networks. After Parliamentary discussion of the shell there is an absence of a clear regulatory framework, operating through democratic and open processes assisted by a public law which was sensitive to interest representation, open and fair procedures, fully reasoned arguments and declarations

---

[126] See the White Paper on *Open Government*. This body is to be established in London.

[127] P. Birkinshaw, *Freedom of Information: The Law, the Practice and the Ideal* (London, Weidenfeld and Nicolson, 1988).

of interest. This is hardly surprising as it continues the tradition of secrecy, informality and non-involvement of the public which characterised, and still characterises, the working of the British State and in particular its quasi-governmental setting. In early 1994, the PAC felt constrained to publish a report stating its concern over a fall in public standards in many of the new arrangements for delivering public services, a decline which led to "money being wasted or otherwise improperly spent".[128] Throughout, we should always remember that the state never withdraws: it merely reforms.

[128]   Public Accounts Committee, *The Proper Conduct of Public Business*, Eighth Report HC 154 (1993/4) (London, HMSO, 1994).

Chapter 5

OMBUDSMEN AND OTHERS

This chapter discusses those bodies, invariably statutory, whose major responsibility is to obtain satisfaction from public authorities for individuals who are aggrieved by decisions, non-decisions, actions or non-actions which amount to maladministration or culpable behaviour. The generic title of most of these grievance-remedial agencies is "Ombudsman" and they exist in relation to central government departments and other specified agencies and non-departmental bodies linked in some way to central government;[1] local government and police authorities and the NHS hospital service including NHS Trusts – but not General Practitioners although the Wilson Report has made important recommendations in this area (see below); Northern Ireland has its own Ombudsmen. In this chapter there will also be an examination of the procedures for registering complaints against the police via the Police Complaints Authority established under the Police and Criminal Evidence Act 1984 (successor to the Police Complaints Board). One of the most dramatic developments in public law throughout the 1980s and 1990s has been the explosion of the ombudsman concept in the private sector, sometimes under statutory authority, sometimes on a voluntary basis. Indeed the proliferation of Ombudsmen has caused the development of a sort of ombudsmen approval society, the founding members comprising the leading statutory and voluntary Ombudsmen. One of the primary *raisons d'être* behind the UK (now British and Irish) Ombudsman Association is concern over the proliferation of the use of the term "Ombudsman" by bodies not in any way independent of those concerns which they are investigating. The Association seeks to establish the criteria which are necessary for the appellation "Ombudsman" and to encourage best practice among Ombudsmen, enhance understanding and publicity for

[1] See the Parliamentary Commissioner Act 1967, Schedule 2 (as extended) for details. The range of bodies listed includes many which are not government departments as described in chapter 2. Complaints must be brought within 12 months.

their work and encourage and safeguard the role of Ombudsmen in the public and private sectors.

The bodies which I focus upon in this chapter have all been created by Parliament to attempt to make good the failures of our political and legal institutions in their respective efforts to rectify the shortcomings of, or assist individuals with grievances against state activities. I shall briefly examine Ombudsmen operating in the private sphere,[2] and the chapter will conclude with a brief discussion of an agency whose statutory responsibilities reflect a phenomenon of both public and private bureaucracy, namely, information held about individuals in the form of vast computerised databanks. The Data Protection Registrar is a regulator and performs ombudsman-like functions, a duality of roles which as we saw has been criticised in relation to the privatised utilities.

The emergence of Ombudsmen in central and local government, the NHS and the appointment of the Police Complaints Board in 1976 illustrated a growing awareness within government of public disquiet over the ability of the institutions of government to handle and deal with complaints about their activities in a fair and responsive manner. The Ombudsmen for central and local government and the Health Service are the most developed independent grievance-remedial devices we possess in the administrative as opposed to the legal or political realms. The Police Complaints Authority differs, as only the most serious complaints will receive its direct attention. These factors make them important subjects for our study. But governmental concessions in providing these bodies were given at a price, as all the bodies are considerably limited in what they can investigate. There were to be no investigations of complaints about policy and its impact, although this constitutes a grey area. Only complaints of an individual and otherwise restricted nature were to be examined, though we shall see how Parliament has provided for the special position of the police.

The Philosophical Underpinnings of the British Ombudsman

It is of interest to note that the introduction of the Parliamentary Commissioner for Administration (PCA) or the Commissioner for

---

2 C. Graham, *The Non-Classical Ombudsman* (Sheffield, Centre for Socio-Legal Studies, University of Sheffield, 1991). On public sector ombudsmen see M. Seneviratne, *Ombudsmen in the Public Sector* (1994).

Local Administration or local government Ombudsman (LGO),[3] established to remedy injustice caused by administrative defects in what are generally relatively mundane causes, should have provoked such opposition. This is all the more curious when one considers that Ombudsmen in the United Kingdom are primarily directed towards righting the individual wrong – only secondarily are they concerned with improving *general* administrative regimes or systems, though it is not difficult to cite general improvements in the quality of administrative practices and decision-making as a result of PCA and LGO reports. Recent reforms in the case of the LGO have facilitated research and work aimed at improving the general quality of administration (Local Government and Housing Act 1989 sections 22 and 23) and the PCA has paid more attention to the cure of systemic failure both by highlighting the amount of time taken to investigate what has gone wrong in the system which led to a complaint and by identifying those cases where changes in practice were introduced to respond to findings of maladministration. His special reports issued under section 10(4) have paid greater attention to systemic failings.[4] Reports of the Health Service Commissioner have become more critical of falling standards, a feature which was particularly noticeable in his report for 1993/94 (HC 499 1993/94). However, any criticism of the "merits" or departmental policy of a decision – as opposed to governmental or party political policy dimensions which are outside the jurisdiction of the PCA in their entirety – is expressly excluded by the legislation establishing the PCA and LGO[5] unless the decision contains maladministration. In 1992, 43 per cent of rejected complaints to the PCA concerned the merits of legislation, administrative decision-making or policy. Where present, it is the maladministration which is to be the object of inquiry, not the merits.[6] In investigations concerning the NHS, the clinical judgment of doctors and consultants – the largest single reason for

---

3 Both the PCA and Local Commissioners are appointed by the Crown and hold office "during good behaviour" subject to various provisions.
4 See, for example, HC 652 1992/3 and HC 13 1993/4.
5 Parliamentary Commissioner Act 1967 section 12(3); Local Government Act 1974 section 34(3). On "departmental policy", that is, what departments are responsible for on a day to day basis, as opposed to "policy questions of political significance" for which Ministers are responsible individually and collectively, see *Fourth Report from the Select Committee on Procedure* (1964/65, HC 303). While the essence of the distinction may be clear *in abstracto*, are Ministers not responsible for *all* policy factors? *Quaere* Executive Next Steps Agencies?
6 Barlow Clowes Report, paragraph 6 p. 2.

refusing jurisdiction – was excluded from the investigatory powers of the Health Commissioner. Lastly, just in case the concessions made by political and administrative powers proved to be too much of a *faux pas*, their decisions, with the sole exception of the Northern Ireland Commissioner for Complaints, cannot be enforced by law against the bodies falling under their jurisdiction. Acceptance of an adverse decision has to be "negotiated" where there is reluctance to accept it. The Local Government Housing Act 1989 has somewhat tortuous provisions to pressurise a recalcitrant authority to accept an Ombudsman's findings which we can examine below.

The office of the PCA owed its origin to Ombudsmen who had operated in Scandinavia for well over a century and a half, and in New Zealand.[7] The original British model – the PCA – differed from its Scandinavian forbears, and Gregory associates this difference with the influence of the Whyatt Report which saw the Ombudsman being an adjunct to Parliament as opposed to an agency independent of the political and administrative regimes.[8] Unlike Scandinavian models, the Whyatt Report recommended that a distinction should be drawn between complaints about the merits of discretionary decisions and those about bad administration such as delay, rudeness or inefficiency, and as we saw, this distinction was maintained in the legislation. Finally Whyatt introduced what has been referred to as the "filter", that is, complaints would first have to be made to a Member of Parliament (or councillor in local government) and then handed on to the Ombudsman. For the PCA and LGO there was to be no direct access and this was a novel feature of the Ombudsman idea. "Whether the Labour Government were right or wrong to cast their P.C. scheme in the form they did, there can be no doubt that . . . planted in their proposals were the seeds of a great deal of misunderstanding and discontent".[9] The PCA's job was to strengthen the position of Parliament in the resolution of grievances against departments. In spite of this official line, a previous Commissioner has doubted the wisdom of the filter[10] and has recommended that he should be invited by a complainant to review the MP's handling of a complaint without the complainant

---

7   Whyatt Report (1961); Gregory and Hutchesson, *The Parliamentary Ombudsman* 1975; for a general comparative study see Caiden, *International Handbook of the Ombudsman*, 1983, Vols I and II.
8   Gregory and Hutchesson, *ibid*.
9   *Ibid*., at 86. See incidentally, I. Scott, "Reforming the Ombudsman . . ." (1994) *Public Law* 27.
10 HC 322 (1983/4).

formally requesting the MP to pass it on to him. The present PCA has supported the removal of the filter.[11] Opposition to this has been expressed not only by government but also by the Select Committee on the PCA, most recently in its report on the relationship between the PCA and the Citizen's Charter and in that on the work, powers and jurisdiction of the Ombudsman.[12] Suffice to say at this point, the filter was removed in the case of the Local Government Ombudsman by the Local Government Act 1988 (section 29 and Schedule 3 paragraph 5(2)).

Policy was to be the concern of Parliament, not the Ombudsman. In the words of Richard Crossman, maladministration was to cover "bias, neglect, inattention, delay, incompetence, ineptitude, perversity, turpitude, arbitrariness and so on." It would have been "a long interesting list." Efforts were to be made to avoid legalistic overtones in the phrase "injustice as a consequence of maladministration"; the meanings of both terms would be "filled out by the practical processes of case work".[13] His concern was not to be with the technical correctness of a decision but whether a public power had been used properly, misused, or abused; that is, with the administrative quality of a decision. If there was an appropriate remedy in a court of law or a tribunal, and it was reasonable to pursue it, then the PCA would decline jurisdiction.[14] Complaints had to be made to the MP within 12 months of notice of the matter constituting the complaint – though this period can be waived.

The Citizen's Charter and the Ombudsman

In 1992 the Select Committee on the PCA investigated the relationship between the Citizen's Charter (CC) and the PCA.[15] If it is true that the PCA is "one of the services of the welfare state",[16] then profound changes in that state structure may call into question the usefulness of the PCA and LGO. Central to the thrust of the Charter is the provision of effective grievance remedial devices operating within the bodies covered by the Charter, a view which I have long held. If these prove to be very effective,

---

11   HC 158 (1991/2) at 12 and HC 650(i) (1992/3) at 10.
12   HC 650 (1992/3) and HC 33 I (1993/4).
13   HC Debs., Vol. 734 cols 51 to 52 (1966/7).
14   PCA Act 1967 section 5(2).
15   Select Committee on the PCA, HC 158 (1991/2).
16   H.W.R. Wade, *Administrative Law (6th edn)* (Oxford, Oxford University Press, 1988) at 82.

will the Ombudsmen become redundant? Or will the existence of internal complaints procedures cause confusion for the public who will fail to distinguish between the internal and external procedures? Might internal bodies be inclined to pre-empt the PCA on "maladministration"? Should there be an expectation that the internal mechanism be exhausted before the PCA is resorted to? On this latter point, the Select Committee voiced its objection and yet the LGO insist that a complaint is made to the appropriate body before it comes to them. While the CC did not highlight the PCA or Health Service Commissioner (HSC), other charters do refer to their work in more detail: the CC did mention that further resistance to the recommendations of the LGO may lead to a power of legal enforcement of their decisions along the lines of the Northern Ireland Commissioner for Complaints (NICC). The PCA in fact believes that the CC has brought his office very useful publicity and has resulted in increased use by the public. The Secretary to the Cabinet expressed the view that there was no need to alter a "machine that works well", but other commentators may have detected a hint of criticism of the PCA in the Charter and have made the point that like all other areas of the public sector, the PCA should be opened up to competition, namely with other complaints mechanisms.[17] The PCA and the Select Committee are alive to the climate in which the public sector, including the PCA, has to operate and the author has no doubt of the importance of the Ombudsman as a safeguard against the wrongful exercise or abuse of power. It was interesting that the press reported that the PCA had been critical of the Government's Deregulation and Contracting Out Bill (1993/4) clauses 57 and 67 allegedly because it might lead to the privatisation of his office. In fact the PCA voiced his concern about a Minister being able to empower a servant of Parliament to do an act.[18]

In his 1993 *Annual Report* (HC 290 1993/4 para.6) the PCA spelt out his approach to Charter Targets and claims for compensation. Where targets amount to promises, failure to meet them may justify compensation. Where they are indicators, failure to meet them may not warrant compensation just as meeting them may not be evidence of a faultless performance.

---

[17] Bradley, "Sachsenhausen, Barlow Clowes and Then?" (1992) *Public Law* 353.
[18] HC Debs. Col. 254 (8 February 1994).

The Parliamentary Commissioner for Administration

Lawyers writing about the PCA have described how he has been a useful adjunct to a system of administrative law;[19] how he has developed a body of case precedents which he can use informally to guide his discretion in future cases in a judicial manner;[20] or that he should not be a court substitute or poor man's lawyer and that lawyers did him a disservice if they cast him in their own image.[21] Certainly only two holders of the office have been lawyers and the first of those stated that his legal background had not made a conscious contribution to his approach.[22] Clearly, holders of the office bring their own talents and *modus operandi* to the task and interpret their powers and duties in a way which they deem appropriate, within of course the parameters of the law. Furthermore, they have to operate in the context and climate in which they find themselves; the political ethos has changed dramatically since the PCA was created over a quarter of a century ago. Consider the impact of consumerism for instance. As I write, a major review of the PCA's and HSC's "Powers, Work and Jurisdiction" is being undertaken by the Select Committee.[23]

Some Facts and Figures

PCA annual reports have revealed how there is considerable confusion in the public eye as to the position and powers of the PCA. As well as receiving many complaints directly from the public, he also receives a significant number which are under the jurisdiction of the LGO, or concern the courts, judges, police, nationalised industries and utilities or other public authority. The PCA himself has voiced disquiet as to what happens to complainants whose complaints are returned to them, though since 1978 he has operated a system whereby if the complainant is willing, he will refer the complaint, if notionally within his jurisdiction, to the relevant MP, asking him or her to re-refer it. Certainly the office appears to be poorly publicised and in a population of over 55 million, it does seem strange that in 1992 he had only 945 complaints

---

19 Wade, Note 16 above, at 90.
20 Bradley, (1980) CLJ 304.
21 Harlow, (1978) MLR 446.
22 Clothier, *Annual Report of the PCA*, 1979.
23 HC 650 (1992/3) and HC 33 I (1993/4); see below for the recommendations.

referred to him[24] (compared with 677 in 1989, 704 in 1990 and 801 in 1991). In 1992, he accepted 269 cases for investigation. In 1991, of 183 cases where an investigation was completed, he concluded that 47.5 per cent of the complaints were wholly justified (87); 42.6 per cent were partly justified (78); 13.1 per cent were not justified or the investigation was discontinued (24). From these figures it would appear that where there is an investigation, the chances of success for a complainant are very high. However, on the one hand the overwhelming majority of complaints are rejected – and this will be after an initial screening without the benefit of any departmental papers or views as the right to inspect only arises after he decides to investigate. On the other hand, departments may concede the point at an early stage before an investigation and this will not be recorded as a "success". It does represent a *de facto* "fast track" procedure although this has not been formerly implemented, as in the case of the Northern Ireland PCA.[25]

The "market shares" of the departments complained against have not changed very much in recent years although there are fluctuations in some departments. One should remember that executive NSAs will assume in some cases responsibility for areas of service which will be complaint intensive. Top of the list in 1993 was the DSS, complaints against which constituted 30 per cent of total referrals, followed by the Inland Revenue at 16 per cent, DoE and Department of Transport with 6 per cent each, Customs and Excise 5 per cent and the Home Office with 3 per cent. Significantly, the Department of Employment witnessed a dramatic fall while the Lord Chancellor's Department claimed 3 per cent. All that these figures reveal is that those departments whose administration brings them into direct contact with the public are more likely to be the subject of a complaint than those which do not have contact, such as the Treasury. Decisions of the latter, while ultimately having a far greater impact on the community or classes of the community, do not have a direct and immediate impact on individuals in a personal form, thereby rendering them unlikely to be the subject of a complaint of maladministration.

For several years the PCA has published his management plan – an innovation of Mr Reid – and he has sought to reduce the

---

[24] It was envisaged that the PCA would receive about 6,000 to 7,000 complaints *per annum*. In Sweden in 1990, the Ombudsmen expected to receive 4,000 complaints from a population of 8 million (Gregory and Pearson, 1992, at 472 to 473.

[25] See HC 650 (iii) (1992/3).

time it takes to issue a report after a full investigation: in 1992, the time taken was 12 months and 13 days; in 1991 it was 13 months and 18 days. In the mid 1980s, the PCA was himself accused by an MP of maladministration because of delays in his investigations.[26] Because of the assumption of responsibilities under the Government's *Open Government* White Paper, the PCA's complement of staff is to be increased from $92\frac{1}{2}$ to $106\frac{1}{2}$. This is a major development in the PCA's jurisdiction and interestingly it has been achieved by extra-statutory concession although "Quite often failure to provide information is a key part of his present work".[27] It was interesting that the Government did not opt for an enforcement mechanism based upon the courts to enforce access rights.

Investigations and Jurisdiction

Set out below is the PCA's own account from his Management Plan 1992/3–1994/5[28] of his method of investigation. Ombudsmen have often described their informal connections and representations to departments operating outside the formal procedure.

"The procedure followed when the Commissioner accepts a complaint for investigation varies in some aspects of detail, but not in matters of general principle, as between PCA and HSC. In the former capacity he is required by statute to give the Principal Officer of the department or body complained against the opportunity to comment on the complaint: this is known as Stage I of an investigation. Stage II begins as soon as possible after receipt of those comments and normally includes an examination of relevant departmental files so as to establish, as far as possible, the facts of the case; whether there has been maladministration on the department's part; and whether, if so, that has caused injustice. Stage II also usually involves interviews or correspondence with officials and, where necessary, the complainant. It continues with the preparation of a draft results report (DRR) setting out the facts and, normally, the provisional findings and conclusion. At Stage III the PCA sends his proposed report to the

---

26 HC 149 (1985/6); and especially HC 315 (iv) (1984/5).
27 HC 605 (ix) 211 (1992/3). This reference was specifically to a case involving salmonella investigation, where the MAFF had been less than forthcoming in their explanation of the rights of farmers (HC 947 (1992/3)) – a single investigation report under section 10(4). The PCA had found maladministration in the MAFF's "lack of frankness".
28 Paragraphs 1.6–9.

Principal Officer concerned, who is invited to check that the
facts in the report are correct (so far as the department are
concerned) and to offer any comments on their presentation.
The Commissioner does not have the executive authority,
either as PCA or as HSC, to impose a remedy upon the body
complained against. Issue of the DRR establishes whether
the department (or health authority) are prepared to offer
the remedy which the Commissioner thinks appropriate for
any injustice which he has found. Securing agreement to a
recommended remedy on occasions takes time and, if the
Commissioner concludes that he is unable to obtain for the
complainant a remedy commensurate with the injustice, he
may lay a special report before each House of Parliament.

An investigation starts with the issue of a summary statement setting out the background to the complaint and those
aspects which have been accepted for investigation. Copies
are sent to the body complained against and, for HSC cases,
to the complainant. It is at Stage II that the HSC procedure
may follow a slightly different course from the PCA procedure. The department (PCA), or the health authority
(HSC), will be asked to send all of the correspondence
and other material relating to the complaint, including in
most HSC cases the clinical and nursing records – particularly where the complaint is about the care or treatment
of someone who has been attending hospital. The body
complained of will also be asked to provide comments on
the complaint . . . . Evidence, either written or oral, may be
sought from *any* persons who may have material information.
Although Parliament has given the Commissioner powers
equivalent to those of the High Court in obtaining evidence
and in respect of contempt, he rarely invokes them and almost
invariably relies on informal interviews. Witnesses are told
that whatever they say may be used in the report of the investigation. The DRR, prepared by the investigating officer, is
normally reviewed by each management level – and checked
for sense, accuracy, comprehensibility and, more recently, for
length – before submission to the Commissioner.

At the end of a PCA investigation, a final results report
(FRR), signed personally by the Commissioner (or, if he is
absent, his Deputy), is sent to the Member who referred the
complaint, who will normally pass a copy to the complainant;
a copy is sent also to the Principal Officer concerned and
to any official identified in the complaint . . . . Statute pre-
scribes those to whom the Commissioner may himself send

FRRs. His reports to them are accorded absolute privilege. It is for recipients to decide what use they make of reports.

The Commissioner reaches his findings on the civil test of "balance of probabilities", rather than by applying that used in criminal proceedings of "beyond all reasonable doubt". The evidence in many cases points so clearly towards a firm finding that there is no practical difference. The reason for the stance adopted by successive Commissioners is that, as explained in paragraph 1.6, remedies (or judgments) are not imposed even though findings are almost invariably accepted by the body complained against. There is no mechanism for appeal, and any subsequent disciplinary action is a matter entirely for that body and then for hearing by tribunal or other judicial process. As an independent scrutineer of administrative practice, the Commissioner gives a view based on equity and common sense."

The PCA has indicated that staff training has become increasingly important. This would appear to be no bad thing, for in a research visit to the PCA's office (which is also the office of the HSC) in 1991, the impression was gained, and to some extent confirmed by a meeting in the Cabinet Office, that people were expected to learn on the job. Being seconded civil servants they would know their way around departments and presumably agencies, would know what to look for and would recognise when files were incomplete. This might strike one as over-sanguine but the PCA has spoken of the advantages of this approach and has examples to support his case.

The PCA has been accommodating in his interpretations of standing of complainants and has allowed representative groups to bring complaints via their MP. Various public bodies, bodies appointed by the Crown and Ministers or government departments and those "wholly or mainly" financed by Parliament are prohibited from making a complaint against departments,[29] thus helping to ensure that the PCA concerns himself with complaints of an *individual* nature as opposed to becoming involved in disputes about relationships between organs of the state. Schedule 3 lists the "Matters" which are not subject to his investigation and as well as covering international relations,[30] extradition, investigation of crime and state security, legal proceedings

---

[29] PCA Act 1967 section 6(1)(*a*) and (*b*).
[30] See, however, Parliamentary Commissioner (Consular Complaints) Act 1981.

and courts martial, the prerogative of mercy and so on, there are also excluded from investigation personnel matters, in the broadest sense, of members of the armed services, civil service or employees of those bodies within the jurisdiction of the PCA.[31] This last exclusion has probably over the years caused the greatest agitation, though the most important exclusion generally is that in paragraph 9 of the Schedule: "Action taken in matters relating to contractual or other commercial transactions, whether within the UK or elsewhere, being transactions of a government department or authority to which this Act applies or other public authority except those concerning the compulsory purchase of land or its disposal as surplus land." This exemption will be addressed in a few moments but we should note the presence of EC Directives which cover this area and breach of these may lead to investigation by the relevant Directorate-General or parties may invoke remedies under the implementing regulations.[32]

What this does not enlighten us about is the fact that many departments or bodies are excluded from the PCA's jurisdiction. In fact the PCA in evidence to his Select Committee believed that a distinct improvement would occur if, instead of listing those bodies which are included – causing redrafting every time a new body is included as occurred in 1987 when many NDPBs were added to the list and from 1988 onwards as NSAs are established – only those bodies which are excluded were listed. These include the Cabinet Office, the Prime Minister's Office, the Parole Board, the Bank of England, most tribunal staff, and the Criminal Injuries Compensation Board. The PCA himself has reported that much time is taken up resolving jurisdictional difficulties. This had occurred when functions had been contracted out by governmental bodies.[33]

Commercial and Contractual Transactions

The exclusion of these transactions has been criticised, *inter alia*, by *Justice*, a Royal Commission and the Select Committee

---

31 See SI 1983 No. 1707. Personnel matters are not excluded in Northern Ireland but this subject was included to address the problem of political and religious discrimination in Northern Ireland and the Ombudsmen in Northern Ireland have had a role in combating such discrimination. The Fair Employment Commission now deals with allegations of discrimination in employment in the province (see chapter 4).

32 The Directives cover supplies, works, utilities and services as well as remedies: EEC 93/36. They are implemented by means of statutory instrument; on utilities see SI 1992/3279 and services SI 3228 1993.

33 HC 650 (1992/3) at 4.

on the PCA as well as by Sir Cecil Clothier himself in his final report as PCA.[34] The Select Committee has recommended that the PCA should investigate complaints "that a department had been improperly influenced in deciding which firms to include among those entitled to tender for contracts, or had made such a decision in an arbitrary manner, or that a department had acted improperly in connection with the withdrawal of a firm's name from the list of approved tenderers." Where companies had been omitted because they had contravened government policy the PCA has opined that this is not an appropriate matter for his investigation, but should be left to the representations of MPs. The Select Committee believed that if such an omission operated inequitably, or not in a uniform manner, then this should be appropriate for investigation.

The Government in its reply[35] argued that commercial relationships and grants to industry where there was a use of "statutory powers involving a wide measure of commercial discretion" should not be subject to review by the PCA. Clearly there are contractual matters which could be more appropriately dealt with by litigation, but the whole administrative side of buying and selling, and the patronage and extent of government pursuit of its objectives by contractual devices attending such activity, are outside the PCA's jurisdiction. On the extremely rare occasions when government contracts have come before courts they have been dealt with in a disappointing manner and appear almost non-justiciable,[36] though we shall have to await and assess what impact the EC Directives on procurement will have in this area.[37] These provide for advertising, elimination of discrimination (between nationals of Member States) and transparency, as well as a requirement that effective remedies for breach be implemented. Some of the hair-splitting judgments on what is within or without the jurisdiction of the PCA border on casuistry – complaints about the communication of confidential information by one department to another he could investigate as they are "administrative", but if the information is used to remove a contractor from a list of

---

[34] In respective order: Justice (1977); Cmnd 6524 (1976); Fourth Report from the Select Committee on the PCA, HC 615 and 444 (1977/8), HC 593 (1979/80) and HC 322 (1983/4).

[35] Cmnd 7449 (1979).

[36] See chapter 4 Notes 109 and 112. They might relate, for instance, to the receipt of "confidential information" by a department.

[37] In local government the Local Government Act 1988 offers some relief where tendering lists and contracts are drawn up or allocated on "non-commercial" considerations.

tenderers, as it has been, that is a commercial matter and excluded by paragraph 9. The limitation of the functions of the PCA as perceived by the Government was brought home clearly when discussing the award of regional development grants to industry under the Industry Act 1972.[38] Grant is provided in the form of a contract, based upon commercial considerations and advice from bodies which are not subject to investigation by the PCA: "The Minister of State did not believe that it would be possible for the PCA to discover whether any improper consideration had entered into the use of the Department's discretion in the period leading up to the award of a contract." When the jurisdiction of the PCA was extended to embrace a large variety of NDPBs, those of a commercial nature such as the Civil Aviation Authority, a nationalised industry, were excluded.

Government is unwilling to have its contractual relationships and powers subjected to scrutiny by the PCA because it does not consider that commercial affairs are "of the very nature of government". The Government's activities as a buyer of goods and services were "quite different from those of its operations which were subject to the PCA's scrutiny".[39] The point is that it *is* exercise of power of government that is in question, but a power that is exercised through the medium of contract, not necessarily statutory command or authorisation, and it is this very power which is inadequately supervised. It is true that the Comptroller and Auditor General can investigate that value for money is achieved in government contracts but this constitutes a very different exercise from an investigation into the fairness and propriety of their allocation or non-allocation. The Select Committee made the point tellingly: "The Government has a duty to administer its purchasing policies fairly and equitably, and if these policies are the subject of complaint then the complaints should be investigated; this is particularly important if any future Government were again to use the award of contracts as a political weapon." This would not entail the questioning of the merits of

---

38   Industrial Development Act 1982, Cooperative Development Agency, etc, Act 1984; see chapter 2 p. 83 above.

39   The argument that some tasks of government are "governmental" and others are not and that the latter ought not to be subject to the same accountability devices as the former, really does open the door for non-governmental government. A converse argument is used to avoid investigation by the Commission for Racial Equality or Equal Opportunities Commission into government activities which are peculiar to government, or "governmental": Race Relations Act 1976 section 75 and *Home Office v CRE* [1981] 1 All ER 1042 and Sex Discrimination Act 1975 sections 29 and 85(1) and *Amin v Entry Clearance Officer* [1983] 2 All ER 865 (HL).

allocation of contracts, the Committee believed. Elsewhere we find that the Supreme Court of Canada has ruled that a provincial Ombudsman has power to investigate the commercial activities of a government commercial body.[40]

There is some ambiguity here in the Select Committee's approach, forced upon it no doubt by the constraints imposed upon the PCA's constitutional limitations. He cannot question the merits of a decision; there is an area of governmental activity where it is felt that because of inadequate accountability devices unjust activities may ensue; the real threat comes when the government uses its powers to achieve political objectives without adequate accountability, and yet political matters are, as the Select Committee themselves said, more appropriately the concern of MPs. If policies themselves are unfair, why should the PCA not be able to criticise them? There is evidence of a more critical approach in the PCA tackling areas which are commercially sensitive – the Barlow Clowes investigation involving the DTI and its regulatory responsibilities of investment businesses being a recent notorious case[41] – and in criticising bad rules.

In one area the PCA and indeed the LGO have been vigilant to maintain their jurisdiction, namely, in those areas where an agent performs duties or powers on behalf of a scheduled body. This is particularly important where government work is contracted out, as occurs with increasing regularity in contemporary Britain. The Act applies to work carried out on behalf of a government department or authority covered by the Act. What will be pursued here will be an allegation of maladministration causing injustice. However, some complaints may relate back to the terms of a contractual specification and improper performance, that is, a breach – matters for which the Ombudsman may not be the best port of call and where complainants will be third parties and for whom the contract is a *res inter alios acta*.

Maladministration and Bad Rules

Although it has rejected a broader definition of "maladministration" as suggested by *Justice*,[42] the Committee has encouraged the PCA to extend the parameters of his own definition. It was felt originally that the PCA could not question statutory rules

40   *British Columbia Development Corp. v Friedman* [1985] 1 WWR 193.
41   R. Gregory and G. Drewry, "Barlow Clowes and the Ombudsman", (1991) *Public Law* 192 and 408.
42   Who recommended that he be empowered to investigate any "unreasonable, unjust or oppressive action" (Justice), Note 34 above.

or departmental administrative rules (primary legislation is not action taken in the course of administrative functions and is *per se* outside the PCA's competence). The rationale of this exclusion was that rule-making was a legislative not an administrative function. *Individual* decisions under statutory or delegated legislative authority or under departmental rules were an appropriate subject of investigation if a complaint was made. The Committee has distinguished between statutory instruments and other forms of delegated legislation. If the former, the PCA cannot question their form, content or merits, though he may examine the effects of an instrument allegedly causing hardship to a complainant and he may ask the department to review its operation and inquire into the steps taken by the department. For the latter category, non-statutory instruments, he may not question their form, content or merits, but his powers to investigate maladministration in the stages leading to the making of the order, or its review, seem to be broader. For departmental rules, the PCA was initially wary of becoming concerned with what are often expressions of department policy. The Select Committee urged the PCA that when a rule was causing hardship or injustice in a particular case under investigation, he should inquire as to what action had been taken to review the rule, and if the rule were found defective, what action had been taken to remedy the particular hardship sustained by the complainant. If the rule had not been revised, it would be open to the PCA to find maladministration in the individual case if there had been deficiencies in the departmental review of the rule. In several special reports published under section 10(4) of his Act the PCA has criticised regulations, and disparities between what a regulation required and the official guidance given to those administering a scheme and he has criticised the operation of a departmental rule. A bolder approach is perhaps being adopted.[43]

There have also been numerous occasions when the PCA has asked a department to review its policy rules but has subsequently found nothing on which to bring a finding of maladministration. A department would have to be very inept to carry out a review of a rule which was so inadequate that it amounted to maladministration. If deficiencies are not present in the review, there is little that the PCA can do if the department perseveres with the rule.[44] It is interesting to note that the PCA has

---

43 See HC 13 (1993/4).

44 Though the Select Committee may put pressure on the department: see, for example, *Knechtl*, 2nd Report, Select Committee on PCA (1970–71) at XII and Cmnd 4846.

investigated the Prison Rules, Rule 33(1) and the departmental rules supplementing it, which are concerned with correspondence between a prisoner and other persons. He found nothing to criticise, although in *Silver v UK*[45] censorship under this rule, and the departmental rules in particular, was found to be in breach of Article 8 of the European Convention of Human Rights. Further, as the PCA did not constitute an "effective remedy" under Article 13 for breaches of the Convention, the British Government was found to be in breach of Article 13. This is to apply international standards to our domestic administration, a task which was never envisaged for the PCA. His task is not to question the content of legality, but to ensure administrative propriety within a given framework of legality.

In the 1992/3 session the PCA roundly criticised departmental rules which delayed compensation payments on new unpaid benefits for disability and living allowance under the "fallow year" rule as too unfavourable to claimants. This criticism was made in a special report under section 10(4) of his Act and is striking for what is, in effect, criticism of departmental policy.[46] It is hoped that this approach will be continued.[47]

Good Administration and Maladministration

What standards of administrative propriety has the PCA insisted upon? Gregory and Hutchesson list the following shortcomings which PCAs have criticised:

(1) Assorted mistakes, errors and oversights.
(2) Failing to impart information or provide an adequate explanation.
(3) Giving inaccurate information and misleading advice.[48]
(4) Misapplication of departmental rules and instructions.
(5) Peremptory or inconsiderate behaviour on the part of officials.
(6) Unjustifiable delay.
(7) One might add not treating, so far as possible, like cases alike.

---

[45] [1983] 5 EHRR 347; and see Birkinshaw (1983) NILQ 269.
[46] See, however, his comments reported in *The Guardian* of 5 June 1992; "The contents of legislation [the article refers to regulations also] and possible need for amendment to it are matters for Parliament itself to consider and not for me."
[47] See HC 652 (1992/3).
[48] And see A. Mowbray, "A Right to Official Advice. The Parliamentary Commissioner's Perspective" (1990) *Public Law* 68.

(8) In his Annual Report for 1993 (paragraph 7) the PCA stated that strict adherence to the letter of the law which causes hardship may constitute maladministration.

(9) He added offering disproportionate redress; failure to inform of rights of appeal; following faulty procedures or not monitoring compliance with adequate procedures.

Further, the PCA has long established that he can question the *quality* of the exercise of discretion in a decision, though it was argued that exercise of discretion was *per se* a judgment upon the *merits* of a decision. The common fault has been a failure by officials to consider all relevant factors in the case in question, and the circumstances in which such failures have occurred have been varied. The PCA has criticised departments for not following all necessary procedures to elicit relevant information, including sometimes the holding of interviews on an informal basis or not allowing appropriate cross-examination at a public inquiry, even if the inquiry was conducted within the strict letter of the Inquiries Procedure Rules. Conversely, Lord Keith in the *Lonrho* litigation[49] involving the takeover of Harrods advised that departments engaged in informal procedures at their peril. The PCA has criticised discrepancies between the information collected by officials, and the way this differs from the advice which they hand on to their Ministers when such advice constitutes the reasons afforded to a complainant for a decision. On occasions he has come close to criticising a decision as wrong because improper or insufficient weight was given to information or evidence, a course of action which takes him perilously close to the merits.[50]

The PCA is given wide powers to obtain information[51] (PCA Act sections 7(2) and 8(1) to (3)) the only exclusion being Cabinet documents.[52] Access to documents is not available to Members

---

49 *Lonrho plc v Secretary of State* [1989] 3 All ER 609 (HL).
50 *The Barlow Clowes Affair*, HC 76 (1989/90), paragraph 4.99. For criticism of the Local Commissioner see *R v Local Commissioner ex parte Croydon LBC* [1989] 1 All ER 1033; see also *R v Local Commissioner ex parte Eastleigh BC* [1988] 3 All ER 151 (CA).
51 Information obtained in an investigation will not necessarily be handed over to the complainant. Under section 68 of the Education Act 1944, when complaints are made to the Secretary of State about an education authority "The Department . . . when confronted with requests to see information obtained from authorities . . . starts with the predisposition not to give it", though they might if circumstances merit it. The PCA agreed with this predisposition, Inv. C 90/82.
52 Section 8(4). Is this still justifiable given the decisions in Public Interest Immunity litigation: *Burmah Oil v Bank of England* [1979] 3 All ER 700 (HL), *Air Canada v Secretary of State* [1983] 1 All ER 910 (HL)?

of Parliament individually;[53] the PCA can ask officials questions which individual MPs cannot; he can get more answers and as his investigation unfolds, more information comes to light. His responsibilities under the Code of Practice on *Open Government* (1994) will cause him to examine documents and files relating to complaints within his jurisdiction to see whether access to information should be given and information is unlikely to be made available to individuals which would not be provided in answer to a Parliamentary Question. However, many areas and government bodies are outside his jurisdiction and in relation to these the PCA will not be able to investigate complaints.[54] He is the acknowledged expert on what constitutes "maladministration" and there has been little doubt that his procedural powers have made the office far more effective in remedying routine but resistant grievances than MPs. This is not to belittle the role of MPs, simply to acknowledge the limits on what they are able to achieve if a department is not prepared to concede a point. MP intervention may, for instance, be able to remedy the most serious cases of injustice, for example, one only has to refer to the role of Chris Mullin MP and the Birmingham Six and the examination of the English criminal justice system that ensued. Furthermore, Rawlings has pointed out in his research that MPs may provide an important role in monitoring a departmental response to PCA reports to see what the department/agency is doing.[55] As the office was established to further the role of Parliament *vis-à-vis* the executive's administrative activities, the relationship of the office with the Select Committee and the role of the Select Committee were seen as essential.

The Role of the Select Committee

The Select Committee was left largely to establish its own role. It discusses the reports of the PCA and those that are published

53 For the position of MPs on select committees see chapter 2 p. 40 *et seq.* and Birkinshaw (1990), at pp. 14–17. Note the Maxwell pension hearings and the Iraqi Supergun inquiries where witnesses, civil servants in the latter case, refused to answer questions with apparent impunity: HC 61 (1991/2) Social Security Committee and HC 86 (1991/2) Trade and Industry Committee.
54 It is important to appreciate that both bodies are outside his jurisdiction, for example, the Cabinet Office as well as functions of departments, for example, foreign affairs, criminal prosecutions, national security and so on.
55 R. Rawlings, "The MPs' Complaints Service" (1990) *Modern L.R.* 22 and 149.

are laid before both Houses, and it may apply pressure to departments to provide remedies. In 1969 it declared its interests as being: examination of the remedies for aggrieved persons, particularly in cases where the PCA has made a special report under section 10(3) (failure to remedy after a finding of injustice caused by maladministration); and secondly the remedial action within departments when his investigations brought to light defects in a *system* of administration. Gregory and Hutchesson describe how out of these two emerged a concern with "administrative policy" – "what departments are responsible for by way of day to day administration, as opposed to policy questions of political significance for which Ministers were responsible".

The sense of the distinction is reasonably clear, though there is a characteristic ambivalence here as Ministers are notionally responsible for *all* policy of their department – reluctant though they may be to accept the implications of such policy.[56] It is possible to indicate changes in administrative practice within departments as a result of Select Committee pressure, and the Government has accepted that changes in administrative rules should be announced in Parliament when the original rules had been announced there,[57] an undertaking which was not adhered to in the notorious case of Matrix Churchill.[58] What of rules not announced? Internal rules of the Inland Revenue have been published after PCA pressure.

The record of the Select Committee has in the past been tinged with some diffidence as it has tended to concentrate on procedural points rather than substantive points of policy. The Select Committee has recommended that the PCA should review legislation where it is not producing the results Parliament intended, though only when MPs were unaware of the consequences of the legislation. They rejected proposals by *Justice* that the PCA could

---

[56] On responsibility and NSAs, see chapter 2 p. 26 *et seq.*

[57] *R v Secretary of State for the Home Department ex parte Ruddock* [1987] 2 All ER 518 and details of changes in telephone tapping criteria.

[58] This was where guidelines concerning the exports of arms to foreign countries were altered without announcement in Parliament. Subsequently, a prosecution was brought against three British businessmen for breaching export embargoes and deception in obtaining export licences for machinery bound for Iraq and whose prosecution was approved by Ministers in spite of the relaxation of the guidelines; one of the businessmen had in fact operated as an undercover agent for British Intelligence at the relevant period. Public Interest Immunity certificates were signed to protect embarrassing evidence. When these were not upheld by the trial judge in the prosecution, the case collapsed and resulted in an inquiry under Scott LJ; witnesses included Mrs Thatcher and Mr Major; see Leigh (1993) and Tompkins (1993).

conduct investigations on his own initiative without a complaint from an MP, though they favoured a follow-up inquiry after a complaint had been lodged where the PCA believed that a department, or section of a department, was not dealing efficiently with its business. A former PCA has been bolder, and while noting that he was the only national Ombudsman not to have the power to investigate on his own initiative, suggested that such an investigation with the Committee or its chairman might be in the public interest.[59] In its review of the *Powers, Work and Jurisdiction of the Ombudsman*, the incumbent Commissioner informed the Select Committee that he did not support the widening of his powers to conduct *sua sponte* investigations. There was no need to create in his office a rigorous inspector-general of government going out "looking for trouble".[60] He was in favour of removing the "filter" via MPs although the Select Committee on various occasions has not appeared to be in favour of this.[61] Among MPs, opinion was evenly divided although some members of the Select Committee openly testified to the fact that their own initial acquaintance with the PCA was happenstance and the PCA cited a case where an MP had written to the PCA stating that he was never going to complain to him again. In response to a questionnaire 54.3 per cent of MPs stated they "never" or "hardly ever" read ombudsmen reports.[62]

I examined the Select Committee's arguments in favour of extending the jurisdiction of the PCA into commercial matters, to which the Government has adamantly and generally refused to cede ground.[63] What success the Select Committee has enjoyed has not been achieved after heroic struggles with the executive, though the legislative extension of the limitation period for claims relating to depreciation of land values caused by public works which resulted after a critical special report of the PCA on the time limits and publication of the scheme by the Department of Transport was an outstanding "victory".[64] Three of the biggest

59 HC 322 (1983/4).
60 HC 650 (1992/3), paragraph 17.
61 See HC 129 (1990/91) paragraphs 28 to 29 and HC 158 (1991/2) paragraph 15.
62 HC 33 I (1993/4), paragraph 25.
63 See, for example HC 650 (ix) (1992/3), at 199 – a memorandum from the Cabinet Office stated that the contractual exemption should remain.
64 Amendments to the scheme were effected by Part 13 of the Local Government Planning and Land Act 1980 and followed the first special report of the PCA under section 10(3) of the 1967 Act (1977–78; HC 666). Inv. 32 C 1004/80.

government "defeats" at the hands of the PCA, *Sachsenhausen,*
Court Line and *Barlow Clowes*, did not follow Select Committee
Reports under section 10(3) of the Act where a remedy is or
may not be forthcoming, but inept ministerial addresses to the
House of Commons.[65] In *Barlow Clowes*, the Government issued
its "Observations"[66] stating why they disagreed with many of
the PCA's findings and conclusions, especially a duty to "third
parties" affected by regulatory failure, but nonetheless accepted
that it would be paying out £150 million in compensation.[67] The
"success" of the Select Committee has been achieved by its very
presence; it instils in senior civil servants the knowledge that they
might have to answer embarrassing questions and it has allowed
a continuing dialogue to be established, formally and informally,
between MPs and civil servants. The Select Committee remains
the body which can hold government to account for haughty and
high-handed actions leading to maladministration. However, the
fact that it chose not to investigate the Barlow Clowes affair
after the PCA's report may give an insight into the limits of
Parliamentary accountability of the executive in the contemporary
state.[68] However, as the PCA had achieved a remedy with which
he was happy it may be that the Committee felt there was little
left to investigate. The efficacy of the Committee *vis-à-vis* the
executive will be tested under the provisions of the Code of
Practice on *Open Government* where the Committee has stated
that when information is refused, the head of the department will
be summoned before the Committee to explain the refusal.[69]

It would be germane to highlight the lack of publicity associated
with his office, the paucity of coverage usually given to his reports
– he publishes quarterly "selections" of his investigations – and

---

65 And single investigation reports by the PCA under section 10(4) of his
     Act.
66 HC 99 (1989/90).
67 A running sore has been maladministration in court services; see section
     110 Courts and Legal Services Act 1990 and the amendment to PCA Act
     Schedule 3 prohibiting investigation by the PCA of action authorised or
     ordered by a judge; see Purchas (1993). In his annual report for 1992/3,
     the PCA reported that problems still existed in relation to jurisdiction over
     the Lord Chancellor's Department (HC 569 (1992/3), paragraph 81) in spite
     of the relaxation of the prohibition. 30 per cent of rejected complaints in
     1992 involved courts, judges and the Crown Prosecution Service (HC 650
     (1992/3) at 26. See C. Harlow in C. Harlow (ed.), *Public Law and Politics*
     (London, Sweet & Maxwell, 1986).
68 Gregory and Drewry, Note 41 above. See also, Parliamentary Commis-
     sioner Act 1994.
69 HC 33 I (1993/4), paragraph 88.

the fact that he remains an object of obscurity in the public eye. Perhaps, the cynic may suggest, the choice of the PCA to police the Code on *Open Government* is an indication of government's attempts not only to minimise successful challenge but to minimise the number of complaints. However, given that the Ombudsman will not be looking at individual injustice but at refusal to allow access which is not justified by the exemptions, it will be reasonable to expect that different types of complainants will be seeking his assistance – public interest groups, campaigners and lobbyists. He has stated his intention to assume a "robust" role for citizens in information complaints.[70] *Barlow Clowes* brought him into rare prominence but that publicity has now largely receded although opinions may differ. It may be that the PCA's work under the Code will help to bring him under a permanent spotlight. However, it is a fact that he cannot enforce his findings upon a reluctant department, and though outright refusal to accept a decision is rare, only on *one* known occasion has the Select Committee constrained a department to remedy an individual injustice caused by maladministration. In 1981, the PCA in his annual report started to list the remedies awarded by departments beyond a mere apology, and some of the individual sums are quite significant, for example, £150 million in the *Barlow Clowes* case, £600,000 to the farmers who had been the victims of MAFF maladministration in the salmonella case[71] and £57,000 compensation because of a mishandling of an application for regional selective assistance.[72] Of course, the amount of compensation awarded, if any is awarded at all, is based upon *ex gratia* considerations by the department, not legal right. Where individual cases raise precedents for a whole *class* of case which it would be difficult to deny, the constitutional principle that significant amounts of public expenditure must be authorised by *specific* legislative authority has been invoked to evade compensation.[73] In the land compensation cases referred to above, for instance, an estimated amount of £8 million was involved in compensation and the figure involved in *Barlow Clowes* doubtless explains why the Government offered such resistance to the report in order to prevent a precedent being established for regulatory failure in such a volatile field as investment business. In a relationship

---

[70]   *Ibid.*, at paragraphs 78 and onward.
[71]   HC 947 1992/3.
[72]   Inv. C 1000/80.
[73]   Payments in *Barlow Clowes* were made out of repayable advances to the Contingency Fund. HC 99 (1989/90).

characterised by negotiation, discretion and political sensitivity, much no doubt depends upon the attitude and temperament of a particular Commissioner. It would be unfair to lay at the PCA's door the shortcomings which ensue from limitations inherent in the PCA's powers and office. Those limitations were deliberately imposed because of constitutional sensitivities and political jealousies. It is a wonder, perhaps, that the PCA has been accepted and has achieved what he has, which probably means that he has not been an unduly burdensome thorn in any important flesh.[74] On the other hand, the Secretary of State was made to eat humble pie in the *Barlow Clowes* episode and various Ministers have testified to the efficacy of the PCA. With this in mind, it is interesting to examine the Select Committee's recommendations from its report on the Powers, Work and Jurisdiction of the Ombudsmen.[75]

The Select Committee's Recommendations

The Committee's remit covered the PCA, HSC and NIPCA. It carried out a survey of MPs' attitudes and approaches to the PCA and in spite of some wide-ranging recommendations, it felt that investigation of the individual complaints should remain the PCA's priority. It was anxious to ensure that adequate funds were provided by the government to ensure the effective achievement of the PCA's "enlarged responsibilities" following *Open Government*. In the light of evidence that "there are many who are ignorant of the PCA's services" it recommended a survey by the Office into public awareness of the PCA and HSC as well

---

[74] This is not to deny that the barbs of the PCA have hit their target with stinging effect. In the first edition of this book I noted the report of an investigation into the Home Office and a forensic scientist whose competence was subsequently questioned. The complaint was made by Mr John Preece who was convicted on the evidence of the scientist and sentenced to life imprisonment. The complaint revealed, according to Mr Jack Ashley MP, "stunning complacency; incompetence and major errors of judgment" on behalf of Home Office officials. The Commissioner criticised the episode as "a pollution of justice at its source" (1983/4; HC 191) for the report. This is not meant as criticism of any past or present Commissioners whose names are "synonymous with long and very thorough investigations." *(The Guardian,* 27 January 1984). It is to acknowledge the constraints imposed upon the office by its legislative and *constitutional* framework. In Sweden, for instance, reform of the penal system was due in large measure to the Ombudsman. It is also noticeable that the Ombudsman has had a more significant impact on administrative *systems* in New Zealand.

[75] HC 33 I (1993/4).

as a "consumer satisfaction survey" into complainants' attitudes about investigations. There was also a recommendation that there should be an annual Parliamentary debate on the work of the Ombudsmen. The Committee felt that there should be restrictions on the use of the term "Ombudsman" and changes to the manner of appointment and financing. Its recommendations for improvement in administration require further comment.

Epitomes of reports showing matters of concern and good practice should be circulated to all departments, and bodies investigated should produce a report identifying how maladministration and failures of service have been rectified. Furthermore, a booklet should be produced on the work of the Ombudsman for civil servants. The Ombudsman may give informal advice to bodies in establishing complaints procedures but not formally approve such procedures (see chapter 2). Interestingly, it was recommended that the Ombudsman be given power under legislation to conduct an "audit" to review the effectiveness of practices and procedures where, for instance, a number of cases have raised concern about standards, but not as an investigation into an individual complaint. To help improve administration and publicise the Office, the Ombudsman should produce occasional publications on good administrative practice. The Committee felt that the PCA should be able to initiate an investigation at the recommendation of the Committee. In spite of the fact that 45 per cent of MPs seldom or never referred complaints to the PCA, the Committee felt that the filter to the PCA and NIPCA should be retained. While the report said nothing about contractual or commercial exclusions, there is a good deal which, if implemented, could significantly enhance the role of the Ombudsman. (For suggestions on the HSC see below).

Complaining about Health Treatment

The Health Service Commissioner (HSC) – who happens to be the PCA – was created by the National Health Services Reorganisation Act 1973 as amended. Consolidated legislation is now in the Health Service Commissioners Act 1993. The HSC reports on complaints made to him from complainants, their relatives or other suitable persons who can make a complaint on behalf of somebody who has died or is unable to act for himself. There *is* direct access to the Commissioner providing the NHS body has been given the opportunity to settle the complaint and a health authority can ask the HSC to investigate a complaint which it has referred to him. The HSC reports to the appropriate Secretary of State rather than to Parliament, though his reports are laid before both Houses. The Select Committee has recommended that he report directly to Parliament.

The most important matter excluded from investigation is a complaint which in his opinion concerns action taken solely in consequence of the exercise of some person's clinical judgment in the provision of diagnosis, care or treatment – in 1992 this involved 25 per cent of rejected complaints. There were 1,176 complaints received in 1991/2, the HSC rejected 540 *in toto*. A record number of 1,384 complaints were received in 1993/4. Also excluded are the judgments of nurses, midwives and others who are not covered by the 1981 procedure for clinical complaints outlined below. The HSC's remit covers any failure in the services provided or failure to provide a service by the various health service bodies listed in the Act, or any other action taken by them or on their behalf. There must be an allegation of hardship or injustice in consequence of the failure or maladministration. He cannot question the merits of a decision taken without maladministration in the exercise of a discretion (1993 Act section 3(4)). The HSC also has jurisdiction over NHS trusts. He cannot investigate complaints against family doctors, dentists, opticians and pharmacists or action taken by a Family Health Service Authority (FHSA) under its formal complaints procedure, but he can investigate other aspects of FHSAs' work such as informal investigation of complaints, closure of surgeries and removal of patients from a doctor's list.[76]

From December 1993 the HSC has started to name all bodies investigated and not simply those involved in cases taken up by the Select Committee on the PCA. In spite of the limitations in his jurisdiction the HSC has been very critical where an authority has not provided a service, as happened at Leeds. His 1993/94 annual report[77] was almost sensational in its criticism of bad standards and practices amounting to an "abnegation of responsibility".

Complaints about Policy

Many complaints are concerned with features which relate to reforms associated with the internal market in health services and are outside the competence of the HSC, although as mentioned

---

[76] The HSC has reported that as a consequence of the decision in *Roy v Kensington etc FPC* [1992] 1 All ER 705 (HL) where there is an allegation of maladministration in the offer by an FHSA of practices and location of practices, these can no longer be investigated (HC 605 (ix) (1992/3) at 177).

[77] HC 499 (1993/4).

he does have jurisdiction over NHS trusts[78] which provide services to GP fundholders and health authorities. There has been considerable reform in provision of health care culminating in the NHS and Community Care Act 1990.[79] There were often splits between Regional Health Authorities and District Health Authorities over relevant strategies: local authorities lost their right to appoint members to DHAs and the majority of crucial appointments to RHAs and DHAs are made by the Secretary of State.[80] NHS trusts are public corporations outside the health authority management structure and are "units actively involved in patient care" (usually hospitals) which are operationally independent although accountable to the Secretary of State and NHS Management Executive. New plans for NHS management were announced in October 1993.[81] NHS trusts are subject to legislation which applies to NHS facilities including the Hospital Complaints Act 1985, the Data Protection Act 1984 and the Access to Health Records Act 1990. Generally, guidance issued by the NHS Management Executive does not apply to trusts, but that on grievance handling does. Annual public meetings held by trusts have been portrayed as rather anaemic affairs[82] and their business plans do not have to be published.

Community Health Councils have a statutory duty to represent the interests of the public in the health service in their districts "and this could include commenting on District Health Authority plans for developing or changing services, assessing how local facilities compare with recommended national standards, investigating facilities for patients or monitoring complaints." A frequent complaint from Community Health Councils is that they are provided with inadequate information for consultation. Before the reorganisation in 1981, for instance, they had sometimes been denied access to relevant papers on, for example, proposed hospital closures prepared for Area Health Authorities.[83] The

---

78   Trusts are separate legal entities and are operationally independent of the health authority management structure. Trust status may be sought by any NHS unit "actively involved in patient care" (Longley, 1993, at 29 to 32).

79   *Ibid.*

80   With a heavy leaning towards those with commercial experience.

81   *Managing the New NHS*, Department of Health, October 1993. The Executive will remain within the Department and RHAs will be reduced from 14 to 8 and will become Regional Offices. Unlike RHAs they will not be subject to requirements for public meetings and the paper was noticeably silent on accountability mechanisms to the public for the new structures. DHAs will combine with FHSAs.

82   *The Guardian*, 1 October 1993.

83   See now *R v NW Thames RHA ex parte Daniels* (1993) *The Independent* 18 June.

Association of CHCs in England and Wales regularly considers and responds to NHS national documents but CHCs are no longer required to submit counter-proposals to DHA plans for services, making "the task of even suggesting that there are any acceptable alternatives extremely difficult" and temporary alterations are outside consultation even though they may well usher in substantial changes.[84] CHCs are likewise "consulted" in applications to establish trusts along with other local bodies. Some DHAs have organised "local meetings" to co-ordinate health and social services planning. Emphasis has been upon informality and co-ordination with parallel exercises conducted by Community Health Councils. The amount of time and quality of assistance given to complainants by CHCs has been shown to be variable, certainly when compared with the copious provision available to doctors from medical defence societies.[85] Government plans involve DHAs assuming the role of consumer advocate although the majority of their membership is appointed by the Secretary of State or her appointees. Surveys reported in *The Guardian*[86] suggest that only one authority in five is ready to meet in public even once a quarter. Two out of three do not allow CHC members to attend private sessions and trust boards do not allow the public, CHC members or the press to attend. Many trusts operated for 18 months before they held their first annual public meeting. There has also been serious disquiet about gagging clauses to prevent employees speaking out about shortcomings in service.[87] The Select Committee has recommended that staff bring their complaints of maladministration to the Committee requesting that they be referred to the HSC.

Complaints by Individuals and Clinical Judgment

On the question of individual complaints, a central feature has been the inability of the HSC to question decisions based upon "clinical judgment". Various official and Select Committee reports urged the Government to reconsider this exclusion,

---

[84] Longley, Note 78 above, at 34 to 35.
[85] C. Hogg, *Complaints about Family Practitioners, Community Health Councils and FHSA Complaints* (London, Greater London Association of CHCs, 1992).
[86] 26 October 1993.
[87] See p. 38 above and the Memorandum from Manufacturing Science Finance to the Select Committee, HC 650 (vi) (1992/3), at 126 to 127. The Committee recommended that effective staff complaints procedures be established and that guidance make it clear that staff may approach MPs for advice, HC 33 I (1993/4), paragraph 124.

especially as about 50 per cent of all complaints related to aspects solely concerned with clinical judgment, and what complainants wanted was "an explanatory mechanism", not compensation.[88] As the Select Committee put it, it was a failure causing widespread public dissatisfaction. "There is a danger that people who only want to establish what happened to them . . . will be driven to expensive and unnecessary litigation." Nonetheless, in its review of the Ombudsman, the Select Committee recommended that clinical judgment remain outside jurisdiction. The medical profession was opposed to such an extension, as were their insurers, but after protracted negotiation between the then DHSS and medical representative bodies, a complaints procedure for complaints other than those relating to family practitioners' services was introduced by Health Circular (81)5, now in HC 88(37).[89] In the memorandum accompanying the 1981 circular was a procedure to be introduced on a trial basis to deal with complaints relating to the exercise of clinical judgment by hospital medical and dental staff. This still applies. The circular has, then, the dual purpose of providing a complaints procedure before the HSC is resorted to, and more importantly allowing a complainant the opportunity for obtaining a "second opinion" on clinical judgment. In the former case, designated senior staff must be appointed to deal with complaints but the task of processing is usually delegated to a member of their staff and district HQ will have a member of staff responsible for co-ordinating complaints for the District General Manager.

The Patients' Charter emphasises that complaints should be considered at as high a level as appropriate. In March 1994, the contract of the chairman of a Welsh health authority was not renewed because of persistent poor performance in the resolution of disputes after serious criticism from the HSC. In July 1994, the Secretary of State, after a critical report from the HSC, announced that unsatisfactory records on complaints procedures would be justification for dismissal of senior personnel.

Complaints about clinical judgment involve the consultant (or doctor) in question who can discuss the matter with the patient, a reply from the consultant or District Manager and if the complainant is not satisfied, the Regional Director of Public Health will discuss the matter with the consultant, the complainant and colleagues. The next stage involves the Director referring the case to two independent consultants who can meet the patient, leading

88 HC 465 (1979/80).
89 Hospital Complaints Procedure Act 1985 section 1.

where necessary to an Independent Professional Review by two consultants nominated by the Joint Consultants' Committee. The complainant can be accompanied at the discussion by a friend or relative, and a GP. The Independent Professional Review provides the "second opinion". The complainant receives a formal reply from the District or Unit Manager stating what action is to be taken, and the issue will generally remain confidential. Interestingly, the discretion of the Director on a referral is subject to the HSC's jurisdiction and there are many cases of complaint.

Uncontroversial as these provisions are, the medical profession was extremely unhappy about the "second opinion" provision and the prospects of "double jeopardy," that is, the procedure would be used by a complainant to elicit information to bring an action in negligence against the authority. A report by the then DHSS stated that the procedure is eligible for complaints "which are substantial, but which do not seem likely to lead to litigation."[90] The procedure dealt with 149 cases in 1990; 184 in 1991 and 236 in 1992.[91] It seems that the procedure is aiming essentially to be a prophylactic device for the future, so that lessons may be learned from past mistakes and adequate explanations offered. However, in well over a half of the concluded cases, the complaint was not resolved to the satisfaction of the complainant. Originally, about 40 per cent of cases considered unsuitable for review were considered to be by complainants who were information-gathering for future litigation. However, there is now an arbitration scheme for medical negligence[92] and rules have been changed to allow far more general pre-action and pre-trial discovery with a view to assisting settlement.[93]

Health authorities (and trusts) are under a duty to monitor complaints made by patients or made on their behalf and arrangements for grievance resolution and summaries have to be provided at quarterly intervals to be considered by the authority or others. Statistical information is seriously inadequate. A great deal of discretion is allowed by the guidelines and although the Department of Health has encouraged a systemic approach, "progress

---

[90] *Report on Operation of Procedure for Independent Review of Complaints*, DHSS, 1983.

[91] HC 650 (ii) (1992/3).

[92] Longley, Note 78 above.

[93] The law has become more accommodating in recent years in allowing greater scope for pre-action discovery in accident cases, *Waugh v British Railways Board* [1980] AC 521; see RSC Ords 24, 38 rr 37, 38 and 39. Only 4 per cent of complaints about medical negligence are litigated.

is spasmodic and monitoring is usually taken to refer to the progress made with individual complaints rather than consideration
of overall organizational deficiencies".[94] Training and publicity
remain patchy. A review of NHS complaints procedures has been
set in motion (the Wilson Committee); the Select Committee
believed that the system was devised for the convenience of providers, not users.[95]

The Wilson Committee reported in May 1994 (*Being Heard*,
HMSO 11 May 1994). It reported that 50,000 complaints were
made against hospitals in England and Wales in 1992, 2,000
against GPs. It recommended that complaints should be resolved
informally wherever possible – most "within days". Where investigation is required, they should be resolved within three weeks,
at most all complaints should be resolved within three months.
A two-tier system is recommended: an immediate response from
"front line staff" and secondly an independent panel to determine
difficult cases possessing a majority of "lay members". Hospitals
and FHSAs (see below) should appoint a complaints officer and
the HSC should have a wider role.

General Practitioners

For family practitioners who are on the NHS lists, there have
been special complaints provisions since 1912, when the state first
contracted with private practitioners for the latter to provide their
services to the public at public expense. Complaint resolution
emerged as an ancillary feature of "value for money" mechanisms
and complaints can be dealt with by service committees. The
bodies are called Family Health Service Authorities. Procedures
are governed by detailed regulations and guidelines.[96] An officer
is appointed to deal *solely* with complaints and a lay conciliator
may be appointed to resolve the complaint informally. Formal
resolution requires a committee which deals with breaches of
service contracts including clinical judgment – many complaints
would not be covered by the breach of service contract formula.
Appeals, held *in camera*, go to the Secretary of State who has
delegated the responsibility to a regional health authority.[97] Parties and witnesses may attend, and legal representation is allowed

---

[94] Longley, Note 78 above, at 70.
[95] HC 33 I (1993/4), paragraphs 95 and onward.
[96] NHS (Service Committee and Tribunal) Regs SI 1992/664.
[97] The position of the Secretary of State could be invidious where s/he dealt
     with a complaint by a patient against a doctor who had been a critic of
     government policy: *The Times*, 15 March 1993.

on appeal to the Secretary of State, but it is excluded at hearings before service committees, even if provided on a voluntary basis, although a doctor will be assisted by a union representative, usually with great experience of such hearings. The CoT and HSC have been very critical of these procedures on a number of grounds and they do seem to be unfairly weighted against the complainant.[98] Longley has observed that the complaints officers may "informally" be assuming the role of a more active conciliator than the appellation would indicate, thereby deflecting cases away from the informal or formal process which might prevent "important issues of collective importance coming to the fore". There may also be increased pressure to monitor the trend of complaints about GPs – which at present there is no duty to perform – as FHSAs review and audit GPs' practices. The secretive nature of the formal hearings before committees, however, means that it is difficult to use information from such hearings for monitoring and managerial purposes. The position is generally unsatisfactory.[99] The Select Committee has recommended that the Ombudsman be empowered to investigate maladministration in the operation of service committees, that the FHSAs (Boards in Scotland) investigate complaints instead of leaving the onus on the complainant and that the HSC be empowered to investigate maladministration on the part of GPs.[100]

The General Medical Council, the doctors' governing body, deals with about 1,600 complaints a year – just over a half of these were rejected because they did not involve an allegation of serious professional misconduct. The GMC has requested broader powers to deal with a wider range of complaint. The nurses' professional body, the UKCCN, has also been very active on the subject of complaints resolution.

Local Government Ombudsmen (LGOs)

General Issues

The Commissions for Local Administration (CLA) were established by Part 3 of the Local Government Act 1974 – one for

---

98 Council on Tribunals AR 1989/90 and 1990/1, at 11 and onward and 1992/3, at 4 to 11.
99 See the Fourth Report of the PCA/HSC (1992/3) where complaints handling was characterised by "under-qualified staff and wholly inadequate supervision".
100 HC 33 I (1993/4), paragraphs 111 to 119.

England and one for Wales. There are three Commissioners (LGOs) covering three regions in England and there is a Commissioner for Wales and one for Scotland. The Act originally required the Secretary of State to designate representative bodies for the Commission in England and for Wales but this requirement was repealed by the Local Government and Housing Act 1989. The Commission is under a duty to review the operation of the Act every three years in relation to the investigation of complaints and to report to relevant departments. Copies are sent to local authority associations. We have already seen in chapter 3 how the CLA has produced Codes of Guidance under the LGHA on *Devising a Complaints System, Council Housing Repairs* and *Good Administrative Practice*. It has taken the lead in establishing the UK Ombudsman Association and promulgating good practice.

Justice, in its 1980 Report on the Local Ombudsman, said that the most thorough investigation of a local authority complaint took place not when it was referred by the complainant to a member or to the council, but when, under the Local Government Act 1974 section 26(5), the Commissioner brought it to the attention of the authority before beginning the formal investigation. It should be noted, however, that every year, more complaints were made directly than through members of authorities. Direct complaints tend not to be frivolous or trivial and about 40 per cent of full investigations each year were into complaints which were initially made directly. All of this meant extra time and expense for the LGO and complainants. About one half of direct complaints disappeared once they were referred back to the complainant, and the LGO felt that they lost heart and as these were often the most vulnerable members of the community, some of those most in need of assistance did not receive it. The *Justice* Report showed how the upper socio-economic brackets were more likely to use the CLA, though it pointed out that treatment was the same for all groups once the complaint was properly referred.

Under the 1988 LGA, the requirement that a complaint had to go through a member of the authority complained against was dropped. The LGO will want to be assured that the authority complained against has had an opportunity to investigate it through its procedures, and if so satisfied s/he will receive the complaint directly. The result has been a dramatic increase in complaints: in the year ending 31 March 1989, the first year of direct access, complaints had increased by 44 per cent over the previous year and in 1990 by a further 24 per cent to 8,733. For the year ending March 1993, 13,307 complaints were made to the LGOs.

Complaints do not have to particularise the nature of the grievance and the Court of Appeal has been generous in its interpretation of the discretion of a Commissioner to accept complaints which are not specifically pleaded, which have by-passed
the member when that requirement existed and which are outside
the 12-month time limit.[101]

The CLA always advocated that it have the power to receive
complaints directly rather than through the member. However,
the vigour with which it applies section 26(5), namely, that there
must be attempted local resolution, may cause problems of its
own. In its 1978 Report, the CLA described a research project which showed that if complainants were interviewed *before*
their complaints were rejected, such interviews often produced
evidence not apparent from the written submission resulting in
the investigation of complaints which would otherwise have been
rejected. There is a danger that complainants will give up if they
are told to try local procedures and they may have justification
for feeling no confidence in them. They are told that they can
come to the LGO if a local settlement is not achieved. But one
wonders if enough is being done to ensure that a barrier to replace
the filter has not been erected. One would feel more confident if
all authorities had developed grievance procedures (see chapter
3) but as of writing, no research had been conducted into the
impact of the CLA's 1992 code on grievances or their existence;
the Sheffield study in 1987 examined the impact of earlier codes.

The annual reports show that there is generally mutual trust
and co-operation between authorities and the Commissioners,
though there are some notable exceptions creating problems, as
we shall see. Commissioners refer to frequent informal contacts
with authorities under investigation and this frequently leads to
the production of more information. The LGO possesses power
to demand information from authorities which is on a par with
that possessed by the PCA in relation to departments,[102] although
LGOs have identified occasions when information has been con-
cealed. When complaints are not rejected at an early stage, for
example, as being outside jurisdiction, the usual practice is for
the Chief Executive to comment, on the understanding that this

---

101 *R v Local Commissioner, etc., ex parte Bradford MBC* [1979] 2 All ER
881.
102 A power effected by section 184 of the Local Government Planning and
Land Act 1980, which in turn reversed a restrictive interpretation of
the LGO's powers by the Divisional Court in *Re A Complaint Against
Liverpool CC* [1977] 2 All ER 650.

may be sent to the complainant; if the Commissioner feels that after consideration of the complaint and comments, it should not be pursued further, his decision and the Chief Executive's comments will be sent to the complainant. Quite often, this will occur after a local settlement. One problem, however, is that the complainant would have to return to the LGO. If the investigation does continue, files will be examined, interviews conducted, and then it may become apparent that the investigation should proceed no further. If it does proceed, it will only at the final stage lead to a formal report which is sent to the authority, to the complainant and to any member who might have been involved. The CLA can make three findings as appropriate: no maladministration; maladministration but no injustice suffered as a consequence; maladministration causing injustice for which the CLA can recommend *ex gratia* compensation from the authority, but only *after* he has investigated and reported. No legal power exists for the authority to make a payment after its own *internal* investigation alone, although in its triennial report of 1993 the CLA has recommended that such a power be explicitly defined in legislation.

The LGO Bailiwick

Like the PCA, the LGO is empowered to investigate complaints alleging injustice causing maladministration. There are prohibitions on what the CLA can investigate and these include: contractual and commercial matters excluding land acquisition and disposal; personnel matters; internal matters of school management or administration; and where the complainant has an alternative avenue of legal or administrative redress unless in the circumstances it would not be reasonable to insist upon the complainant pursuing such relief.[103] Legal proceedings and criminal matters are outside their jurisdiction as are complaints "affecting all or most of the inhabitants of the Authority's area". From 1981 housing complaints have topped planning complaints as the leading subject-matter of complaints properly referred.

Extending the Scope of the Ombudsman

The Commissioners generally speak well of their relationship with authorities, but their reports still indicate that a significant number of authorities are displaying a hostile reaction to the CLA.

---

[103] See *R v Local Commissioner ex parte Croydon LBC* [1989] 1 All ER 1033.

The Government has not accepted the need for an extension of the LGO's jurisdiction into contractual or commercial matters, which, when one considers the Salmon Commission Report[104] and notorious events in local authority administration, is a surprising omission. The LGA 1988 does set out a framework of rights for frustrated bidders and tenderers whereby they are entitled to have bids or requests included in selected lists of tenderers or tenders for contracts refused only for commercial reasons, to receive reasons for decisions and to have recourse to the courts where the Act's provisions are broken. The LGO has in fact taken a more robust line in pursuing commercial matters than has the PCA, and like the PCA, the LGO can examine allegations of maladministration against those acting as agents for local authorities, that is, providing services under contract. Matters of internal school management remain beyond the investigatory powers of the LGO (see chapter 3), although it may investigate the actions of an LEA in dealing with such a matter. The CLA has recommended in its 1993 Triennial Review that it should be empowered to investigate complaints concerning internal management of schools. The LGOs cannot investigate on their own initiatives – either without a complaint (as is possible with the Ombudsman in Sweden, Finland, Canadian Provinces and New Zealand) or on the request of an authority where no complaint has been made, although the Review recommended such a power. In 1986, the Widdicombe Report recommended that the LGO should be empowered to take cases to the courts where there were, *inter alia*, persistent breaches of the law by an authority. The Government did not accept such a proposal but created the post of monitoring officer to report to the authority on possible illegal action and maladministration (chapter 3, p. 134). The 1993 Triennial Review also recommended modifications to the exclusion concerning personnel matters and, crucially, to contractual matters relating to tendering.

Several consequences flowed from the Local Government and Housing Act 1989. The first was that the Representative Body which represented local authority associations and which had persistently obstructed the Local Commission in its recommendations for reform was abolished. Furthermore, the CLA was no longer to be financed by local authorities but by central government revenue support grant. The CLA has power to appoint advisory commissioners and has specific power to issue guidance to authorities on good administrative practice (see p. 100).

104   Cmnd 6524 (1976).

The departure of the Representative Body is no sad loss. Under the Local Government Planning and Land Act 1980, the Secretary of State was empowered to issue or approve Code(s) of Practice concerning the publication by authorities of information about their functions for their community. The CLA requested the DoE that the Code on Rate Demands should contain information about authorities' *own* grievance procedures as well as how to complain to the LGO. The RB opposed this. In the event, the information was restricted to "possible supplementary information that might be published in association with rate demand notes" and a CLA survey showed that very few authorities gave any information at all on these topics. We have seen the more recent powers of the CLA to provide guidance and how such has been provided on complaints procedures.

Enforcing Decisions

The more intractable problem has concerned the minority of authorities which do not comply with a Commissioner's final report. The only sanction for a Commissioner is to publish a "further report" setting out the facts and giving it maximum publicity, although the LGHA 1989 introduced some additional powers effective from 1990 (section 26(2) to (2)C). Basically authorities are given three months from the date of receipt of an adverse report to notify the LGO of what action they are taking or proposing to take. The authority will be given a further three months to take the action. Where the outcome is unsatisfactory, the LGO may issue a further report recommending necessary remedial action by the authority and what is required to prevent similar injustices in the future. The same time limits apply. Where the authority intends not to act upon the further report, it must be considered by the whole council. Any member named in the report must not vote on the issue and independent reports must be made where reports are presented to the council by parties interested in the LGO report (section 28). Where the LGO remains dissatisfied, s/he may require publicity in the local press of a statement to be agreed between the authority and the LGO which will contain material as required by the LGO and, if the authority wishes, the authority's reasons for non-compliance. The LGO has power to cause it to be published at the authority's expense (section 26 (2D)–(H)). Furthermore a New National Code of Local Authority Conduct has been produced and members must declare to be guided by the Code in their actions. Where a LGO adverse report finds maladministration and a breach of the

Code by a member,[105] that member must be named in the report with particulars of the breach unless the LGO considers it unjust (sections 31–32).

In 1992/93, 17 further reports were issued which is remarkably consistent in numerical but not percentage terms with the position a decade earlier: in 1982/83, 20 further reports were issued. Since 1974, 302 further reports have been issued and the CLA has reported 201 cases of "unsatisfactory outcomes". More daunting is the fact that in only one case has there been a satisfactory outcome following publication of a statement by an authority. The attitude of the Representative Body when it existed and local authority associations has sometimes been reprehensible; the Association of District Councils for instance advised authorities not to minute any informal practices they may have relating to non-statutory participatory and consultation exercises with neighbours and third parties on planning applications. Such a practice would probably amount to maladministration but it is a graphic illustration of the defensive posture which did local government little good.

It may well be that the LGO will have to be invested with powers to seek enforcement of his recommendations through court orders as exists for the Northern Ireland Complaints' Commissioner, where courts can also quantify the complainant's loss. In cases of persistent breach the Attorney General (NI) may seek enforcement through the High Court though obviously these powers relate to the problem of religious and political discrimination practised by many local authorities in Northern Ireland at the time the Ombudsman was introduced into the province.[106] *Justice* has supported this proposal in the past and more crucially the Citizen's Charter suggested there may be a need for legal enforcement if authorities continue to be recalcitrant, the Government having rejected the proposal when it was made in the Widdicombe Report. The CLA obviously is unwilling to prejudice its relationship with authorities generally by resorting to legal enforcement, but there have been some signs that the CLA has recognised the distinct possibility, however.[107] On one matter, the 1980 *Justice* report was disappointing. It saw the CLA as a remedy for individual grievances essentially, and underplayed the role it could perform

---

105   Breach of the Code does not of itself amount to maladministration but may be *prima facie* evidence of such.
106   A famous case involving the NICC and the courts concerned the prohibition of the use of publicly owned facilities for the playing of Gaelic games.
107   See in the past the 1983 Annual Report Report of the CLA and, for example, Inv. 994/C/81.

in improving standards of general administration. A reading of Commissioners' Reports has brought home the sensitivity of individual commissioners to the balance to be struck between the requirements of administrative efficiency, administrative necessity and individual justice, not only for the complainant but for whole classes of complainants. Since 1974 a particular skill has been displayed by particular local commissioners, I feel, that is not often repeated elsewhere in our public administration. The skill is in achieving a balance between public efficiency and individual justice. It remains reprehensible that the Commission has not been taken too seriously in certain quarters of local authority administration.

Impact upon Administration

It has been noticeable how over the years the types of complaint investigated have changed, reflecting changes in the bodies over whom the LGOs have jurisdiction. Now, HATs have been included, as have UDCs (planning functions only) and the National Rivers Authority (flood defence and land drainage), housing benefits and admission and expulsion decisions of grant-maintained schools. In spite of the embargo on commercial matters, the CLA has nudged away at certain restrictions so that concessionary bus passes are within jurisdiction as are complaints about market operations and provision of moorings. On the general contractual and commercial exclusion the Government has been adamant. 1992/3 the LGOs received 13,307 complaints (1982/3 2,753 referred through a member); 13,617 complaints were determined in that year; 12,862 concluded after initial inquiries; 336 formal investigations were discontinued; formal investigation reports were issued in 419 cases with 339 findings of maladministration with injustice, 42 of maladministration and 38 of no maladministration. 2,114 complaints were settled locally and 17 further reports were issued. The average length of time in investigations where there is a formal report is $70\frac{1}{2}$ weeks (this includes investigations which were discontinued without the need for a formal report) and this was six weeks better than the target set in the 1991/2 business plan, although it is interesting to compare it with 43 weeks in 1982/3, but one should note the dramatic increase in complaints in that decade. The average time taken to deal with a complaint which was not subject to a full investigation was 14 weeks – two weeks less than the target.

I have already spoken about the detailed guidance published by the CLA, in particular that on complaints systems and good administrative practice which includes examples of common errors. In July 1993, Bulletins for authorities were launched with examples of errors and a Guide to the Local Ombudsman Service has been published which is updated every six months. In the Annual Report for 1992/3 the reasons for finding maladministration were set out – 37 grounds were established. Delay is the largest single factor and failing to comply with the law is second. The CLA has insisted that authorities give reasons for decisions which are clear, precise and informative; provide correct information and accurate advice; obtain and give access to all relevant information in the making of a decision; allow interviews and representations to be made; and has insisted on "fair play" in administration, to a far greater extent than would be insisted upon by law,[108] and that authorities generally get their procedures right for the future by drawing up their own codes of practice or establishing more obvious domestic grievance procedures.[109] Failure to monitor progress of an issue, to abide by undertakings, to publish policies or formulate policies for action are listed. Some of their recommendations have involved expenditure of large sums of money, for example, £100,000 to a community group, although three-quarters of the sum would be provided by central government.[110] The LGO has come much closer to questioning the merits of a decision than has the PCA, though the statement: "The decision was taken with maladministration and I therefore am able to question the merits"[111] is unusually sanguine.[112] Generous accommodation for "standing" has been afforded to representative groups bringing complaints. The CLA and individual Commissioners have done far more to publicise their service than has the PCA. The LGHA 1989 imposed duties upon the *authority* to consider the report where there is an adverse finding – which might be satisfied by placing the report before a committee but the *full Council* must consider a further report where one is

---

108 "An Ombudsman's task is not to decide whether authorities were entitled to take particular decisions as a matter of law, but to establish whether their decisions were taken with or without maladministration. Compliance with the law gives no immunity from maladministration. Acceptable administrative action lies within the frame of a wider (and less precise) concept than action within the law": Pat Cook, 1983 Report, Inv., 387/77. See the comments of Lord Diplock in *Nat. Fed. of Self Employed etc v Inland Revenue Commissioners* [1982] AC 617.

109 Inv. 945/C/81.

110 Inv. 13/C/80.

111 Inv. 9/5/82.

112 On an attempt to establish the distinction between the role of the CLA and the use of the ballot box to change a decision, see Inv. 11/S/82.

issued (sections 26 and 28). A greater use of interviews, especially for members of lower socio-economic groups, would clearly be worthwhile to help those who have difficulty cutting through the thickets of public administration. On this point Widdicombe recommended a right of *sua sponte* investigation where the LGO suspects the possibility of maladministration in an authority, but this has not been accepted.

Ombudsmen and the Courts

Both the PCA and the CLA are subject to the supervisory jurisdiction of the High Court on an application for judicial review.[113] In the case of the LGO the courts have allowed review of the exercise of their powers and in a manner which could be very inhibiting. In the *Croydon* case[114] the LGO had investigated complaints about the way in which an education appeals panel operating under the Education Act 1980 had dealt with a case. The fact that the appeal body was operating judicially did not bar the LGO's investigation because the investigation was into the refusal to consider the merits of the individual case and concerned the way in which a decision was made. However, when considering whether or not to decline jurisdiction because the person had a remedy through the courts, the LGO did not have to ask whether the complainant would succeed but whether a legal remedy could be provided. The LGO was also under a continuing duty to consider the appropriateness of judicial relief at any stage in his investigation, so that a transfer might take place – the indigence of a plaintiff was not referred to although LGOs have stated that that is a factor they would consider when exercising their discretion to investigate. Where there was a specialist tribunal established to hear the complaint (the panel) and the relief the LGO could offer was the same as the court, the LGO should consider giving way to the courts especially where there were no safeguards to protect the public bodies, that is, the requirement

[113] *R v PCA ex parte Dyer* [1994] 1 All ER 375 (QBD); this case and an earlier case show that the widest of leeway will be given to PCA discretion: *Re Fletcher's Application* [1970] 2 All ER 527 established the stand-off position of the courts. In *Dyer*, the complainant challenged, unsuccessfully, the PCA's refusal to take up some complaints and to allow her to see the preliminary draft report which is sent to the department complained against. The LGO has been successfully challenged; see below. See *Halifax BS v Edell* [1992] 3 All ER 389 (Ch. D) on the Building Societies Ombudsman and note that under the Social Security Act 1990, the Pensions Ombudsman is subject to a right of appeal to the High Court.

[114] [1989] 1 All ER 1033 (QBD).

for leave, provision of costs and so on. On the facts of the case the LGO was wrong to have found maladministration on the part of the panel as they had made the decision correctly. However, more generally, the decision could prove very difficult for the LGOs if strictly applied, especially as maladministration and illegality do often meet in a twilight zone.[115] It should be noted that Woolf LJ did not rule the investigation unlawful but the finding alone.

The PCA has written about the advantages and relative merits of Ombudsman investigations and judicial decisions,[116] and the relationship between Ombudsmen and tribunals has been the subject of a study by the Administrative Review Council in Australia.[117]

Complaints against the Police

There has been widespread public disquiet over a range of issues covering relationships between police and the local community. These include: total distrust by deprived urban communities, especially black communities, of the police and the exercise of their powers; allegations of police corruption; allegations of police violence and deaths due to violence while in police custody; police tactics at, or against those travelling to, demonstrations and pickets; "fire brigade" and other forms of policing such as the use of the former Special Patrol Groups, mutual aid and Support Units; the role of special divisions in "political" investigations; and the subject of police powers enacted on a uniform statutory basis in the much criticised, and seldom applauded, Police and Criminal Evidence Act 1984. Centripetal tendencies evidenced by the establishment of regional crime squads, the Police National Reporting Centre, the Police National Computer and further recommendations for police reorganisation and the creation of a super national investigatory unit not unlike the FBI have alarmed those who believe that a force should operate and be accountable locally. It is always too easy, and therefore simplistic to cast the police as the repressive arm of a "strong state", enforcing a class system of justice at the expense of working or lower classes or minority groups under the guise of maintaining an independent "rule of law". It cannot be overlooked, however,

---

115 See *R v CLA ex parte Eastleigh BC* [1988] QB 855 (CA); see also the dicta of Lord Diplock in *Nat Fed*, Note 108 above.
116 Reid, 1993.
117 Administrative Review Council (Australia) (1985): N. Lewis and P. Birkinshaw, *When Citizens Complain: Reforming Justice and Administration* (Buckingham, Open University Press, 1993).

that authoritarian elements in the police may be afforded unnecessary encouragement to abuse their extensive powers if the methods of obtaining accountability, complaint resolution and forming relations with local communities are inadequate. Increasing informal, and indeed formal, centralisation of administration is often cited as a factor encouraging such tendencies. Many of the proposals affecting police administration and accountability and which seek to introduce greater efficiency and responsiveness into police performance similar to those introduced elsewhere in the public sector are as unpopular with the police as they are with sections of public opinion.[118] I say a little more about this in a moment (and see my Preface above).

Control over and Accountability of the Police

It is often remarked that the police are accountable to the community in two respects. First, by the law itself in as much as they are charged with enforcing the law impartially in the name of the community, though in reality it would be virtually impossible to obtain a mandamus directed against a Chief Constable directing him to perform his duties;[119] and inasmuch as the police are answerable to the ordinary criminal and civil law of the land for their actions. Second, the police are accountable under Acts of Parliament to *local* police authorities which are special committees of local authorities, with variations for "combined forces".[120] Though "officers of the Crown", the police are paid by local authorities except in London, but they are "servants" of neither.[121] Responsibility lies to central government through HM Inspectors of Constabulary and, ultimately, to the Home

---

[118] The Sheehy Report (Cm, 2280, 1993) on police responsibilities and rewards sought to introduce market incentives into police work: fixed term appointments, performance-related pay. It met with unprecedented opposition from the police.

[119] *R v Commissioner of Police of the Metropolis ex parte Blackburn* [1968] 2 QB 118 (CA); *R v Chief Constable of Devon and Cornwall ex parte Central Electricity Generating Board* [1981] 3 WLR 867 (CA).

[120] Often referred to as police committees, membership comprises two-thirds county councillors and one-third magistrates. Prior to 1964, they were referred to as "Watch Committees". For combined forces they are referred to as police authorities. On proposed amendments to their constitution see the text below and the Police and Magistrates' Courts Act 1994 (PMCA).

[121] *Fisher v Oldham Corporation* [1930] 2 KB 364. A police officer is liable individually for any torts committed on duty and by virtue of section 48 of the Police Act 1964, the Chief Constable is liable vicariously for any tort committed by an officer in the course of his employment. If such an action is successful, damages are paid out of the police fund. On limits to actions in negligence, see pp. 272–275 below.

Secretary or relevant Secretary of State, who is now empowered to issue specific directions to police authorities where the Inspectors make an adverse report.[122] The Secretary of State may determine objectives for policing by authorities and set performance targets and issue codes of practice. The authority must determine local policing objectives and policing plans setting out priorities and expected financial resources. The Chief Constable must have regard to the plan "in discharging his functions". In London the police authority is the Home Secretary.

The argument has often been advanced that from the 19th century onwards, police forces outside London have been subject to centralisation of administration at both a formal and informal level and that local accountability to the "Watch Committee", as it was called, gradually diminished in significance and efficiency. In England and Wales in 1857, there were 239 separate forces; today there are 43. If the Home Office's 1993 recommendations come to fruition[123] there will be an estimated reduction by 20. With increasing informal control over police activities from the Home Office and increasing resort to highly technological aids, over 30 years ago the *Royal Commission on the Police*[124] stated that in exercise of his power over general policy matters and policing activities of an operational nature, the Chief Constable "should be free from the conventional processes of democratic control and influence". Police authorities in England and Wales are charged, however, with the duty of ensuring "the maintenance of an efficient and effective police force" – the physical side of policing. The Chief Constable is statutorily responsible for the "direction and control" of forces. In Scotland the role of the

---

[122] For example, for Scotland, Secretary of State for Scotland. The Inspectorate may issue or refuse to issue a certificate of effectiveness. The Home Secretary has power to award and withhold 50 per cent of a force's expenditure. It has been argued that the Home Secretary can direct the Metropolitan Commissioner more specifically than he can Chief Constables of other forces by virtue of the Metropolitan Police Act 1829, section 1, though see Lord Denning in *ex parte Blackburn* [1968] 2 QB 118 (Hartley and Griffith, *Government and Law,* 1981). Nb section 15 Police and Magistrates' Courts Act 1994. And see Marshall, *Constitutional Conventions,* 1984, at 120 to 121. In a crucial decision the Court of Appeal has held that the prerogative power still has a role to play in the relationship between the Home Secretary and the chief of police so that the Police Authority may be bypassed: *R v Secretary of State for the Home Department ex parte Northumbria Police Authority* [1988] 1 All ER 556 (CA): the case concerned the issue of plastic bullets and CS gas.

[123] Home Office, Cm. 2281, 1993.

[124] Cmnd 1728, 1962.

police authority is similar, though it has a different composition. In Northern Ireland, an independent police authority was introduced in 1988.[125]

Chief Constables present annual reports to the authorities – these vary enormously in utility and content as their subject-matter is within the discretion of the Chief Constable. Surveys in the past have found that as few as ten authorities in England and Wales regularly used their power to call for special reports from the Chief Constable. As regards public access to meetings of the authorities, the Local Government Access to Information Act 1985 applies to police authorities although research carried out by the author in 1988/9 showed public interest to be indifferent and the statute does not alter the immunities that the Chief Constable has over policy information. The exclusions and exemptions under that statute regarding public admission afford ample scope to remove interested members of the public from what they may regard as meaningful observation. London has no police authority apart from the Home Secretary and this has been a cause of grave concern for many London boroughs which have felt that there has been inadequate accountability to local communities in the boroughs. The White Paper of 1993 on *Police Reform*[126] recommended an advisory body to assist the Home Secretary in oversight of the Metropolitan force.

Finally, the policy authority has power to ask for, if the Home Secretary approves, the resignation of the Chief Constable in the interests of efficiency or effectiveness (Police Act 1964, section 5(4) as amended). The power of the authority to suspend chief officers under the Police Regulations is restricted by regulations which necessitate the approval of the Police Complaints Authority (POLCA) before suspension.[127]

The relationship between the Authority and the Chief Constable has been described as one of co-operation and compromise in which the operational independence of the Chief Constable does not have to give way in subordination and obedience to a democratically elected local body and as a relationship which seeks to protect the independence of the police from central political direction. Although the Government has resiled from the full rigour of the Sheehy proposals on marketisation of police operations, or police responsibilities and rewards, it has retained

---

[125] See HC 395 (1988/9) for its first Annual Report.
[126] Cm. 2281. Section 13 PMCA 1994 allows councillors to question police authorities on the discharge of their functions.
[127] SI 1985 519 reg. 23.

some attenuated recommendations such as fixed term contracts for senior staff, which it has been claimed will help to reduce the operational independence of senior officers,[128] and some features of performance related pay. Police reform has been described as profoundly centralising.[129] Central government will "set the key objectives which it expects the police to secure", states the paper, and "local police authorities will be strengthened and made more effective", along with police authority arrangements for the metropolis outside the Home Office. However, says Reiner,

> "The 'strengthened' police authorities will be much less accountable to local people . . . . The two-thirds component of locally elected councillors will be reduced to a half . . . authorities will be sixteen members . . . and the non-elected eight will comprise three JPs and 'five local people appointed by the Home Secretary'. The Home Secretary will also appoint the authority's chairperson, who will have a casting vote."[130]

As I write, the Home Secretary, under enormous pressure from the House of Lords, has modified his proposals.

Complaints against the Police (sections 84–90 PACE)

The method of registering complaints against the police was revamped in 1976 by the Police Act of that year which emerged after ten years of discussion and which created the Police Complaints Board (PCB). It has been suggested that the 1976 Act, despite police protestations, "did little more than confirm the long standing right of police to investigate themselves."[131] Sir Cyril Phillips, chairman of the PCB, rejected the idea of a totally independent complaints system and informed Lord Scarman: "Much would be lost if responsibility for receiving and investigating complaints were removed from the police . . . . The system, by and large, is working well."

Lord Scarman did not concur. Outlining the factors behind the violent rioting in Brixton in 1981, he focused upon a collapse of

---

128   Making accountability "calculative and contractual" (Reiner, NLJ, 1993, at 1096); given the preponderance of government appointees on police authorities this will make senior police officers susceptible to a government line when their fixed term contracts are up for renewal.
129   Reiner, *ibid.* See above.
130   Reiner points out that no consultation took place with independent experts. *Ibid.*, at 1126.
131   Humphrey in *Policing the Police* (ed. Hain) 1979. Investigations take place under section 49(1) of the Police Act 1964. See Goldsmith (1990).

the police liaison committee in 1979; "hard" policing methods; an absence of consultation with the community and a deep distrust by the community of the independence of the complaints procedure.[132] "Unless and until there is a system for judging complaints against the police, which commands the support of the public, there will be no way in which the atmosphere of distrust and suspicion between the police and the community in places like Brixton can be dispelled" – a point that was repeated in Liverpool and Manchester. His recommendations for a more sensitive and racially enlightened training of police officers (including eventually the acceptance of his recommendation that racially discriminatory or prejudicial behaviour should be a specific disciplinary offence)[133] and his suggestion for a revamped complaints procedure and for the creation of a statutory duty upon Chief Officers of Police and police authorities to liaise through more localised committees have, to a greater or lesser degree, experienced realisation. Liaison in London, he recommended, should be at borough or district level. On the complaints system generally, he expressed the belief that the existing procedure was more concerned with internal disciplinary matters rather than satisfying the complainant and that it lacked "a sufficiently convincing independent element." His specific recommendations were for a conciliation procedure for less serious complaints which would operate informally, greater use of outside police officers to investigate more serious complaints and the use of an "independent" supervisor, for example, the chairman of the PCB.

After various reports and replies and one aborted Bill,[134] the Government elected for a three-tier system of complaints handling. These procedures were outlined in the same Bill, which significantly extended the powers of the police in England and Wales, attracting criticism from the Church, the legal, medical

---

132   Scarman, Cmnd 8427, 1981. Complainants would face the criminal standard of proof (see text). "Double jeopardy" and the DPP's (Crown Prosecution Service) decisions on prosecutions are examined in the text at pp. 235–236 below. Often those complaining are, unsurprisingly, on the receiving end of enforcement of the law. Use of prosecution powers for tactical purposes, "tit for tat" and making complaints likewise have been observed (HC 631, 1979/80). Scarman did refer generally to the absence of channels through which black members of the community could articulate their grievances.

133   Police and Criminal Evidence Act 1984, section 101(1)(b), though cf PMCA 1994 section 37(e). See: *Racism Awareness Training for the Police*, Home Office Research and Planning Unit, 1984, E. Cashmore and E. McLaughlin, *Out of Order: Policing Black People*, 1991.

134   The Triennial Report of the PCB Cmnd 7966; the Plowden Report, Cmnd 8193; the Home Affairs Committee, (1981/2) HC 98, 1 and the Government Reply, Cmnd 8681 (1982).

and journalist professions. The drafters of what became PACE do, on the surface, appear to have made more of a conscious effort to make the procedure more autonomous and "independent". The PCB was replaced by the Police Complaints Authority (POLCA). The Authority is to consist of a chairman, appointed by Her Majesty, that is, the Prime Minister in reality, and eight other members appointed by the Secretary of State. No former "constable" may be a member, members can be whole-time or part-time and there will be two deputy chairmen of the Authority which is to be a body corporate. Schedule 4 deals with length of office, removal from office, remuneration, appointment of staff and the establishing of regional offices with the consent of the Secretary of State and the Treasury.

The Complaints Procedure

Turning to complaints made by members of the public, or made on their behalf and with their written consent, against a member of the police force, the chief officer of police for the area is under a duty "to take any steps that appear to him to be desirable for the purposes of obtaining or preserving evidence relating to the conduct complained of", and to record the making of the complaint if he considers he is the "appropriate authority" to deal with it. If he is not, he has to send the complaint, or particulars of it if not in writing, to the "appropriate authority". The chief officer or appropriate authority determines whether the complaint can be dealt with informally or formally and a chief inspector[135] or superior officer may assist in the making of such a decision. If the chief officer, etc., determines that it shall be investigated formally, he has to appoint an officer to investigate, and he may request a chief officer from another area to supply an investigating officer. If the request is made, an officer must be provided. Informal investigation requires the consent of the complainant and concerns complaints that would not justify a criminal or disciplinary charge if proved.[136] About 65 per cent of complaints are informally resolved.[137] There are separate provisions for complaints against officers above the rank of chief superintendent.[138]

---

[135] The Government have proposed the abolition of the rank of chief inspector and chief superintendent.
[136] Details concerning the informal complaints procedure are in regulation SI 1985 No. 671.
[137] HO Statistical Bulletin, 12 March 1992.
[138] This may take the form of a sub-committee of the Police Authority as recommended by the Home Office.

The last tier concerns those complaints which the chief officer has to refer to the Authority and these include complaints concerning death or serious injury and those covered by statutory regulations. The chief officer also has power to refer to the Authority any complaint which is not required to be referred. The Authority has power to require submission of a complaint which has not been referred by the chief officer, etc., and the latter may refer any *indication* of commission of a criminal or disciplinary offence by officers of chief superintendent rank or below not contained in a complaint to the Authority because of their gravity or exceptional circumstances. The Authority shall supervise investigations which they receive on a mandatory reference (apart from those under SI 1985 No. 673 where there is a discretion) and they must supervise other investigations, including those into specific allegations and so on, where they consider it desirable in the public interest that they should do so. The Authority has power to approve the appointment of investigating officers for supervised investigations. Supervised inquiry reports are sent to the Authority and the chief officer, etc., and the complainant may be sent, "if practicable to do so", a copy of the Authority's "appropriate statement" to the chief officer, etc., stating whether the Authority is satisfied with the investigation, or if not why not. If the complaint is not supervised, only the chief officer, etc., receives a copy of the investigating officer's report. Regulations provide for supply of a copy of the complaint to the complainant and the officer investigated.[139] Complaints

---

[139] Until 1994 case law had established that public interest immunity protects the investigation and statements taken for that investigation but not the original complainant's complaint, that is, that the documents cannot be obtained by a litigant wishing to use them to sue the police: *Neilson v Langharne* [1981] 1 QB 736 (CA); *Makanjuola v Commissioner of Metropolitan Police* [1992] 3 All ER 617 (CA); *Halford v Sharples* [1992] 3 All ER 624 (CA); see, however, *Peach v Commissioner of Metropolitan Police* [1986] 2 All ER 129 (CA) on predominant purpose for holding an investigation; this general immunity was interpreted to prevent the police using documents in civil proceedings to defend themselves or to sue, they may only be used for the complaint investigation or disciplinary proceedings against the police: *R v Chief Constable of West Midlands Police ex parte Wiley* (1993) *The Times*, 30 September (CA), a decision which put the police in a comparable position with complainants. However, the House of Lords has reversed both *Neilson* and *Wiley* removing the class basis of public interest immunity, although a contents basis of protection may be made out on the specific facts of a case: *R v Chief Constable of Nottinghamshire Police ex parte Wiley* [1994] 3 All ER 420 (HL). Note also that a complaint containing malice destroys the privilege in a complaint from the complainant's perspective, leaving the complainant open to actions in defamation: *Fraser v Mirza The Scotsman* 4 March (1993) (HL).

about "direction or control", that is, policy are not covered by the procedure, and nor are complaints about conduct which have been, or are, the subject of criminal or disciplinary proceedings.

The chief officer decides whether the investigation has revealed that a criminal offence has been committed, and if so he must refer the report to the Director of Public Prosecutions (DPP). The Authority has to be informed, after the DPP has decided upon the criminal issue if referred to him, whether disciplinary proceedings are being brought; if not, why not. The Authority can direct a chief officer to refer a report to the DPP, although this power is to be removed, or to bring disciplinary "proceedings" himself, and may ask for "such information as they may reasonably require" to discharge this last function. Police committees must keep themselves informed of the manner in which complaints against members of the force are dealt with. The Authority must not disclose information received, though they do make various reports to the Secretary of State.[140] Regulations provide for provision of information to the Authority.[141] The PMCA 1994 has amended some of the details of these provisions to reduce the discretion of the Chief Officer of Police on references to the DPP and to alter the wording from disciplinary "charges" to "proceedings".

Significantly "double jeopardy" has been amended. This was where the former PCB had interpreted the decision of the DPP not to prosecute a criminal charge,[142] to necessitate that disciplinary charges should not be directed to be brought where the same issues had to be proved in a disciplinary charge as in the criminal charge. This had caused great controversy and a ruling from the High Court that a fixed practice by the PCB was *ultra vires*.[143] The details of the Home Office advice on this topic are contained in guidance issued by the Secretary of State.[144]

---

140 When requested to do so; when the "gravity or exceptional circumstances" of a subject necessitates, in their opinion, a report; a triennial report on the working of the complaints machinery (removed under PMCA), and an annual report.

141 SI 1985 520.

142 But where the officer is tried and found not guilty, s/he will not face disciplinary charges involving the same facts, see PACE section 104(1) and (2) now removed by PMCA.

143 In exercising his discretion to prosecute or not, the DPP sought a degree of probability of success of at least 51 per cent, that is, higher than a normal prosecution. See *R v PCB ex parte Madden* [1983] 2 All ER 353 and the fettering of discretion by the PCB. *The Guardian* estimated that 20,000 cases could possibly be affected, 23 December 1982.

144 Home Office, *Police Complaints and Discipline Procedures*, Cmnd 9072 (London, HMSO, 1983), paragraph 5.13 to 14.

The POLCA is not an independent Ombudsman, although considerable effort has been invested to present the Authority as a truly impartial entity. It is true to say that the police will still investigate the vast majority of complaints themselves without supervision from the POLCA and that apart from the informal procedure, the likelihood in practice is that the formal investigations will be considered as a matter of internal discipline; and it is interesting to note that the disciplinary rules were amended in conjunction with the PACE reforms.[145] In fact, significant changes can be expected in police discipline concerning removal of inefficient police officers, or those not guilty of disciplinary offences and dismissal for redundancy, even though the Sheehy report has not been accepted.[146] A Home Office consultation paper[147] has suggested a movement away from discipline to management in a way that would recast the whole of the complaints process; indeed it questions in many cases whether "complaint" is a justified term.

In an area as sensitive as police complaints controversy is bound to be rife. After his initial recommendations, Lord Scarman had to call a press conference to counter police allegations that he had undermined police confidence. The Home Affairs Committee reported a motion of no confidence in the POLCA by the Police Federation; the latter has also supported the case for an independent Ombudsman and there has been considerable difficulty over the restrictions imposed on the POLCA in its use of information, restrictions which do not affect the police.[148] The editor of the *Police Review* has described the proposed changes in police organisation and pay as ushering in a "Police State".[149] Civil liberties groups have voiced their disquiet over the procedures

---

145   Indeed, the Legend to Part 9 of the Act is "Complaints and Discipline". Officers are to be given the opportunity to comment on complaints processed informally. A police officer found guilty of a disciplinary charge can appeal to the Secretary of State, who will issue guidance to chief officers on complaints and discipline. The Home Secretary has bowed to pressure from the Police Federation to allow officers facing disciplinary charges involving a possibility of dismissal, demotion or resignation, to be legally represented; see *Maynard v Osmond* [1977] 1 All ER 64, and PACE section 102. In December 1993, a disciplinary tribunal dismissed an officer in the Metropolitan force of the rank of Assistant Commissioner, the highest ranking officer to be so dismissed.

146   Home Secretary, 28 October 1993. See now PMCA 1994.

147   *Review of Police Disciplinary Procedures*, 1993.

148   Though see Note 139 above.

149   14 May 1993, at 16 to 17.

by stating that they would not invoke them but rely instead on civil suits before the courts. Delay in dealing with complaints has been described as "endemic".[150] After five years of prompting, POLCA began to record the number of complaints alleging racially discriminatory behaviour in October 1990. However, the investigation of police malpractices and misdemeanours can prove to be one of the most impenetrable of areas, as John Stalker found out when conducting investigations in Northern Ireland.[151] The problems encountered on the mainland have involved corruption affecting groups, stations and even Regional Crime Squads. Particularly intractable has been the difficulty of obtaining information where groups of wrong-doers have been involved in serious criminal behaviour.

POLCA has been highly critical of certain aspects of police practice. It has been critical of the secrecy attending disciplinary hearings and the lack of public or press access to those hearings, which was regarded by the police as an intrusion into "internal police discipline".[152] A complainant may attend but not be present at the verdict. Information on the outcome and punishment are "scanty", for example: "there was an appropriate finding and punishment". POLCA has also suggested that there should be a two-tier disciplinary procedure to deal with less serious offences where the burden of proof would be less onerous than that required at present before all hearings, namely, the criminal standard. This has been taken up by the Home Office,[153] which suggested a four-stage procedure to deal with poor performance and invited comments upon the form of "misconduct" procedures. These would move away from the court or quasi-judicial ethos and would be more investigatory and the panel would comprise senior police officers with power of dismissal. A right of appeal would exist to an industrial tribunal.

In the first triennial review of the POLCA it rejected calls by chief police officers that a complaint should be investigated or made a disciplinary charge only where it had been specifically detailed by the complainant. A "complaint about the conduct" POLCA believed should be redefined to include all wrongdoings which emerged in the course of an investigation or otherwise.

---

150   POLCA Annual Report, 1991, paragraph 4.1. See also R. Clayton and H. Tomlinson, *Civil Actions Against the Police* (2nd edn 1994).
151   J. Stalker, *Stalker* (London, 1988). He was investigating the alleged "shoot to kill" policy in Northern Ireland and was dismissed from the investigation in notorious circumstances.
152   Home Affairs Committee HC 179 (1991/2) paragraph 32.
153   Note 147 above.

Complaints run at about 35,000 *per annum*, but this should not be confused with complaint cases which often contain several complaints. In 1986 cases referred to the POLCA numbered 3,688; in 1990 it was 5,078 and in 1992 4,476 of which 697 were supervised under section 87 and 60 under section 88, that is, there was no formal complaint but a need for supervision because of the possibility of a disciplinary or criminal offence. Forces are set a target of 120 days to complete an investigation and the POLCA has reduced to 32 days its consideration of the disciplinary aspects. Under 1990 regulations the POLCA can grant dispensation to a force not to investigate and in 1992 dispensation was granted in 31 per cent of complaints (6,035); in 1991 it was 22 per cent. Of 9,200 cases of complaint (many of which involve more than one complaint) completed in 1992, 904 (9.8 per cent) resulted in some form of action, from disciplinary charges to advice – 49 resulted in criminal charges. In 75 cases disciplinary charges were preferred where the relevant authority had recommended no charges; of these, 17 were subsequently withdrawn after agreement about another form of admonishment.

One point of interest concerns the highly publicised dispute between the Special Branch and the Security Service over jurisdictional clashes relating to anti-terrorism and organised crime investigations. The Security Service's activities involving individuals are investigated under procedures contained in the Security Service Act 1989 and involve investigation and decision upon complaints by a tribunal and a Commissioner who publishes an annual report after vetting by the Prime Minister. The procedures are not unlike those available under the Interception of Communications Act 1985.[154] The Intelligence Service is to be placed on a similar statutory footing. Security and Intelligence concentrate much of their effort on Northern Ireland and it should be noted in passing that an Independent Assessor of Military Complaints in Northern Ireland produced a first annual report in 1994 (HC 369 (1993/4)).

Local Consultation

General accountability is to be provided by the statutory duty upon the police authority, after consulting the chief constable, to make arrangements which they are under a duty to review "from time to time" in each police area to obtain "the views

---

[154]   P. Birkinshaw, *Freedom of Information: The Law, the Practice and the Ideal* (London, Weidenfeld and Nicolson, 1988).

of the people in that area about matters concerning the policing of the area" and for obtaining co-operation in crime prevention. Separate arrangements are to be made for London, centring on each borough or each district as appropriate. The Commissioner has to take account of guidance issued by the Secretary of State, and "shall consult" the council of each London borough or district about the appropriate arrangements. The Secretary of State has a general power to ask for reports on the arrangements and to require their review.

One should immediately note the vacuousness of many of these provisions. What, for instance, will the bodies be allowed to discuss? How will the subjects be chosen? How will membership be comprised? There is a good amount of discretion suffusing statutory duties, which will no doubt be supplemented by well-intended administrative guidelines urging full consultation. There is no provision ensuring that the chief constable, or commissioner, takes a "serious look" at the views of the bodies. Non-statutory interim procedures had been available for such consultation prior to the enactment of the duty described above, and the Home Office issued *Guidelines on Consultation with the Community*.[155] This provided little detail on the points of membership and administration outlined at the beginning of the paragraph, law enforcement, and those operational aspects of policing which it would be wrong to make the subject of local consultation. Clearly, there are policy and investigatory matters which it would be inappropriate to discuss if it hindered criminal investigation. But policy is a term which many feel has been invoked to ensure no discussion with the community or their representatives on aspects of policing that affect the local community in a general fashion, and it is difficult to believe that there will be a widespread change in police attitudes on this topic. Even Lord Scarman believed that not all operational matters should be ruled out of discussion, so that the community could be heard "not only in the development of policing policy but in the planning of many, though not all, operations against crime".

The actual practices of police forces under the non-statutory liaison schemes varied enormously, from those which had appeared to do "nothing except comply with the Home Office guidelines" or which appeared non-existent, to one urban authority which had spelt out the topics for discussion: constitution, membership, and so on. Such administrative details were common in

---

[155] June 1982, and see Home Office Circular 62/89.

the examples, but the terms of reference for discussion were almost uniquely detailed. These included:

(1) provision of a forum for police and community representatives to discuss local policing problems and other matters of mutual concern;
(2) to promote feedback from the community on particular and general policy strategies and modes of operation;
(3) to enable the community to appreciate problems faced by the police in enforcing the law in that community;
(4) to encourage co-operation between the police and the community in the determination of priorities and the development of agreed strategies to deal with particular local problems;
(5) to discuss the effects of past police operations;
(6) to discuss the general implications of any pattern of complaints in the area and the provision of practical advice and assistance to members of the community in dealing with the police;
(7) lay visits to police stations.

The above items do represent important issues which it would be appropriate to set down as statutory *minima*. Formerly, trial schemes of lay visits to Metropolitan police stations established by the Home Office have been poorly responded to by London boroughs. In 1989, the Home Office issued Circular 62/89 on consultation arrangements under section 106 and while observing that formal machinery now existed in all London boroughs and in most parts of England and Wales, it noted widely varying attitudes by the police on the sharing of information, the absence of ethnic minorities and young people and a "predominance of people well used to committees: professional and middle class white people".[156]

Data Protection

The Data Protection Act 1984, which seeks to "protect individuals against potential misuse of personal information held about them on computers", was enacted in July 1984. The Government opted for a Data Protection Registrar (DPR) to establish the public register of data users and computer bureaux which the public may examine. It will be his responsibility to ensure that all data users and computer bureaux fulfil their statutory obligations

[156] Paragraph 24.

and comply with the eight data protection principles. The Home Office press release described the Data Protection Registrar as "an Ombudsman for data subjects [who] will investigate complaints from individuals who believe that data relating to them are being held in breach of the principles." Representative groups of data users (holders) will be encouraged by him to draw up codes of good practice. Data users have a right of appeal against the Data Protection Registrar's decisions to a Data Protection Tribunal. Certain data will remain outside the protection of the Act. There are also non-disclosure and subject access exemptions. The Act is a regulatory measure which provides a grievance remedial function and it applies to holders of information in the private and public sectors. In the White Paper on *Open Government* there were proposals to allow a statutory right of access to public sector documents in paper form with an enforcement mechanism built upon or similar to the DPR.[157]

In 1991 there were 164,000 registered users of personal data. In the year 1991/2 there were 1,747 complaints to the office – a decrease of 400 or so from the previous year, but in 1992/3 the number of complaints rose to 4,590. In a survey conducted by the DPR, in spite of the fact that access to personal information was seen as an increasingly important topic by the public, only 9 per cent were "spontaneously aware of the Data Protection Act".[158]

Private Sector Ombudsmen

As well as the above we have a prisons Ombudsman (adjudicator) and a pensions Ombudsman, against whose decisions a right of appeal exists to the High Court, and various uncertain hybrids such as the Security and Interceptions Commissioners and Tribunals, even an official to hear from those security and intelligence officers who feel pangs of conscience about their duties. There are commissioners to assist trade unionists against trade unions and to help those who are the victims of unlawful industrial action. But it is the extension of the ombudsman procedure concept into the private sector that has been a staggering development since the early 1980s. There are Ombudsmen for financial services, professional services (including accountants),

---

[157] An EC Directive, in draft form as of writing, would have wide implications for our domestic data protection and privacy laws.
[158] DPR Annual Report, 1992/3, paragraph 68.

media and press, telephone information services, even Ombudsmen in some universities; there is a Commissioner for the rights of trade union members and under the Trade Union Reform and Employment Rights Act 1993, a Commissioner for Protection Against Unlawful Industrial Action to assist "citizens" in actions against trade unions – not an ombudsman role but one which has been suggested, and rejected, for other Ombudsmen to assist litigants against public bodies (see chapter 6 p. 259). It constitutes an expansion of public law technique into the private sector realm with certain modifications: the basis of the jurisdiction is often, though not invariably, voluntary and they are primarily concerned with individual wrong-righting rather than overall system improvement,[159] so that they are more obviously a form of Alternative Dispute Resolution and they may operate with set compulsory enforcement powers relating to jurisdiction such as in the case of the Insurance Ombudsman (IO) and Building Societies Ombudsman (BSO) whose jurisdiction is binding up to £100,000 and voluntary thereafter. Being voluntary, the schemes only apply to those who are members, although the Government may pressurise firms into becoming members by informal means or the threat of statutory regulation, and although they are not bound by concepts of maladministration to the extent that public sector Ombudsmen are, they are generally concerned with the administrative quality of a decision as opposed to merits and discretion.[160] Some private sector Ombudsmen are statutory, for example, the Building Societies Ombudsman, the Legal Services Ombudsman and the Pensions Ombudsman, but they are closer in spirit to the "voluntary" bodies than the public sector variety although in the case of one purely voluntary Ombudsman, the Insurance Ombudsman, the court has ruled that it is not subject to public law review.[161] All publish annual reports but none publish individual case reports, even in anonymised form, apart from brief summaries. Investigators in private bodies tend to be professionally qualified whereas state Ombudsmen are civil servants or operate along civil service lines – one of the reasons one commentator has suggested why their reports are so long, taking the form of novelettes. Some of the voluntary Ombudsmen have been particularly critical of bad practices operating to the detriment of consumers and this has been notable in banking.

---

[159] See, however, Graham, 1991.
[160] *Halifax BS v Edell* [1992] 3 All ER 389.
[161] *R v IOB ex parte Aegon Life Ass.* (1994) *The Times* 7 January.

For all the Ombudsmen, the UK Ombudsman Association has agreed that criteria should apply to warrant the designation "Ombudsman". The major criteria are: independence of those subject to investigation although there may be minority representation on the body to whom the Ombudsman reports; fixed term and secure appointments and independence in deciding whether a complaint is within jurisdiction; accessibility and here we should note that the NCC[162] reported that only around a quarter of people surveyed had heard of the Building Society Ombudsman, Insurance Ombudsman or Banking Ombudsman.[163] The 1992 Code of Banking Practice stipulates that all banks and building societies must have internal grievance procedures and details of how to make further complaint. The IO and BSO have rated highly on accessibility but poorly in terms of perceived fairness.[164] Some of this feeling may be due to the fact that, as Birds and Graham have reported in the case of the IO, his formal role is investigator but his terms of reference allow him to act as conciliator, arbitrator and adjudicator[165] – a confusion of roles which seems to complainants to be too compromising.

The jurisdiction, manner of appointment and powers of Ombudsmen should be matters of public knowledge and they should be able to investigate complaints without the need for prior consent from those complained against; they should have a right to acquire all relevant information, allow access to the complainant to such information except for special and justifiable reasons, and should be required to act in a fair manner, make reasoned and fair decisions and communicate to the parties the reason for their decisions. Unless otherwise specified in statute, there should be direct access to Ombudsmen, bodies investigated should have their own internal complaints procedures which are clearly publicised and the existence of the Ombudsmen should also be publicised by the bodies. There should be a requirement that decisions will be implemented by the parties investigated or a "reasonable expectation" that they will be implemented and powers of publicity where they are not implemented. They should also report publicly at least annually.

---

162   NCC (1993).
163   Graham, Seneviratne and James, 1993.
164   NCC, Note 162 above, at 41.
165   J. Birds and C. Graham, *Complaints against Insurance Companies* (Sheffield, University of Sheffield Faculty of Law, 1992).

Conclusion

Ombudsmen have been described as "an institutionalised form of public conscience".[166] Lewis and others[167] have seen in the Ombudsmen a procedure for seeking out systemic abuse in a way that courts and tribunals are ill-equipped to do. The point has been made before that an Ombudsmen Commission would seem to offer an opportunity to make more coherent the operation of our plethora of public sector Ombudsmen. A similar body could be created for private sector Ombudsmen on a sectoral basis, for example, financial services, broadcasting and media and so on, with compulsory membership and compulsory powers of decision. Can there be any justification for separate offices in the public sector for central government and local government and the NHS?[168] In the case of the first and last the division is artificial as they occupy the same building and both offices are held by the same person. Furthermore, it has become apparent that different Ombudsmen are applying different criteria in recommending awards of compensation for the sheer "bother" and injury to feelings of complainants, known by some as the "buggeration" factor, although William Reid prefers the term *"solatium"*. In all cases, there is a need for greater publicity for the Ombudsmen. All surveys show they are not as well known by consumers as they ought to be. Indeed, the multiplicity of schemes in one area creates what has been called a "bugger's muddle".[169] We have still not used anything like the full potential of the ombudsmen procedures to engage in system improvement and overhaul.

[166] Caiden, 1983.
[167] Lewis and Graham, 1991; Lewis and Birkinshaw, Note 117 above.
[168] See sections 17 and 18 of the HSC Act 1993 and the passing of information and consultation between the PCA and the HSC.
[169] Retiring Ombudsman of LAUTRO in 1989.

Chapter 6

THE COURTS

The New Judiciary

This book has described and analysed the non-judicial means of remedying grievances against the state. However, the role of the courts cannot be overlooked for a variety of reasons. First of all their say prevails over all the other grievance procedures we have discussed; they have the power to correct the activities of all who act under public power whether its basis be statutory, prerogative or in some sense voluntary, that is, the government has allowed an organising interest to regulate an activity as a surrogate for the state.[1] Generally courts display a reluctance to intervene in a dispute until an appropriate and relevant grievance procedure has been exhausted unless an egregious error has been perpetrated in the procedure. Secondly, while the actual extent of the influence of the courts is a matter for empirical research with some role for informed speculation, there is little doubt that the growing importance of judicial review and sophistication of the law that is being applied has had an impact upon governmental thinking.[2] In 1987, for instance, the Treasury Solicitor's Department and Cabinet Office produced a rather testy document which advised civil servants how to minimise opportunities for judicial review.[3] A further factor is that courts and judges also operate at an important symbolic level even in this age of general scepticism and disenchantment among the public concerning the operations of the political process.[4] A new generation of senior judges has assumed the role of active spokesmen for legal reform[5] and

---

[1] On the relationship between statutory disciplinary action and private actions, see *R v ICA etc ex parte Brindle* (1994) *The Times* 12 January (CA).
[2] See Waldegrave, 1993, pp. 18 and 24 above.
[3] *The Judge over your Shoulder* (1987).
[4] Large numbers of complaints are made to the PCA about courts, judges and the prosecution service: see chapter 5 Note 000.
[5] Sir H. Woolf, "Public Law–Private Law: Why the Divide?" (1986) Public Law 220; *Protection of the Public: A New Challenge* (London, Stevens, 1990); "Judicial Review: A Possible Programme for Reform" (1992) Public Law 221.

government critic in an extra-judicial capacity in a manner that casts them as the informed voice of wisdom, experience and rationality while the Ministers appear as ideologues unprepared to listen to rational arguments or as demagogues pandering to populism who simply have right on their side.[6] Fourthly, and one could add to the list but space forbids, there have been strikingly important decisions which have received national prominence where the courts have started to dismantle the chains of ancient prerogative which cloak the operations of government even to this day and the repurcussions of which could have a dramatic impact upon official thinking. Even the common law itself seems revitalised so that it can, in some judicial eyes at least, provide a protection which is as good as, perhaps surpasses, that provided by the European Convention on Human Rights.[7]

As I shall explain in a moment, although it is difficult to establish whether some of these developments are a reaction against or are positively influenced by the increasing impact of European legal thought in our law, there are certain ingrained and cultural features of our law which need to be addressed if we are to extract the optimum from the judicial contribution to administrative justice – including the reorganisation of the court structure insofar as it impacts upon the public law side of justice.[8] Other items would involve judicial appointments and training, the structure of the professions and elevation to Queen's Counsel, the price of legal services and the nature of legal service which best promotes the public interest. As was said many years ago, so long as lawyers take comfort in the neutrality of the marketplace to provide the optimum kind of legal practice and lawyer, then lawyers can take comfort in the neutrality of their product and ultimately in the system of justice that they help to administer.[9] A market-based

---

6 Browne-Wilkinson, 1988; Woolf, 1992; Purchas, 1993. The debate sparked off by Lord Woolf's criticism of the Home Secretary's suggested alterations to penal policy was the highlight. An obvious increase in stridency of tone and critical content has been detectable since the government papers on reform of the legal profession and the Courts and Legal Services Act 1990. See the article by Sir F. Purchas (1994) concerning the position of Wood J. as President of the Employment Appeal Tribunal and criticism of his conduct over appeals by the Lord Chancellor.

7 Sir J. Laws, "Is the High Court the Guardian of Fundamental Human Rights?" (1993) *Public Law* 59; and see Sir N. Browne Wilkinson, "The Infiltration of a Bill of Rights" (1992) *Public Law* 397, and *Times Newspapers v Derbyshire CC* [1993] 1 All ER 1011 (HL).

8 N. Lewis and P. Birkinshaw, *When Citizens Complain: Reforming Justice and Administration* (Buckingham, Open University Press, 1993).

9 S. Scheingold, *The Politics of Rights* (Yale University Press, 1974).

system of legal services is only neutral if the market is neutral. Markets are not neutral; they are money sensitive and power responsive. Our system of justice still needs to address the poverty of the theory which legitimates the dispensation of justice through the courts in the contemporary British state.

The constitution settlement of the 17th century ensured that there would be no "independent" safeguard which was "somewhat fundamental" to act as a corrective to governmental excesses.[10] The supremacy of common law and its proprietary basis over other forms of law is well recorded,[11] as is the supremacy of Parliament over common law.[12] What is of present interest are two developing themes in our public law.

The European Impact

The first has been the increasing reminders from the European Commission and Court of Human Rights of the failure of judicially developed law in the United Kingdom to provide adequate protection for individuals in the field of human rights.[13] Even

10 Impeachment was the preserve of Parliament and it has not been used against an unpopular Minister since 1715. Criminal impeachment was last employed in 1805: Roberts, *The Growth of Responsible Government in Stuart England*, 1966; Berger, *Impeachment* 1973. For an account of the origins of ministerial responsibility, see Roberts, *op. cit.*

11 Both the *cursus scaccarii* of the Court of Exchequer – "the nearest approach to a body of administrative law that the English legal system has ever known" and the Court itself being the closest to an administrative court in England when exercising its revenue jurisdiction (W.S. Holdsworth, *A History of English Law (Vol. 1)* (7th edn, rev. 1966) at 238–39, – and the Star Chamber and prerogative courts developed "tendencies" towards a public law system as opposed to distinct forms of judicial relief. The 17th century ensured that the common law would succeed in having these pre-Restoration developments interpreted as historical aberrations.

12 And see *Burmah Oil v Lord Advocate* [1965] AC 75 and War Damage Act 1965; *Shah v Barnet LBC* [1983] 1 All ER 226 (HL) and Education Fees and Awards Act 1983 and inclusion in 1993 of a clause in the TU Reform and Employment Rights Bill to reverse the impact of a decision of the Court of Appeal that industrial action by teachers was in furtherance of a trade dispute and therefore immune from civil suit: *Associated Newspapers v Wilson* [1993] IRLR 336 (CA) and s 13 TU etc Act 1993. Judicial decisions are frequently nullified by statutory regulations, see generally: Prosser, *The Test Case Strategy*, 1983. On a judicially created fundamental Bill of Rights protection for freedom of speech in Australia see: *Australian Capitol TV Pty v Commonwealth of Australia* [1992] 66 ALJR 695 and Lee, 1993.

13 *Silver v UK* [1983] 5 EHRR 347; *Malone v UK* [1984] 7 EHRR 14; *Campbell & Fell v UK* judgment 28 June 1984; *Campbell and Cosans v UK* (1982) 2 EHRR 293; most graphically the *Spycatcher* episode: *Observer*

though the Convention is not part of our domestic law,[14] the areas affected by decisions of the Court and Commission and the prompting these have given to legislative reform and judicial development are becoming legion. The Committee of Ministers of the Council of Europe has made its influence felt with its recommendations on Good Administrative Practice.[15] Up to 6,000 applications to the Commission each year[16] and delays of up to five years and eight months before cases were heard by the Court have prompted reform of those institutions which were announced at the Vienna Summit of Heads of State and Government in October 1993. The major innovations include a new permanent court to which individual applicants will have right of access and which will screen cases in committees of three judges and hear cases in chambers of seven judges. Chambers will place themselves at the disposal of parties to attempt to achieve a friendly settlement. In exceptional circumstances the court will sit in a Grand Chamber of 17 judges. The Commission will go and the Committee of Ministers will no longer have jurisdiction over cases alleging breaches of human rights although it will supervise compliance with the court's judgments. The Protocol No. 11 was signed by Foreign Ministers on 11 May 1994 and must be ratified by all members of the Convention "as soon as possible".

European Community law, which *is* a part of our domestic law, made a less dramatic entry at the judicial level, although its potential was felt in the UK in early cases concerning equal opportunities and sex discrimination.[17] However, there can be

---

13 Continued
    and Guardian Newspapers v UK [1991] 14 EHRR 153; *Hewitt and Harman v UK* [1992] 14 EHRR 657; and on prisoners' rights *Campbell v UK* [1993] 15 EHRR 137. See *Pratt and Another v Attorney General of Jamaica and Another* [1993] 4 All ER 769 (PC) and the Privy Council's protection of fundamental rights.

14 Originally the provisions of the Convention were not relevant considerations to be taken into account in the exercise of a Ministerial discretion: *R v Secretary of State etc. ex parte Kirkwood* [1984] 1 WLR 913. The Convention is prayed in aid as a guide to the interpretation of statutes and now also, it seems, the common law: *Brind v Secretary of State for the Home Department* [1993] 3 All ER 1011 (HL), but not regulations where they are clear and are authorised by statute: *ibid.*

15 R (80) 2, 11 March 1980 (see Justice/All Souls, *Administrative Justice: Some Necessary Reforms*, Oxford, Oxford University Press, 1988).

16 Article 25 allows individual petition; this Article is ratified periodically.

17 *McCarthys v Smith* [1981] QB 180 (CJEC and CA); *EC Commission v UK of GB and NI* [1984] 1 All ER 353 (CJEC); *Johnston v Chief Constable of the RUC* [1986] 3 All ER 135 (CJEC). See the interesting article by Lord Lester (1994).

no doubt that the field of EC law has entered into popular
legal consciousness, if not popular consciousness, with several
judgments which have had a revolutionary impact upon judicial
redress against state organs and with new areas of liability opening
up hitherto closed areas of governmental activities.[18] The court
has interpreted directives in such a way as to confer direct legal
effect upon individuals, that is, in a manner which creates individual rights based upon EC law before domestic courts. This was
achieved first of all against state bodies,[19] then against emanations
of the state[20] and, who knows, we might find directives being
invoked successfully against private concerns such as employers
in the private sector, banks and insurance companies.[21] Domestic
law must, the ECJ has stated, be interpreted in accordance with
operative directives even where they have not been implemented
or properly implemented into domestic law.[22] Barriers to relief
in domestic law have been interpreted not to bar relief in EC
law where a community remedy is available.[23] The most dramatic
development from an English if not quite a British perspective was
the decision in *Factortame (No. 2)*,[24] after the European Court
had ruled that any national impediments to the realisation of
Community law must be removed.[25] The end result was, the
House of Lords held, that an act of Parliament itself had to be
disapplied by injunction if it contravened Community law. The
role of the ECJ, investigation of complaints and breaches of EC
law by the Commission and the co-ordination and harmonisation
of laws throughout the Community have had a culture-changing

18   *Francovich* [1992] IRLR 84; *Emmot* [1991] 3 CMLR 894; *Marleasing* [1992]
      1 CMLR 305.
19   *Van Duyn v Home Office (No. 2)* [1975] 3 All ER 190 (CJEC). An "indi-
      vidual" does not include a local authority: see *Wychavon D.C.*, Note 67
      below.
20   *Marshall v Southampton AHA* [1986] 2 All ER 584 (CJEC); *Foster v British
      Gas plc* [1990] 3 All ER 897 (CJEC) and [1991] 2 AC 306 (HL); *Marshall
      v Southampton etc. Health Authority (No. 2)* [1993] 4 All ER 586 (CJEC).
      And of course the Transfer of Undertakings and Protection of Employment
      saga: *Commission of the EC v UK* JEC, 8 June 1994.
21   W. van Gerven, *The Horizontal Effect of Directive Provisions Revisited –
      The Reality of Catchwords* (University of Hull, Institute of European Public
      Law, 1993).
22   See *Marleasing*, Note 18 above.
23   *Emmot*, Note 18 above; *Marshall (no. 2)*, Note 20 above. *Marshall* is of
      enormous significance.
24   [1991] 1 AC 603.
25   And see *EOC v Secretary of State for Employment* [1994] 1 All ER 910
      (HL).

impact in those areas where EC law operates,[26] to such an effect that, and quite rightly, constitutional theorists and lawyers are addressing the fundamental questions of public law to the operation of EC law.[27]

The Creation of Coherent Public Law

The second theme is the much acclaimed[28] judicial development or creation of a "procedural public law" and a "coherent system of administrative law". The statement of Lord Diplock that there has been "progress towards a *comprehensive system* of administrative law that I regard as having been *the greatest achievement of the English courts* in my judicial lifetime" captures the mood.[29] The decision of the Law Lords in 1984 that executive action under the royal prerogative was reviewable in a court of law – at least in those subject areas which are appropriate for judicial review – was a landmark.[30] In that case, however, the Law Lords held that the government ban on trade union membership at General Communications Headquarters was not unlawful *because* the Government had established that the ban was necessary in "the interests of national security". The onus was upon the Government to establish such a ground. In other cases, courts have held that statutory language should be interpreted in a manner which necessitates that a factual basis is established before an executive discretion is exercised. In *Tameside, Khawaja, Guardian Newspapers* and the *GCHQ* decisions[31] the courts would not accept the bare assertion

---

[26]   F. Snyder, "The Effectiveness of European Community Law: Institutions, Processes, Tools and Techniques" (1993) Modern L.R. 19. An interesting case on the limits of its operation occurred in *Society for the Protection of Unborn Children v Grogan* (1991) *The Times* 7 October (ECJ), and see *Open Door Counselling Ltd etc v Ireland* (1992) *The Times* 5 November (ECt HR).

[27]   P. Craig (1992) *Oxford Jo. of L.S.* 552; C. Harlow, "A Community of Interests? Making the Most of European Law" (1993) *Mod.L.R.* 331; Sir G. Slynn, *Introducing a European Legal Order* (London, Stevens, 1992).

[28]   Especially by the judiciary.

[29]   *IRC v National Federation of Self Employed and Small Businesses* [1982] AC 617.

[30]   *Council of Civil Service Unions v Minister for Civil Service* [1984] 3 All ER 935 (HL). There was doubt expressed by Lords Fraser and Brightman whether the Royal Prerogative itself, as opposed to power delegated under it, was reviewable, though Lords Diplock, Scarman and Roskill suggested it was. See *Burt v Governor etc. of NZ* (1992) 18 May (CA NZ).

[31]   *Secretary of State for Education and Science v Tameside MBC* [1977] AC 1014; *Khawaja v Secretary of State for the Home Department* [1983] 2 WLR 321 (HL); *Secretary of State for Defence v Guardian Newspapers* [1984] 3

of the executive, or the *ex facie* reasonableness of executive discretionary action.[32] Courts have, however, afforded great respect to the integrity of complex statutory processes leading to decision by the Secretary of State and have shown a reluctance to intervene in such cases or in cases where a commercial judgment has been exercised by a non-departmental body.[33] The *GCHQ* decision was also the occasion when Lord Diplock suggested a coherent categorisation of judicial review under the heads of: "illegality" (*ultra vires* proper); "irrationality" (unreasonableness, abuse and so on, of discretion); "procedural impropriety" (breach of fair procedure/natural justice or failing to follow a proper procedure). He added "proportionality" as developed by French, German and EC law. This may involve a review of the *merits* of a decision if it suggests "overkill" or excessive punishment or where the decision is out of proportion to legitimate objectives, that is, an unwarranted interference with human rights – a reversal of the Jesuitical motto that ends justify means.[34] It would apply where a scheme or policy adopted by governors/administrators or on their

---

[31]   Continued
       WLR 986 (HL); GCHQ decision, Note 30 above. *Khawaja* established that the scope of review in *habeas corpus* was not confined to the "reasonableness" of the authority's *ex facie* case, but could establish the factual basis of the charge which the authorities would have to prove on a balance of probabilities. There was timely judicial support for Lord Atkin's dissenting judgment in *Liversidge v Anderson* [1942] AC 206. See *R v Secretary of State for the Home Department ex parte Ali* [1984] 1 WLR 663.

[32]   Though it would be too ambitious to suggest the development of a "substantial evidence" test as in the USA. For the basic test on judicial treatment of facts, see *Edwards v Bairstow* [1956] AC 14 and *Global Plant v Secretary of State* [1972] 1 QB 139. Statutory applications to quash under the Town and Country Planning Act 1971 (now 1990) have frequently been the occasion for a probing inquiry into facts supporting a decision: *Colleen Properties v Minister of Housing and Local Government* [1971] 1 WLR 433; *Niarchos (London) v Secretary of State for the Environment* (1977) 76 LGR 480; *Prest v Secretary of State for Wales* (1983) 81 LGR 193 (CA).

[33]   *R v Secretary of State for Trade and Industry ex parte Lonhro* [1989] 2 All ER 609 (HL); *R v ITVC ex parte TSW Broadcasting* [1992] *The Times* 30 March (HL); note on closure of the coal mines and consultation: *R v British Coal Board ex parte Vardy* (1992) *The Times* 30 December.

[34]   It is a far more probing test for the review of a discretion than provided by Lord Greene in *Associated Provincial Picture Houses v Wednesbury Corporation* [1984] 1 KB 223 (CA); see *Padfield v Minister of Agriculture, Fisheries and Food* [1968] AC 997. In *Brind*, Note 14 above, the House of Lords denied that proportionality was a discrete ground of review in British law but other cases have been more circumspect, see Jowell and Lester, *Public Law* (1987) 368 and *R v Secretary of State for Transport ex parte Pegasus Hols Ltd* [1989] 2 All ER 481 and Recommendation R (80) 2 of the Committee of Ministers of the European Council, 11 March 1980.

behalf is simply not justified by the weight of evidence. One can discern the courts, nagging away at the administration and the evolution of a duty to provide reasons or reasoned decisions in a widening variety of adverse circumstances.[35]

A development of singular importance was the reformulation of RSC Order 53, the *Application of Judicial Review*.[36] This has made more coherent the procedure for application for judicial review so that *all* forms of relief, that is, certiorari, prohibition, mandamus, as well as declarations and injunctions, can be applied for in one proceeding, and can be coupled with each other and a claim for damages.[37] Relief under Order 53 is discretionary and is not given as of right.[38] Recent decisions have insisted that review of a decision or action of a public body or official must be made by Order 53 procedure[39] unless the applicant can show

---

[35] *Doody v Secretary of State for the Home Department* [1993] 3 All ER 92 (HL). See, however, *R v HEFC ex parte IDS* [1994] 1 All ER 651 (QBD) and for the high water mark, *R v Lambeth LBC ex parte Walters* (1993) 26 HLR 170 (QBD).

[36] Now contained in statute: Supreme Court Act 1981 section 31; Order 53 is in SI 1977 No. 1955; and see SI 1980 No. 2000. Order 53 is a *procedural* and not a *substantive* reform, so that it cannot take away pre-existing rights: *Wandsworth LBC v Winder* [1984] 3 All ER 976 (HL).

[37] Certiorari is a device used to quash decisions of, originally, an inferior judicial body which were outside its jurisdictional powers or contained an error of law on the face of the record. Prohibition was an instruction to an inferior judicial body not to continue exceeding its jurisdiction. Their scope has long since transcended judicial or quasi-judicial bodies. Mandamus is an instruction ordering a public body or official to perform his lawful duties, for example, exercise a discretion properly. The best treatment of public law remedies is in de Smith, *Judicial Review of Administrative Action*, 1980 (new edition H. Woolf and J. Jowell pending). See Law Commission, Working Paper No. 40, 1970; Law Commission No. 73, Cmnd 6407 (1976); and Law Commission Consultation Paper No. 126 (1993).

[38] Sir T. Bingham, "Should Public Law Remedies be Discretionary?" (1991) Public Law 64. It may be refused if, for example, the applicant has behaved badly or is undeserving or the application is made after "undue delay" and if successful would be "likely to cause substantial hardship to, or substantially prejudice the rights of any person or would be detrimental to good administration": Order 53, r. 4; Supreme Court Act 1981 section 31(6). The time limit for application is three months, but this would not appear to be a right, as "undue delay" *might* defeat the application on the grounds stated above even within three months: SI 1980 No. 2000. See *Carswell v Dairy Produce Quota for England and Wales* [1990] 2 AC 738; *R v Secretary of State ex parte Furneaux* [1994] 2 All ER 652 (CA). The three-month period is subject to statutory or rule of court limitations upon seeking review, for example, the six-week rule in planning cases for an application to quash.

[39] O'Reilly v Mackman [1983] AC 120. See for Scotland *Brown v Hamilton DC* (1983) *Scots Law Times* 397 and see for judicial review in Scotland:

a breach of a private right,[40] in which case he may proceed by private action;[41] or he may raise the issue collaterally as a defence or attack in other proceedings.[42] In *Roy's* case[43] the House of Lords gave further consideration to this approach, holding that the existence of public law features in a dispute did not dictate the necessity of judicial review proceedings where the private law rights dominated the issue, and appropriate relief could only be awarded in private law proceedings.[44]

A "Crown Office List" has been established which will be handled by judges who are, and who will become, more expert in "procedural public law".[45] As of writing, 18 judges are assigned to the list and they are assisted by deputy High Court judges especially in homeless litigation. Furthermore, judges themselves have been in the vanguard of those suggesting wide-ranging reforms

---

39   Continued
     Wolffe (1992); if an individual is seeking review of a private body's decision or action, private law procedure and not Order 53 *is* the necessary procedure: *Law v National Greyhound Racing Club* [1983] 1 WLR 1302 (CA) though cf. *R v Disciplinary Committee of the Jockey Club ex p. Aga Khan* [1993] 2 All ER 853 (CA); where the body is acting as a surrogate for the state and performing essential regulatory responsibilities it may be subject to public law review: *R v City Panel on Take-overs ex parte Datafin* [1987] 1 All ER 564 (CA). Public law tests of natural justice are applicable in many private relationships: *McInnes v Onslow-Fane* [1978] 1 WLR 1520; but tests of "reasonableness" in the exercise of a private discretion are rarely applicable unless a statute has introduced them: see for New Zealand *Finnegan v NZRFU Inc.* [1985] 2 NZLR 159 (NZCA); and note generally decisions on restraint of trade.

40   Such as breach of contract, breach of duty of care, interference with proprietary right or misfeasance of public office and so on, that is, a "cause of action".

41   As witness for instance the discussion of quasi-government in Chapter 4 and the intermediate nature of many quasi-governmental institutions. See, for example, *Peabody Housing Ass. v Green* [1978] 38 P & CR 644 for the position of housing associations. The case law is becoming legion; see Borrie (1989). Under Order 53, r. 9(5) if proceedings are commenced by judicial review but it becomes apparent that they should have been commenced by writ the court hearing the application can treat the matter as if it commenced by writ: see for an unhelpful decision: *R v Secretary of State for the Home Department ex parte Dew* [1987] 2 All ER 1049.

42   *Wandsworth LBC v Winder* [1984] 3 All ER 976; *Roy v Kensington etc. Family Health Practitioner Committee* [1992] 1 All ER 705 (HL).

43   Note 42 above.

44   See Law Commission, *Administrative Law: Judicial Review and Statutory Appeals*, Consultation Paper no. 126 (London, HMSO, 1993). Fredman and Morris (1994) have argued for a unified procedure for review for public and private bodies.

45   Sir L. Blom-Cooper, "The New Face of Judicial Review" (1982) *Public Law* 250.

in the realisation of justice against the state, reforms which are not simply centred on adapting ancient prerogative writs to the requirements of the late 20th century but which have suggested significant developments in the judicial apparatus and procedures on the public law side.[46]

How Coherent?

All is not quite a picture of coherence. The public/private division is far from clear-cut in many situations.[47] While the range of bodies over which judicial review may be exercised has developed significantly to include what in law would be considered private bodies but which are exercising regulatory powers as a surrogate for the state, the occasions when parties may challenge decision-making by public bodies through private action can be unclear,[48] as indeed are the range of bodies which are subject to judicial review. Exercise by a public body of its contractual powers would appear not to be susceptible, generally, to Order 53 relief although the employment status of Crown servants and officers has produced complications.[49] Withdrawal of licences would be a matter for judicial review.[50] The scope of the award of declarations and injunctions under Order 53 is still uncertain and has been hampered by conceptualisations pre-dating the reform of Order 53, although in *M v Home Office*[51] the Law Lords held that interim injunctions could issue against the officers of the Crown in public law proceedings and when acting in their official capacity notwithstanding the Crown Proceedings Act 1947. The decision

---

46 See Note 5 above.
47 Law Commission Working Paper No. 126 (1993).
48 See for example, *Gillick v DHSS* [1985] 3 All ER 402 (HL).
49 *R v Post Office ex parte Byrne* [1975] ICR 221; *R v BBC ex parte Lavelle* [1983] 1 All ER 241; *R v East Berkshire Health Authority ex parte Walsh* [1984] 3 All ER 425 (CA), though failure to *incorporate* statutory contractual terms by public employers may be reviewable under Order 53, *sed quaere? R v Secretary of State ex parte Benwell* [1984] 3 WLR 843 (Order 53 only remedy available on the facts). See *Mclaren v Home Office* [1990] ICR 824 (CA) and *R v Lord Chancellor's Department ex parte Nangle* [1991] IRLR 343.
50 *R v Barnsley MBC ex parte Hook* [1976] 3 All ER 452 (CA); *R v Birmingham City Council ex parte Dredger* [1993] *The Times* 28 January. See *Mercury Communications Ltd v Director General of Telecommunications* (28 February 1994, QBD), which was an application to strike out a request for a declaration that the DGT's interpretation of British Telecom's licence, clause 13, was incorrect. The judge refused to rule that private law procedure was an "abuse".
51 [1993] 3 All ER 537 (HL).

reversed *Factortame (No. 1)*[52] where it was held that they could not. *Factortame (No. 2)*[53] only allowed the award of an injunction where there was an arguable breach of EC law. Now domestic law and court orders and undertakings given to court may be protected by the order and by the court's contempt jurisdiction if need be, even where the contemnor is an officer of the Crown.[54]

In their desire to protect public bodies from vexatious and tardy litigants, the courts have insisted that judicial review of a "public" body, or one exercising public powers, must be sought by Order 53 when exercising its public jurisdiction – the "exclusivity principle". This procedure requires leave,[55] is subject to a strict time limit and removes some of the procedural advantages of private action to establish the facts.[56] The case law has emphasised that there may be exceptions to this general rule, and *Roy* above illustrates such an exception. The House of Lords has ruled that the Social Security Commissioners have power to rule on the vires of a regulation which is a matter of dispute before them – a power which the Court of Appeal had denied to the Commissioners – rather than be forced to remit the matter to Order 53 review. There are clearly implications for other tribunals and lower courts and the extent of their review powers, although a number of problems relating to collateral challenge remain unresolved.[57] The Law Commission has set out a series of possible options for reform, stating its preferred choice to be one where Order 53 was only insisted upon where no private law issue was raised in the proceedings.[58]

52 [1990] 2 AC 85.
53 [1991] 1 AC 603.
54 Lord Woolf in *M v Home Office*, Note 51 above, believed that an injunction could be issued prior to leave being obtained; "in a case of real urgency . . . the fact that leave had not been granted is a mere technicality" (at 565). See also Note 25 above.
55 Judicial review is a two-stage process: leave to apply followed by full hearing which can be expedited; see *R v Commissioner etc. ex parte Stipplechoice* [1985] 2 All ER 465 (CA) and some dogged defence of the right to appeal where leave is refused. All proceedings take place in London. Cross-examination and discovery can take place but they are rare. In Scotland there is no leave requirement; in Northern Ireland leave may be given without a hearing: B. Hadfield and E. Weaver (1994) *Public Law* 12.
56 *O'Reilly v Mackman* [1983] 2 AC 237; *Roy v Kensington etc. Family Health Practitioner Committee* [1992] 1 All ER 705 (HL).
57 *Chief Adjudication Officer v Foster* [1993] 1 All ER 705 (HL) and Bradley, (1993) *Public Law* 218; *Quietlynn v Plymouth City Council* [1988] QB 114; *Bugg v DPP* [1993] 2 All ER 815 (QBD).
58 Con. Paper no. 126, 1993, paragraphs 18 to 20.

A detailed empirical study of Order 53 procedure has high-lighted a variety of difficulties associated with judicial review and should be set beside the somewhat sanguine congratulatory accounts offered by the Justice/All Souls Review of Administrative Justice (1988) of the Order 53 reforms and judicial comments praising the new dawn of judicial review.[59] Chief among the problems identified are delay, the crucial importance and complexity of the leave stage in seeking review, a stage which does not receive the same degree of attention in commentaries as the substantive hearings, inconsistent application of criteria or application of inconsistent criteria by judges in allowing leave, leading to notable disparities in figures on leave by different judges and the presumption that leave is used to relieve the pressure on court dockets and the administration – that it is a judicial pressure valve. Several judicial decisions at full hearing would encourage such a reading.[60] The fact that applicants for relief frequently lack information or documents from public authorities heightens the opacity of the leave process, thereby enhancing the opportunities for bodies to prevaricate and prove obstinate.[61] Furthermore, in peremptory haste, the procedure governing appeal against a decision of the High Court to the Court of Appeal on a judicial review was reformed so that appeal is no longer automatic but leave must be sought.[62] Immigration is not included in these provisions.

Barriers to the Use of Courts

One had confidence in speaking more optimistically of the generous accommodation given to the interpretation of "sufficient interest" when determining which applicants may invoke the courts in judicial review. The *National Federation* case suggested that each case be dealt with by reference to its context and background.[63] If an applicant can raise a suspicion of unlawful

---

[59] *Parr v Wyre BC* [1983] HLR 41 (CA), Donaldson LJ; Sir H. Woolf (1990), Note 5 above, at 101.

[60] *Ex parte Swati* [1986] 1 All ER 717 (CA) and *Puhlhofer v Hillingdon LBC* [1986] AC 484.

[61] Sunkin, Bridges and Meszaros, (1993); Law Commission Paper 126 (1993), paragraphs 5.3 to 11.

[62] Bridges and Cragg, (1993) NLJ 1745 and SI 1993/2133 (L20).

[63] *IRC v National Federation of the Self Employed and Small Businesses* [1982] AC 617 and Supreme Court Act 1981 section 31(3). For *locus standi* in private law litigation see: *Gouriet v Union of Post Office Workers* [1978] AC 435 and *Barrs v Bethell* [1982] Ch. 294. *Gillick v DHSS* [1985] 3 All

activity in the exercise of public power, no matter how recondite
the power, sufficient interest may be established to make a
challenge.[64] Whether this will make a difference to the likelihood
of success at the full hearing is another issue.[65] However, a
post-*Federation* trend setting more restrictive tests for judicial
review can be witnessed. These decisions seem to display an
antipathy towards public interest litigators whether privately or
publicly funded. In the former case, the existence of a statutory
body to advise on ancient monuments removed the necessity of
an "outside" body with acknowledged experts addressing the court
on the scheduling of a site as a monument of national importance
when a challenge was made to the Secretary of State's exercise
of discretion.[66] In the latter, the Court of Appeal held that the
Equal Opportunities Commission did not have *locus standi* in a
public law issue concerning the UK's Community law obligations
in relation to equal opportunities although this aspect of the
judgment was overruled by the House of Lords.[67] The EOC

63 Continued
    ER 402 (HL), where a parent sought a declaration in private law that
    advice in a DHSS circular on prescription of contraceptives to a girl under
    16 was unlawful; and *Att.-Gen. v Able* [1984] 3 WLR 845. See also Local
    Government Act 1972 section 222 where local authorities can institute civil
    proceedings "protecting and promoting" the interests of local inhabitants:
    Kirklees MBC v Wickes Building Supplies Ltd [1992] 3 All ER 717.
64 In *R v Secretary of State for Social Services ex parte GLC*, [1984] *The
    Times* 16 August the Child Poverty Action Group but not the GLC had
    sufficient interest to bring an application under Order 53 on behalf of
    unidentified claimants wrongfully deprived of supplementary benefit. See
    further Cane (1990) and the interesting *R v AG ex parte ICI plc* [1987] 1
    CMLR 72 (CA).
65 See, for example *R v IBA ex parte Whitehouse* (1984) 81 LSGaz 1992 and
    R v Secretary of State for the Environment ex parte Ward [1984] 1 WLR
    834. In *Ward's* case, there is a statement to the effect that although a party
    may not have a private interest to found an action for breach of statutory
    duty, he may well have "sufficient interest" for Order 53 review. And see
    R v Horsham DC ex parte Wenman (1992) HLR 669. In prison cases where
    courts have ruled that breach of a statute or statutory rules does not confer
    a right of action, prisoners have sufficient interest to challenge the vires of
    fairness of the exercise of powers under statutory powers. On the inability
    of a prisoner suing for breach of the Prison Rules, see *R v Deputy Governor
    of Parkhurst Prison ex parte Hague* [1991] 3 All ER 733 (HL).
66 *R v Secretary of State for the Environment ex parte Rose Theatre Trust*
    [1990] 1 QB 504 (Schiemann, 1990); *R v Secretary of State for Employment
    ex parte Equal Opportunities Commission* [1993] 1 All ER 1022.
67 [1994] All ER 910 (HL). The EOC had *locus* by virtue of its statutory
    remit under Part VI Sex Discrimination Act 1975. See *R v HM Inspec-
    torate of Pollution and MAFF ex parte Greenpeace* (1993) 29 September
    (unreported). "Greenpeace" had *locus standi* to challenge HMI's decision

sought to challenge the Secretary of State's opinion that the UK was not in breach of Community law and his statement that no amending legislation would be introduced because there was no breach requiring legislation.[68] Dicta from the former case stated that "The decision . . . was . . . 'one of those governmental decisions in respect of which the ordinary citizen does not have a sufficient interest to entitle him to obtain leave to move for judicial review' even though this may well leave an unlawful act by a Minister unrebuked."[69] Given those sentiments, one cannot envisage the role of the courts changing dramatically in assisting in the resolution of grievances against the state unless a reform such as Lord Woolf's recommended Director of Civil Proceedings were introduced.[70] Such a development seems unlikely for the fore-seeable future. The Director would assist litigants against public bodies and would initiate actions and help develop principles of public law. Woolf envisaged that the Director's appointment and activities would be "independent" of politics.[71]

In the United States, courts have expanded the ambit of litigation by use of class actions, modified rules on *locus standi* and the *Brandeis Brief*.[72] Courts have also insisted that regulatory agencies

[67] Continued
      varying authorisations for radioactive waste discharge. Cf. *Wychavon D.C. v Secretary of State for the Environment* (1994) *The Times* 7 January: local authority not an "individual" capable of invoking directly effective provisions of EC law against Secretary of State.

[68] One of the majority judgments in the *EOC* case in the Court of Appeal, Note 66, related *locus* to the object of attack, an opinion as opposed to a decision or action or inaction, and this case raises a series of issues which the Law Commission has addressed. What are the limits of judicial review *vis-à-vis* opinions, guidance and other non-executive or evanescent "activities"? See the interesting *Good v Epping Forest DC* [1992] 3 PLR 103. In the *EOC* case in the House of Lords, the majority held that the EOC had *locus standi* and that a declaration could be issued that British legislation was inconsistent with EC provisions; but an expression of opinion could not be the subject of review.

[69] Law Commission, Note 61 above, paragraph 9.17, quoting Schiemann J.

[70] Woolf, 1986, 1990, Note 5 above.

[71] See Widdicombe (1986), paragraphs 9.87 and onward and Employment Act 1988 section 19 and the role of the Trade Union Commissioner, and TU Reform and Employment Rights Act 1993 and the role of the Commissioner for Protection Against Unlawful Industrial Action and an *actio popularis* against such action.

[72] The brain-child of Louis Brandeis (*Muller v Oregon* 208 US 412 (1908), it is a device for introducing social, economic and wider implications of a possible decision before the court. His brief contained two pages of legal argument and over 100 pages on the social and physiological benefits of reducing the working hours of women. Similarly in the USA *amicus* briefs for interested groups are a widely used device to widen the range of

promulgate policy by rule-making – sometimes after negotiation
with interested parties and those wishing to make comment – and
not adjudication wherever possible, a development which has
helped to create far greater opportunities for legal process to be
used as a starting point for the mobilisation of collective rights and
interests.[73] There are many opportunities for interested parties to
participate in varying degrees of formality in agency rule-making
which are far more advanced than any British analogue. Doubtless a constitutional culture which emphasises the importance of
due process of law and equal protection of the law provides much
of an impetus for the use of law as a medium to raise issues
of wide political concern in a manner which would be alien in
British courts. It is also true to say that the American political
and legislative processes had become so controlled by powerful
vested interests, and the agencies alternated in their symbiotic
relationships with the regulated so frequently that it was difficult
to assess who was regulating whom; in these circumstances the
courts became the only channel through which the small man,
the "new propertied" man, could register his stake in the constitutional scheme of things. What can prevent courts, however,
becoming the preserve of the mighty?

Let us examine how frequently Order 53 is invoked and relief
granted. The figures below give details of applications for judicial
review applications. There has been a marked, indeed dramatic,
increase in numbers of applications in the period 1981 to 1992; in
1968 there were 87 applications for leave with 24 orders granted,
a figure which had grown by 1977 to 376 and 29 respectively.[74]
What these figures do not reveal are the problems and difficulties
for litigants posed by existing procedures.

For appeals from bodies exercising statutory administrative,
judicial or quasi-judicial functions, the issue of standing for an

72   Continued
     argument before courts in cases dealing with constitutional rights. *Amicus*
     briefs in the important case of *Regents of University of California v Bakke*
     438 US 265 (1978), which concerned reverse discrimination, ran to three
     volumes. See Prosser, *The Test Case Strategy*, 1983.
73   Rule-making is prospective, collective and legislative as opposed to adjudi-
     cation which is usually but not exclusively retrospective and individualistic,
     see Shapiro, 78 Harv. LR 921 (1965). Prospective overruling by courts
     has attracted much attention: see Lewis (1988). On executive delegated
     legislation and congressional restraint, see Chadha 51 *US Law Week* 4907
     (1983). On the post "rights revolution" period see Sunstein (1990).
74   S.A. de Smith, *Judicial Review of Administrative Action* (4th edn) (ed.
     J.M. Evans) (London, Stevens, 1980).

Table A

Applications for Leave Received, Allowed and Refused/Not Proceeded With, 1981–1992

| | Total applications received | | | Allowed | | Refused/not proceeded with | |
	No.	% increase from previous year	from 1981	No.	%	No.	%
1981	558	–	–	382	71%	158	29%
1982	685	23%	23%	468	68%	217	32%
1983	850	24%	52%	621	69%	229	25%
1984	915	8%	64%	701	77%	214	23%
1985	1169	28%	109%	781	67%	382	33%
1986	816	–30%	46%	578	71%	238	29%
1987	1529	87%	174%	767	59%	532	41%
1988	1229	–20%	120%	695	55%	578	45%
1989	1580	29%	183%	905	59%	645	41%
1990	2129	35%	281%	902	52%	823	48%
1991	2089	–2%	274%	923	50%	929	50%
1992	2439	17%	337%	1123	47%	1268	53%

Table B

Substantive Hearings Allowed and Dismissed and Cases Withdrawn, 1981–1992

	Total applications determined	Allowed	Dismissed	% Successful	Cases withdrawn
1981	315	131	184	42%	39
1982	298	148	150	50%	n/a
1983	311	162	149	52%	n/a
1984	380	188	197	48%	n/a
1985	501	211	290	42%	n/a
1986	404	178	226	44%	n/a
1987	506	216	290	43%	n/a
1988	409	177	232	43%	293
1989	387	187	200	48%	179
1990	448	282	166	63%	88
1991	636	434	202	68%	168
1992	504	262	242	52%	366

Source: Crown Judicial Statistics (1981–85), Judicial Statistics (1986–91) and Crown Office (1992) (Sunkin, Bridges and Meszaros, Note 60 above). The author gratefully acknowleges the permission of Sunkin *et al.* and the Public Law Project to reproduce these tables.

appellant is usually straightforward if a party has been involved in a two-cornered encounter with an authority over the issue of a licence, grant, permission, and so on.[75] More difficult are those cases such as planning, compulsory purchase or environmental matters where statute allows a "person aggrieved" to apply to the High Court, usually to have a decision by an authority or Minister quashed within a specified period (often six weeks) on the grounds that it was not within the powers of the Act.[76] Courts have been quite accommodating to applicants in their interpretation of the grounds of "statutory quashing".[77] Conversely "person aggrieved" was for many years given a narrow interpretation in litigation and has been interpreted to mean a person with a *specific legal* interest in the issue.[78] In *Buxton v Minister of Housing and Local Government*[79] the plaintiff sought to set aside a grant of planning permission on the grounds of a blatant impropriety by the Ministry. Because in law the development proposed would not constitute a nuisance to his land, he had no legal grievance against the authority and, therefore, was not a "person aggrieved" entitled to seek an order to quash. However, judicial approaches have moved on and have suggested that any person allowed to participate in the proceedings, for example, a public inquiry, should have the right to make the application to the court.[80] In the *Southend* case, Woolf LJ has even drawn a parallel between "person aggrieved" and "sufficient interest" for judicial review[81] – although we should bear in mind that some judicial decisions seem to be restricting the ambit of "sufficient interest" (see above).

An important development came in the *People Before Profit*

---

75 For a list of statutory rights of challenge, see Law Commission (1993), Note 44 above paragraphs 121 to 135.

76 For example, Town and Country Planning Act 1990, sections 284, 287 and 288. See *R v Secretary of State for the Environment ex parte Ostler* [1977] QB 122, and for the PCA on the same case (1976) 77 HC 524, at 16 to 18; *R v Cornwall CC ex parte Huntingdon* [1992] 3 All ER 556 (QBD).

77 See Note 32 above.

78 The authorities for this proposition are cases dealing with the interests of creditors in bankruptcy proceedings in the 19th century, not quite the appropriate analogy of planning and environmental decisions of the late 20th century. See now *Cook v Southend BC* [1990] 1 All ER 243 (CA).

79 [1961] 1 QB 278 (QBD).

80 *Turner v Secretary of State for the Environment* (1973) 28 P & CR 123 and *Bizony v Secretary of State for the Environment* (1975) 239 EG 281. The discussion of inquiries in chapter 2 pp. 65 *et seq.* should be recalled at this point.

81 *Cook v Southend BC* [1990] 1 All ER 243 (CA).

litigation[82] where an action group had participated at a month-long inquiry into a proposed local plan (see chapter 3) of the local authority. The authority overrode the inspector's report which supported various objections made at the inquiry by the group against the plan, and rather peremptorily awarded planning permission in accordance with the plan. After the inquiry, the group became incorporated as a company limited by guarantee which meant technically it was a different legal entity from the group which objected at the inquiry and it sought to challenge the action of the authority. It sought relief by judicial review under Order 53. It was held that it was a body with "sufficient interest" as it was essentially the same group and legal technicalities ought not to defeat the merits. This seems to be a wider interpretation of standing than would have been afforded by the "person aggrieved" formulation, so common in specific statutory provisions allowing applications to quash, at least until the *Southend* case. Never-theless, the judge held with "very great regret" that the group's application failed on other grounds. Objectors had only a limited right of ultimate objection even though the inquiry had come out almost entirely in their favour. Indeed, the judge thought "public inquiries very often may have no useful purpose at all . . . I am slightly perturbed that a public inquiry can take place and its findings be so favourable and yet the authority can dismiss it virtually out of hand . . . the objectors won after a month's inquiry and lost after a few minutes consideration by the (planning) committee." Had leave to proceed been granted, £5,000 security for costs would have been sought by the judge. And this brings us to the non-legal dimension restricting judicial relief against the state – money. Cuts in legal aid have been a widely publicised feature of conflict between the professions and a Treasury-driven Lord Chancellor's Department. As the latter has been quick to point out, legal aid expenditure was set to rise to £2 billion by 1995; in 1987–8 the bill was £426 million. The effect of cuts and the introduction of arrangements such as "franchising" legal aid practice[83] are predicted to reduce significantly the number of practices providing legal aid service.

---

[82]   *R v Hammersmith and Fulham LBC ex parte People Before Profit* (1982) LGR 322 (QBD).

[83]   Law firms which meet the Legal Aid Board's quality criteria will be granted a franchise in one or more of nine areas of work. This will lead to quicker payment of fees and freedom from some administrative controls. The Board will monitor and audit franchises.

Taking on the Powerful

The state is its own financier – at our expense. In the field of litigation it is a "repeat player" while most litigants are "one-shotters".[84] To the latter, litigation is an unusual and often daunting experience. The former possess the expertise, the resources, the time; litigation is an occupational hazard and the costs do not fall on individual shoulders. Not all who litigate against the state are "one-shotters" of course, and to achieve some semblance of opportunity to use law as a device for protecting rights or interests, individuals often merge into groups advocating causes or issues and utilise devices such as the "Test Case" strategy.[85] Harlow and Rawlings have shown how the use of the strategy, or the use of courts to advance political causes has a long heritage in England. Financing such litigation is nonetheless problematical unless privately supported. The award of legal aid displays a structural antipathy against collective action[86] and posits whether the hypothetical individual would risk his own money on litigation. Public interest law groups or neighbourhood law centres which provide a free legal service to areas and issues which law has tended to neglect, rely upon public funding and charity. The latter (there were 57 at the end of 1992, 6 of which faced crippling cuts) are always at risk that public funding will cease if they act "politically" which is a frequent complaint where they

---

84 M. Galanter, "Why the 'Haves' come out ahead: speculations on the Limits of Legal Change", (1974) 9 *Law and Society Review* 95. C. Harlow and R. Rawlings, *Pressure through Law* (London, Routledge, 1992).

85 Prosser, *The Test Case Strategy*, 1983; Harlow and Rawlings, *Op. cit.* 1992.

86 *R v LAB ex parte Hughes* (1992) NLJ 1304 (CA): what is of benefit to an *individual*: law centres submit a very small number of claims for judicial review, information provided at IALS seminar on Public Law and Legal Services, March 1993 by D. Forbes. See the thoughtful essay by P. Lewis (1973). See also the Royal Commission on Legal Services, Cmnd 7648 (1979), below and the Government Response Cmnd 9077 (1983) and the Green and White Papers on the legal profession (Cm. 570 and Cm. 740 (1989). The Government places full emphasis upon the independent legal profession operating upon market principles and "legal aid from public funds should be available in appropriate cases for *individuals* who have inadequate resources". The Government "looks to the professions to maintain standards" of vitality and independence and to maintain "freedom under the law". It rejected a Council for Legal Services and Ministerial Responsibility for legal services in any particular area. Legal aid for "groups" is available in some cases (*Legal Aid Handbook*, 1993, paragraph 16.1 onward) though individuals should learn to "pool their resources". All in all, the response was really an apologia for the *status quo*.

are challenging their paymasters for failing in public duties in housing, social services, public health, and so on, or where they are challenging a government agency or influential institution. The problems encountered by the Community Development Project were referred to in Chapter 3. The Project's use of legal processes, *inter alia*, to ventilate collective grievances about inadequate housing policies, bureaucratic high-handedness, arbitrary management and allocation of capital were not tolerated. It was seen as being all the more offensive when the public purse was funding the activity.

Is there something improper about the use of legal processes for such purposes? The Law Centres Federation in a criticism of the Royal Commission on Legal Services[87] stated 29 examples of work which they perform of a kind not catered for by private practitioners. These examples

"should be uncontentious – each involved the provision of advice and assistance on matters relating to English law, albeit delivered in innovative fashion (and) have generated controversy and subjected the centres involved to outspoken attack. Regrettably, this seems bound up with the fact that law centre services are different from those traditionally provided, and because they are provided to different individuals and groups from those who had previously had access to legal resources . . . these novel ways of working involve acting on issues and against people or institutions who have previously been relatively immune from effective legal action."

The Government has favoured advice centres but it has been reported that almost 90 per cent of their work involves a legal issue which is simply not recognised because of the absence of legally qualified advisers.[88] The Legal Action Group has called for a Legal Services Commission to run the legal aid programme, ensure equal access to justice, educate the public about their rights, monitor the effects of the law and legal system on poorer clients and to carry out research into legal aid.[89]

Inevitably, reaction from frustrated campaigners included the belief that law, and legal process, are a sham, unable to live up to its rhetoric if asked to strike against vested interests of a public or private nature. Certainly law has not assisted in the creation of a surrogate political process for those unable to utilise political

[87] *Response to the Royal Commission on Legal Services*, 1979.
[88] D. Forbes, "Advice Services and Public Law", IALS 19 March 1993.
[89] *A Strategy for Justice*, LAG, 1992.

mechanisms or influence political elites. Groups or individuals may be far more interested in influencing the outcome of a decision by participating in its making rather than attacking it after the event. The United States has developed certain participatory procedures in public decision-making which offer more formal guarantees of opportunity for interested parties to contribute to decision-making than any British analogue. Agency rule-making is a clear example, and there are specific and general obligations in federal law for interested parties to be informed and provided with opportunity to make comment upon proposed rules, provide counter-arguments to others' comments and judicially developed tests to ensure that the agency takes a "hard look" at the comments. This process can be supplemented by hearings and oral presentation of argument.[90] Many government departments and local authorities in the United Kingdom make efforts to contact interested groups and individuals before bills, draft instruments, or bye-laws become law. A leading administrative lawyer, Professor Wade, has spoken of the widespread practice of consultation by governmental bodies in relation to delegated legislation in the United Kingdom. It remains very often a discretionary and administrative practice, and even when duties to consult are enshrined in statute, they rarely provide opportunities which citizens can encash in terms of hard legal rights to participate.[91] In exempting most of the information in the policy-making process from that which will be available under its provisions for open government, it is unlikely that much will change dramatically where the government hold a firm line on achieving a particular policy.[92]

In English law, there is no general presumption that parties will be consulted before legislative provisions or administrative rules are brought into effect, regardless of their ultimate importance or

---

[90]   The so-called "hybrid" procedures, which are discussed briefly elsewhere (p. 67–70). These have been subject to attack but have survived.

[91]   See Chapters 2, 3 and 4 above. See *Aylesbury Mushrooms v Agricultural, Horticultural and Forestry Industry Training Board* [1972] 1 All ER 280 (QBD) and *Lee v Department of Education and Science* (1967) LGR 211. Note *R v Aylesbury Crown Court ex parte Chahal* [1976] RTR 489 (DC); *Findlay v Secretary of State for the Home Department* [1984] 3 WLR 1159; *R v Secretary of State for Trade and Industry ex parte USTI* [1992] 1 All ER 212 (QBD); *R v British Coal Board ex parte Vardy* [1992] *The Times* 30 December (failure to consult over closure of pits in breach of EC and domestic law – target for pit closures nonetheless well on the way by 30 December 1993).

[92]   See *Vardy*, Note 91 above and see Hansard Society, *Making the Law* (Hansard Society Commission, 1993), especially chapter 3.

impact upon individuals.[93] This the Law Society discovered when the Lord Chancellor was held not to be under a duty to consult the Society before announcing cuts in legal aid eligibility.[94] When a general discretion to consult interested parties before making statutory orders or recommendations is present, the discretion is that of the designated official or politicians and though not unreviewable, it is extremely difficult to upset in practice. Courts have shown greater sensitivity in affording procedural protection to those who stand to be particularly affected by implementation of a policy, and have even held that fairness requires that such parties should have access to the reports of government advisers upon which a policy rests[95] and that identifiable groups should be consulted where change in a policy will detrimentally affect that group.[96] Where the courts can identify an individual interest that will suffer adversely as the consequence of an exercise of discretion, they have shown themselves vigilant in insisting upon opportunities to have one's say, know reasons for adverse decisions, even to know what others have said about the particular case.[97] What the courts are doing is protecting and advancing the realm of "legitimate expectation". In the formulation of broader policy, there has been little in the way of judicial insistence that a "hard look" is taken of views expressed where consultation does take place; that all parties are *fully* informed; and that reasons are provided as a matter of course even though there is no statutory duty to provide them. There is no doubt that administrative lawyers and a cadre of forward-looking judges have done much to raise consciousness, but many changes rely in practice upon goodwill rather than legal duty.

---

[93] *Bates v Lord Hailsham of St Marylebone* [1972] 1 WLR 1373. *R v Secretary of State ex parte USTI* [1992] 1 All ER 212. It is different if there is an *individual decision* depriving somebody of something – either a right, a privilege or a "legitimate expectation". And see: *Mahon v Air NZ Ltd* [1984] 3 All ER 201 (PC), and Lord Roskill in the *GCHQ* litigation, Note 30 above.

[94] *R v Lord Chancellor ex parte Law Society* (1993) *The Independent* 22 June.

[95] See the *ex parte USTI* decision, Note 92 above, but see also the discussion of *Bushell* and note the White Paper on *Open Government* pp. 38–39 above – such information is unlikely to be covered by the code of practice.

[96] See Lord Roskill in the *GCHQ* case, Note 30 above.

[97] See *Doody*, Note 35 above.

The Courts

Some Transatlantic Experiences

The United States has afforded a more favourable climate in which law can be used as a method of mobilising political resources. This was achieved by liberalising the rules on standing and the development of class actions – a procedural device enabling a litigant whose claims are shared by, or similar to numerous other individuals to litigate on behalf of their interests in court. If s/he wins, then remedial action and possibly large damages can be awarded to other members of the class. If s/he loses the individual claim, the court can deal with the class issue independently.[98] "Lawsuits involving the validity of governmental action or inaction, rather than asserting private rights, have come to dominate Federal Civil Dockets".[99]

Throughout the 1970s, the Supreme Court sought to confine the wider interpretation given to standing in the 1960s. This approach continued throughout the 1980s. Various cases have restricted the tests for standing[100] although *Duke Power Co. v Carolina Environmental Study Group* has reaffirmed the sufficiency of environmental interests as a basis for standing. Freedom of information legislation can be invoked by a "busy body" – even by a non-US citizen – and specific federal legislation can negative a restrictive interpretation of standing.[101]

Class actions have similarly been under judicial attack. Their use has been restricted in school segregation cases, civil rights, apportionment, environmental, consumer or other collective law suits aiming to vindicate rights of a more political nature to achieve social change.[102] The Supreme Court has treated the class as numerous individual claimants and claims and not as "a single jural entity capable of suing and being sued . . . constituted ad hoc for the very purpose of conducting a particular litigation and that its principal or only unifying characteristic is often the legal relationship or grievance in controversy". The onslaught on class

---

[98] A. Chayes, "Developments in the Law – Class Actions" (1976) 89 *Harv. LR* 1318.

[99] A. Chayes, "Public Law Litigation and the Warren Court" (1982) 96 *Harv. LR* 4.

[100] *Sierra Club v Morton* 405 US 727 (1972); *Valley Forge Christian College v Americans United for Separation of Church and State* 102 SCt 752 (1982); *Simon v Eastern Kentucky Welfare Rights Org.* 426 US 26 (1976).

[101] For example on environmental legislation. See, however, *Weinberger v Romero-Barcelo* 456 US 305 (1982) and *Amoco Production Co. v Village of Gambell* 480 US 531 (1987).

[102] See Chayes, Note 99.

actions has been more successful than that upon standing, and has concentrated on abstract legal and procedural technicalities.[103] Chayes concludes:

> "In standing cases . . . affluent or middle class plaintiffs seeking to vindicate environmental values seem to do pretty well . . . The losers (in class actions) are unwed mothers looking for child support, blacks, other minorities and the poor challenging patterns of police brutality or demanding access to adequate housing or medical services."

However, liberal tests for standing have been under sustained attack.[104]

American courts have a far wider range of remedial devices at their disposal to give effect to their decisions in litigation of a public, as opposed to a private nature. A declaration or court order upholding constitutional or legal rights in such litigation has been well described as merely the starting point of the realisation of those rights in practice.[105] The development of particular forms of relief against public bodies to ensure that judicial decisions are implemented by large defendant bureaucracies has been a persistent theme in litigation since the 1960s. The special forms of relief owe their origin to judgments addressing segregated education and housing systems and reform of state penitentiary systems. Courts employed "special masters" who are administrative assistants to the court and who in prison cases aided "in implementing decrees in suits challenging conditions of confinement". Through "masters" the court will be supplied with "feed-back" on how its judgment is being implemented throughout a particular system. Their duties include fact-finding, investigating and reporting to the court after its decisions.[106] Stewart and Sunstein[107] describe the reaction of the courts in the United States to the "administrative state" with the creation of remedies "designed to increase public participation in agency decision-making". These they describe as rights of defence against unlawful action; rights of action and initiation whereby the courts have enjoined public bodies to make a decision conferring rights or benefits upon those

---

[103] *Zahn v Int. Paper Co.* 414 US 156 (1973); *Eisen Carlisle and Jaquelin* 417 US 156 (1974); *General Telephone Co. v Falcon* 102 SCt 2364 (1982).
[104] *Allen v Wright* 468 US 737 (1984); *Center for Auto Safety v Thomas* 847 F. 2d 843 (DC Circ. 1988).
[105] Scheingold, *The Politics of Rights*, 1974.
[106] See (1979) 88 Yale LJ 1062.
[107] "Public Programs and Private Rights", (1982) 95 *Harv. LR* 1193.

seeking relief and which are very wide-ranging in impact as it
seems the courts have been shaping the substantive outcome of
the eventual decision of the body; lastly the "new property" hearing right concerned with legislative entitlement and the protection
of interests by procedural fairness. Recent years have seen a
judicial retrenchment in respect of the wide nature of judicial
intervention in the provision of remedies against public bodies.[108]
Nevertheless, commentators appear generally sanguine that the
surrogate political process provided by courts in the United States
has still left a powerful apparatus through which alternative votes
may be registered.

There have been onslaughts against these developments by the
Executive and Supreme Court.[109] There have been restrictive rulings in freedom of information suits; a form of "proportionality"
has been invoked as a means of statutory interpretation to assess
whether the aggregate social costs of legislation are proportionate
to the aggregate social welfare from its implementation; court
decisions have made it easier for employers to utilise discriminatory employment practices;[110] and a judicial presumption has
developed against judicial review of agency inaction.[111]

Some Domestic Difficulties

Enough has been said to suggest that I am doubtful of the ability
of our courts to develop a public law framework for litigation
comparable with the United States. That law is used, and has been
used for generations, for highly political strategies is obvious.[112]
Attempts at creating such a public law framework through our
courts and through the legal profession as presently organised
should be viewed with scepticism given that English law in its
structure, thought and culture is individualistic. At various stages,
the common law has shown a remarkable strength and resili-
ence when defending individuals against state excesses. But its
philosophy has been the protection of property and proprietary

---

[108] Tobias, 74 *Cornell LR* 270 (1989); Sunstein, Note 73 above; Vreeland, 57
       Chicago LR 279 (1990).
[109] On the executive side, see Executive Order 12,291,46 *Federal Register* 13193
       – placing limits on future rule-making; on the judicial side *Vermont Yankee*
       98 SCt 1197 (1978) limiting the contribution of "hybrid procedures" in
       rule-making and *Industrial Union Dept. AFL C 10 v American Petroleum
       Institute* 448 US 607 (1980). See Note 104 above.
[110] *Ward C. Packing Co. v Antonio* 109 SCt 2115 (1989).
[111] *Heckler v Cheney* 470 US 821 (1985).
[112] Harlow and Rawlings, Note 84 above.

interests, and not all can rest content that such a philosophy is appropriate to form a basis of protection for the range of needs and interests of citizens in a changing state structure. The point can be made by examining some of the technicalities involved in obtaining remedies against the state.

It seems that public law has been restricted to judicial review, statutory applications to quash and certain appeals.[113] The power to award damages on review under Order 53, r. 7 will seem now to have little application in practice.[114] To obtain damages, a citizen is best advised to sue in an action begun by writ or originating summons to vindicate a *private* right against a public body. When one sues a public body in a cause of action,[115] one asserts rights of an individual nature which the common law or statute provides.[116] Although expressed to be common law, the state has many effective immunities from a liability in common

---

[113] This is not an observation with which I would agree. The objection will be taken that our constitutional law transcends these matters. Most of the corpus of constitutional law deals with the rules and conventions governing relationships between the various organs of the state and are not justiciable at the suit of individuals before the courts.

[114] Note Lord Scarman in *RC v Rossminster* [1980] 1 All ER 80 at 105. Restitution is not available under judicial review: Goff LJ in *Winder* and see *Woolwich BS v IRC* [1992] 3 All ER 737 (HL) and the *Hammersmith* case, Note 119 below. An order to pay sums by way of grant under statute does not attract interest: *Sherriff (No. 2)* (1988) *The Independent* 12 January.

[115] Raising an estoppel against a public authority – that an official has made a representation to you which you have acted upon to your detriment or that it would be unfair for the authority to ignore can be *enforced* by Order 53: *R v Liverpool Corporation ex parte Liverpool Taxi Fleet Operators' Association* [1972] 2 QB 299; *Att.-Gen. of Hong Kong v Ng Yuen Shiu* [1983] 2 All ER 346 (PC); *R v RC ex parte Preston* [1983] 2 All ER 300 as well as by raising a defence to enforcement proceedings, etc. More of a sword than a shield? *Preston* was reversed on appeal [1984] 3 All ER 625. Note *Ex parte Khan* [1985] 1 All ER 40 (CA); see *R v IRC ex parte MFK etc. Ltd* (1989) NLJ 1343 (QBD) and *Matrix Securities Ltd v IRC* [1994] 1 All ER 769 (HL).

[116] For the liability of the Crown, see Crown Proceedings Act 1947 and Hogg. *Liability of the Crown in Australia, New Zealand and the U.K.*, 2nd edn, 1989. The Crown it appears cannot be sued for breach of a statutory duty unless the duty binds others apart from the Crown. The Crown is not bound by a statute unless the statute states that it is; and the Crown can take the benefit of a statute though not bound by it: *Town Investments v Department of the Environment* [1977] 2 WLR 450 (HL); *Lord Advocate v Dumbarton DC* [1990] 1 All ER 1 (HL). For public corporations many of the statutory duties are so vague as to be virtually non-justiciable at the suit of an individual in private law but may raise questions of public law providing a *locus* can be established. The Citizen's Charter programme is reviewing the extent of Crown immunities.

with its citizens. This derives partly from legal quirks and accidents and partly from the privileged position of the Crown and public bodies which operate not as persons with a natural and private capacity, but with a capacity framed in statutory and, for the Crown, prerogative and personal powers.[117] So, for instance, governments cannot be estopped from developing or changing policy by pleas that they have acted or conducted themselves in a manner which an individual has relied upon or that they have made contracts or representations to which they must be bound if this prevents them from exercising their statutory or prerogative powers.[118] Likewise, public bodies cannot be held to representations or agreements made by themselves or servants which would result in them increasing their *vires* although it may be that the developing law of restitution will be of increasing utility here.[119] To allow authorities to be bound by such representations would be to encourage *ultra vires* activity – even though a perfectly innocent victim may suffer.[120] Decisions since the early 1970s have attempted to allow representees to insist that public bodies stand by their representations where this would have the effect not of abusing, exceeding, or not exercising statutory powers, but of rendering performance of those powers fairer.[121] The creation of a nuisance under statutory authority will carry no liability when Parliament has authorised, expressly or impliedly, the nuisance.[122]

Private actions against public bodies where the essence of the claim is negligence in the exercise of a statutory power are unlikely to meet with success when one is attacking the

---

117 And officials, as Lord Woolf reminded us in *M v Home Office* [1993] 3 All ER 537 (HL), possess an individual and personal responsibility; for Dicey this is what the Rule of Law meant.

118 *The Amphitrite* [1921] 3 KB 500 (BD); see also *Laker Airways v Department of Trade* [1977] QB 643 (CA).

119 A recent helpful discussion is in *Western Fish Products v Penwith DC* [1981] 2 All ER 204 (CA). The question of law was made notorious in the "interest rates swaps" saga involving local authorities and city institutions; *Hammersmith and Fulham LBC v Hazell* [1991] 1 All ER 545 (HL) (Loughlin 1990 and 1991). In subsequent cases, restitutionary orders were made: *WLG v Islington LBC* (1993) *The Independent* 25 February (QBD) and on appeal (1994) *The Independent* 5 January (CA). Some plaintiffs sought to rely upon fraudulent misrepresentation.

120 The case law in such instances is obscure and has caused confusion, often to avoid injustice. The services of the PCA and LGO should be recalled in this context.

121 See Note 115 above.

122 *Allen v Gulf Oil Refining Co.* [1981] AC 101 (HL).

policy element of the decision, unless one can show that the decision is *ultra vires and* that it constitutes a breach of duty owed to the plaintiff in law to exercise reasonable care and that the breach has caused the plaintiff harm which was foreseeable and compensable.[123] The last decade has witnessed a judicial diffidence to find actionable breaches in the exercise of what may be termed regulatory powers and operational powers which require some judgment in their exercise – most obviously in the case of the police and financial regulators.[124] These points are well developed elsewhere.[125] Should liability be established, compensation is paid out of the public purse which has many other demands upon it. The end result is that it is very difficult to succeed in actions against public bodies in private law where there is the additional burden of establishing that the activity is *ultra vires*, or where it is part of a complicated statutory scheme or where the issue under attack involves a question of judgment. The conclusion is difficult to avoid that sometimes acts of plain negligence in appropriate conditions of proximity are escaping liability. The common law has thrown the risk or burden in these relationships upon private parties, to the advantage of the state and public purse. Parliament itself has often provided immunity from suits in negligence for regulatory authorities.[126] Furthermore there is no liability for *ultra vires* activity *per se* unless a public body or official acts negligently, or maliciously or knowingly

---

[123]   *Dorset Yacht Co. v Home Office* [1970] AC 1004; *Anns v Merton London Borough Council* [1978] AC 728; *Department of Health and Social Security v Kinnear* (1984) 134 New LJ 886; *Lonrho v Tebbit* [1991] 4 All ER 973 (Ch. D). See the interesting judgment of Kennedy L J in *Stovin v Wise (Norfolk CC, third party)* [1994] 3 All ER 467 (CA).

[124]   *Hill v Chief Constable of West Yorkshire* [1989] AC 53; *Alexandrou v Oxford* [1993] 4 All ER 328 (CA); *Ancell v McDermott* [1993] 4 All ER 355 (CA); see also *Rigby v Chief Constable of Northamptonshire* [1985] 1 WLR 1242. On the exercise of supervisory and regulatory powers: *Yuen Kun-Yeu v AG of Hong Kong* [1988] AC 175; *Rowling v Takaro Properties Ltd* [1988] 2 WLR 418 (PC); *Davis v Radcliffe* [1990] 2 All ER 536 (PC). See *X v Bedfordshire CC* (1993) *New Law Journal* 1783 – no duty owed to child under Child Care legislation by local authority to protect child against parental abuse. *Wood v Law Society* (1993) *New L.J.* 1475 held that in investigating complaints, the Law Society was acting quasi judicially and did not owe a duty of care.

[125]   P. Craig, *Administrative Law (2nd edn)* (London, Sweet & Maxwell, 1989), chapter 15; P. Cane, *Introduction to Administrative Law (2nd edn)* (Oxford, Oxford University Press, 1992), chapter 12.

[126]   Banking Act 1987 ss 1(4) and 2(7) and Financial Services Act 1986 s. 187.

outside their powers or jurisdiction.[127] This is a heavy burden
for plaintiffs to overcome. A remedy in damages for loss caused
by "wrong administrative action" and "excessive or unreasonable
delay" has been recommended by the Justice/All Souls committee
reviewing administrative justice,[128] a recommendation which Sir
Harry Woolf could not "wholly endorse".[129]

Statutory schemes to compensate individuals for decisions rendering them the victims of the collective welfare, as in planning
decisions or compulsory purchase causing blight, have gone some
way to redress some of the deficiencies caused by common law,
though the impetus of these decisions has been to move from a
liability in law to conferral of a benefit under an administrative
discretion.[130]

The most significant development in this area has involved EC
law, particularly the case of *Francovich*.[131] When the European
Court held that, providing the appropriate conditions were established, a Member State that has failed to implement or properly
implement a Directive may find itself liable in damages to a
person or body who has suffered damage as a consequence of
that non-implementation,[132] it squeezed into a ball many of the
arguments concerning powers, control, inactivity, negligence and

---

127 *Dunlop v Woollahra Municipal Council* [1981] 2 WLR 693 (PC); *Bourgoin
SA v Ministry of Agriculture* [1986] 1 CMLR 267 (CA); *R v Knowsley MBC
ex parte Maguire* (1992) *The Times* 26 June and *Racz v Home Office* [1994]
1 All ER 97 (HL). But see the implications of the *Francovich*, *Emmot*
and *Marshall (No. 2)* decisions of the CJEC. For punitive damages and
oppressive government action, see *Rookes v Barnard* [1964] AC 1129 and
the limits imposed in *AB v SW Water Services Ltd* [1993] 1 All ER 609
and *Deane v Ealing LBC* [1993] ICR 685 (CA) and see Race Relations
(Remedies) Act 1994.
128 See Note 15 above.
129 Woolf, 1990, Note 5 above, at 57.
130 For example, Land Compensation Act 1973; Vaccine Damage Payment Act
1979; Planning and Compensation Act 1991 and Reinsurance and Acts
of Terrorism Act 1993. Note the provision made for haemophiliacs who
became aids victims having contracted the condition as a consequence of
contaminated substances used by the NHS. The PCA rejected the complaint
which was eventually litigated: *Re HIV Haemophiliac Litigation* (1990) NLJ
1349 (CA) on discovery. For similar litigation in France, see Errera, (1993)
Public Law 537. See PCA Fourth Report (1992/3) on compensation for
slaughtered poultry; and Harlow (1982).
131 [1992] IRLR 84 (CJEC).
132 The relevant conditions are: that the provisions must be capable of being
directly effective, that is, they attribute rights to individuals, their content
must be capable of being identified from the provisions of the Directive
and there must be a causal link between failure to implement or implement
properly and the damage suffered by the individuals.

liability that have clouded this area since the decision of the *East Suffolk Rivers Catchment Board* case,[133] if not before. In *Francovich* there was inactivity; there was unlawful action by virtue of non-implementation. This was the base upon which liability was established[134] although it remains to be seen what possible defences may be invoked by the state to avoid liability.

When a challenge is made to the legality of action or decision-making of public bodies, the presumption is *omnia praesumuntur rite esse acta* or "all is as it should be", which the plaintiff must displace on a balance of probabilities.[135] To establish the details of a decision will invariably require discovery of documentation where all the necessary evidence is not present on the record of the proceedings as is usual in "judicial" processes. Discovery and inspection, although obtainable under judicial review, are awarded sparingly and for limited purposes.[136] We have witnessed considerable erosion of judicial deference to pleas of public interest immunity by Ministers or senior civil servants, in other words, that it is against the public interest to allow documents to be handed to a litigant, so that even Cabinet documents can be the subject of an order for discovery.[137] Papers concerned with the governmental process at ministerial level have been the subject of applications for discovery and pleas of immunity, and it seems clear that in appropriate circumstances and subject to the interests of state security and diplomatic relations, they can be inspected by the judge if the applicant can persuade the judge that there is a "reasonable probability" that the documentation is very likely to assist his case and that it is necessary to dispose fairly of the case. A mere "hunch" that they might assist is not sufficient to cause the judge to look at the papers before s/he decides where the interests of justice lie: in discovery and inspection to assist the litigant in their cause, or against discovery and inspection to protect the

---

133 [1941] AC 74. The duty in *Francovich* was to implement Directives; in *East Suffolk* to exercise discretion lawfully.
134 Under Article 5 EC Treaty and to guarantee the effectiveness of EC law and rights thereunder and see on the latter point Articles 169 to 171 as amended by the Maastricht Treaty.
135 For a graphic illustration see *Cannock Chase DC v Kelly* [1978] 1 WLR 1 (CA), the facts of which are now amended by statute. In the absence of evidence to the contrary, public bodies are presumed to have acted properly.
136 Law Commission, Consultation Paper No. 126, 1993, chapter 8.
137 See Lords Scarman and Keith in *Burmah Oil Co. v Bank of England and Att.-Gen.* [1979] 3 All ER 700 (HL); and Lord Fraser in *Air Canada v Secretary of State for Trade (No. 2)* [1983] 2 AC 394 (HL), doubting *dicta* of Lord Reid in *Conway v Rimmer* [1968] AC 910.

public interest of security, frankness and confidentiality in public administration. The test which has to be satisfied before a judge inspects is an onerous one.[138]

Public interest immunity is not confined to organs of central government, but its exact parameters are unclear.[139] There are indications that courts may be more amenable to ministerial pleas for immunity when based upon considerations of security and public order.[140]

Relief under Order 53 is discretionary, not as of right, and reference has been made to time limits and procedural points. Delay can defeat an application either at the leave stage or at the full hearing and in any event the time limit for bringing an application for leave is three months.[141] These points and others have been the subject of a paper by the Law Commission.[142] The prerogative orders operate so as to insist that public bodies exercise their powers or duties properly and this is usually satisfied by a reconsideration of the issue, even if the public body comes to the same conclusion as the initial one. The court is concerned with *process* not substance.[143] Mandamus is a difficult remedy to obtain as its award may well impose financial obligations upon a public body if it is instructed to perform a public duty[144] and mandatory injunctions are likewise difficult to obtain. A declaration cannot be awarded on an interim basis nor, it would seem, according to some unfortunate decisions, can a ruling be made upon the legality of advisory opinions,[145] although the decision

---

138   Pleas against the state bodies invariably involve an allegation of *ultra vires* or questionable activity and at a functional level this is inevitably impossible to prove without evidence in the bodies' possession. "The task of the court was to decide the case fairly between the parties on the evidence available, and not to ascertain some independent truth by seeking out evidence of its own accord", believed the majority in the *Air Canada* decision. The individual has to have some independent evidence of his or her own before s/he can ask the court for more.

139   *D v NSPCC* [1978] AC 171; *SRC v Nassé* [1979] 3 All ER 700 (HL).

140   *Makanjuola v Commissioner of Met. Police* [1992] 3 All ER 617 (CA) though see *R v Chief Constable West Midlands Police ex parte Wiley* [1994] 3 All ER 420 (HL); *Balfour v FCO* [1994] 2 All ER 588 (CA).

141   See p. 253 above.

142   Note 44 above, chapters 4 and 14.

143   See r. 9(4), and also *Shah v Barnet BC* [1983] 1 All ER 226 at 239, 240 per Lord Scarman on limitations of mandamus; *Chief Constable of North Wales Police v Evans* [1982] 3 All ER 141 (HL).

144   *R v Bristol Corporation ex parte Hendy* [1974] 1 All ER 1047 (CA); and see *R v Secretary of State for Social Services ex parte CPAG* (1988) *The Independent* 11 October (CA).

145   Law Commission, Note 142 above, paragraphs 2.12–13.

in *M v Home Office*[146] has facilitated the award of injunctions against the Crown's officers, but such awards invariably require a cross-undertaking as to damages.[147]

Courts appear reluctant to enforce statutory obligations upon public bodies where to do so would cause significant public expenditure. In cases concerned with the control of housing conditions under the Public Health Act 1936 (now Part III Environmental Protection Act 1990) the Divisional Court has given clear guidelines to magistrates on the exercise of their discretion if asked to issue a nuisance order under section 94(2) against an authority. The end effect was to moderate significantly the power of the nuisance order and the expense upon the authority, and a subsequent House of Lords decision effectively endorsed the approach of the Divisional Court.[148] Statutory obligations are interpreted benevolently for the authority. Under the Housing (Homeless Persons) Act, Lord Denning said that the decision-making of authorities should be looked at "benevolently" *vis-à-vis* homeless applicants, a sentiment echoed in a somewhat high-handed tone by Lord Brightman.[149] Even when a tenant won in litigation against a public landlord which was found to be in breach of statutory covenants, the judgments were framed so as to give clear guidelines to authorities on how to circumscribe the apparent effects of the decision.[150] McAuslan argues that these cases should be compared with the frequent occasions when courts give succour to private landlords – often property companies – when local authorities claim the former are breaking their duties under Housing and Public Health Acts. The picture painted is often of a beleaguered individual beset by rapacious authority – a cameo which is often difficult to reconcile with the facts.[151]

As I write, environmental law has been seen to offer greater opportunity to those in inner city areas and elsewhere to help establish a healthier and better environment than previous

---

146 [1993] 3 All ER 537 (HL).
147 This is where the person seeking the injunction has to undertake to make good any financial loss suffered by the enjoined party as a consequence of the award of the injunction. Where the Crown or a public body seeks an injunction to enforce the law, such an undertaking is not usually requested, but may be: *Hoffman La Roche v Secretary of State for Trade and Industry* [1974] 2 All ER 1128 (HL); *Kirklees BC v Wickes BS Ltd* [1992] 3 All ER 717 (HL).
148 *Nottingham City DC v Newton* [1974] 1 WLR 923; *Salford CC v McNally* [1975] 2 All ER 860 (HL).
149 *Pulhoffer v Hillingdon LBC* [1986] 1 All ER 467.
150 *Liverpool City Council v Irwin* [1976] 2 All ER 39.
151 McAuslan, 1980, at 195 to 210.

legislation. Here there has been access to information regulations under EC directives, an Environmental Protection Act 1990
and Water Act 1989 (now consolidated) and public registers of
those causing pollution. Opportunities have been found to work
alongside regulatory regimes administering "integrated pollution
control" and to utilise individual prosecutions for breaches of
emission and pollution limits. This new-found optimism should be
seen in the context of the Government's proposals outlined in the
Queen's Speech in 1993 to allow widespread deregulation of controls which stood as an impediment to business and enterprise and
which, the Government claimed, sapped initiative. Unnecessary
red tape and bureaucratic excesses are easy targets; one should
not overlook the fact that much regulation concerning safety and
health has been introduced to counter and remove abuses and
dangerous practices by those intent on making profit regardless
of the human cost.

Conclusion

We live at a time of profound change in our public and private
life, change with which our formal constitutional apparatus is
ill-equipped to cope. This poses a fundamental dilemma. Inertia
against change is the bias of the formal British Constitution and
those who manage its operation. On the surface all appears the
same in much the same way that Macaulay remarked that after
the Glorious Revolution of 1688/9 nothing had really changed in
respect of most law and governmental institutions: "Not a single
new right was given to the people".[152] This was a contradiction in
terms: a revolution revealing a "profound reverence for the past"
where the Crown was constitutionalised but not, one might add,
the executive. Beneath the surface irremediable change had been
wrought. The constitution in formal terms today is the same as
that which the Government inherited in 1979; the machinery of
government, which is not the same thing as a constitution, has
changed irreversibly.

Law is a special product of this inertia. The important biases
operate at a systemic not a personal level. Law is presented as
something which is beyond personal preferences and above political conflict. Yet its method is to transmute conflicts of political,
economic and social moment into disputes between *individuals*
based upon individual entitlement and duty. The techniques of

---

[152]   *History of England*, Vol. III (1889) at 1306.

law operate to conceal the biases inhering in its structure. A conflict, for instance, about the best way of producing a suitable transport policy for the urban environment becomes an issue concerned with the fiduciary duties owed by an authority to its beneficiaries as if the former were a private trust.[153]

The idea of law often conveys a basic set of moral imperatives or a belief that legal processes can provide an opportunity to establish what basic moral imperatives are and what they dictate in particular circumstances, or how they should inform the working of public institutions and how those institutions should treat citizens. If we expect something of this order from our courts we will face disappointment. If judges attempt it without sufficient training, and without significant changes in judicial and professional culture, the results could be disastrous. On the whole the judiciary do their job pretty well and independently. But in the interface of law and politics, it is a narrow job protecting a rather narrow range of interests. Law's promise is about more than this. Senior judges may look with expectation on the possibilities of "procedural public law", but it is doubtful whether the role of our courts, free from prior restraint, is going to alter significantly in resolving grievances or providing remedies against the state.

Just in case the judiciary prompt our public administration under Order 53 to engage in a re-examination of its values, then these concomitant contributions towards a greater openness and accountability would be desirable were judicial involvement to engender a movement towards "responsive" and "reflexive" law.[154] The former concentrates upon the purposive quality of law and its encouragement for affected communities to participate in government and administration. The latter sees law providing "regulated autonomy . . . which will redefine and redistribute property rights (and) create the structural premises for a decentralised integration of society by supporting integrative mechanisms within autonomous social systems . . . (relying) on procedural norms that regulate processes, organisations and

[153] The "Fares Fair" dispute in *Bromley LBC v GLC* [1982] 1 All ER 129 (CA & HL). Or the respective merits of alternative educational philosophies become an issue of abstruse and pettifogging statutory construction of terms such as "reasonable" on the presumption that such vague terms are susceptible to definitive objective analysis: *Tameside* and section 68 of the Education Act 1944. See also: *Hammersmith and Fulham LBC v Secretary of State for the Environment* [1990] 3 All ER 589 (QBD, CA, HL).

[154] Nonet and Selznick, *Towards Responsive Law*, 1978; Teubner, "Substantive and Reflexive Elements in Modern Law", (1983) 17 *Law and Society Review* 239.

distribution of rights and competencies":[155] in other words,
regulated self-rule. One has only to see the development of
this as a practice in finance, professional administration and
industrial and commercial operations to realise that that is how
law is used by governments today: a framework is created under
law in which organised interests may regulate themselves under
rule-books, codes of practice and Ombudsmen. The courts' task is
to interpret the procedural rules governing these bodies and their
codes to the extent that government has not excluded judicial
interpretation. As I have remarked elsewhere, what is lacking is a
suitable constitutional dimension to these developments, the substantive norms guiding the standards of the content of delegated
rules and codes and the absence of appropriate and suitably qualified institutions/bodies to oversee this vast amount of delegated
power – power delegated by the state. An American authority has
expressed the task confronting public law in the United States in
the following terms, and I believe they are increasingly relevant
in a British and European context:

> "One of the major tasks of modern public law is to develop
> structures to decrease the likelihood of regulatory failure and
> to introduce . . . constitutional safeguards into a dramatically
> changed system of government. For the most part remedies
> must come from non-judicial institutions. Structural reform
> should be high on the agenda here."[156]

---

155 G. Teubner, "Substantive and Reflexive Elements in Modern Law" (1983)
     17 *Law and Society Review* 239, at 254 to 255.
156 Sunstein (1990), at 229 to 230. The quotation is modified to account for
     the fact that Sunstein is referring to a written constitution.

Chapter 7

REMEDIES – AN OVERVIEW

It was commonplace, recently, to read about the increasing inability of law, legal process and the representative institutions of government to operate as effective control mechanisms over the exercise of power by the contemporary state. Writers argued that we had seen an increasing resort to administration and government intervention causing the development of a bureaucratic-regulatory form of law and government to accompany the managerial state.[1]

This was characterised by the widest delegation of powers and conferral of discretion by political overlords to their subordinates. The society in which such developments had taken place, it was argued, would have little need for a form of law that was based upon an individualistic outlook which placed the supremacy of individualism and individual property rights at the centre of its universe. The administrative state had swept aside the supremacy of the individual, which was seen as a thin cover for individual rapacity and had placed its emphasis upon collective welfare, as interpreted by elected politicians and officials, and intervention to redress the inequalities wrought by the operation of the market. The current political rhetoric, however, emphasises privatisation, deregulation, a minimal state and the supremacy of individualistic, or *gesellschaft* law. In the last decade and a half there has been a far greater centralisation of power reclaimed or arrogated by central government. Discretionary power has been concentrated in the centre and delegated under various programmes to public and private actors and partnerships between the two. In the Autumn Statement of 1992, the Chancellor announced changes in the use of privately raised finance to enable public and private sector bodies to work together more effectively, that is, to get

---

[1] E. Kamenka and A. Tay, "Beyond Bourgeois Individualism" in Kamenka and Kneale (eds), *Feudalism and Beyond* (1975); R.M. Unger, *Law in Modern Society. Toward a Criticism of Social Theory* (New York, Free Press, 1976).

private finance to help public services.[2] As I write a call has gone out from the Government for a public/private initiative to establish new schools for select/special groups.

In the case of both public and private sector actors, market competition and market substitutes and greater attention to the delivery of services by contract specification and contract compliance have been introduced. The result has not been the removal of government or discretion; it has been rather to give them new expression: the empowering state confers its powers to allow others to help themselves. So, for instance, we find far greater responsibility for managerial discretion given to chief executives and their subordinates in the new agencies; contracting out of services necessitates far greater choice in setting specifications and assessing compliance, discretion in setting appropriate standards and establishing consumer contact points especially in relation to complaints and feed-back. New guidance issued by HM Treasury in 1992 on market testing allows suppliers to use greater flexibility and innovation in their response to public bodies.[3] For the service recipients it does not really matter whether the service provider or file holder is a public or private entity; discretion at the level of delivery will not be any less than at present under payments of social fund, national insurance or social security income support, or in extracting child payments from absent parents, or in disciplining prisoners. Even where regimes of payment are rights-based, discretion may be reduced, never eradicated.

The latest developments in what may be termed "managerial government" or "entrepreneurial government" may be very creative but they inevitably involve a wide element of choice and power to act. We have seen the deliberate attempts to keep the courts out of many of the new "public law contracts" between departments and agencies and bodies within the NHS; the interpretation of these arrangements is not ombudsmen territory[4] and the Public Accounts Committee quite understandably is not geared to righting individual grievances. In the public contracts for service delivery, terms should deal with details of service,

---

2   Citizen's Charter Annual Report 1992, Cm. 2101, at 58.
3   *Ibid.*, at 59.
4   As opposed to maladministration in the service of the contractor, which will be. However, one can imagine a case of a contractor arguing that s/he has complied faithfully with the specifications which were as a matter of policy accepted as adequate by the department or agency and that this is what a complaint is concerned with. Will the Ombudsman interpret contracts which the department claims represents its assessment of the merits of a level of service?

price and quality, provisions for monitoring and inspection, for penalties for complaint handling[5] and for arbitration. Citizens must be afforded direct rights to complain in such "contractual relationships".[6]

What has been learned from the lessons of previous chapters? We still find ourselves in an administrative/regulatory state. It is a contradiction in terms to talk about the state without accepting a governmental and regulatory role, whether such roles are conducted through formal or informal processes, public or private places. Such roles are still considerable and all-pervasive if protean and less certain. They have thrown up a host of opportunities, procedures and practices through which grievances may be redressed, opinions expressed and participation allowed. To what effect? Some general points will follow on these matters.

What Lessons are there for the Future?

Grievance redress is an essential feature of accountability. It is not a discrete activity concerned with settling gripes, picking bones or rubbishing public servants or their surrogates. In raising the profile of grievance redress, the Citizen's Charter has performed an invaluable service. Where it lacks is in addressing an appropriate constitutional dimension – a social contract addresses the totality of a citizen's worth and contribution, and not simply his or her expectations from an economic marketplace. If we really are attempting to re-invent British government we cannot ignore government's role in helping citizens to develop as social beings as well as economic agents. Nor can we, as Norman Lewis and I have said elsewhere, allow government to abandon its obligations to deliver an effective justice system and effective methods for overseeing the operation of a system of justice. The CC has promoted the importance of obtaining public attitudes to service and the importance of complaining, devising adequate procedures for complaints and responding to information from complaints and surveys. The strategic importance of complaints as a management tool is a feature which has yet to be fully accepted in public and private concerns. But encouraging consumerism as opposed to citizenship does not mean that the customer is always right. Anyone in a position of power and responsibility

---

5   This is evident from a study of the tender documents for Strangeways Prison.

6   N. Lewis, *How to Reinvent British Government* (London, European Policy Forum, 1993).

will know that sometimes the answer has to be "No"; what is important is that there is a suitable mechanism through which a challenge may be made and that the reasons for that response are properly explained.

I have said enough about the ingredients of a good complaints procedure not to necessitate repetition. The CC has indicated what should accompany a good complaints procedure to reduce the necessity of complaining: competition in service delivery and the introduction of capital markets are obvious features; others include performance-related pay and the ending of anonymity of public servants. The former is controversial because of the need for appropriate criteria to assess what should be key elements in a good performance and what should happen if they are met but other corners are cut to achieve good ratings. A way to avoid complaints about non-delivery of a service is to ensure that unlawful action of service staff cannot prevent delivery; to this end the Government has legislated that those affected by such industrial action may sue those responsible; this pays scant regard to the fact that those non-performing are themselves consumers of other services, possessing not just one status identity. It also reduces to nought the grievances of employees who simply cannot make effective protest without taking unlawful action given the removal of so many immunities from industrial action.[7] Provision of information about service targets and standards of performance and publication of indicators of performance can indeed help to explain what legitimate expectations are, and learning from mistakes discovered from complaints should help to reduce repetition of the same mistakes or shortcomings. Inspection and audit are vital aspects in revealing systemic and serious shortcomings in government activities; witness the prison reports of Inspector Judge Tumim or the reports of the Public Accounts Committee (PAC).

What we find so often is that there is no adequate mechanism to ensure that government responds in a responsible and constructive manner.[8] What we do not know very much about is peoples' perceptions of complaining; why do some complain and not others? Are the obstreperous and pushy with an unjustified

---

7   *Meade v Haringey LBC* [1979] ICR 494 (CA). Prison officers were prevented from taking industrial action by temporary injunction on the ground that they may arguably be in an analogous position to the police: *The Times* 19 November 1993.

8   It has been reported that some departments have stamped documents "Not for eyes of PAC", *The Guardian*, 23 November 1993.

claim more likely not only to complain but to succeed? The Employment Service informed me that the incidence of complaining and the nature of complaints increased and changed noticeably as recession bit into socio-economic groups in a way that was previously unknown. The further inquiry which I can only touch upon here but which Norman Lewis and I have written upon at length elsewhere concerns the optimum form of procedure for different types of complaint or grievance.[9] Procedures should possess the following features, all of which were recognised long before the CC emerged from Downing Street and the Cabinet Office.

(1) *Accessibility*. The practices and procedures which were examined were invariably precipitated by the need for government to legitimate the exercise of power where the traditional methods for providing or achieving control and accountability were either ineffective or too far removed from most members of society. Generally, procedures for remedying grievances must be accessible, open and well-publicised. They should also be provided free or at minimal cost. There are still many examples of procedures which are neither accessible nor open and of whose existence most members of society are ignorant. Surveys have shown low levels of awareness of how to complain about, for example, courts, GPs and hospitals, schools and immigration officials. Over 80 per cent of people surveyed by Charterline (see chapter 1) felt they needed more information about where to make a complaint (*If Things Go Wrong . . . Access to Complaints Systems*, Citizen's Charter Complaints Task Force, No. 1, June 1994). Where this is the case, the utility of such procedures is singularly impaired. Where there is a real need for confidentiality, it should be respected. It is also essential that procedures be as informal as possible unless there are going to be differences of fact or disputed versions of events. Friends or companions should be allowed to accompany the complainant. An "in-house" procedure is adequate providing appropriate training is given to staff and an independent element is present where it might appear that attitudes or perceptions are entrenched on the complainant's side and on that of the service provider. The development of internal adjudicators/Ombudsmen in the Inland Revenue and prisons – though I repeat that in the case of prisons transferring a responsibility for discipline as well as conferring a grievance remedial brief to one person was, I feel, misplaced – and the resort to internal review by officers in the

---

9   N. Lewis and P. Birkinshaw, *When Citizens Complain: Reforming Justice and Administration* (Buckingham, Open University Press, 1993).

Social Fund are steps in the right direction. Rigorous control of standards and training by superiors who are independent of the department concerned is necessary. The efforts of the Social Fund Inspector are to be applauded but there is a case for transferring this responsibility out of the department altogether to a completely separate body. The same might be said of adjudicators, most commonly found in employment and social security, who are still appointed as departmental officials.

(2) *Effectiveness.* Procedures must be effective and must be shaped appropriately for the task in hand; their powers must be adequate and their objects clearly thought out and published. This may often necessitate a greater degree of clarity on the part of government and officials or contractors. This has sometimes been sadly lacking, as witness the Commission for Racial Equality in its earlier days, the DSS,[10] numerous local authorities, the regulatory agencies overseeing privatised industries (see chapter 4); in fact the absence of an overseeing body to offer expert guidance on all facets of administrative justice along the lines of the Administrative Review Council of federal government in Australia or the Administrative Conference of the United States is patently obvious in the somewhat haphazard hotchpotch that we have created,[11] a point I pick up below. Complainants must be informed at all stages how their complaint is progressing, and this must be processed as expeditiously as the circumstances allow. Time limits should be reasonable and strictly complied with unless injustice ensues. Enactment of codes of good administrative practice should be considered where desirable, and too much should not be left to good will and attitude, vital though these are. The Government still remain to be convinced of the need for legislative provisions. They are the ones which, however, tend to be taken most seriously. Grievance procedures must operate against an established set of published performance criteria to set realistic standards for the body or area of activity against which complaints are made with an effective input from those for whom the service exists. In establishing such criteria, interested groups must be given fair and equal access to the process involved. Much needs to be done here to make sure that the process does not become dominated by "self-interested

---

10   For a complaints procedure that no-one knew about in the former DHSS, see "The Citizen's Charter and the Ombudsman", HC 158 (1991/2) at 2 Qus. 6 and 7 and *The Guardian*, 2 August 1991.

11   Lewis and Birkinshaw, Note 9 above.

hustlers". Decisions should usually be binding upon the body complained against; the complainant should generally be free to pursue other remedies if desired.

(3) *User friendliness.* Numerous studies show that most people will not complain even when justified in so doing. Obviously cultural and structural reasons have their role to play. There is fear of reprisal, the reluctance to upset what may be a continuing relationship, a lack of information, the feeling of futility induced by a lopsided contest. Many are inarticulate and have a phobia about confrontation or are simply mesmerised by the complexity of bureaucratic arrangements – in education for instance there have been six major statutes introducing wholesale change since 1980; the machinery of central and local government has been subject to fundamental reorganisation, as have the utilities. The pace and degree of change has been blistering even for seasoned Whitehall watchers. Perhaps the encouragement to complain so evident in the CC misses the target. Perhaps consumers do not want simply to complain about inadequate teaching, or waiting lists in hospital, but rather about a reorganisation which they feel alienating. In education reforms, for instance, Feintuck has observed that the Education Reform Act 1988 (ERA), in encouraging opting out, raised expectations of increased choice and accountability that have not been met; accountability was to be based on parental choice and ERA did not empower parents sufficiently. ERA deliberately sought to undermine the ability of local authorities to plan and manage the local education system, atomised local power, relocating power often in relatively unaccountable NDPBs, and widened the discretion of central government without imposing any appropriate new safeguards against abuse. More recent developments, he argues, have introduced a corporatist-like (see chapter 4) relationship between central government and elites who dominate the grant-maintained sector subject to only minimal external scrutiny.[12] This may be the real object of complaint but the parent may perceive the problem in terms of a less favoured school rather than inadequate teaching. Furthermore, research by the NCC suggests that parental ignorance of complaints procedures under ERA was substantial. The complaints procedures involving GPs are amongst the most consumer-resistant in operation: the onus is on the complainants

[12]   M. Feintuck, *Accountability and Choice in Schooling* (Buckingham, Open University Press, 1994).

to prove their case; no investigation as such is undertaken by the relevant committee (see chapter 5 and HC 33 I (1993/4)).

In NHS Trust applications, Longley has observed how the statutory consultation provisions, in which the views of the public are actively sought, result in the views of the public being submitted to the Secretary of State by the Regional Health Authority which organises the procedure along with Trust applicants through public meetings. These are at the discretion of the RHAs and applicants. The CHC has to be consulted but other consultations are again subject to discretion, for example, with representatives of the local profession, NHS employees, and the local community. Longley argues that the consultation period is too short (three months), that insufficient information is provided to make consultation meaningful and that the organisation of ballots is specifically excluded from the consultation. The consultation process only commences after the business plan and detailed applications have been prepared. Longley continues:

> "Amongst the eight key factors on which Trust applications are to focus in order to obtain the approval of the Secretary of State are the 'overall aims of the Trust and the benefits for the patients and the local community' and the 'way in which services will be developed and quality assured'. These are obviously matters about which the public as consumers either individually or collectively might have an interest and might wish to express a view."[13]

Goriely has pointed out that in the negotiations concerning legal aid reform the Legal Aid Board did not seek the views of the end user of legal services – the public. Are clients not in a position to make judgments about professional services? Goriely argues that work carried out by the NAO and the Legal Aid Board shows that there are many aspects of work which lay clients are competent to judge. For example, whether the client was informed about the costs of services, whether the solicitor listened and understood the client's problems, kept in touch and gave clear advice and whether any complaints were dealt with in a positive way. "A solicitor who does not understand what the client wants cannot begin to offer an appropriate service."[14] If we are to target resources to those most in need, is it not appropriate that we

---

[13] D. Longley, *Public Law and Health Service Accountability* (Buckingham, Open University Press, 1993).
[14] Goriely, *Consumer Policy Review*, April 1993.

establish who those most in need are, what their needs are and what service they require?[15]

(4) *Responsiveness.* Procedures and practices must operate in a responsive manner. This embraces qualities such as openness; giving of good reasons; providing interviews and explanations orally or in writing and in detail when requested. Complaints should be properly logged, and close liaison should take place between the policy divisions and those divisions where complaints are received so that where necessary policy can be framed, or programmes developed, with the lessons of such complaints in mind. The CC has been correct to emphasise the central role that complaints should assume in enhancing managerial performance. One can see this idea developing. In the financial services field and indeed in the case of the Legal Services Ombudsman, the schemes are used to act as quality control devices and in the case of the former, complaints procedures are seen as an integral part of the regulatory process.[16] It will be interesting to see what research into the impact of the CC will show in terms of respon- sive procedures; detailed work on the police complaints process has shown that in 100 supervised cases only in four were there meetings with complainants or other interested parties.[17] The degree of impartiality necessary to handle a grievance is obviously a factor of importance, as is the kind of procedure adopted. Sometimes what is needed is an effective means of achieving conciliation. Sometimes independent arbitration after an informal hearing may be desirable or an independently chaired tribunal conducted on formal but not legalistic lines, or a public hearing to press one's case and challenge others. All currently exist; are they as effective and is good practice as widespread as it ought to be?

(5) *Policy.* It will be argued that all the above suggestions are directed towards complaints about the "administrative method" and its impact upon individuals or groups; there is nothing about real participation in shaping policy-making, that is, the "political objectives" of governors.[18] We have seen how policy and merits have, expressly or effectively, been excluded from public discussion.

---

15 New LJ 1993, at 497.
16 Graham, 1991.
17 M. Maguire, "Complaints Against the Police: The British Experience", in A. Goldsmith, *Complaints Against the Police: A Comparative Study* (Oxford, Oxford University Press, 1990).
18 Sir D. Wass, *Government and the Governed* (London, Routledge and Kegan Paul, 1984).

The White Paper on *Open Government* excludes access to virtually all aspects of policy information. "Information" may be held back where its disclosure would harm the frankness and disclosure of internal discussion – an exemption couched in very wide terms to protect all aspects of the policy-making process. A ccmmitment to publish the facts and analysis of the facts behind major policy decisions after their announcement is weakened by being restricted to that which the "Government considers relevant and important". Policy is the prerogative of Cabinet and respected advisers or designated officials and trustees. In some cases statements explaining why policies were adopted will be made to elected representatives. In other cases they are not made. I have discussed the arguments for revised procedures to act as "Big Inquiries" into major programmes (see chapter 2) as well as consultation on policy proposals. Short of a decentralised and radically altered system of participatory government,[19] what reforms would be desirable to subject policy-making to independent and effective scrutiny? It is obvious that I am not satisfied with Parliament's ability by itself to act as a continuing and effective overseer of policy. It can deliver dramatic and effective rebukes for haughty government. But government is invariably too big, too professional and too adroit for Parliament. A balance has to be struck between government without effective restraint, and government which is in the hands of powerful minority interest groups and which cannot govern.

The former Permanent Secretary to the Treasury, Sir Douglas Wass, produced some interesting ideas a decade ago which have been studiously ignored by government ever since. Wass argued for a large, single, permanent Royal Commission "from which panels would be drawn to carry out specific studies".[20] The Commission "would decide which issues to investigate, what terms of reference to give its panels and who should sit on them".[21] Appointed for a fixed period on the advice of the Prime Minister, it could co-opt specialist advisers and would appoint its own executive and Chairman. Where desirable "a dialogue could be established with appropriate Select Committees". It would possess a "limitless" remit into constitutional and major change,

---

[19]   And which with the fullness of time, who knows? On practical advice to achieve more effective participation see Beresford and Croft (1992).

[20]   Wass, Note 18 above.

[21]   Wass saw the Commission possessing about 200 members. Appointment would be by the Crown on the recommendation of the Prime Minister. Clearly one must be alive to dangers of patronage and this method of appointment is not adequate by itself.

drawing membership from the professions, commerce, industry and banking, education, social services and so on. It would be an advisory and recommendatory body, not an executive one. This is not quite a realisation of John Stuart Mill's: "Nothing less can be ultimately desirable than the admission of all to a share in the sovereign power of the State", but it is an important idea and one that government cynicism ought not to be allowed to destroy. Of course time has moved on and it may be that the consensus politics to which the idea seems attached is too distant a memory either to be accepted by governments for the foreseeable future or to fit into the world of privatised policy-making and rule by management consultant. The arrogance of government, which I take to be a weakness likely to afflict all governments, may dismiss such measures but once a government ignores advice built upon expertise, experience and wisdom the road to ruin beckons.

My own attitude is to look with favour on the creation of an independent and prestigious overseer of public administration, possibly developing the Wass model. The Council on Tribunals was deliberately starved of such potential and the Administrative Conference of the United States (ACUS) established in 1964 to "identify causes of inefficiency, delay and unfairness in administration" may hold some useful lessons. Engaging a full-time chairman and staff, it subcontracts its research to outside experts. It comprises nine standing committees dealing with specialised topics.[22] It is essential that such a body's membership is independent of government and that its recommendations are responded to in a reasoned and constructive manner by government. In 1994, ACUS had to justify to Congress its continuation. It was successful in securing its budget for a further year.

The Australian Administrative Review Council[23] has a brief to examine the whole range of administrative justice in federal government, including the courts, and is a body which has won the admiration of myself and colleagues. Recently and following a report on *Rule-Making by Commonwealth Agencies*,[24] legislation is expected which will require mandatory consultation with the community before the making of "important" rules – these duties will be enforceable through the courts. Given the enormous resort to rule-making as a feature of bureaucratic existence –

---

[22] For example, regulation of business; public access and information; grants, benefits and contracts; judicial review; rule-making and so on.

[23] Lewis and Birkinshaw, Note 9 above.

[24] ARC, 1992.

public or private – the potential for this as a democratic vehicle is enormous. The ARC's annual report for 1992/3 has details of its work on the applicability of judicial review to government business enterprises, with possible ways of ensuring that there are adequate complaints mechanisms in place for health, housing and community services.

Horses for Courses

By which I mean the most appropriate fora for different types of dispute. In my description of complaints processes and means of seeking redress I may be justly criticised for casting fog where others had shone light. This area quite understandably has been a lawyers' paradise[25] and has recently been addressed by the author.[26] I can only offer a few concluding comments.

The best work in the public law tradition in the UK has been sensitive to the fuller realisation of fair play and justice in widely differing contexts and procedures. In some subjects collective welfare is paramount; in others individual entitlement. Some political contexts are more likely to veer towards a formal framework of justice; others will emphasise a substantive model of justice. The former will pursue justice according to the rules of procedure; the latter according to ideals of a perceived "good life". In the latter case "substantive" means a justice dependent upon principles of "felt rightness" or correctness, or appropriateness derived from religion, an economic order, a legal system or some other value system. Both of these categories of justice may be broken down further into sub-categories of an irrational or rational nature where rationality means predictability or reckonability of outcome. This is of course Weber's formulation from almost a century ago. Substantive irrational justice is a tyrant's paradise; formal rational justice – the closest many believe to a modern legal system – can become dehumanising and alienating.

---

[25]   The following is a highly selective list: W. Robson, *Justice and Administrative Law* (1928); H.W.R. Wade, *Towards Administrative Justice* (1963); J. Jowell, *Law and Bureaucracy* (1975); L. Fuller, "The Forms and Limits of Adjudication" (1978) 92 *Harvard L.R.* 353; J. Mashaw, *Bureaucratic Justice* (1983) and *Due Process in the Administrative State* (1985); C. Harlow and R. Rawlings, *Law and Administration* (London, Weidenfeld and Nicolson, 1984); P. Craig, *Administrative Law (2nd edn)* (London, Sweet & Maxwell, 1989); Sunstein, *After the Rights Revolution* (Harvard UP, 1990).

[26]   See Note 9 above.

In choosing particular procedures, or no procedures, to settle or negotiate disputes, one must be alive to the fact that that choice will be susceptible to greater or lesser degrees to particular substantive/emotional/rational/political/economic pressures. I would hope for procedures in different contexts which help in their own way to fulfil democratic expectations: that we all count as individuals and that we are all part of a collective enterprise which is, or should be, humanising in its efforts and objectives. If processual or procedural justice does not aim for these substantive ideals then it is a poor process.

BIBLIOGRAPHY

Abel-Smith, B. and Stevens, R. (1968) *Lawyers and the Courts.* London, Heinemann.

Administrative Review Council of the Commonwealth of Australia. (1985) *The Relationship Between the Ombudsman and the Administrative Appeals Tribunal.* Report No 22. Canberra, ARC.

Appleby, G. and Ellis, E. (1984) "Formal Investigations: The Commission for Racial Equality and the Equal Opportunities Commission as Law Enforcement Agencies." *Public Law* 236.

Armstrong, Sir R. (1987) *The Duties and Responsibilities of Civil Servants in Relation to Ministers.* London, Cabinet Office.

Arthurs, H. W. (1985) *Without the Law.* University of Toronto Press.

Ashford, D. (1981) *Policy and Politics in Britain.* Oxford, Blackwell.

Bains, M. (1972) *The New Local Authorities: Management and Structure.* London, HMSO.

Baldwin, R. (1978) "A British Regulatory Agency and the 'Skytrain' decision." *Public Law* 57.

Baldwin, R. (1980) "A Quango Unleashed . . .". *58 Pub. Admin.* 287.

Baldwin, R. (1985) *Regulating the Airlines: Administrative Justice and Agency Discretion.* Oxford, Clarendon Press.

Barker, A. (ed.) (1982) *Quangos in Britain. Governments and the Networks of Public Policy Making.*

Barron, A. and Scott, C. (1992) "The Citizen's Charter Programme." *Modern L. R.* 526.

Beresford, P. and Croft, S. (1992) *Citizen Involvement: A Practical Guide for Change.* London, Macmillan.

Bingham, T. Sir (1991) "Should Public Law Remedies be Discretionary?" *Public Law* 64.

Birds, J. and Graham, C. (1992) *Complaints Against Insurance Companies.* University of Sheffield, Faculty of Law.

Birkinshaw, P. (1982) "Homelessness and the Law: the Effects and Response to Legislation." *5 Urban Law and Policy* 255.

Birkinshaw, P. (1985) *Grievances, Remedies and the State* (1st edn). London, Sweet & Maxwell.

294

Birkinshaw, P. (1986) *Open Government, Freedom of Information and Local Government.* Local Government Legal Society Trust.

Birkinshaw, P. (1988) *Freedom of Information: the Law, the Practice and the Ideal.* London, Weidenfeld and Nicolson.

Birkinshaw, P. (1990) *Government and Information: the Law Relating to Access, Disclosure and Regulation.* London, Butterworths.

Birkinshaw, P. (1991a) *Reforming the Secret State.* Buckingham, Open University Press.

Birkinshaw, P. (1991b) *Freedom of Information: the US Experience.* Hull University Law School, Studies in Law.

Birkinshaw, P. (1993a) "'I only ask for information' – the White Paper on Open Government." *Public Law* 557.

Birkinshaw, P. (1993b) "Citizenship and Privacy" in Blackburn, R. (ed.) *Rights of Citizenship.* London, Mansell.

Birkinshaw, P., Harden, I. and Lewis, N. (1990) *Government By Moonlight: the Hybrid Parts of the State.* London, Unwin Hyman.

Blom-Cooper, L. Sir (1982) "The New Face of Judicial Review . . ." *Public Law* 250.

Borrie, Sir G. (1989) "The Regulation of Public and Private Power." *Public Law* 552.

Bradley, A. (1992) "Sachsenhausen, Barlow Clowes – and then?" *Public Law* 353.

Browne-Wilkinson, N. Sir (1988) "The Independence of the Judiciary in the 1980s." *Public Law* 88.

Browne-Wilkinson, N. Sir (1992) "The Infiltration of a Bill of Rights." *Public Law* 397.

Cabinet Office (Ibbs Report) (1988) *Improving Management in Government: the Next Steps.* London, HMSO.

Cabinet Office, Efficiency Unit. (1990) *Scrutiny of Ministerial Correspondence.* London, HMSO.

Cabinet Office and HM Treasury (1992) *Non-Departmental Public Bodies: A Guide for Departments.* London, Cabinet Office.

Caiden, G. (1983) *International Handbook of the Ombudsman, Vols I and II.* Connecticut, Greenwood.

Cane, P. (1990) "Statutes, Standing and Representation." *Public Law* 386.

Cane, P. (1992) *Introduction to Administrative Law (2nd edn).* Oxford, OUP.

Carson, W.G. (1981) *The Other Price of Britain's Oil.* Martin Robertson.

Cawson, A. (ed.) (1985) *Organised Interests and the State: Studies in Meso Corporatism.* London, Sage.

Chamberlayne, P. (1978) "The Politics of Participation." *4 The London Journal* 47.

Charter 88. (1994) *Extra Governmental Organisations in the UK and their Accountability.* London, Charter 88.

Chayes, A. (1976) "Developments in the Law – Class Actions." *89 Harv. LR* 1318.

Chayes, A. (1982) "Public Law Litigation and the Warren Court" *96 Harv. LR* 4.

Cockburn, C. (1977) *The Local State.* London, Pluto Press.

Coleman, F. (1993) "All in the Best Possible Taste." *Public Law* 488.

Council on Tribunals (1990) HC 64 *Annual Report 1990/91.* London, HMSO.

Craig, P. (1992) "Once Upon a Time in the West: Direct Effectiveness and Federalism." *Oxford Journal of Legal Studies* 552.

Craig, P. (1989) *Administrative Law (2nd edn).* London, Sweet & Maxwell.

Crawford, C. (1988) "Complaints, Codes and Ombudsmen in Local Government." *Public Law* 246.

Crouch, C. and Dore, R. (1990) *Corporatism and Accountability.* Oxford, OUP.

Daintith, T. (1979) "Regulation by Contract: the New Prerogative." *32 Current Legal Problems* 41.

Daintith, T. (1982) "Legal Analysis of Economic Policy." *Journal of Law and Society* 191.

Davies, A. (1979) *What's Wrong with Quangos?* London, OCPU.

Davies, A. and Willman, J. (1991) *What Next? Agencies, Departments and the Civil Service.* London, Institute for Public Policy Research.

Department of the Environment (DoE). (1993) *An Evaluation of the Local Authority Reports to Tenants Regimes by Marsh, A.* et al. London, HMSO.

de Smith, S.A. (1980) *Judicial Review of Administrative Action* (4th edn, Evans, J.M.). London, Stevens.

Dicey, A.V. (1914) *Law and Public Opinion in England.* London, Macmillan (1963 repr.).

Dienel, P. (1989) "The Citizen as Assessor: Planning Public Services" in *Providing Public Services that Serve the Public* (ed. Epstein, J.). London, Anglo-German Foundation.

Dworkin, R. (1978) in *Men of Ideas* ed. B. Magee. Oxford, Oxford University Press.

Dyson, K. (1980) *The State Tradition in Western Europe*. Oxford, Martin Robertson.

Farmer, (1974) *Tribunals and Government*. London, Weidenfeld and Nicolson.

Feintuck, M. (1994) *Accountability and Choice in Schooling*. Buckingham, Open UP.

Franklin, M. and Norton, P. (eds) (1993) *Parliamentary Questions*. Oxford, Clarendon Press.

Franks, Sir O. (1957) *Report of the Committee on Administrative Tribunals and Enquiries*. Cmnd 218. London, HMSO.

Fredman, S. and Morris, G. (1994) "The Costs of Exclusivity: Public and Private Re-examined." *Public Law* 69.

Friedmann, K. (1974) *Comparative Aspects of Complaint and Attitudes Towards Complaining in Canada and the UK*.

Friedmann, W. (1971) *The State and the Rule of Law in a Mixed Economy*. London, Stevens.

Fuller, L. (1978) "The Forms and Limits of Adjudication." *92 Harv. LR*. 353.

Fulton, (1968) *Report of the Committee on the Civil Service*. Cmnd 3638. London, HMSO.

Galanter, M. (1974) "Why the 'Haves' Come Out Ahead: Speculations on the Limits of Legal Change." *9 Law and Society Rev.* 95.

Ganz, G. (1972) "Allocation of Decision-making Functions." *Public Law* 215 and 299.

Ganz, G. (1977) *Government and Industry*. Professional Books.

Genn, H. (1993) "Tribunals and Informal Justice." *Modern LR* 393.

Genn, H. and Genn, Y. (1989) *The Effectiveness of Representation at Tribunals*. London, Lord Chancellor's Department.

Gibbons, T. (1991) *Regulating the Media*. London, Sweet & Maxwell.

Goldsmith, A. (1990) *Complaints Against the Police: A Comparative Study*. Oxford, OUP.

Goldsworthy, D. (1991) *Setting Up Next Steps*. London, HMSO.

Graham, C. (1991) *The Non-Classical Ombudsman*. Sheffield, Centre for Socio-Legal Studies, University of Sheffield.

Graham, C. and Prosser, A. (1991) *Privatising Public Enterprises*. Oxford, Clarendon Press.

Graham, C., Seneviratne, M. and James, R. (1993) "Publicising the Bank and Building Societies Ombudsman Schemes." *Consumer Policy Review* 85.

Gregory, R. and Drewry, G. (1991) "Barlow Clowes and the Ombudsman." *Public Law* 192 and 408.

Gregory, R. and Pearson, J. (1992) "The Parliamentary Ombudsman After Twenty-five Years." *70 Public Administration* 469.

Gower, (1984) *Review of Investor Protection* Cmnd 9125. London, HMSO.

Griffith, J.A.G. (1966) *Central Departments and Local Authorities*. Allen & Unwin.

Griffith, J.A.G. (1974) *Parliamentary Scrutiny of Government Bills*. Allen & Unwin.

Griffith, J.A.G. and Ryle, M. (1989) *Parliament*. London, Sweet & Maxwell.

Gyford, J. (1991) *Local Government and the Public*. Macmillan.

Hague *et al.* (1975) *Public Policy and Private Interests*.

Hambleton, R. (1978) *Policy, Planning and Local Government*.

H.M. Treasury (1992) *Executive Agencies: A Guide to Setting Targets and Measuring Performance*. London, HMSO.

Hansard Society. (1993) *Making the Law*. Hansard Society Commission.

Harden, I. (1988) "A Constitution for Quangos." *Public Law* 27.

Harden, I. (1992) *The Contracting State*. Buckingham, Open UP.

Harden, I. and Lewis, N. (1986) *The Noble Lie: The British Constitution and the Rule of Law*. London, Hutchinson.

Harlow, C. (1982) *Compensation and Government Torts*. London, Sweet & Maxwell.

Harlow, C. (1986) in Harlow, C. (ed.) *Public Law and Politics*. London, Sweet & Maxwell.

Harlow, C. (1993) "A Community of Interests? Making the Most of European Law." *Mod. LR* 331.

Harlow, C. and Drewry, G. (1990) "A 'Cutting Edge'? The Parliamentary Commissioner and MPs." *Public Law* 745.

Harlow, C. and Rawlings, R. (1984) *Law and Administration*. London, Weidenfeld and Nicolson.

Harlow, C. and Rawlings, R. (1992) *Pressure Through Law*. London, Routledge.

Harris, N. (1992) *Complaints about Schooling*. London, National Consumer Council.

Harrison, M.L. (1984) *Corporatism and the Welfare State*. Aldershot, Gower.

Hawkins, K. (1984) *Environment and Enforcement*. Oxford, OUP.

Hawkins, K. and Thomas, J. (eds) (1984) *Enforcing Regulation*.

Hedemann-Robinson, M. (1994) "The Individual and the EC Ombudsman." *New LJ* 609.

Hirschman, A. (1970) *Exit, Voice and Loyalty: Response to Decline in Firms, Organisations and States*. Cambridge, CUP.

Hogg, C. (1992) *Complaints about family practitioners, Community Health Councils and FHSA complaints.* London, Greater London Association of CHCs.

Holdsworth, W.S. (1966) *A History of English Law Vol. 1.* 7th edn revised. London, Methuen and Sweet & Maxwell.

Holland, P. and Fallon, M. (1978) *The Quango Explosion.*

Home Office. (1985) *Police Complaints and Discipline Procedures.* Cmnd 9072 (1983). London, HMSO.

Hood, C. (1973) "The Rise and Rise of the British Quango." *New Society,* August 16.

Johnson, N. (1977) *In Search of the Constitution.* Methuen.

Jones, G. (1979) "Central – Local Relations, Finance and the Law." *2 Urban Law and Policy* 25.

Jowell, J. (1975) *Law and Bureaucracy.* Port Washington, N.Y., Dunellen.

Jowell, J. and Lester, A. (1987) "Beyond Wednesbury: Substantive Principles of Administrative Law." *Public Law* 368.

Justice (1976) *The Citizen and the Public Agencies.* London, Justice.

Justice (1977) *Our Fettered Ombudsman.* London, Justice.

Justice (1980) *The Local Ombudsman: The First Five Years.* London, Justice.

Justice/All Souls (1988) *Administrative Justice: Some Necessary Reforms.* Oxford, OUP.

Kamenka, E. and Tay, A. (1975) "Beyond Bourgeois Individualism . . ." in *Feudalism and Beyond* (Kamenka and Kneale eds).

Lambert *et al.* (1978) *Housing Policy and the State.*

Law Centres' Federation (1979) *Response to the Royal Commission on Legal Services.*

Law Commission (1993) Consultation Paper No 126. *Administrative Law: Judicial Review and Statutory Appeals.* London, HMSO.

Laws, J. Sir (1993) "Is the High Court the Guardian of Fundamental Human Rights?" *Public Law* 59.

Lawson, N. (1992) *The View from No. 11. Memoirs of a Tory Radical.* London, Bantam.

Layfield, F. (1976) *Report of the Committee on Local Government Finance* Cmnd 6453. London, HMSO.

Leach, S., Stewart, J. and Walsh, K. (1993) *The Changing Organisation and Management of Local Government.*

Lee, H. (1993) "The Australian High Court and Implied Fundamental Guarantees." *Public Law* 606.

Leigh, I. (1993) "Matrix Churchill, Supergun and the Scott Inquiry." *Public Law* 630.

Lester, Lord A. (1994) "Discrimination: What can Lawyers Learn from History." *Public Law* 224.

Lewis, C. (1988) "Retrospective and Prospective Rulings in Administrative Law." *Public Law* 78.

Lewis, N. (1981) "Towards a Sociology of Lawyering in Public Administration." *Northern Ireland Legal Quarterly* 89.

Lewis, N. (1989) "Regulating Non-Governmental Bodies: Privatization, Accountability and the Public-Private Divide." in *The Changing Constitution* (eds Jowell, J. and Oliver, D.) Oxford, OUP.

Lewis, N. (1992) *Inner City Regeneration*. Buckingham, Open UP.

Lewis, N. (1993) *How to Reinvent British Government*. London, European Policy Forum.

Lewis, N. and Birkinshaw, P. (1979a) "Local Authorities and the Resolution of Grievances – Some Second Thoughts." *Local Government Studies* 7.

Lewis, N. and Birkinshaw, P. (1979b) "Taking Complaints Seriously" in Partington, M. and Jowell, J. *Welfare Law and Policy*. London, Frances Pinter.

Lewis, N. and Birkinshaw, P. (1993) *When Citizens Complain: Reforming Justice and Administration*. Buckingham, Open University Press.

Lewis, N. and Harden, I. (1982) "Law and the Local State." *Urban Law and Policy* 65.

Lewis, N. and Harden, I. (1983) "Privatisation, De-regulation and Constitutionality: Some Anglo-American Comparisons." *34 Northern Ireland Legal Quarterly* 207.

Lewis, N. and Livock, R. (1979) "Council House Allocation Procedures." *Urban Law and Policy* 133.

Lewis, N. and Wiles, P. (1984) "The Post Corporatist State?" *Journal of Law and Society* 65.

Llewellyn, K. "The Normative, the Legal and the Law Jobs: the Problem of Juristic Method." (1940) *49 Yale Law Journal* 1355.

Longley, D. (1993) *Public Law and Health Service Accountability*. Buckingham, Open UP.

Loughlin, M. (1986) *Local Government in the Modern State*. London, Sweet & Maxwell.

Loughlin, M. (1990 and 1991) "Innovative Financing in Local Government . . ." (1990) *Public Law* 372; (1991) *Public Law* 568.

McAuslan, P. (1980) *The Ideologies of Planning Law.*

McAuslan, P. (1987) "The Widdicombe Report: Local Government Business or Politics?" *Public Law* 154.

McAuslan, P. and McEldowney, J. (1985) *Law, Legitimacy and the Constitution.* London, Sweet & Maxwell.

McCrudden, C. (1987) "The Commission for Racial Equality: Formal Investigations in the Shadow of Judicial Review." In Baldwin, R. and McCrudden, C. *Regulation and Public Law.* London, Weidenfeld and Nicolson.

McGougan, A. (1990) "The Importance of Being Honest." *Media Law and Practice* 17.

Maguire, M. (1990) "Complaints Against the Police: The British Experience." in Goldsmith, A. (1990).

Maitland, F.W. (1900) *Introduction to Otto Gierke: Political Theories of the Middle Ages.* Cambridge, Cambridge University Press.

Maitland, F.W. (1901) "The Crown as Corporation." *18 Law Quarterly Review* 131.

Maitland, F.W. (1955) *The Constitutional History of England.* Cambridge, CUP.

Marshall, G. (1971) *Constitutional Theory.* Oxford, Oxford UP.

Marshall, G. (1993) "The Maastricht Proceedings." *Public Law* 402.

Mashaw, J.L. (1983) *Bureaucratic Justice.* Yale UP.

Mashaw, J.L. (1985) *Due Process in the Administrative State.* Yale UP.

Maud Sir J. (1967) *Report of the Committee on the Management of Local Government.* London, HMSO.

Meredith, P. (1984) "Falling Rolls and the Reorganisation of Schools." *Journal of Social Welfare Law* 208.

Middlemas, K. (1979) *Politics in Industrial Society.* London, Macmillan.

Middlemas, K. (1983) *Industry, Unions and Government.* London, Macmillan.

Morrell, F. (1977) *From the Electors of Bristol.* Spokesman Pamphlet No 57.

Morrison, H. (1933) *Socialisation and Transport.*

Mowbray, A. (1990) "A Right to Official Advice. The Parliamentary Commissioner's Perspective." *Public Law* 68.

National Consumer Council (1991) *The Gas Industry.* London, NCC.

National Consumer Council (1993) *Ombudsman Services.* London, National Consumer Council.

Norton, P. (1982) "'Dear Minister . . .' The Importance of MP to Minister Correspondence." *Parliamentary Affairs* 59.

OCPU (1979) *The Big Public Inquiry.* London, Justice, Outer Circle Policy Unit.

Osborne, D. and Gaebler, T. *Reinventing Government.* New York, Addison Wesley.

Paris and Blackaby (1979) "Not Much Improvement." In Kantor (ed.) *The Governable City.*

Poggi, G. (1978) *The Development of the Modern State.* London, Hutchinson.

Prosser, A.J. (1977) "Poverty, Ideology and Legality . . ." *4 British Journal of Law and Society* 539.

Prosser, A. (1983) *Test Cases for the Poor.* London, CPAG.

Prosser, A.J. (1986) *Nationalised Industries and Public Control.* Oxford, Blackwell.

Public Accounts Committee (1994) *The Proper Conduct of Public Business,* Eighth Report (1993/4). London, HMSO.

Purchas, Sir F. (1993) "The Constitution in the Market Place." *New LJ* 1604.

Purchas, Sir F. (1994) "Lord Mackay and the Judiciary." *New LJ* 527.

Purdue, M. (1991) *Planning Appeals: A Critique.* Buckingham, Open UP.

Rawlings, R. (1986a) *The Complaints Industry: A Review of Sociolegal Research on Aspects of Administrative Justice.* London, ESRC.

Rawlings, R. (1986b) "Parliamentary Redress of Grievance." In Harlow, C. (ed.) *Public Law and Politics.* London, Sweet & Maxwell.

Rawlings, R. (1990) "The MPs' Complaints Service." *Modern LR* 22 and 149.

Reade, (1984) "Town and Country Planning." In *Corporatism and the Welfare State* (ed. Harrison, M.L.).

Reid, W. (1993) "What's the good of law in a case o' the kind?" *Public Law* 221.

Reiner, R. (1993) "Responsibilities and Reforms." *New Law Journal* 1096.

Robson, W. (1928) *Justice and Administrative Law.*

Royal Town Planning Institute (1982) *The Public and Planning: Means to Better Participation.*

Sainsbury, R. and Eardley, T. (1992) "Housing Benefit Review Boards." *Public Law* 551.

Scarman, Lord (1981) *The Brixton Disorders, 10–12 April 1981,* Cmnd 8427. London, HMSO.

Scheingold, S. (1974) *The Politics of Rights.* Yale UP.
Schiemann, K. Sir (1990) *"Locus Standi." Public Law* 342.
Seneviratne, M. (1991) *Complaints Procedures in Local Government*, PhD Thesis, University of Sheffield.
Seneviratne, M. (1994) *Ombudsmen in the Public Sector.* Buckingham, Open University Press.
Sheffield (1987) Lewis, N. *et al. Complaints Procedures in Local Government.* University of Sheffield.
Skeffington Report (1969) *Report of the Committee on Public Participation in Planning: People and Planning.* London, HMSO.
Slynn, G. Sir (1992) *Introducing a European Legal Order.* London, Stevens.
Smith, B. (ed.) (1975) *The New Political Economy: the Public Use of the Private Sector.*
Smith, B. and Hague, D. (1971) *The Dilemma of Accountability in Modern Government: Independence versus Control.* London, Macmillan.
Snyder, F. (1993) "The Effectiveness of European Community Law: Institutions, Processes, Tools and Techniques." *Modern LR* 19.
Society of Local Authority Chief Executives (1978) *Ad Hoc Inquiries in Local Government.* Solace.
Stalker, J. (1988) *Stalker.* London.
Stewart, J.D. (1992) *Accountability to the Public.* London, European Policy Forum.
Stewart, R. *et al.* (1978) "Vermont Yankee and the Evolution of Administrative Procedure." *91 Harv. LR* 1804.
Stewart, R. and Sunstein, C. (1982) "Public Programs and Private Rights." *95 Harv. LR* 1193.
Streek, W. and Schmitter, P. (eds) (1985) *Private Interest Government.* London, Sage.
Summers, R. (1971) "The Technique Element in Law." *59 California Law Rev.* 733.
Sunkin, M. *et al.* (1993) *Judicial Review in Perspective.* The Public Law Project, London.
Sunstein, C. (1990) *After the Rights Revolution.* Harvard UP.
Teubner, G. (1983) "Substantive and Reflexive Elements in Modern Law." *17 Law and Society Review* 239.
Titmus, R. (1971) "Welfare Rights, Law and Discretion." *42 Political Quarterly* 113.
Tomkins, A. "Public Interest Immunity after Matrix Churchill." *Public Law* 650.
Trubeck, D. (1977) "Complexity and Contradiction in the Legal Order." *11 Law and Society* 529.
Turpin, C. (1972) *Government Contracts.* London, Penguin Books.

Turpin, C. (1989) *Government Procurement and Contracts.* Harlow, Longman.

Unger, R.M. (1976) *Law in Modern Society. Toward a Criticism of Social Theory.* New York, Free Press.

van Gerven, W. (1993) *The Horizontal Effect of Directive Provisions Revisited – The Reality of Catchwords.* University of Hull, Institute of European Public Law.

Veljanovski, C. (1993) *The Future of Industry Regulation in the UK.* London, European Policy Forum.

Wade, H.W.R. (1963) *Towards Administrative Justice.* University of Michigan Press.

Wade, H.W.R. (1988) *Administrative Law* (6th edn). Oxford University Press.

Waldegrave, W. (1993) *The Reality of Reform and Accountability in Today's Public Service.* London, CIPFA.

Wass, D. Sir (1984) *Government and the Governed.* London, RKP.

Whyatt, Sir J. (1961) *The Citizen and the Administration: The Redress of Grievances.* London, Stevens.

Widdicombe, D. (1986) *The Conduct of Local Authority Business,* Cmnd 9797. London, HMSO.

Wikeley, N. and Young, R. (1992) "The Administration of Benefits in Britain." *Public Law* 238.

Winkler, J.T. (1975) "The Industry Act 1975 In Context." *British Journal of Law and Society* 103.

Wolffe, W.J. "The Scope of Judicial Review in Scots Law." *Public Law* 625.

Woolf, Sir H. (1986) "Public Law – Private Law: Why the Divide?" *Public Law* 220.

Woolf, Sir H. (1990) *Protection of the Public: A New Challenge.* London, Stevens.

Woolf, Sir H. (1991) *Prison Disturbances.* Cm 1456. London, HMSO.

Woolf, Sir H. (1992) "Judicial Review: A Possible Programme for Reform." *Public Law* 221.

Wraith, R. and Hutchesson, P. (1973) *Administrative Tribunals.* London, George Allen and Unwin.

Wraith, R. and Lamb, G. (1971) *Public Inquiries as an Instrument of Government.* London, George Allen and Unwin.

Wyner, A. (ed.) (1973) *Executive Ombudsmen in the USA.* Berkeley, University of California.

INDEX